ARMENIAN APOCRYPHA
RELATING TO BIBLICAL HEROES

EARLY JUDAISM AND ITS LITERATURE

Rodney A. Werline, Editor

Editorial Board:
Randall D. Chesnutt
Kelley N. Coblentz Bautch
Maxine L. Grossman
Jan Joosten
James S. McLaren
Carol Newsom

Number 49

ARMENIAN APOCRYPHA
RELATING TO BIBLICAL HEROES

BY

MICHAEL E. STONE

Atlanta

Copyright © 2019 by Michael E. Stone

All rights reserved. No part of this work may be reproduced or transmitted in any form or by any means, electronic or mechanical, including photocopying and recording, or by means of any information storage or retrieval system, except as may be expressly permitted by the 1976 Copyright Act or in writing from the publisher. Requests for permission should be addressed in writing to the Rights and Permissions Office, SBL Press, 825 Houston Mill Road, Atlanta, GA 30329 USA.

Library of Congress Cataloging-in-Publication Data

Names: Stone, Michael E., 1938- author.
Title: Armenian Apocrypha relating to biblical heroes / by Michael E. Stone.
Description: Atlanta : SBL Press, 2019. | Series: Early Judaism and its literature ; Number 49 | In Armenian and English; some of the English is a translation from Armenian. | Includes bibliographical references and index.
Identifiers: LCCN 2019000480 (print) | LCCN 2019006337 (ebook) | ISBN 9780884143550 (ebk.) | ISBN 9781628372373 (pbk. : alk. paper) | ISBN 9780884143543 (hbk. : alk. paper)
Subjects: LCSH: Apocryphal books. | Apocryphal books—Translations into Armenian—Criticism, Textual.
Classification: LCC BS1696 (ebook) | LCC BS1696 .S7662 2019 (print) | DDC 229/.9049—dc23
LC record available at h]ps://lccn.loc.gov/2019000480

Printed on acid-free paper.

Table of Contents

Preface	ix
List of Manuscripts	xi
List of Texts	xii
Signs and Abbreviations	xiii
Procedural Matters	xiii
Abbreviations	xv

1. THE NUMBER AND THE TWELVE CLASSES OF ANGELS — 1
   - Introductory Remarks — 1
   - Text — 2
   - Translation — 3

2. AN EXORCISM IN THE NAME OF ADAM — 4
   - Introductory Remarks — 4
   - Text — 5
   - Translation — 5

3. THE CONSTRUCTION OF NOAH'S ARK — 7
   - Introductory Remarks — 7
   - Excursus — 9
   - Text — 11
   - Translation — 12
   - Some Other Noah Traditions — 13

4. CONCERNING ABRAHAM — 15
   - Introductory Remarks — 15
   - Text — 15
   - Critical Apparatus — 17
   - Translation — 17

5. ABRAHAM AND THE IDOLS — 20
   - Introductory Remarks — 20
   - Texts and Translations — 22

CONTENTS

6. SUPPLICATION ABOUT THE SODOMITES AND GOMORREANS 24
   Introductory Remarks 24
   Story of Father Abraham §§17–21 26
   Supplication concerning the Men of Sodom and Gomorra 28

7. BRIEF HISTORY OF JOSHUA SON OF NUN 57
   Introductory Remarks 57
   Text 61
   Critical Apparatus 77
   Translation 82

8. THE STORY OF THE ARK OF THE COVENANT 109
   Introductory Remarks 109
   Text 110
   Critical Apparatus 114
   Translation 115

9. CONCERNING THE ARK OF GOD 123
   Introductory Remarks 123
   Text 124
   Translation 126

10. CONCERNING SOLOMON AND THE BUILDING OF THE TEMPLE 128
    Introductory Remarks 128
    Text 130
    Translation 132

11. SIGNS AND WONDERS OF THE TEMPLE 137
    Introductory Remarks 137
    Text 140
    Translation 141

12. KING SOLOMON: FOUR SHORT TEXTS 143
    Introductory Remarks 143
    Solomon Texts 1 and 2 149
    Text 6. King Solomon's Ring 162
    Text 7. Solomon and the Bubu Bird 167

13. PRAISE OF THE PROPHETS 171
    Introductory Remarks 171
    Texts and Translations 172

14. THE SHORT STORY OF THE PROPHET ELIJAH 175
    Notes on the Texts in M6092 and M101 175

Edition of the Extract in M6092	176
Extract from M101	178
15. HEZEKIAH AND MANASSEH	180
Introductory Remarks	180
Text	182
Translation	188
16. JEREMIAH, SUSANNA, AND THE TWO ELDERS	197
Introductory Remarks	197
Text	197
Translation	200
17. THE NINEVEHITES	204
Introductory Remarks	204
Text	205
Translation	206
18. STORY OF DANIEL	207
Introductory Remarks	207
Text	209
Translation	212
19. EZRA SALATHIEL	218
Introductory Remarks	218
Text 1	219
Text 2	220
Text 3. Questions of Ezra	222
Text 4. The Oldest Manuscript of *4 Ezra*	224
Sample Readings and Stemmatic Discussion	225
Bibliography	229
Index of Subjects	235
Index of Ancient Sources	247
Index of Manuscripts	256

Preface

This book is the fifth member of a series which I commenced with the publication of *Armenian Apocrypha Relating to Patriarchs and Prophets* in 1982. Initially, my aim was to search unstudied Armenian manuscripts with the hope of discovering works dating back to Second Temple times, like those treatises of Philo of Alexandria that survive only in Armenian translation. From this initial aim, the project developed into the search for reworkings of biblical traditions, stories, and persons in Armenian. These are of interest both because they sometimes do preserve ancient traditions and also because they reflect a rich tradition of biblical exegesis and commentary, much of it in genres of the older apocryphal and pseudepigraphical literature.

The whole project would have been impossible without the help given, down to his death in 1996, by Archbishop Norayr Bogharian, who until his ninetieth birthday, was keeper of Manuscripts of the Armenian Patriarchate of Jerusalem. His help is evident in particular in the earlier volumes of this series. All the way through I have also enjoyed the support of the Maštoc‘ Matenadaran, Institute of Ancient Manuscripts in Erevan, Armenia, under three directors, Sen Arevšatyan, Hrachea Tamrazyan, and present director Vahan Tēr-Ghevontyan. I also acknowledge here the most constructive scholarly cooperation of Dr. Gēorg Tēr Vardanean, curator of manuscripts of the Matenadaran and of members of his department's staff as well as of colleagues there. Over the years I have been able to pass many delightful and fruitful months rummaging among the Matenadaran's extraordinary collections.

A number of friends have supported me in this labor, and to them thanks must be given. The late Archbishop Shahe Ajamian, Gohar Muradyan, Aram Topchyan, Theo M. van Lint, and Abraham Terian each helped in very significant ways, often saving me from my own mistakes.

I am also indebted to financial support for this project over the years, given by the Israel Academy of Sciences and Humanities (first volume), the Hebrew University of Jerusalem, and, consistently over recent decades, the Israel Science Foundation. The present book was supported by Israel Science Foundation grant no. 1123/16.

The book has benefitted from the support of my research assistants, Tomer Doitch, Michal Emanuel, and Samuel Rausnitz in 2016–2017 and Nathaniel Amsalem, Guy Shulberg, and Maria Ushakova in 2017–2018. Without their help, it would have been a much more difficult task.

The SBL Press series on Early Jewish Literature (once part of Septuagint and Cognate Studies), SBL Press, and its director Bob Buller have given volumes of recent years a warm and welcoming home. Gratitude is expressed to the series editor Rod Werline.

The first volume in this series in 1982 was dedicated to my two children. This volume, being completed in 2019, I dedicate to my great-granddaughters, Yael Nira Mazal and Shir Tsabari, and Nogah Yaacov-Avni, and to the blessed memory of Nira, my life-partner, whose life was a blessing for all who knew her.

List of Manuscripts Containing Texts Newly Published

Manuscript, folios	Date (CE)	Text no.	Title
J0652, p. 490–491	angular *notrgir*	12	Solomon Texts 1–3
M101, 399r–401r	1740	14	The Short Story of the Prophet Elijah
M101, 401v	1740	17	The Ninevehites
M682, 8r	1679	4	Concerning Abraham
M724, 169v–173v	1736	19	Ezra Salathiel
M10986, 83v–84v	seventeenth century	10	Concerning Solomon and the Building of the Temple
M1134, 81r–84r	1695	18	Story of Daniel
M1500, 359v	1271–1288	12	Solomon Text 1.1
M2168, 310v–327r	seventeenth century	7	Brief History of Joshua Son of Nun
M2242, 24v–31v	seventeenth century	6	Supplication about the Sodomites and Gomorreans
M2245, 148r–148v	1689	1	The Number and the Twelve Classes of Angels
M4618, 131v	1675–1706	5	Abraham and the Idols
M4618, 132r–132v	1675–1706	12	Paralipomena
M4618, 132r–133r	1675–1706	12	Solomon Texts 1–2, 6–7
M4618, 142v–143v	1675–1706	15	Hezekiah and Manasseh
M4618, 146v–148v	1675–1706	7	Brief History of Joshua Son of Nun
M4618, 53r	1675–1706	3	The Construction of Noah's Ark
M5531, 66r–66v	eighteenth century	13	Praise of the Prophets
M5607, 308r–309r	1278	16	Jeremiah, Susanna, and the Two Elders
M5571, 212r–218r	1657–1659	6	Supplication about the Sodomites and Gomorreans
M5607, 67r–81r	1278	19	Ezra Salathiel
M5933, 27r–27v	fourteenth century	11	Signs and Wonders of the Temple
M6092, 343v–351v 353r	seventeenth century	7	Brief History of Joshua Son of Nun
M6092, 351v–353r	seventeenth century	14	The Short Story of the Prophet Elijah
M6340, 55v–58r	1651	8	The Story of the Ark of the Covenant
M9100, 35r–37r	1686	9	Concerning the Ark of God
Urbat'agirk	1512	2	An Exorcism in the Name of Adam

LIST OF TEXTS PUBLISHED HERE AND THEIR MANUSCRIPTS

Title	Manuscript	Year (CE)	Text no.
Abraham and the Idols	M4618	1675–1706	5
An Exorcism in the Name of Adam	Urbatʻagirk	1512	2
An Exorcism in the Name of Adam	V1957	n/a	2
Brief History of Joshua Son of Nun	M2168	seventeenth century	7
Brief History of Joshua Son of Nun	M6092	seventeenth century	7
Concerning Abraham	M0682	1679	4
Concerning Solomon and the Building of the Temple	M10986	seventeenth century	10
Concerning the Ark of God	M9100	1686	9
Concerning the Story of the Ark of the Testament	LOB Egerton708	eighteenth century	9
Ezra Salathiel	M5607	1278	19
Ezra Salathiel	M724	1736	19
Hezekiah and Manasseh	M4618	1675–1706	15
Jeremiah, Susanna, and the Two Elders	M5607	1278	16
Paralipomena	M4618	1675–1706	12
Praise of the Prophets	M5531	eighteenth century	13
Signs and Wonders of the Temple	M5933	fourteenth century	11
Solomon Text 1.1	M1500	1271–1288	12
Solomon Texts 1–2	J2558	1615	12
Solomon Texts 1–2, 6–7	M4618	1675–1706	12
Solomon Texts 1–3	J0652	angular *notrgir*	12
Story of Daniel	M1134	1695	18
Supplication about the Sodomites and Gomorreans	M2242	seventeenth century	6
Supplication about the Sodomites and Gomorreans	M5571	1657–1659	6
The Ninevehites	M0101	1740	17
The Number and the Twelve Classes of Angels	M2245	1689	1
The Short Story of the Prophet Elijah	M0101	1740	14
The Short Story of the Prophet Elijah	M6092	seventeenth century	14
The Story of the Ark of the Covenant	M6340	1651	8

Signs and Abbreviations

dtg	dittography
fol(s).	folio, folios
hkt	homoeoarkton
hmt	homoeoteleuton
OG	Old Greek
om	omit/s
p(p).	page(s)
p.m.	prima manu, designates text written by the original scribe
s.m.	secunda manu, designates text written by a later scribe
Th.	Theodotion
vel sim.	or the like
( )	words introduced into a translation by the editor for comprehensibility's sake
< >	words introduced into a diplomatic text from another source, including emendation
[ ]	lacuna in the manuscript
{ }	corrupt text
∞	transpose

Procedural Matters

In the Armenian Bible, 1–2 Samuel and 1–2 Kings are numbered as 1–4 Kingdoms (Reigns). In this volume, however, to make it easier for the reader, I follow the ordinary English usage and denote them as 1–2 Samuel and 1–2 Kings. In this book, with respect to Psalms and certain chapters of the historical books, the Masoretic numbering is followed by the different LXX numbering in parentheses. A similar practice is followed in those occasional instances in which there is a difference of verse numbering between these two versifications.

The manuscript sigla in this volume follow the system developed by Bernard Coulie in "Liste des sigles utilisés pour désigner les manuscrits," *Supplements* to *Répertoire des bibliothèques et des catalogues de manuscrits arméniens*, ed. Bernard Coulie, Corpus Christianorum (Turnhout: Brepols, 1992). Transcriptions follow the rules of the *Revue des études arméniennes*.

References to works in the *Armenian Apocrypha* series are referred to by the volume's short title and the number and short titles of the text in that volume. Works within the present volume are referred to by number and short title.

Editor's remarks in the critical apparatuses are always preceded by a colon.

Abbreviations

Cited Catalogues of Manuscripts of the Matenadaran

Short Catalogue 1
Eganyan, O., A. Zeyt'unyan, and P'. Ant'abyan. Vol. 1 of Ցուցակ ձեռագրաց Մաշտոցի անվան Մատենադարանի (*Catalogue of Manuscripts of the Maštoc' Matenadaran*). Erevan: Academy of Sciences, 1965.

Short Catalogue 2
Eganyan, O., A. Zeyt'unyan, and P'. Ant'abyan. Vol. 2 of Ցուցակ ձեռագրաց Մաշտոցի անվան Մատենադարանի (*Catalogue of Manuscripts of the Maštoc' Matenadaran*). Erevan: Academy of Sciences, 1970.

Short Catalogue 3
Malkhasyan, Armen. Vol. 3 of Ցուցակ ձեռագրաց Մաշտոցի անուան Մատենադարանի (*Catalogue of Manuscripts of the Maštoc' Matenadaran*). Erevan: Erevan State University Press, 2007.

General Catalogue 1
Eganyan, O., A. Zeyt'unyan, and P'. Ant'abyan. Vol. 1 of Մայր ցուցակ հայերէն ձեռագրաց Մաշտոցի անուան Մատենադարանի (*Grand Catalogue of the Armenian Manuscripts of the Maštoc' Matenadaran*). Erevan: Academy of Sciences, 1984.

General Catalogue 3
Eganyan, O. Vol. 3 of Մայր ցուցակ հայերէն ձեռագրաց Մաշտոցի անուան Մատենադարանի (*General Catalogue of Armenian Manuscripts of the Maštoc' Matenadaran*). Erevan: Nairi, 2007.

General Catalogue 4
Kēoškeryan, A., and Y. K'ēosēyan. Vol. 4 of Մայր ցուցակ հայերէն ձեռագրաց Մաշտոցի անուան Մատենադարանի (*General Catalogue of Armenian Manuscripts of the Maštoc' Matenadaran*). Erevan: Nairi, 2008.

General Catalogue 7
Tēr Vardanyan, Gēorg. Vol. 7 of Մայր ցուցակ հայերէն ձեռագրաց

Մաշտոցի անուան Մատենադարանի (General Catalogue of Armenian Manuscripts of the Maštocʻ Matenadaran). Erevan: Nairi, 2012.

OTHER BIBLIOGRAPHIC ABBREVIATIONS

ANRW	*Aufstieg und Niedergang der römischen Welt: Geschichte und Kultur Roms im Spiegel der neueren Forschung*. Part 2, *Principat*. Edited by Hildegard Temporini and Wolfgang Haase. Berlin: de Gruyter, 1972–.
BGAMB	*Beiträge zur Geschichte des alten Mönchtums und des Benediktinerordens*
CBQ	*Catholic Biblical Quarterly*
CEJL	Commentaries on Early Jewish Literature
CSCO	Corpus Scriptorum Christianorum Orientalium
EJL	Early Jewish Literature
Gen. Rab.	Midrash Genesis Rabba (Berešit Rabba)
Ginzberg, Legends	Ginzberg, Louis. *The Legends of the Jews*. 7 vols. Philadelphia: Jewish Publication Society of America, 1909–1938.
HTR	*Harvard Theological Review*
HUAS	Hebrew University Armenian Series
IJS	Institute of Jewish Studies
JE	*The Jewish Encyclopedia*
JJS	*Journal of Jewish Studies*
JSHRZ	Jüdische Schriften aus hellenistisch-römischer Zeit
JSJSup	Supplements to *Journal of Jewish Studies*
JSP	*Journal for the Study of the Pseudepigrapha*
JTS	*Journal of Theological Studies*
MH	Մատենագիրք Հայոց (Ancient Armenian Literature)
OLA	Orientalia Louvaniensa Analecta
OED	*Oxford English Dictionary*
PhA	*Philosophia Antiqua*
RB	*Revue Biblique*
REArm	*Revue des études arméniennes*
SAC	Studies in Antiquity and Christianity
SBLDS	Society of Biblical Literature Dissertation Series
SD	Studies and Documents
SPCK	Society for the Promotion of Christian Knowledge
SVTP	Studia in Veteris Testamenti Pseudepigrapha
TU	Texte und Untersuchungen
UPATS	University of Pennsylvania Armenian Texts and Studies

YJS	Yale Judaica Series
Yovsēpʻianc'	Yovsēpʻianc', Sargis. *Անկանոն գիրք Հին Կտակարանաց* (*Uncanonical Books of the Old Testament*). Venice: Mekhitarist Press, 1896.
WZKM	*Wiener Zeitschrift für die Kunde des Morgenlandes*

Abbreviations for Ancient Sources

m. ʾAbot	ʾAbot
Apoc. Ab.	Apocalypse of Abraham
3 Apoc. Bar.	3 Baruch (Greek Apocalypse)
Ascen. Isa.	Mart. Ascen. Isa. 6–11
m. Ber.	Berakot
1 En.	1 Enoch
Gen. Rab.	Genesis Rabbah
Jub.	Jubilees
Liv. Pro.	Lives of the Prophets
b. Mak.	Makkot
Pen. Adam	Penitence of Adam
Pr. Man.	Prayer of Manasseh
Ps.-Ezekiel	4QPseudo-Ezekiel
Ques. Ezra	Questions of Ezra
y. Sanh.	Sanhedrin
T. Ab.	Testament of Abraham
T. Jos.	Testament of Joseph
T. Reu.	Testament of Reuben
T. Sol.	Testament of Solomon
b. Yebam.	Yebamot

1. The Number and the Twelve Classes of Angels

Introductory Remarks

This short piece occurs in M2245 on fols. 148r–148v. It has its own title and is clearly demarcated. This manuscript is a *Miscellany*, copied in 1689, perhaps in Adrianopolis (Edirne, Turkey).[1] It contains a number of apocryphal works, and other writings included in it may well have apocryphal content. Known texts include: *Question concerning the Archangels*[2] and *The Fall of the Angels*, fols. 114v–115r;[3] *Third Story of Joseph*, 330r–349v;[4] *Generations from Adam to Christ*, fols. 271r–272r.[5] So far unpublished is *Questions of St. Gregory*, fols. 235r–238v, a text dealing with individual eschatology.[6]

The intent of the text I am presenting here is unclear compared with the numerous lists of angelic ranks and classes that I have published previously.[7] Thus, *Angels and Biblical Heroes 3.1 Angelology Text 2* and other texts as well are apotropaic and *Angels and Biblical Heroes 3.5 The Praise of the Angels* deals with the praises sung by the heavenly hierarchy. Other writings discuss the list of nine angelic classes as a type of the ranks of the church hierarchy,

---

1. *General Catalogue* 7, 619–28.
2. Michael E. Stone, *Armenian Apocrypha Relating to Angels and Biblical Heroes*, EJL 45 (Atlanta: SBL Press, 2016), 72–75.
3. Stone, *Angels and Biblical Heroes*, 72–77.
4. Stone, *Angels and Biblical Heroes*, 176–229.
5. Stone, *Angels and Biblical Heroes*, 41–50.
6. I am preparing an edition of this text, which is discussed in "The Questions of St. Gregory: The First Recension," *Le Muséon* 131 (2018): 141–71. Currently I am preparing a further study on this work
7. Stone, *Angels and Biblical Heroes*, 65–111.

and so forth. Such texts, composed with a distinct purpose, may be seen in the published collections of angelological material.[8]

The present text seems to know two traditions of angelic classes, one of nine classes and the other of twelve. In the manuscript, this text is followed by a short list of the four types of wood of which the cross was constructed.[9] The two texts are not related.

This edition is a diplomatic copy of the manuscript, not normalizing the quite numerous spelling anomalies. However, when an abbreviation is resolved, I have used standard ancient Armenian spelling, it being impossible to determine which spelling the scribe might have used. I have not included detailed comments, since a number of very similar texts have been fully annotated in my *Angels and Biblical Heroes*.

Text

Title/ Յաղագս Հրեշտակաց թվոյն եւ դասուց ԲԺն. (12) մնցն:[10]

1/ Բայց մեք վերջացետալքս ի թուոց նոցա եւ ի բարձրութենէ եւ ի պայծառութենէ, զի. Թ. դասք են նորա եւ ամենայն դասք ԲԺն. (12) զունդք, զոր առաքեալքն նահապետութեան ասէ. եւ ամենայն զունդք հազարք հազարաց, եւ բիւրք բիւրաց:

2/ Բարձր քան զմիմեանս, որպէս երկինք քան զերկիր, պայծառ քան զմիմեանս, որպէս արեգակն քան զլուսին: Եւ մէկ / fol. 148v / դասն շատ է քան զամենայն մարդկութիւնս. եւ զօրագոյնք են քան զամենայն արբս, որպէս հրեշտակք քան զմարդ:

---

8. Michael E. Stone, "Some Armenian Angelological and Uranographical Texts," *Le Muséon* 105 (1992): 147–57; Stone, "Some Further Armenian Angelological Texts," in *Apocrypha, Pseudepigrapha and Armenian Studies: Collected Papers*, 2 vols., OLA 144–144 (Leuven: Peeters, 2006), 1:427–35; Stone, *Angels and Biblical Heroes*, 65–112. There are also rather a lot of angelic names in the apotropaic and allied prayers and invocations published by Frédéric Feydit, *Amulettes de l'Arménie chrétienne*, Bibliothèque arménienne de la Fondation Calouste Gulbenkian (Venice: St. Lazare, 1986) and in Sargis Harut'unyan, Հայ հմայական և ժողովրդական աղօթքներ (*Armenian Incantations and Folk Prayers*) (Erevan: Erevan State University Press, 2006).

9. The wood of the cross was the object of considerable speculations. In Armenian it is featured, among others, in the two texts called *Adam Fragments* and in *Words of Adam to Seth*. On both of these see Michael E. Stone, *Armenian Apocrypha Relating to Patriarchs and Prophets* (Jerusalem: Israel Academy of Sciences, 1982), 2–13. This topic is widespread and we cannot document it here. Among other works, see Esther C. Quinn, *The Quest of Seth for the Oil of Life* (Chicago: University of Chicago Press, 1962).

10. This abbreviation could not be resolved satisfactorily.

1. THE NUMBER AND THE TWELVE CLASSES OF ANGELS

3/ Եւ են անդի խնսարի. Աթոռք Քերոբէք, Սերոբէք, Տերութիւնք, Զօրութիւնք, Իշխանութիւնք, Պետութիւնք, Հրեշտակապետք, Հրեշտակք:[11]

TRANSLATION

0/ Concerning the Number and the Twelve Classes of Angels

1/ But we having come to an end of their classes and elevation and brightness. For their classes are nine and each class is composed of twelve groups, which are the highly ranked emissaries[12] according to, "and each host of a thousand thousands, and myriads of myriads."[13]

2/ (They are) higher than one another as the heavens are (higher) than the earth; brighter than one another as the sun is than the moon. And one class is more numerous than all mankind, and they are stronger than all men, just as the angels (are) than a man.

3/ And descending from there they are: Thrones, Cherubs, Seraphs, Dominions, Powers, Rules, Chiefs, Archangels, Angels.

---

11. This is the standard list of nine angelic classes, widespread in Armenian literature. See Stone, *Angels and Biblical Heroes*, 66.

12. Taking նահապետութեան adjectivally (A. Terian). առաքեալքս is plural and the verb ասէ is singular.

13. Dan 7:10.

2. An Exorcism in the Name of Adam

Introductory Remarks

The first printed book in Armenian is the *Urbatʻagirkʻ*, that is, *The Book of Friday*, published in Venice in 1512. As well as prayers and a gospel extract, it contains a number of exorcisms. The whole book has been studied and translated into Italian with ample annotation by Alessandro Orengo.[1] The particular text I present here is an exorcism, a type of composition instances of which are found in many Armenian exorcisitic or apotropaic manuscripts, amulets, and other works of similar character.[2] This brief text expresses and refers to a number of apocryphal traditions relating to Adam and Satan, which are pertinent to the present volume. In the text below, the pagination follows that of the printed *Urbatʻagirkʻ*. No text printed in Feydit's collection of Armenian amulets corresponds to this particular one.[3]

The edition I give here is based on the printed text of 1512 (= O). Dr. Orengo collated two Venice Mekhitarist manuscripts with it, V927 and V1957. No significant variants were found except for the reading following my edition of the text given here.

Sigla
O = Printed ed.   M = MS V927   V = MS V1957

---

1. Alessandro Orengo,"*Owrbatʻagirkʻ*' (*Il Libro Del Venerdi*), Atti della Accademia Nazionale dei Lincei 388 (Rome: Accademia Nazionale dei Lincei, 1991), 371–538. Dr. Orengo most kindly drew my attention to this brief document many years ago. I judge it appropriate to publish the Armenian text with an English translation in this volume because of the apocryphal traditions it comprises.

2. For edited Armenian amulet and magical texts and for some translations see: Feydit, *Amulettes de l'Arménie chrétienne*; Harutʻunyan, *Armenian Incantations*; and Yoav Loeff, "Four Texts from the Oldest Known Armenian Amulet Scroll: Matenadaran 115 (1428) with Introduction and Translation" (MA thesis, Hebrew University of Jerusalem, 2002).

3. Feydit, *Amulettes de l'Arménie chrétienne*.

2. AN EXORCISM IN THE NAME OF ADAM

Text

Urbatagirkʻ/ p. 0 / Երդմնեցուցանեմ զձեզ ի յանուն այն, որ ետ Ադամայ զմագաղաթն լուսաւոր, / p. 1 /գրեաց կտակս եւ կնքեաց եւ եդ ի գանձն իւրում եւ ասէ. «Իջանեմ ես երկիր, ուստի ստեղծայ»:

Եւ ապայ փչեաց ի նայ շունչ կենդանի: Խաւսեցաւ նայ ցՏէր եւ ասէ.

«Ես եմ սատանայ եւ զգեստն Ադամայ ունիմ: Եւ զամենայն արարածս տուեալ է ի ձեռս քո, անդ եդի զնա»:

Parallel text in V:

Գրեաց կնքեաց եդ ի գանձի իւրում եւ ասաց. «Իջանեմ յերկիր, ուստի ստեղծի. յորժամ անցքէ զիմ պատուիրանն, զզեցո զնա լուսեղէն փառօքն»:[4]

Translation

I adjure you in that Name of the One who gave Adam the luminous parchment.[5] He[6] wrote this testament[7] and sealed (it) and placed (it) in his

---

4. Dr. Orengo most graciously provided me with the variant readings of the two manuscript copies noted above. I do not present them here.

5. I.e., God. This is the letter that, according to apocryphal Armenian tradition, was given to Adam, preserved in his treasury, and passed down the generations until the Magi brought it from the East to newborn Christ. The letter was supposed to predict the coming of Christ. Orengo (*Urbatʻagirkʻ*, 409, n. 141) gives information about this tradition. A further discussion along with the translation of a relevant passage from the *Infancy Gospel* is to be found in Michael E. Stone, *Adam's Contract with Satan: The Legend of the Cheirograph of Adam* (Bloomington: Indiana University Press, 2002), 71–72; Igor Dorfmann-Lazarev, "The Cave of the Nativity Revisited: Memory of the Primeval Beings in the Armenian *Lord's Infancy* and Cognate Sources," in *Mélanges Jean-Pierre Mahé*, ed. Aram Mardirossian, Agnès Ouzounian, and Constantin Zuckerman, Travaux et Mémoires 18 (Paris: Association des Amis de Centre d'Histoire et Civilization de Byzance, 2014), 285–333 and particularly 312 and 326–33. I advance a hypothesis that Eve is depicted on a fifth-century mosaic clasping God's document in her hand; see the plate on p. 334 of Dorfmann-Lazarev's article.

6. Apparently, Adam.

7. More than one work circulated in antiquity under the title *Testament of Adam*. See Stephen Edward Robinson, *The Testament of Adam: An Examination of the Syriac and Greek Traditions*, SBLDS 52 (Chico CA: Scholars Press, 1982); Robinson, "Testament of Adam," in *Apocalyptic Literature and Testaments*, vol. 1 of *The Old Testament Pseudepigrapha*, ed. James H. Charlesworth (Garden City, NY: Doubleday, 1983), 989–95; Robinson, "The Testament of Adam: An Updated *Arbeitbericht*," *JSP* 5 (1989): 95–100. See for ancient

treasury.[8] And he said, "I descend to earth whence I was created." And then He (God) blew the breath (spirit) of life into him (Adam).

That one[9] spoke to the Lord and said, "I am Satan and I have the garment of Adam.[10] And[11] all creations have been given into your hand. There I put it."[12]

Parallel text in V:

He (Adam) wrote, sealed, placed (it) in his treasury, and said, "I descend to earth whence I was created. When the sentence concerning me is over, I will wear it in luminous glory."

"When he will transgress my commandment, put it on with luminous glory."[13]

---

testimonia to *Testament of Adam* and various works in diverse languages bearing this or a similar title: Michael E. Stone, *A History of the Literature of Adam and Eve*, EJL 3 (Atlanta: Scholars Press, 1992), 77–78, 82, 85–87, 95–97, 100, 111.

8. The tradition of Adam's treasury was connected with the notion of the Cave of Treasures, and that was very widespread. Its most famous instance is the Syriac work, *Cave of Treasures*, 21.12. See the edition of Carol Bezold, *Die Schatzhöhle, syrisch und deutsch herausgegeben* (Leipzig: Hinrichs, 1888).

9. I.e., the fallen angel who is also Satan.

10. The tradition of Adam's garment is complex and cannot be discussed here. The reference is more likely to be to the garments of light he wore in the Garden than to those God made for him (Gen 3:21), though this second interpretation cannot be ruled out. The tradition of the garments of light is ancient and widespread in Jewish and Christian texts. On the Armenian traditions concerning Adam, see Michael E. Stone, *Adam and Eve in the Armenian Tradition, Fifth through Seventeenth Centuries*. EJL 38 (Atlanta: Society of Biblical Literature, 2013).

11. Perhaps the speaker changes here.

12. The last words are obscure.

13. Here apparently God is the speaker.

3. The Construction of Noah's Ark

Introductory Remarks

Manuscript M4618 has been the source from which a number of the works edited in this volume were drawn. It is described in the *Short Catalogue* of Matenadaran manuscripts. The manuscript is a *Miscellany* composed of different parts, copied by different scribes, dated to 1569, 1693, 1695, and 1706. The text presented here is on fol. 53r[1] in the section copied by Ignatius of Amida who wrote the greater part of the manuscript. The rest of the manuscript was copied by Grigor (fols. 79r–93r), Vardan *vardapet* (fols. 178r–200v), and an unknown scribe (fols. 162r–167v). The manuscript was copied in Van between 1675 and 1706.

This codex contains a number of apocryphal texts. Those texts listed in the *Short Catalogue* of the Matenadaran in Erevan include: *History of Adam and Eve*,[2] *Flight of Christ to Egypt*,[3] *Noah's Ark* (apparently, the present text), *The Oil That They Found in the Albanian*[4] *Books, The Fall of Satanel and Adam*,[5] *The Deception of Adam, Adam's Sons*,[6] *King Hezekiah*,[7] *Isaiah*.[8] Other works, listed in our own notes and in the detailed description, include *Questions of St. Gregory* (fols. 9r–10v) and *Concerning the Tower*,[9] (fols.

---

1. My thanks are expressed to Kʻnar Harutʻunyan of the Matenadaran who kindly verified my long-hand copy of this text made some years ago against the manuscript. Dr. Gēorg Tēr Vardanyan graciously made a draft of the full description of this manuscript available to me and here I have extracted fom it material relevant to the Armenian Apocryphal literature.
2. Folios 1r–6r.
3. Folios 45r–46v.
4. A Caucasian Christian people called the Ałuankʻ in Armenian.
5. Folios 133v–140r, including text parallel to W. Lowndes Lipscomb, *The Armenian Apocryphal Adam Literature*, UPATS 8 (Atlanta: Scholars Press, 1990), 108–27.
6. Folios 138r–140r; see Lipscomb, *Apocryphal Adam Literature*, 142–71.
7. Folios 142v–144r.
8. Folios 13r–14v.
9. The Tower of Babel is intended.

-7-

43r–44r). *Story concerning Abraham* is found on fols. 53v–55 and is another copy of *Abraham Text 2*, edited some years ago.¹⁰ Text no. 12, *King Solomon: Four Short Texts* is published from this manuscript. In general, the texts of apocryphal interest are to be found in the first 160 folios of the manuscript. Some time ago I made public some details of and extracts from a work on Abraham,¹¹ and a short composition on calendar titled *Concerning the Millennia II* has also been published, from this manuscript.¹² In addition *Concerning the Places of Hell* was published from fols. 146r–146v of the same manuscript. Many of its riches, however, have not yet been mined.

In the present book I publish a number of texts from this interesting volume, including text no. 12 *Concerning King Solomon* (fols. 133v–135r); text no. 7, *Brief History of Joshua Son of Nun* (fols. 146v–148v); and text no. 15, *Hezekiah and Manasseh* (fols. 142r–143v).

Texts dealing with Noah are not uncommon, but I am familiar with no other apocryphal text than the one presented here that contains such details about the construction of the Ark. In addition, the tradition about the craftsman Nersēs remains mysterious. Of previously published texts relating to Noah, note *The Story of Noah*, which forms part of a longer biblical retelling called *Biblical Paraphrases* and *Sermon concerning the Flood*.¹³

The text I am presenting here overlaps with material found in the fourteenth-century work Գիրք հարցմանց (*The Book of Questions*), by Grigor Tatʻewacʻi (1346–1409/10) in the chapter titled Վասն Նոյեան տապանին (*Concerning Noah's Ark*). For its first three sections our text runs parallel to but is shorter than Grigor Tatʻewacʻi's *Book of Questions*.¹⁴ However, from the words եւ արուեստաւորին "and the craftsman's" in section 4 on, there ensues material that is not contained in *Book of Questions*. Its source is unknown, as are traditions about the existence of the craftsman and his name. Indeed, usually stress is laid up on Noah's building the Ark himself. The text is formulated in the standard erotapokritic form of question and answer.

---

10. I published this from an older manuscript, M8531 in Michael E. Stone, *Armenian Apocrypha Relating to Abraham*, EJL 37 (Atlanta: Society of Biblical Literature, 2012), 36–50.

11. Stone, *Armenian Apocrypha Relating to Abraham*, 237–38.

12. Stone, *Angels and Biblical Heroes*, 35–36, text 3.2.

13. Michael E. Stone, *Armenian Apocrypha Relating to Adam and Eve*, SVTP 14 (Leiden: Brill, 1996), 174–79.

14. See Grigor Tatʻewacʻi, Գիրք հարցմանց (*Book of Questions*), repr. ed. (Jerusalem: St. James Press, 1993), 293.

3. THE CONSTRUCTION OF NOAH'S ARK

Following this text, for convenience's sake I have given an extract from *The Story of Noah* mentioned above, which also deals with the construction of the Ark and draws a rather different picture. In the section titled "Some Other Noah Traditions," I present next a further narrative of the same events, taken from the Armenian Adam apocryphon titled *Concerning the Good Tidings of Seth*. For this text I draw upon Lipscomb's text and translation.[15]

EXCURSUS: QUESTIONS AND ANSWERS AND OTHER SCHOLASTIC TEXTS IN THE ARMENIAN APOCRYPHA

There exist in Armenian, as in many other Christian languages, documents composed of texts of questions and answers about the Bible, often elucidating details of the biblical narratives. This genre of texts is widespread.

Among the oldest such texts in Armenian are the two surviving "Question and Answer" treatises of Philo's that are preserved in Armenian, his *Questions on Genesis* and *Questions on Exodus*. His *Questions on Genesis* is preserved fully, but only segments of *Questions on Exodus* survive. This genre's origins lie in the Hellenistic exegetical tradition and it was adopted in late antiquity as an exegetical and polemical tool.

Before the emergence of patristic and the polemical Question and Answer treatises, there were literary forms of Second Temple Jewish literature that cultivated series of questions set in the mouth of a biblical hero, or of a saint or other significant figure and answers given by angels or God. Thus, as well as texts in which the questions are posed by an anonymous interlocutor, there are dialogic compositions in which the questions are asked by a named hero. Such elenchic dialogues are to be found in many apocalyptic revelatory texts, an early example being the *Book of the Watchers*. Not dissimilar series of questions occur in heavenly ascent visions such as *3 Baruch*; and in the Dialogic Dispute form, so beloved particularly of *4 Ezra*.

For examples of such texts in published Armenian, see *Questions of Ezra*[16] and *Questions of St. Gregory*.[17] Apocrypha in this genre include the questions apocalyptic seers ask of angels in the course of heavenly journeys

---

15. Lipscomb, *Armenian Apocryphal Adam Literature*, 196–200. This is cited by permission. Another form of this text is to be found in the other recension of *Concerning the Good Tidings of Seth* in Lipscomb, *Armenian Apocryphal Adam Literature*, 279–80.

16. Michael E. Stone, "A New Edition and Translation of the Questions of Ezra," in *Solving Riddles and Untying Knots: Biblical, Epigraphic, and Semitic Studies in Honor of Jonas C. Greenfield*, ed. Ziony Zevit, Seymour Gitin, and Michael Sokoloff (Winona Lake, IN: Eisenbrauns, 1995), 293–316.

17. Stone, "Questions of St. Gregory."

and the angelic responses. There are also texts that seem to be answers to questions like those posted by elenchic texts, but in which the questions themselves are not recorded.

There are medieval Armenian assemblies of questions and answers on narratives from the Hebrew Bible. The most famous are, perhaps, the *Book of Questions* of Vanakan vardapet Taušecʻi (1181–1251) and the *Book of Questions* of Grigor Tatʻewacʻi (1346–1409), but a number of other texts exist, some attributed and some anonymous.

In the present collection of parabiblical texts, we find both "Question and Answer" texts, and also documents presenting lists of statements that appear to be answers to questions that are either not preserved or else deliberately omitted. Such texts in the medieval period seem to have emerged from the University Monasteries and other similar learned contexts.

Moreover, in addition to the Question and Answer genre, in medieval Armenian apocryphal texts we find further hints of a learned, scholarly origin of various features. These include citations of multiple authorities' views on a certain issue, consultation of multiple manuscripts in the attempt to clarify a textual difficulty, and application of material from a very specific genre as a rhetorical tool.[18]

Some instances in this book are the following:

(1) Instances of resolving exegetical difficulties in the biblical story.

> No. 4, *Concerning Abraham*. This document is a single segment of *Abraham 5 Genealogy of Abraham*. That document is a series of units of information, each a self-sufficient paragraph, that could readily have been answers to questions.

(2) Instances in which the author draws on learned and scholastic traditions.

> No. 3, *The Construction of Noah's Ark*. This text draws from *Book of Questions* of Grigor Tatʻewacʻi and supplements that with other, elsewhere unknown traditions.
>
> No. 7, *Brief History of Joshua*. Interest in natural science is exhibited in §43, which includes a passage either from a metallurgic work, or

---

18. It is my hope to conduct a further study of such features of these Bible-related texts with the aim of gaining insight into at least one nexus of the genesis of the Armenian parabiblical texts, that is, the scholastic tradition. Other features relevant to such an enquiry are the calendary, astronomical, and astrological knowledge exhibited by some documents.

3. THE CONSTRUCTION OF NOAH'S ARK

from some *Physiologus*-like catalogue of wondrous beasts and natural phenomena.

No. 1, *The Number and the Twelve Classes of Angels* starts with 1/ Բայց մեք վերջացեալքս ի թուող նոցա եւ ի բարձրութենէ եւ ի պայծառութենէ, "1/ But we having come to an end of their classes and elevation and brightness." This phrasing in the opening of the indicates its scholastic origins, though not necessarily branding it as erotapokritic.

No. 6, *Supplication about the Sodomites and Gomorreans*, §§24–25 takes care to avoid contradictions in the biblical text by stressing details that are not treated in the biblical story, responding to an apparent contradiction.

The passage §§28–29 seems to draw on an erotapokritic source in its discussion of the Dead Sea and the divine destruction of Sodom. This source included questions about notable natural phenomena as well as exegetical difficulties in the biblical text. This source was in Question and Answer form, as is betrayed by the words, "If someone were to say that God judged mercilessly and did not give a sign first …" (§29). The answer forestalled the question.

No. 7, *Brief History of Joshua*, §63 discusses the astronomical ramifications of Joshua's halting of the sun and moon. Here there is astronomical theory, including the ideas of the constellations and the decans, brought to bear on the standing still of the sun and moon. This appears to be a response to a question and adduces current astronomical and astrological ideas to make its point.

Text

Title/ Վասն Նոյեա տապանակի հարց:
1// fol. 53r / Թէ որպէս Նոյեան տապանին ձեւն եւ չէնքն:
2/ Ասէ գիրն, թէ չորեքանկիւնի. ներքոյ եւ արտաքոյ նաւթիւ ծեփեալ, որ է կուպրն, զի մի վնասեցի.
3/ Երկայն ԳՃ. (300) կանգուն. եւ լայն Ծ. (50) եւ բարձր Լ. (30): ԺԵ. (15) կանգուն հաւասար բարձրացոյց. եւ ի ԺԵ.ն (15) նրբեցոյց, զի չորն վիժեցի. նման է սագաշէն եկեղեցւոյ:
4/ Եւ դուռն յետուստ կողմանէ, զի դիւրաւ մտցեն կենդանիքն: Եւ արուեստաւորին անունն Ներսէս է: Այնքան ողջախոհ էր Նոյ, որ Լ (30) ամն մի անգամ մերձենայր ի կինն:
5/ Եւ ի Ճ. (100) ամն Գ. (3) որդիք ծնաւ՝ Սեմ, Քամ, Յաբեթդ, եւ ապա սկսաւ շինել զտապանն, եւ Ճ. (100) ամն կատարեցաւ: Հարցին գնա, թէ՝ «զինչ գործես». եւ նա ասէր, թէ՝ «ձեր մեղացն բարկացեալ

է Աստուած. շրիեղեղ կու տայ»: Տրտմէին եւ տարակուսէին, բայց սովորական յաղթէր: Կատակ արարեալ ծիծաղէին, ուտէին ըմպէին, կանայս առնէին:

Translation

Title/ Question Concerning Noah's Ark:

1/ Of what form[19] and construction is Noah's Ark?

2/ Scripture says that it was four-cornered.[20] It was plastered inside and outside with tar,[21] which is bitumen, so that it would not be damaged.

3/ Its length was three hundred cubits and its width was fifty cubits and its height was thirty (that is: cubits).[22] He raised it to a level of fifteen cubits, and at fifteen cubits he narrowed (it), so that the water would fall. It is like a gable of a church.[23]

4/ And the door was from the stern, so that the animals might enter easily. And the craftsman's name is Nersēs.[24] Noah was so chaste that he approached his wife only once[25] during thirty years[26]

5/ And in the one hundredth year he begot three sons, Shem, Ham, Japheth. And then he began to build the Ark and in the one hundredth year it

---

19. The text opens with է, which is far from usual and indicated that this is an extract from a text or a crystallized oral retelling.

20. That is, square or rectangular.

21. Genesis 6:14 relates that Noah is to cover the Ark with pitch. Genesis does not describe it as a rectangular box, but this is its shape in early Christian representations of it, see Ruth A. Clements, "A Shelter amid the Flood: Noah's Ark in Early Jewish and Christian Art," in *Noah and His Books*, ed. Michael E. Stone, Aryeh Amihay, and Vered Hillel, EJL 28 (Atlanta: Society of Biblical Literature, 2010), 277–99 and particularly 278–87.

22. These are the measurements given in Gen 6:15.

23. Exactly what is intended in Gen 6:16 by "finish it to a cubit above" is unclear, but regardless, it does not mention a change of dimensions at the height of fifteen cubits.

24. The implications of this phrase are unclear. Is Nersēs the same person as Noah, or is he a workman employed by Noah? This is unique.

25. The Armenian tradition makes much of Noah's chastity. This is how the phrase "walked with God" (Gen 6:9) is understood. See in *Sodomites* published here, §30 and the extract from *Concerning the Good Tidings of Seth* given at the end of the present section. This is a standard Armenian Christian approach to the text.

26. The period of thirty years between births is to be found in many apocryphal stories. Some striking instances occur, such as *History of Adam and His Grandsons* §§1–12, which sets at a space of thirty years between each of the following events: Adam's first intercourse with Eve and the birth of Cain, the begetting of Abel, and the killing of Abel. In Stone, *Armenian Apocrypha Relating to Adam and Eve*, 92 there is an extensive note on this topic.

was completed.[27] They asked him, "What are you doing?" and he said, "God is wrath at your sins; He will bring a Flood." They were sad and doubted, but their habitude won out.[28] They joked and smiled; they were eating and drinking and taking women.[29]

Some Other Noah Traditions

The Story of Noah

2. Եւ հարիւր տարին ապա կատարեցաւ. եւ ձայն կացնին եւ ուրախին, դրին եւ սղոցին ասէր, թէ գայ ջրհեղեղն. եւ ոչ հաւատային:

2. And a hundred years then were completed. And the sound of axes, and of adzes, of chisels and of saws, said that the flood was coming. And they did not believe.

Concerning the Good Tidings of Seth[30]

24. Now God became angry at them because of their many sins, and he wished to drown them. 25. God commanded Noah to build an ark and to marry. 26. When an angel came and told Noah to marry, he did not want to marry, for he was five hundred years old.[31]

27. And the angel said, "You must fulfill God's commands, for he is about to destroy this world with water; he will drown everything, and you will become a new Adam, for this world will be filled with your seed.[32] 28. Noah said, "How long shall I live in this world?"

29. The angel said, "You are five hundred years old; you must live another four hundred years." 30. Noah said, "Four hundred years pass like a dream

---

27. According to Gen 5:31, Noah begat his three sons at the age of five hundred, and the flood came when he was six hundred years old (Gen 7:6). This is the chronology of §5 in our text here.

28. The idea of his contemporaries mocking Noah is in part derived from Gen 6:9, which says that Noah "was blameless in his generation."

29. His contemporaries were, in the retelling of this story, the sons of Cain and the wayward sons of Seth. In the apocryphal Armenian Adam books these themes of their promiscuity and gluttony occur repeatedly. See Lipscomb, *Armenian Adam Literature*.

30. Stone, *Patriarchs and Prophets*, 88.

31. Observe the stress on his chastity in §34 of *3 Construction* above.

32. The idea of Noah as founder of humanity after the Flood, resembling Adam, is to be found in *4 Ezra* 3:9–11, a work also extant in Armenian.

in the night.³³ Why should I corrupt my virginity on account of one transitory dream?" 31. The angel said, "They are the Lord's commands; you cannot hinder them."

32. Noah said, "I do not know if there remains a chaste woman whom I might marry." 33. The angel said, "There is one pure virgin <from the line of Seth who has kept her virginity unstained>, whose name is Noemzara;³⁴ marry her."

34. And he began to build an ark. Its length was one hundred and fifty cubits and its width fifty, and its height was thirty cubits. 35. And the angel went away from him. 36. And Noah married.

37 *Text of Y*: And while he was building the ark, the axe cried out, the hatchet cried out, the saw cried out, <and> the wood cried out. "Behold a flood is coming and it will destroy this world!"

38. *Text of B*: 38a. Then Noah heard the cry of the axe, he went <and> related to everyone that a flood was coming. Every man scorned him. But Noah was determined about the Ark. 38b. Everyone would go and see the design of the ark; they would hear the cry of the axe and the hatchet, the saw and the hand-saw which said, "A flood is coming!" 38c. They would scorn and say, "Look at the ignorance of Noah, who says a flood is coming!" 38d. Noah went forth, <and> upon a high hill he was building the ark, <and he said>, "The water will come up to here and will rise higher." He built the ark for eighty years.

38e. The angel came to Noah and said, "Take three women from Seth's line for your sons, and these are their names: Zanazan, Zarmanazan, <and> Yereknazan. 38f. And these three women are still young virgins, and of Seth's seed. But your sons may not marry <them> until you go out of the Ark. But you, enter that ark, because a flood is coming!" For when Noah married and began building the Ark he had three sons. And these were their names: Shem, Ham, and Japheth.

---

33. A fairly common simile in the Hebrew Bible, compare Isa 29:7, Ps 73(72):20, Ps 90(89):5, Job 20:8.

34. This is the name of Noah's wife in many sources, already starting with 1Q20 (Genesis Apocryphon) 6:7, *Jub.* 4:33, Stone, *Armenian Apocrypha Relating to Adam and Eve*, 97.

4. Concerning Abraham

Introductory Remarks

This text is preserved on fol. 8r of M682, a *Miscellany,* copied in 1679.[1] It is for the most part another version of a segment of *Abraham 5, Genealogy of Abraham.*[2] The passage deals briefly with a number of genealogical traditions relating to Abraham, Isaac, and Jacob and their spouses. In *Abraham 5, Genealogy of Abraham* this material is embedded in a longer collection of miscellaneous traditions relating to the biblical past.[3]

In greater detail, we may say that *Concerning Abraham,* §§1–9 on fol. 8r of M682 is another form of *Abraham 5, Genealogy of Abraham.* §§1–6 correspond in content to *Abraham 5, Genealogy of Abraham.* It is noteworthy that, while in §§1–4 the two texts are rather similar, §§5–6 of *Concerning Abraham* present a rather different form of the parallel material that is found in *Abraham 5 Genealogy of Abraham.*[4] Subsequently, in §10 it contains an unique tradition concerning Abraham's brother Haran and his death, there retailing an idea known to other Abraham texts, but not formulated by them in the wording used here.[5] We give the text and translation of the document with a collation down to the end of the parallel material in §8. In addition, the list of trials that occurs in §2 is embedded in *Abraham 5, Genealogy of Abraham,* §2. This passage also occurs in manuscripts as an independent document and is published as such in *Abraham 13, The Ten Trials of Abraham.*

Text

M682 1/ Թարայ հայրն Աբրահամու ծնաւ զնաքովր, զԱռան եւ զԱբրահամ: Եւ ի ԺԸ. (18) ամին Աբրահամ Ճանաչեաց զԱստուած. եւ

---

1. *General Catalogue* 3, 310–16.
2. Stone, *Abraham,* 78–85.
3. Stone, *Abraham,* 78–85.
4. The section divisions in M0682 are not identical to those in *Abraham Text 5.*
5. Compare with *Abraham Texts* 4.6 and 10.9.

ի Կ. (60) ամին ասաց Աստուած ելանել յերկրէն, որ եւ բնակեցան, ի Խառան:

2/ Եւ ՀԵ. (75) ամին դարձեալ ել ի Խառանայ եւ յըստանեացն եւ պանդխտեցաւ ի զՊաղեստին եւ Ժ. (10) փորձանաց հանդիպեցաւ:

3/ Նախ՝ ելանելն յերկրէն եւ բնակիլն ի մէջ օտարաց:

Բ՝ քարշիլն Սառայի փարոնի:

Գ՝ բաժանիլն Ղովտայ:

Դ՝ ոչ ինչ առնուլն յաւարէն Սողոմայ:

Ե՝ քարշիլն Սառայի Աբիմելէքայ:

Զ՝ ի ծերութեան թլփատիլն:

Է՝ տալ զՀագար ի ձեռն Սառայի:

Ը՝ ի բաց հանելն Հագարայ:

Թ՝ աւետեացն Աստուծոյ ոչ երկմտելն:

Ժ՝ որդին պատարագել:

4/ Վասն այսց հաճոյ եղեւ Աստուծոյ, եւ արար զնա հայր բազմաց: Ի ՁԶ. (86) ամին ծնաւ զԻսմայէլ ի Հագարայ, ի ՂԹ. (99) ամին թլփատեցաւ, ի Ճ. (100) ամին ծնաւ զԻսահակ, ի Ղ. (90) ամին Սառայի. եւ մեռաւ Սառայ ՃԻԷ. (127) ամաց:

5/ Եւ էառ կին Աբրահամ զՔետուր, յորմէ ծնաւ որդիս Զ. (6): Մինն զմինն եսպան, եւ այլքն լցին զերկիր, որոց մի են թուրք, որ եւ Պալհաւունիք կոչին՝ Պահլ քաղաքին անուամբ, եւ Արշակունիք՝ յաղագս Արշակայ քաջին:

6/ Եւ մեռաւ Աբրահամ ՃԽԵ. (145) ամաց: Իսահակ էառ կին զՌեբեկայ՝ թոռն Նաքովրայ եղբօրն Աբրահամու: Խ. (40) ամին իւրոյ առաւ, բայց ոչ մերձեցաւ մինչ ի Ի. (20) ամն: Եւ ի Կ. (60) ամին Իսահակայ ծնանի Ռեբեկայ գՅակոբ եւ զԵսաւ:

7/ Եսաւ էր վայրագ, զազանամիտ, անասնաբարոյ, մարդատեաց, որովայնամոլ, անձնասէր եւ ոչ աստուածասէր. վասն որոյ զանդրանկութիւնն վաճառեաց Յակոբայ: Եւ Յակոբ փախեալ յԵսաւայ գնաց ի Խառան եւ էառ զերկուսին դուստերն Լաբանայ քեռոյն իւրոյ. Բ. (2) նաժշտցքն:

8/ Այս են ծնունդքն Յակոբայ՝ Ռուբէն, Շմաւոն, Ղեւի, Յուդա, Իսաքար, Զաբուղոն, եւ Դինա քոյր նոցա՝ ի Լիայէ կնոջէն.

Դան եւ Նեփթաղիմ՝ Ջեղփայէ աղախնոյ նորին.

9/ Գաղ եւ Ասեր ի Բալլայէ աղախոյն Հռաքելի.

Յովսէփ եւ Բենիամին ի Հռաքելայ: Եւ մեռանի Իսահակ ՃՁ. (180) ամաց:

10/ Բայց թէ էր ասաց գիրն թէ մեռաւ Առան՝ եղբայրն Աբրահամու, առաջի հօր իւրոյ Թարայի: Վասն զի ոչ էր մեռեալ որդի յառաջ

4. CONCERNING ABRAHAM

քան զհայրն յԱդամայ հետև. ե[.]ւա զի զծնունդ չորոյն արար. վասն բնութեանս սահմանի ոչ մեռաւ, այլ յառաջ քան զհայրն:

Critical Apparatus

The lemma is M0682 and the variants are readings in which the published text *Abraham 5, Genealogy of Abraham*, differs from it.

1/ հայրն Աբրահամու] om | Աբրահամ ծանաչեաց] ∞ | և ի2°] ի | ելանել "to go forth"] ել յերկրէ և յազգէ քումմէ "go forth from your land and family"

2/ դարձեալ om | և յրնտանեացն և պանդխտեցաւ ի զՊադեստին] ի Պադեստին | և4°] ուր և

3/ ելանել | և բնակին ի մէջ օտարաց] և յազգէն "and the family" | ի փարոնի] փարաւնէ | առնուլ | յԱբիմելէքէ | հանել | Հազարայ] + որդովքն | պատարագելն — բազմաց] om

4/ Իսմայէլ ի Հազարայ] զԻսմայէլ | ի ճ] ճ | ի Դ ամին Սառայի] և Սառայ Դ ամաց | որդիս Ձ] + զԸմրամ և զՅեկդան և զՁմադան և զՄադիան և զՅեսբոկ և զՍովէ : "Ēmram and Yekdan and Zmadan and Madian and Yesbok and Sovē"

5/ սպան | Պահլ — անուամբ] յաղագս Պահլ քաղաքին "on account of the city Pahl"

6/ զՌեբեկայ | Խ ամին — զԵսաւ] om

7/ և Եսաւ] Եսաւ էր | յորովանամոլ | ոլայ] + ասաց Աստուած զՅակոբ սիրեցի և զԵսաւ ատեցի "God said, I loved Jacob and Esau I hated" | զանդրանկութիւնն — Յակոբայ] om | և Յակոբ | իւրոյ] + զԼիա և զՌաքէլ "Leah and Rachel" | Բ նաժշտացքն] om

8/ այս — Յակոբայ] և ծնաւ որդիս ԺԲ "and he begot 12 sons"

9/ և մեռանի Իսահակ] Իսահակ մեռանի

Translation

1/ Terah, Abraham's father, begot Nahor, Haran, and Abraham. And in his 18th year, Abraham recognized God. And in his 60th year, God said to go forth from the land which they inhabited, to Haran.[6]

---

6. Gen 11:31. According to *Jub.* 11:28 Abraham was fourteen years old when he recognized God.

2/ And in the 75th year, again he went forth from Haran and from his family.[7] And he sojourned in Palestine, and he encountered ten trials.[8]

3/ First, the going forth from his land and residing among strangers.

2. Sarah's being taken away by Pharaoh.[9]

3. The separation from Lot.[10]

4. Not taking anything from the booty of Sodom.[11]

5. Sarah's being taken away by Abimelech.[12]

6. Being circumcised in old age.[13]

7. Delivering Hagar into Sarah's power.[14]

8. Expelling Hagar.[15]

9. Not doubting God's announcement.[16]

10. The offering of his son.[17]

4/ On account of these he was pleasing to God and He made him a father of many. In the 86th year he begot Ishmael from Hagar.[18] And in the 99th year he was circumcised.[19] In the 100th year he begot Isaac[20] in Sarah's 90th year. And Sara died at 127 years.[21]

5/ And Abraham took Keturah as wife, from whom he begot six sons.[22] They killed one another, and the remainder filled the earth. One of these were the Turks,[23] who are also called Palhavunis, after the name of the city of Bahl, and the Arsacids on account of Arsaces the Valorous.[24]

---

7. Gen 12:4–5; Jub. 12:12 also says that he was sixty when he went forth.
8. Gen 12:1–13:11.
9. Gen 12:15–20.
10. Gen 13:11.
11. Gen 14:22–23.
12. Gen 20:2–18.
13. Gen 17:24.
14. Gen 21:12.
15. Gen 21:14.
16. I.e., of Isaac's birth. This is related in Gen 18:1–16.
17. Gen 22:2–13.
18. Gen 16:16.
19. Gen 17:2–13.
20. Gen 21:5.
21. Gen 23:1.
22. Gen 25:1–2.
23. Movsēs Xorenac'i 2.8 mentions an individual T'urk', a grandson of Hayk who was the eponymous ancestor of the Armenians. Our author has taken the -k' to be a plural ending and identified T'urk' with the Turks. That is not appropriate.
24. This section seems dependent on Movsēs Xorenac'i, whose aim at this point was to trace the Noachic ancestry of the Armenians; see Movsēs Xorenac'i 2.1 and Robert W.

4. CONCERNING ABRAHAM

6/ And Abraham died at 175 years (of age).[25] Isaac married Rebecca, Nahor Abraham's brother's granddaughter.[26] He was married in his 40th year,[27] but he did not draw near to her until the 20th year.[28] In Isaac's 60th year Rebecca bore Jacob and Esau.[29]

7/ Esau was savage, brutal, bestial, misanthropic, gluttonous, self-loving and not God-loving. On account of this he sold the rights of the first-born to Jacob.[30] And Jacob fled from Esau.[31] He went to Haran. And he took (that is, married) the two daughters of Laban his uncle with two handmaidens.[32]

8/ These are the descendants of Jacob:[33] Reuben, Simeon, Levi, Judah, Issachar, Zebulun and Dina, their sister from his wife Leah;

Dan and Naphtali from her handmaiden Zilpah;

9/ Gad and Asher from Bilhah, Rachel's handmaiden;

Joseph and Benjamin from Rachel. And Isaac died at (the age of) 180 years.[34]

10/ But, why does Scripture say that Haran, Abraham's brother, died before his father Terah? Because from Adam on, no son had died before his father. [ ] that he brought about the begetting of the mule, on account of which he did not die at his natural term, but before his father.[35]

Thomson, *Moses Khorenats'i: History of the Armenians*, rev. ed. (Ann Arbor: Caravan, 2006), 128.

25. Gen 25:7–8.
26. Gen 24:67.
27. Gen 25:20.
28. Apparently, after they married. See the similar assertion about Noah in *3 Construction of the Ark* below.
29. Gen 25:25–26.
30. Gen 25:33.
31. Compare Gen 35:1.
32. All this genealogical material is in accordance with Genesis.
33. Gen 35:23–26, Exod 1:1–4.
34. Gen 35:28.
35. The same consideration is to be found in *Abraham Text* 2.6; see Stone, *Abraham*, 43–44 n. 30. See also *Abraham Texts* 4.6, 10.9. This miscegenation of the horse and the ass is not mentioned in the Hebrew traditions about this subject.

5. Abraham and the Idols

Introductory Remarks

This brief document is preserved in M4618 on fol. 131v.[1] It is a filler, written in a different hand to that of the scribe of the main part of the manuscript. It is followed by two further passages, each written by a different scribe.[2] This page of writing, then, preserves three units of text dealing with details of biblical and parabiblical narratives and copied by three different individuals. Here these three passages are denoted A, B, and C. Moreover, the section of fol. 131v copied by the first scribe, that is, passage A, is itself composed of three textual fragments. The first fragment of A is about Abraham and the sale of idols, the second fragment deals with John the Baptist's food, and the third with King Solomon the wise. The provenance of all of these fragments remains unknown and only one of them has been published.[3]

Thus, there are three fillers on fol. 131v each copied by a different scribe. The first filler (A) opens with a tradition about Abraham. The following two filler passages (B and C) are lacunose, for a section of the left-hand part of the page has been torn off. The second passage deals with Satan and his son; the third is *List of 12 Literate Nations*.[4] None of them draws an explicit moral

---

1. See on the manuscript the "Introductory Remarks" to 3 *The Construction of Noah's Ark*, above, pp. 7–8.
2. This is clear from the image. The manuscript is described briefly in *Short Catalogue* 1, 1247–48.
3. Michael E. Stone, "Three Apocryphal Fragments from Armenian Manuscripts," in *A Teacher for All Generations: Essays in Honor of James Vanderkam*, ed. Eric F. Mason et al., JSJSup 153 (Leiden: Brill, 2012), 2.939–46.
4. I published this in Stone, *Armenian Apocrypha Relating to Adam and Eve*, 163. It occurs in numerous copies, far more than were at my disposal when I edited it in the 1990s. An apparently rather early form of it is to be found in the *Chronography of Philo of Tikor* (MH, 5. §§104–106); see also in manuscript M2679, fol 36v of the year 981 CE. I have noted the following further copies: M268, fol. 152v; M537, fols. 233v–234r; M605, fol. 135; M8494, fol. 215r; P0121, 149r–151r. Undoubtedly still more copies exist.

5. ABRAHAM AND THE IDOLS

or has any homiletic features. Here I am publishing all of section A, the first of these units of text.

The various stories relating Abraham's recognition of God should be dealt with in a separate monograph. In my study of the Armenian Abraham Saga[5] I dealt with the three chief narratives, and one very rare one. The first of them is the story of how God, through Abraham, saved Terah's field from the depredations of the crows.[6] The second narrative relates Abraham's discovery of God through the contemplation of the heavens.[7] This narrative is widespread in Jewish and Christian texts,[8] as in *Abraham 2.3, The Story of Father Abraham*, and it is sometimes combined with either the story of the ravens or the third tale, that of Terah, idol maker.[9] A fourth, rarely encountered story is that God's saving of Lot brought Abraham to recognize Him. This is found in *Abraham 11, The Story of Terah and of Father Abraham* §31.[10]

The third story, the one featured here, describes Terah, Abraham's father, as involved in the manufacture and sale of idols. Like the present document, various other traditions also relate incidents highlighting the idols' impotence. In the present text, the idols fall into filth and Abraham subsequently recognizes their powerlessness. This is a good example of descriptions of such incidents and their implications.[11] However, as it stands in the present manuscript this incident is incomplete and Abraham's consequent recognition of God is not mentioned.[12]

---

5. Stone, *Abraham*.

6. Birds: Stone, *Abraham*, 18–19, 43, 51–53, 148, 193. The origins of the bird story are discussed there. For further relevant references in that book to this and the other stories of Abraham's discovery of God, its index may be consulted.

7. Astronomical: Stone, *Abraham*, 51–53, 148, 193; see also Louis Ginzberg, *The Legends of the Jews*, 7 vols. (Philadelphia: Jewish Publication Society of America, 1909–1938), 5:210 n. 6.

8. See, Ginzberg, *Legends of the Jews*, 5:210 n. 6. See *Abraham Texts* 8.5, 11.2, 15.2 and compare *Gen. Rab.* 38:28. For different versions of the story of Abraham and the idols, see Bernhard Beer, *Leben Abrahams nach Auffassung der jüdischen Sagan* (Leipzig: Leiner, 1859), 9–11; compare *Tanḥuma Lek Leka* 2.2. see also *Apoc. Ab.* 1–3.

9. Discussed on the following page.

10. Stone, *Abraham*, 156. This is an unusual position for this incident. To maintain that Abraham only recognized God at the time of the Sodom events raises narrative difficulties, when compared with the biblical text.

11. Re. idols: see discussion in Stone, *Abraham*, 147 and index s.v., as well as Ginzberg, *Legends of the Jews*, 5:215–18.

12. A more complex variant of this story, including an ass bearing idols falling, is to be found in *Apoc. Ab.* 1–3.

Texts and Translations

Abraham and the Idols and Two Other Incidents

M4618 1/ Թարա՝ հայրն Աբրահամու, կուռք կու շիներ, եւ Աբրահամ ծախեր։ Եւ օր մի տարաւ ի շուկայն իշարեր մի կուռք։ Եւ յանկարծակի անկաւ էշն ի չամուրն,[13] եւ կուռքն ամենայն ջարդեցան, եւ Աբրահամ փախեաւ ի հօրէն։

1/ Terah, Abraham's father, built idols and Abraham sold them. One day, he was bringing a donkey-load of idols to the market. Suddenly the donkey fell into the filth and all the idols were broken into pieces and Abraham fled from his father.[14]

John the Baptist's Food

2/ Սուրբն Յովհաննէս մկրտիչն ի տեղին, ուր բնակեր, Փառան կոչի, որպէս ասի։ Եւ կերակուր նորա՝ մարախ եւ մեղր վայրենի։ Մարախն խոտ է. ի Հրէաստան յոլով լինի։ Ամառն գծին ուտեր եւ գձմեռն՝ գտակն։ Եւ մեղրն վայրենի պիծակի մեղրն է։

2/ St. John the Baptist (was) in the place called P'aran where he dwelt,[15] as is related. And his food was locusts[16] and wild honey.[17] The locust is a

---

13. In preparing my previous edition of this document in Stone, *Abraham*, 238, I could not identify this word. It eventuates that it is the Turkish word *čamur*, which means "dirt, filth."

14. This is part of one of the stories of Abraham's discovery of God: I have already published the text on Abraham with a translation in *Abraham*, 238.

15. Nowhere in the New Testament is P'aran (Paran) related to John the Baptist. However, it is a desert or wilderness, see Gen 21:21, Num 10:12, 12:16 etc. John was in the wilderness according to Matt 3:1, Mark 1:4, etc. So, a medieval author being unfamiliar with the geography of the Holy Land, could connect the name Paran with the wilderness of John the Baptist.

16. John's diet is mentioned in Matt 3:4 and Mark 1:6 as "locusts and wild honey." The Greek ἀκρίδες designates the insect. The Armenian author, worried apparently by John's eating the insects, explains that the word մարախ "locust" means a sort of grass. NBHL notes its occasional equivalence with մատուտսակ, a sweet root. By what seems to be a strange coincidence, "locust" in English may also designate both the insect and a number of sorts of tree, including the carob; see *OED*, s.v. In fact, in Middle Eastern diets, locusts (the insects) were eaten, notably by Bedouin, and they are regarded as permitted food by the rabbis (see *m. Ber.* 6:3). So, of course, were the pods of the carob.

17. See Matt 3:4, Mark 1:6.

sort of grass; it is in all Judea. In the summer he ate the sprouts, and in winter, the lower part; and wild honey is wasp honey.

Solomon's Saying

3/ Զի՞նչ է, որ ասէ Սողոմոն, թէ Ռ (1,000) ծով՝ մէջ մէկ նաւի: Պատասխանի.՝ Սուրբ [Աստուա]ծածինն¹⁸ է:
Ձգայլու ձագն յուսումն տվին. և ասէին, թէ՝ «այբ, բեն, գիմ», և նա ասէր. «այծ, բուծ, գառն»:

3/ What is that which Solomon said, "A thousand sea(s), in one ship."¹⁹
Answer: It is the holy Theotokos.
They gave a wolf cub to be taught: and they were saying, "ayb, ben, gim"; and it (the cub) said, "goat, ewe lamb, lamb."²⁰

---

18. A tear has carried away the first part of this word, adding to the obscurity of the preceding.
19. The meaning and the source of this Solomonic saying itself are not evident. Obviously, the Theotokos was thought to have given birth to Christ. How the "thousand ships" relate to Christ is obscure. It is not drawn from the biblical books of Solomon, or from *Questions of the Queen*, which exists in Armenian: See below text no. 10, *Concerning Soloθ mon* and text no. 11, *Signs and Wonders* dealing with Solomon. On the various traditions about Solomon, see also Pablo A. Torijano, *Solomon the Esoteric King: From King to Magus, Development of a Tradition*, JSJSup 72 (Leiden: Brill, 2002). Many Solomon legends are published in St. John Drelinc Seymour, *Tales of King Solomon* (London: Oxford University Press, 1924).
20. This is a wisdom saying: on being taught the first three letters *ayb, ben, gim*, the wolf cub responds with the names of three beasts on which wolves prey and the names of which start with these three letters. One might summarize the moral of the tale as "a wolf in sheep's clothing is still a wolf." This is a clearly parabolic story.

6. Supplication about the Sodomites and Gomorreans

Introductory Remarks

The *Supplication about the Sodomites and Gomorreans* (henceforth: *Sodomites*) is published for the first time here from two manuscripts:

The first, M5571 was written in Smyrna and Surat (India) by Petros in the years 1657–1659 and the text occurs on fols. 212r–218r.[1] The manuscript, described so far only in the *Short Catalogue* of the Matenadaran, Maštocʻ Institute of Ancient Manuscripts in Erevan, is titled *Partial Bible*.[2] However, it also contains some pseudepigraphical texts. In addition to a copy of *Sermon Concerning the Flood*,[3] it also preserves *Adam, Eve and the Incarnation*, which has been published.[4] The script is a fairly unskilled *notrgir*, with many odd spellings. Here M5571 served as the text and is edited diplomatically. Any changes from its text, be they editorial or be they drawn from M2242, are enclosed in pointed brackets, <>.

The second manuscript, M2242, belonging to the same library, is of the seventeenth century, provenance unknown. The manuscript is a *Miscellany* and the text occurs on fols. 24v–31v. *Sermon concerning the Flood* precedes this text and occurs on fols. 18v–31v. Following it is *Sermon concerning the Three Youths*.[5] It is written in a clear, regular *notrgir* hand. *Sodomites* is followed by *Third Story of Joseph*.[6]

Both manuscripts M5571 and M2242 are written in Ancient Armenian with a liberal admixture of Middle Armenian forms. Such are անել (§10),

---

1. *Short Catalogue* 2, 210.
2. Stone, *Armenian Apocrypha Relating to Adam and Eve*, 8–9.
3. Stone, *Armenian Apocrypha Relating to Adam and Eve*, 174–83.
4. See Stone, *Armenian Apocrypha Relating to Adam and Eve*, 20–79; Michael E. Stone, "Adam, Eve and the Incarnation," *St. Nersess Theological Review* 2 (1997): 167–79; reprinted in Stone, *Apocrypha, Pseudepigrapha and Armenian Studies*, 1.213–25.
5. I.e., the three companions of Daniel. This is unpublished.
6. This document was published in Stone, *Angels and Biblical Heroes*, 176–228.

6. SUPPLICATION ABOUT THE SODOMITES AND GOMORREANS

կայրեմ (§16), ճամփու (§18), մտալ (§20), etc. In addition, M5571 has some spelling peculiarities. None of them is consistent and they are recorded in the apparatus. These include: բ — ք; ձ — գ; ց — ծ; ու — ոյ. It also quite often omits the letter *ho* (h) in instances such as աշխարի, and the like, see §§3, 29, 30, etc.

Sodomites is a greatly expanded form of the narrative found in *Abraham Text 2 Story of Father Abraham*, §§17–21. For convenience's sake, we reproduce that section of text and translation below preceding the edition of the new document.

Sodomites follows the biblical storyline in Gen 18–19 and also introduces passages mentioning or relevant to Sodom from elsewhere in the Bible. Examples additional to Gen 14, are the use of Gen 13:10 (§27), Lev 19:13 (§12), Ezek 16:49 (§12). In addition to its more or less direct quotations, it is impregnated with many biblical turns of phrase. Thus, we may conclude that it draws directly on *Story of Father Abraham* and, adding to that base, the rhetoric of the text utilizes citations and allusions to the Bible.

The document also offers explanations of exegetical difficulties in the text. Often, in our view, these are introduced to forestall or serve as responses to questions that are posed or could be posed in elenchic texts. Such texts, raising queries and difficulties discerned in the biblical text, sometimes present their questions in sequential biblical order and on other occasions focus them around a single text or incident. Indeed, in §31 a remnant of an underlying questions text survives: it reads, "And if a man asks, …" See further examples noted in the remarks on §§2, 25, 30.

Here, then we present the following:

- *Story of Father Abraham* §§ 17–21, drawn from the edition and translation thereof.[7]
- The text of *Sodomites* drawn from M5571, in a diplomatic edition.
- The Critical Apparatus presenting points at which the copy in M2242 differs from M5571.
- The translation of *Sodomites* with annotations.

---

7. Stone, *Abraham*, 40–41 and 48–50. The text is reproduced by permission.

Story of Father Abraham §§17–21

Text

17/ Եւ ասէ Տէրն ցԱբրահամ. «Աղաղակ Սոդոմացոցն եւ Գոմորացոց ելաւաջի իմ»։ Եւ ասէ Աբրահամ. «Մ՛ի կորուսեր արդարն ընդ ամբարբշտին»։ Եւ ելաց առաջի Աստուծոյ Աբրահամ, երկիր եպագ եւ ասէ. «Տէր, ես հող եւ մոխիր եմ. զհողդ եւ մոխիրդ հետ քեզ խոսելոյ արժան արիր։ Թէ Ծ. (50) արդար / fols. 88v / գտան ի մէջ նոցա, կու կորուսանի՞ ալլոց մեղացն»։ Եւ ասէ Տէրն. «Ոչ կորուսից»։ «Թէ պակաս լինի Ե՛ (5).»։ Ասէ Տէրն. «Թող լինի ԽԵ. (45)»։ Եւ եկն ի ԽՋ. (46), Ի. (20), Ժ. (10) արդար։ Դ. (4) էր՝ Ղովտ եւ կինն եւ աղջիկն. այլ արդար ոչ գտաւ։ Եւ զի՞նչ է չարիք նոցա։ Արուազետ էին՝ որդն հետ որդի, հետ անասնոց, անողորմ էին դիմաց աղքատին, դուռն փակէին դէմ աղքատաց եւ ապա հաց ուտէին։ Աստար հուրն հանդիպէր փոխանակ պատուէլոյն եւ կերակրելոյն բռնէին, հետոն չարիք գործէին։

18/ Եւ ասէ Տէրն. Բ հրեշտակացն, թէ՝ «Գնացէք ի Սոդոմ եւ զԱբրահամու եղբաւր որդին զՂովտ իւր տանովն հանեցէք Աբրահամ/ fol. 89r /ու սիրուն համար»։ Եւ Աբրահամ երկիր եպագ Աստուծոյ։ Եւ գնաց Աստուած, մեկնեցո ի տեղոցէն։ Եւ եկին Բ. հրեշտակն ի Սոդոմ, եւ Ղովտ նստէր առ դռանն. եւ նա իւր բարի վարպետէն Աբրահամէ էր ուսեալ զհուրրնկալութիւն։ Եւ երկիր եպագ, զոր տեսեալ Ղովտ զգեղեցկութիւն պատկերի նոցա։ Ասաց ի միտս, թէ սոցա նման գեղեցիկ մարդ ի քաղաքս չէ մտեր. քաղաքացիքս սոցա զլուխս մեծ չար կու բերեն։

19/ Կամէր Ղովտ զաղտ պահել եւ ծածուկ ճանփու դնել, զի մի իմասցին չարագործքն։ Ի քուն մտեալ էր. պատեցին զտունն Ղովտայ։ Ծածկել ջանաց Ղովտ, այլ տեսեալ էին մէջ քաղաքին։ Յառաջն պատեցին զտունն, / fol. 89v / զի մի զաղտ դռնով փախիցէ։ Ասացին Ղովդա, թէ՝ «Ու՞ր են արքն, որ մտին ի տուն քո։ Տո՛ւր մեզ»։ Եւ ել Ղովտ առ նոսա յետ նա փականել զդուռն։ Դարձեալ սկսաւ աղաչել զնոսա Ղովտ, թէ՝ «Բ դուստր ունիմ հարսնացու. ձեզ տամ զնոսա»։ Սովրեալ էին յարուագիստութիւն, որ ի կին մարդ ոչ նայէին ամենեւին։

20/ Իբրեւ զիտացին հրեշտակքն զՂովտա վիշտն, բացին զդուռն. զՂովտ ի տուն առին։ Եւ փիտեցին յերեսա նոցա, կուրացան։ Եւ ասին հրեշտակն ցՂովտ. «Անմիտ, դու գիտե՛ մեք մեղաւոր մարդ եմք։ Մեք հրեշտակք ամենակալին եմք»։ Եւ ասին ցՂովտ. «Է քո աստ ընդանի, հա՞ն»։ Եւ ել Ղովտ եւ ասաց փեսա/ fol. 90r /ային, որ առնելոց էին զդստերսն, եւ ոչ հաւատացին, այլ ծաղր արարեալ։ Եւ ասին

6. SUPPLICATION ABOUT THE SODOMITES AND GOMORREANS

հրեշտակն ցՂովտ. «Ջամենայն գիշերս աշխատ եղար եւ չգիտեր զոք արժանի»:

21/ Կալան գձեռանէ նոցա եւ հանին արտաքոյ քաղաքին: Դարձաւ կինն Ղովտա յետս եւ եղեւ արձան աղի: Սոդոմացի էր կինն. պատուիրեցին հրեշտակքն յետս չդառնալ: Մնաց Ղովտ եւ Բ դստերքն: Գնացին փութով: Հուր եւ ծըծում<բ> առ հասարակ թափեցաւ: Մէկ ժամ այրեցաւ մարդ, անասուն, այգի: Եւ ապա սեւ ջուր թանձր, իբրեւ զկուպրն, ի վեր երեկ յանդընդոց: Որպէս մեռած մարդ ոչ շարժի, այսպէս մեռած ծով անւանի, եւ Յորդանան անցանէ: Ոչ ի գետի / fol. 90v / ջրէն ի ծովն խառնի, եւ ոչ ծովէն ի գետն:

Translation

17/ And the Lord said to Abraham, "The cry of the Sodomites and the Gomorreans has ascended before me." And Abraham said, "Do not destroy the righteous with the wicked." And Abraham wept before God, he bowed down and said, "Lord, I am dust and ashes. You made me, this dust and ashes, worthy to speak with you. If fifty righteous are found among them, will it (that is, the city) be destroyed (because) of the sins of the others?" And the Lord said, "I will not destroy (it)." "And if five lack?" The Lord said, "Let there be forty-five." And he came to forty-six, twenty, ten righteous. There were four (righteous)—Lot and his wife, and the daughters. No other righteous person was found. And what was their evil? They were homosexuals, male with male, and with beasts; they were merciless towards the poor; they shut the door against the poor and then ate bread; a foreign guest encountered instead of honor and nurture, (that) they seized (him), they did evil with (to) him.

18/ And the Lord said to the two angels, "Go to Sodom and bring forth Lot, Abraham's nephew, with his household, for the love of Abraham." And Abraham bowed down to God. And God went, departed from that place. And the two angels came to Sodom, and Lot was sitting by the gate and he had learned hospitality from his good teacher Abraham. And he bowed down, to those the beauty of whose countenance Lot had seen. He said to himself, "A man as beautiful as them has not entered the city. These citizens (dwellers in this city) will bring great evil on their heads."

19/ Lot wanted to keep (it) secret, and secretly to set (them) on the way, so that evildoers should not learn of it. When he fell asleep, they surrounded Lot's house. Lot tried to hide, but they had been seen (them) in the city. First, they surrounded the house, so that he should not secretly flee by the door. They said to Lot, "Where are the men who entered your house? Give (them) to us." And Lot went out to them, closing the door behind him. Again, Lot began to beseech them, "I have two marriageable daughters. I give them to you." They were so used to lying with men that they completely ignored women.

20/ When the angels apprehended Lot's difficulty, they opened the door; they took Lot into the house. And they blew in their faces; they became blind. And the angels said to Lot, "Foolish one, do you consider that we are sinful men? We are angels of the Omnipotent." And they said to Lot, "Bring forth whoever is your family here." And Lot went forth and he said to his sons-in-law, who were going to take his daughters (i.e., in marriage) and they did not believe, but mocked. And the angels said to Lot, "All this night you labored and you did not know who was worthy (i.e., of being saved)."

21/ They took them by the hand and brought them out of the city. Lot's wife turned back and became a pillar of salt. The woman was from Sodom; the angels commanded not to turn around. Lot and his two daughters remained. They went quickly. Fire and sulphur poured down equally. Men, beasts, vineyards were burnt all at once. And then black water, thick as sulphur came up from hell. Just as a dead man does not move, thus it is named the Dead Sea. And the Jordan passes through. Nothing of the river water is mixed with the sea and nothing of the sea with the river.

SUPPLICATION CONCERNING THE MEN OF SODOM AND GOMORRA

Text

M5571 Title/ Աղաղակ վասն սոդոմացւոց եւ գոմերացոց

1/ [Ե]ւ ասէ Տէր ցԱբրահամ. «Աղաղակ սոդոմացւոցս եւ գոմերացոց եւ առաջի իմ. եւ արդ էջեալ տեսից ըստ աղաղակին վճարել ինէ կեանք նոցա։ Ապա թէ ոչ, զի գիտացից»։ Աստուած ոչ ի կարծիսն դատարի, որ քննէ զսիրտս եւ զերիկամունս։

2/ Եւ ոչ թէ չգիտէր Աստուած զչարիս նոցա, այլ օրէնս հաստատէ դատաւորաց եւ թագաւորաց՝ նախ քննէլ եւ ստուգել[8] զիրաւն, եւ ապա տալ զվճիռն.[9] Զի[10] թէ Աստուած, որ ծածկազէտ է եւ ամենիմաստ. առանձ[11] հարցման եւ քննութեան եւ դատաստանի չէ պարտ տալ վճիռ. զի կարճ է գիտութիւն մարդոյս, ոչ գիտեն գձշմարիսն։

---
8. ւ above line p.m.
9. ջ above line p.m.
10. եւ erased before զի.
11. sic!

6. SUPPLICATION ABOUT THE SODOMITES AND GOMORREANS   29

3/ Այլ պարտ է մատնած եւ գչարախօսա‹ծ› մարդն Լ. (30) օր երկաթով կապել եւ դնել ի բանդ, մինչեւ զան Բ. (2) կամ Գ. (3) վկայք եւ յատնել սուտն եւ իրաւն։ Եւ ապա, թէ տուկանելոյ լինի կամ սպանելու, որք տուզանեն եւ սպանանեն, եւ թէ անմեղ լինի, ազատեն։ / fol. 212v / Չէ պարտ դատապարտել եւ իշխանաց՝ մէկից մէկ աւատալ մատնողին, գուցէ առ նախանձու լիցի մատնութիւն, եւ սպանանեն զանմեղն։ Եւ թէպէտ փոշիմանեն յետոյ, այլ ոչ կարեն կենդանացնել, եւ լինի մարդասպան եւ անմեղ արեան պարտական։ Վասն իւրոյ մեծ իմաստութեան դատաւորաց եւ թագաւորաց մէկից մէկն ոչ լսէ բանսարկու մարդոյն, այլ քննել ստոգ եւ ապա տատել ըստ արժանաց։

4/ Չի դատաւորն կամ թագաւորն յորժամ աթոռ նստի, աթոռ նորա նման պիտի աթոռոյն Աստուծոյ, ոչ նիւթական այլ գործ դատաստանի։ Եւ որպէս զարդարեն զաթոռն եւ նստի թագաւորն, նոյնպէս եւ որ ընդ իշխանութեամբն է, նա զարդարեալ եղեցի իրաւամ‹բ›ք։

5/ Իսկ աղաղակն ի հրեշտակաց, կամ ի տարերաց, կամ ի գրկերոց լինի. զի ամեն մարդի[12] հրեշտակ կա պահապան՝ հաւատացելոցն Բ. (2), անհաւատիցն Ա. (1), եւ թագաւորացն Քրիստոս է պահապան, եւ հոգեւոր մարմաւոր իշխանաց հրեշտկապետք են պահապանք, եւ քաղաք‹ի› եւ երկրի դաշտ հրեշտակաց են պահապանք։ Յորժամ մարդն բարի լինի եւ պտղաբեր ծառ, գնան հրեշտակ‹ք› եւ զոհանան Աստուծոյ։ Եւ մին հրեշտակն մնա եւ գիշերն պահէ զմարդն, զի մի նեղեցգցէ կամ խեղդեցցէ դեւն զմարդն։ Եւ մին հրեշտակն առնու զաւուր բարի գործքն մարդոյն՝ զպա‹հ›սն եւ զաղօթքն, զարտասուքն եւ զողորմութիւնն, եւ որպէս զարմադան տանի դնէ առաջի Աստուծոյ եւ զոհանա բարեգործ մարդոյն։

6/ Եւ յետ ամեն առաւոտու լուսանալոյն Աստուծոյ ողորմութեան դուռն կու բացուի դեմ աշխարհիս, գայր հրեշտակն, եւ ական թօթափելին հասանի օգնութիւն մարդոյն։ Եւ բերէ Աստուծոյ բարի ողորմութիւն եւ օգնական լինի մարդոյն եւ պահեն ամէն չարէ, եւ աջողի բարին։

7/ Իսկ յորժամ չար լինի մարդն եւ անպտուղ ի բարի գործոց. / fol. 213r / յանժամ պահապան հրեշտակն գնա առաջի Աստուծոյ, զանգատի եւ աղաղակէ, թէ՝ «Չարագործ է մարդն այն եւ ոչ ունի պտուղ բարի, որ բերեմ առաջի Աստուծոյ։ Բարձ գնա ի կենաց եւ զիս այլ ուրիշ բարի եւ պտղաբեր մարդոյ դիր պահապան։ Որպէս թագաւոր զոք կատէ, այզէպան կու դնէ այզոյ իւրդ, եւ աղին ոչ տա

---

12. An anomalous form for մարդոյ.

պտուղ. ադա՛շէ զթազաւորն եւ ասէ. «քակեա զայգին եւ զիս պտղաբեր այգւոյ դիր պահապան, զի բերից զքեզ[13] պտուղ եւ մի եղից ամօթով»:

8/ Երկրորդ զանկնատն եւ ադադական տարերաց լինի, որ ձանձ<ր>անա ի յարուազետ եւ ի <զաղ>րազործ մարդկանէ: Տաղտկանան եւ ադադակէն առ Աստուած, զի այսպիսիքն ծանրաբեռն են յաշխարհիս վերայ, որ հանապազ ապականեն զերկիր մեղօք: Որպէս մարդ ի ծանր բեռացն նեղանա, կամի բաց ընկենուլ, այսպէս եւ տարերքս նեղանան այնպիսացն եւ ադադակէն առ Աստուած եւ խնդրէն զբարձունս յաշխարհիս:

9/ Երրորդ զանգատն եւ ադադական ի զրկելոց, ըստ այնմն. «Զրկեալ ի ձեռս ադադակէ, եւ բողոք հնձողաց եհաս ականջս Տեառն զօրութեանց»: Չի որբն եւ զայրին եւ ադքատքն անտէր են եւ չունեն զոք օգնական: Որբցն հայր եւ արանց դատաւոր Աստուած է: Յորժամ անիրաւատ եւ անողորմ մարդ զրկէ զնոսա, նոքա չունին զոք օգնական առ Աստուած. ադադակէն, եւ ադադակ նոցա <ի վեր անցանէ> քան զղաս հրեշտակաց եւ մտանէ առաջի Աստուծոյ եւ զԱստուած ի բարկութիւն շարժէ ի վերայ անողորմ զրկողացն. եւ բողոք հնձողացն:

10/ Յորժամ մարդ ամառն շող ժամանակին մարդոյ <հունձն> տայ անել եւ վարձն կտրէ, եւ նոքա ադադակէն առ Աստուած եւ զԱստուած ի բարկութիւն շարժէն, որպէս ասէ Մովսէս. «Որ հատանէ զվարձս վարձկանի, ընդ արիւնահեղսն եղիցէն»: Չվարձքն ի վարձն թէ կտրէ մարդ, արիւնահեղիցն[14] եւ մարդասպանութեան կարգն է: Պարտ է պահմանաւ զմարդն վարձել եւ, երբ կատարի ժամանակն, / fol. 213v /զվարձն բոլոր տալ եւ հալալութիւն խնդրել: Վասն այն ասէ[15]՝ զերկինքն Աստուած ըստ իւրում մեծութիւնունի, զերկանմնութեամբն. թեպետ զինտ զամենայն, այլ ներէ ողորմութեամբ: Իսկ հրեշտակաց եւ զրկելոց ադադական շարժէ Աստուած ի բարկութիւն:

11/ Իսկ Աբրահամ կայր առաջի քադաքիցն եւ ահազին դատաւորին, որ յայտնելով նմա գշարհսն սոդոմաեցոց, շարժէ զնա ի բարեխօսութեան այնոցիկ, զորոց ամբաստանէ: Մարգարէն ասէ. «Անօրէնութիւն քո Սոդոմ լիութեամբ հացի եւ յղ<փ>ութիւն զինոյ, զի յօրն յայն, որ ձեռն ադքատ ոչ կարկառէր, եւ որ առ մարդիք ինքեն, առ

---

13. It is quite possible that զքեզ (acc. with nota accusativi) is corrupt for ցքեզ "to you." On confusion of ց and զ, see Michael E. Stone and Vered Hillel, "Index of Variants," in *The Armenian Version of the Testaments of the Twelve Patriarchs: Edition, Apparatus, Translation and Commentary*, HUAS 11 (Leuven: Peeters, 2012), no. 50.

14. ե above line.

15. է above line.

6. SUPPLICATION ABOUT THE SODOMITES AND GOMORREANS

Աստուած ամբարիշտ է»։ Իսկ Աբրահամ աղաչէր ոչ վասն արդարոց՝ այլ վասն մեղաւորաց, գիտելով թէ արդարն ապրի առանց բարեխօսի։

12/ Եւ ասէ Աբրահամ. «Քաւ լիցի քեզ, որ դատես զամենայն երկիր. մի արասցես զայդ դատաստան. ամենայն երկիր լի է մեղօք», ասէ. «եւ դուն ես ողորմութեամբ, զի մինն մի կորուսանէր ստուգութեամբ, ապա թէ խիստ բարկացեալ ես՝ խնդրեմ ի քէն». ասէ. «զի զարդարն մի կորուսանէր ընդ ամբարիշտն»։ Եւ ելաց Աբրահամ առաջի Աստուծոյ։

13/ Եւ ասէ Տէր Աստուած gԱբրահամ, թէ՝ «Ե. (5) քաղաք է երկրով. թէ ի մէջն նոցա արդար գտանի, քո սիրոյդ համար եւ արդարոց սիրուն համար մեղաց»։ Եւ անկեալ Աբրահամ ի վերայ երեսաց, երկիր եպագ Աստուծոյ եւ ասէ. «Տէր, ես հող եմ եւ մոխիր, զհողս եւ զմոխիրս հետ քեզ խօսելոյ արժանեան արարեր։ Յերբ դու այտ<պ>էս ողորմած եւ մարդասէր ես, այն Ե. (5) քաղաքէն թէ Ծ. (50) արդար գտանի ի մէջ նոցա, վասն Ծ. (50) արդարոցն կու ներեա <այլոց> մեղաւորացն»։ Եւ ասէ Տէր. «Ոչ կորուսից, թէ գտանի Ծ. (50) արդար ի մէջ նոցա»։

14/ Եւ ասէ Աբրահամ. «Տէր, թէ ողորմած լինիս, այլ եւս ամ{բ} արձակիմ, թէ պակաս լինի Ե. (5)»։ Եւ ասէ Տէրն. / fol. 214r /«Թող լինի Խե. (45)»։ Եւ եկն ի Խ. (40) եւ Լ. (30) եւ Ի. (20), մինչեւ Ժ. (10)։ Եւ թէ վասն էր Ծ. (50) թիւ բուռն եհար։ Զի Ծ. (50) թիւն ազատ արարեր <ըստ> օրինացն. ոչ միայն մարդիք, այլ եւ գերկիր եւ զանասուն ազատեր, եւ զդիակեր մայրն կենակիր առներ։

Վեցիւր բովանդակէ զինդիրն, որով շարժ<ի> մարմինն, եւ լինի ապականացու մարդն. եւ վեցեկի շարժմամբ շարժի մարդ առաքինութիւն կամ ի չարութիւն, զի կարասցէ արդար անապականութիւն աձել զապականեալ մեղօք։ Խե. (45)՝ որդեծնութեան անդրանիկն, Խ. (40)՝ շնչաբերութիւն արուի, Լ. (30)՝ կատարելութիւն մարդկային ազգի հասակի եւ իմաստութեան, Ի. (20)՝ թիւն զինուորութեան, Ժ. (10)՝ կատարելութեան, որ ունի հիմն, գչորս թիւն գԺ. (10) ծնանի։ Ընդ որ ոչ էր արժան անցանել անկատարն, եւ զի ծածուկ է զազգասիրութիւն, ազգն չորս էր՝ Ղովտ եւ կինն, եւ Բ. (2) որդիքն դստերքն, եւ չորրորդ կինն, որ պաղեցաւ։

15/ Եւ յայտնի է զի Ա. (1) արդար ոչ գտաւ ի մէջ[16] նոցա։ Եւ զի՞նչ էր չարիք նոցա, որ այնպէս բարկացեալ էր նոցա Աստուած։ Ասէ, զի արուագէտ էին որձն հետ որձի, յետ անասնց եւ զրաստի խառնակէին հանապաղ։ Եւ Բ. (2) զի անողորմ են եւ ձեռն աղքատ ոչ մեկնէին, զդուռն փակէին ի դէմ աղքատաց եւ ապա հաց ուտէին։ Օտարական հ<իւ>րն որ հանդիպէր, փոխանակ պատուելոյն եւ

---
16. Erased q precedes.

կերարկելոյն՝ բռնէին յետոև չարիք գործէին։ Անողորմ էին, վասն այն ոչ գտան Աստուծոյ ողորմութիւն։ Ինչ մարդ դէմ աղքատին եւ օտարականին դուռն փակէ, Աստուծոյ ողորութեան եւ արքաութեան դուռն փակուի[17] դէմ այնպիսոյն եւ այլ ոչ բացուի։[18] Եւ զի բոլորովիմք չար էին եւ չունէին մասն բարեաց, վասն այն կորեան, զի անմասն ի բարոյ՝ չարն, վաղն մահ լինի։

16/ Եւ ասէ Տէր Բ. (2) հրեշտակացն. թէ «Գնացէք ի Սոդոմ եւ զԱբրահամու եղբօր որդին իւր / fol. 214v / զՂովտ տանէն հանիցէք՝ Աբրահամու սիրուն համար, որ յետ առաւոտուն լուսանալուն զե. (5) քաղաքն կայրեմ[19] հրով»։ Եւ Աբրահամն երկիր եպազ Աստուծոյ եւ գնաց։ Եւ Աստուած մեկնեցաւ ի տեղոջէն, քանզի Աստուած ի տեղի ոչ է, այլ տեղիքն Աստուած է. եւ ի սիրելեացն ոչ մեկնի, այլ ծածկէ անեղն զինքն խնաելով <յեղականպս>։

17/ Եւ եկին. Բ. (2) հրեշտակն ի Սոդոմ. յորժամ բարի առնէ[20] Աստուած, ի մէջ երկուցն կացեալ երեւի։ Իսկ պատուհասն ի ձեռն <երկուց>[21]՝ խնաող եւ տանջողական զօրութեան, որ ըստ գործուն կոչեն բարի։ Եւ չար առաքեաց ի նոսա տանջանս ի ձեռն հրեշտակի չարի, իբրեւ ստակող անդրա<ն>կացն եզիպտացոց։ Թազաւոր բարի զպարզեւ ձեռամք տա եւ զպատակումն դահճօք վճարէ։

Եւ եկին Բ. (2) հրեշտակն ի Սոդոմ ընդ երեկս, զի այնժամ հիւրք խնդրէին օթեւանս. այլ ատ Աբրահամ ի մէջօրէի եկին, զի արժանի էր Տեառն լուսու, իսկ Սոդոմ ընդ երեկս, զի այլ ոչ էր ծագեալ նոցա արեգակն։

18/ Եւ Ղովտ նստեր առ դրանն Սոդոմա նման իւրոց վարդապետին Աբրահամու. զի որպես <աշակերտի> բարո չէ հնար թէ ոչ մասամբ ինչ նմա<նի> վարդապետի իւրոյ, նոյնպէս եւ նա իւր բարի վարդապետէն Աբրահամու հոր եղբօրէն էր ուսեալ զհիւրընկալութիւնն եւ զաղքատսիրութիւն։

Եւ երկիր եպազ իբրեւ զակն անկատար ծառայից եւ բռնադատէ տանել ի տունն իւր, կասկածելով ի չարեաց նոցա։ Նոքա զի հրեշտակք էին, գեղեցիկ պատկերով երեւեցան։ Որպէս մեք, յորժամ զգեղեցկապատկեր մարդ տեսանեմք, վկայեմք եւ ասեմք, թէ հրեշտակաց կերպարանք ունէին։ Զոր տեսեալ Ղովտո զգեղեցկութիւն պատկերի նոցա, ասաց ի միտս իւր թէ. «Սոցա նման գեղեցիկ մարդ ի քաղաքս

---

17. Postclassical form.
18. Postclassical form.
19. Postclassical form.
20. է written over ե.
21. The text of M5571 has corruptly երաց < *Բg.

6. SUPPLICATION ABOUT THE SODOMITES AND GOMORREANS

չեմ տեսեալ. թէ այս չարգործ քաղաքացիքս իմացան, սցա գլուխն մեծ չար կու բերեն»: Վասն այդ / fol. 215r / մեծարեաց իւր տունն. եւ նոքա ասեն. «Ոչ այդպէս, այլ ի քաղաքամիջի աստ ազգուք»: Եւ Ղովտ բռնադատեաց զնոսա եւ տարաւ ի տունն իւր ասելով. «Վասն Աստուծոյ մտէք ի տուն իմ եւ առ իս ազերուք»: Կամէր Ղովտ զաղտ պատուել եւ ծածուկ ճանփու դնել, զի մի իմասցեն չարագործծքն քաղաքացոց նման իրի:

Նախ առ Աբրահամ տարաւ գիրեշտակս, ցուցանելով, թէ որպիսի բարի ծառայս ունի երկրի, որ[22] վասն սոդոմաեցցոն կոռուստեանն ադաչէր եւ զգերին անդրէն դարձուցանէր, որում ի դեպ էր խնդրել ընդ սատակումն քանանցոց. զի նմա խոստացեալ էր գերկիրն:

19/ Եւ ապա առ <Սոդոմ>[23] առաքէ գիրեշտակս, գիտելով թէ որպէս չարք էին եւ ոտար<ատեացք>, որ եւ իրաւի է ոտարացուցանէ զնոսա ի կենաց աստի, որք բռնեն երկրի: Արար եւ Ղովտ պատրաստութիւն կերակրող բաղարճ. ոչ նկանակ պարկեշտոս եւ խորհրդաւորս, որ գոր օրինական դնէ: Չի չունէր խմորն <ի> Սոդոմա չարեացն. եւ թէպէտ[24] անմեղ էր, այլ ոչ էր իմաստուն իբրեւ զԱբրահամ:

20/ Եւ մինչչեւ ի քուն մտալ էր սոդոմաեցցոն, պատեցին զտունն Ղովտա երիտասարդաց մինչեւ գծերսն: Եւ թէպէտ ծածկէլ> չանաց զնոսա Ղովտ, այլ տեսեալ էին ի մէջ քաղաքին եւ հարցանէին զմիմիանս, թէ՝ «զի՞նչ եղեն»: Եւ մատնեցին՝ ոտար այրն Ղովտ տարաւ ի տունն իւր:

Եւ ապա յայտ է զկատաղումն նոցա, զի ոչ անկատար տղայութիւն եւ ոչ ցամաքեալ ծերութիւն դատարեցուցանէր զնոսա ի մեղաց: Եւ զեն[25] պիտի երկարել զպղծութիւն, թէ ի հրեղէնս ոչ էին մտաբերել՝ թերեւս ոչ հրով, այլայլով պատուհասով կատարեալք էին: Առաջն պատեցին զտունն, զի մի զաղտաղոնով փախուցանէ:

21/ Ապա ասացին Ղովտա, թէ՝ «Ու՞ր են արքն, որ մտին առ քեզ. տուր ի մեզ, զի գիտասցուք զնոսա»: Եւ ել Ղովտ առ նոսա, / fol. 215v / եւ ընդանեացն հրամաեաց յետնափակ առնել գդուռն, եւ ասէ առ նոսա Ղովտ. «Որովհետեւ մտին արքն այնոբիկ ընդ յարկաւ գերանաց իմոց, մի՛ գործէք չար ինչ ընդ նոսա»: Եւ նոքա ասեն. «Մատեր բնակել պանդխտութեամբք, դատաստան<աւ> եւս կամէլ դատել զմեզ: Դու մեկ ոտարական մարդ ես: Երկրի մերում բնակեցար, ուզես

---

22. ն above line.
23. Ադամ "Adam" of the text must be an error. M2242 has the reading given here.
24. ւս above line p.m.
25. This unclear word is not translated. Perhaps < զայն, so read "that abomination."

իշխանութեամբ դատաստան առնես ի վերայ մեր։ <Դո՞ւ ես մեր խրատատու։ Տուր մեզ, ասեն,> ապա թէ ոչ, զ<չ>արիս նոցա ի գլուխ քո անցուցիք»։ Եւ դարձեալ սկսաւ ադաչել զնոսա Ղովտ եւ ասէ. «Բ. (2) դուստր ունեմ հարսնուցու. ձեզ տամ զնոսա։ Արարէք ընդ նոցա, զինչ եւ կամիք ձերէն։ Արանցն այնոցիկ մի մեղանչէք, որով<հետեւ> մտին ի տունն իմ»։ Եւ յորժամ ասաց զանունն դստերացն, սկսան զանել զնա։

22/ Եւ այնպէս սովորեալ էին արուագիտութիւն, որ ի կին մարդ ոչ նաէին ամենեւին, զոր օրինակ փոխանակ հացի շան աղբ ուտէին, եւ կամ փոխանակ ոչխարի մսի՝ շան մի ուտէին։ Այսպէս վառեալ էին արտօրէն խառնակութեամբ՝ փոխանակ օրինաւոր ամուսնութեան։

23/ Իբրեւ զիտացին հրեշտակքն[26] զՂովտա վիշտն, որում կայր, բացին զդուռն եւ կալան զուսագլուխն ի զՂովտ ի տուն առին։ Եւ փչեցին յերեսս նոցա, եւ ան ժամայն կուրացան, եւ զտունն արդարուն փրկեցին։ Եւ սրտից նոցա զզութեան ցաւոց եաուն՝ ապաշաւանդա դառնալ։ Այլ սովորական մոլեգնութեան ոչ էտ թոյլ, այլ գիշերուն կարծէին զմուտն։ Եւ ափափելով խնդրէին զդուռն, մինչեւ լքան եւ թուլացան։

24/ Եւ ասեն հրեշտակքն զՂովտ. «Անմիտ, դու գիտե՞ս՝ մեք մարմնաւոր մարդ ենք.[27] մեք հրեշտակք Աստուծոյ ամենակալի ենք»։ Յիշեցին այսպէս զԱբրահամու պաղատանս եւ ասեն զՂովտ. «Է քո աստ <ընդտանիք>, հա՛ն աստի, զի թէ արժ/ fol. 216v /անի <լինին կելոյ>՝ հաւատացեալ, ելցեն եւ ոչ կ<ո>րիցին»։ Որպէս եղեն իսկ՝ զի վասն այն դարձաւ գերին Սոդոմայ, զի ոչ այնմ, այլ այս էին արժանի։

Եւ էլ Ղովտ եւ ասաց փեսային, որ առնելոց էին զդստերս նորա, եւ այլ ընդանեաց եւ բարեկամաց. եւ ոչ հաւատացին, այլ ծաղր արարեալ հիմարութեան համարեցան զբանն։

25/ Եւ իբրեւ այգ եղեւ, ասեն զՂովտ. «Զամենայն գիշերս աշխատեցար եւ չգտել զոք արժանի։ Արի՛ սակաւուք եւ ե՞լ»։ Եւ ի սաստիկ երկիւղէն ցնորեցաւ եւ յափշեցաւ։ Կալան զձեռանէ նոցա եւ հանին չորս բաց։ Խօսին ընդ նմին. «Փութա՛յ», ասեն, «ապրեցո՛յ զանձն քո»։ Գիտին, զինչ գործելոց էին դստերքն։ Եւ կինն հանեալ, եղին զնա արտաքո քաղաքին եւ ասեն զնոսա. «Փութով զնացէք, զի յորժամ լուսանա եւ ծագէ արեգակն, ի բարձր լեառն ելանէք, եւ ամենեւին յետս մի՛ նաէք»։ Դարձաւ կինն Ղովտա յետս եւ եղեւ արձայն աղի։

---

26. բ above the line p.m.
27. Postclassical form, occurring here and elsewhere.

6. SUPPLICATION ABOUT THE SODOMITES AND GOMORREANS   35

Սոդոմայեցի էր կինն Ղովտա, որում պատուիրեցին հրեշտակքն չդառնալ յետս, զի նշանակ թերահաւատութեան <է>:

26/ Ասէ. «Մի[28] թերահաւատիք, զոր լուաք: Կամ չհաւատացաք, կամ այլ ընդանիս ունէր աղի Տէր, կամ ոտնահար եղեւ, զոր ոչ է արժան ումէք առնելն Աստուծոյ: Եղելոցն ընդ անկումն թշնամոյն ասէ մի՛ ուրախանալ, վասն այսորիկ առցան աղի եղեւ, զի հայեցցի եւ մի առցի ի պաշտոն»: Եւ մնաց Ղովտ եւ Բ. (2) դստերքն, եւ զնացին փոութով եւ ոչ կարացին ի լեառն հասանել:

27/ Եւ էր քաղաք մի փոքրիկ եզր երկրին Սեգովր անուն: Խնդրեաց Ղովտ ի հրեշտակացն եւ ասաց, թէ՝ «Ի՞նչ ողորմած էք: Ես այլ ոչ կարեմ գնալ: Թող այս փոքր քաղաքս ազատ լինի, զի անկայց եւ ապրեցայց <ի>[29] նմա: Եւ չէ փոքր, այլ մեծ երախտիք է ինձ»: Վասն Աբրահամու աղօթիցն եւ սիրուն համար թող այս Ա. (1) / fol. 216v / քաղաքս փրկէ: Չի սակաւ անմեղ էր, քան զայլ քաղաքս, եւ թէ զուին Ժ. (10) արդարք: Չի լիշատակ մնասցէ պարարտութեան երկրին, որ ձեզ մօն է երկիրն եւ Ե. (5) թագաւոր կարէր պահել: Այտ է, զի դրախտի նման ամառն, եւ ձմեռն անպակաս է բարին եւ պտուղն: Եւ որպէս զդրախտն ոչ կարացին ժառանգել վասն մեղաց, նոյնպէս եւ սոդոմացիքն վասն մեղաց իւրեաց զրկեցան այնպիսի բարերի երկրէն:

28/ Եւ ասեն ցնա հրեշտակքն, թէ՝ «Ահա արարածք մեծարանս եթեսաց քոց. ոչ հրեշտակացն է այս բանս, այլ՝ Տեառն[30] հրեշտակաց՝ ապրիլ ի Սեգովրա, որ կոչի հաբերէն փոքր ասացած»:

Արեգակն ծագեաց, եւ Ղովտ եմուտ ի Սեգովր, եւ տեղեաց Տէր Աստուած ի Տեառնէ հուր եւ ծծումբ երկնային՝ նման հուրն շրջապատ: Եւ զդ անտ[31], որպէս թէ <կոտորեալ> հրուն զգենուր ծծումբ: Եւ տեղուր անձրեւ հրալի. ոչ միայն զմարդ, այլ եւ զանասունս, զշինուած եւ զանդաստան առ հասարակ այրէր, զի մեծացի պատուհասն թշնամեաց թագաւորին մեծի, եւ զչար ճճիս. եւ զկատաղի զազանս ի յորջս եւ ի <դաղարս> իւրեանց:

Սատակելով որ մեղօք նոցա շաղախեալ էր, պատժօք նոցա տոչորեցից. եւ այսպէս հուր եւ ծծումբ առ հասարակ թափեցաւ ի վերայ բոլոր երկրին մարդաչափ[32] բարձր: Եւ ի մէջ ժամն այրեաց առ հասարակ զմարդն եւ զանասուն, զդրախտ եւ զայգի: Եւ ապա սեւ ջուր՝ թանձր իբրեւ զկուպր, վեր երեկ յանդընդոց եւ ծածկեաց

---

28. M5571 actually reads Մմի, through dittography.
29. M5571 omits.
30. է erased here.
31. M2242 adds: այլ յորժամ կամի Աստուած անզուն զոյանայ.
32. A vertical line precedes.

գերկիրն։ Եւ որպէս մեռած մարդն ոչ շարժի, այսպէս մեռած ծով անուանի։

29/ Եւ Յորդանան անցանէ ընդ մէջ։ Ոչ ի գ<ե>տի ջրէն ի ծովն խառնի, եւ ոչ ծովէն ի գետն։ Եւ զարնանային ժամանակն շուրջու բոլոր ծովին ծաղկի ծառն եւ պտուղ բռնէ. եւ յորժամ կտրեն զպտուղն, մէջն մոխիր է կրակէ։ Եւ յերկնից / fol. 217r / իջեալ հուրն վառի ի ծովուն տակն, ծուխն ելանէ եւ նստի ի վերայ ծովուն, իբրեւ գ<բալ> եւ զմառախուղ։ Եւ այսպէս մնա հուրն վառ մինչեւ ի կատարած աշխար<հ>ի։ Այսպէս եւ յորժամ վերջին հուրն այրէ զաշխարհս, ապա սողոմաեցոց հուրն խառնի եւ տանջանքն կազմի մեղաւորաց։

Թէ ասիցէ ոք, թէ անողորմ դատեցաւ Աստուած եւ նշան ոչ արար նախ, ըստուկապէս նշանս չարար, այլ ամենայն երկրի նշան Սոդում արար։ Եւ զի առ մին անողորմ երեւեալ՝ ամենայն երկրի ողորմեցի՝ խրատելով ահ եւ երկիւղ մեծի աղէտին։

30/ Ատտար ցանգութիւն տիրանց ի վերայ նոցա. օտար հրով վերուստ ի վայր եկեալ բոցակէզ եղեն, իբրեւ զփուշ, ուստի խլի ի վերայ արմատոցն այրի՝ նշանակ ահագին դատաստանին Աստուծոյ յայնպիսի գործս կատարելոցն։ Չի ահ մեծ է անկանել ի ձեռս Աստուծոյ կենդանւոյ։

Եւ նոքա որպէս փոխեցին զաստուածադիր կարգն եւ թակեցին զարդար ամուսնութիւն, եւ Աստուծոյ արարչութեան եւ բարի կարքոյն հակառակ գործեցին, նոյնպէս երկինքն փոխեաց կարքն իւր եւ, փոխանակ անձրեւին, հուր իջոյց ի վերուստ եւ այրեաց զնոսա։ Չի եւ ամենայն մարդ, որ ծնանի եւ գա աշխարհս, քանի որ կարէ, մարդ պարտ է սրբութեամբ կուս կենալ։ Եւ յորժամ ոչ կարէ մեղաց համբերել եր, պարտ է աստուածային օրինսքն հալալ կին առնուլ։

Եւ իւր հալալին յետ կատարել մեղաց կարիքն. այս է աստուածադիր կարքն եւ բանական օրէնքն։ Որպէս ի սկզբանէ արար Աստուած արու եւ էգ՝ վասն աճմանն եւ որդեծնութեան։ Եւ արուագիտութեան եւ անասնագիտութեան հակառակ է Աստուծոյ բարի կամացն եւ արարչութեան։ Եւ քան զամենայն մեղաւոր առաւել ատելի են Աստուծոյ. արտաբր օրինաց եւ անթողելի մեղօք մեղանչեն, քանց գշուն պիղծ են, եւ քան գէշ խառնակ։ Եւ ոչինչ կենդանի որդն առ որդն ոք երթա՝ ոչ շուն եւ ոչ էշ։ Եւ որք գնան, առաւել / fol. 217v / պիղծ, խառնակ եւ անսուրբ են, քան գշուն եւ գէշ, եւ գրկեալ են ի շնոր<հ>ացն Աստուծոյ։

Եւ ոչ են արժանի մտանել ի տունն Աստուծոյ եւ յաղորդել ի սուրբ խորհրդոյն։ Եւ որպէս աններելի մեղք է, <որ էգն մօտ էգն երթա,

6. SUPPLICATION ABOUT THE SODOMITES AND GOMORREANS

այլ> որ արիւն մօտ արիւն[33] երթա, նոյնպէս անթողելի մեղք է, որ <էգն մօտ էգն երթայ>: Այլ <արուին> եւ էգին է հրաման խառնման եւ միաւորութեան աստուածային օրինօքն:

31/ Եւ թէ հարցանէ մարդ, թէ՝ «Յիմա այլ շատ մարդիք կան արուազետ. վասն էր ոչ այրէ Աստուած հրով»: Զսոդոմացիքն այրեց, աշխար<հ>ի օրինակ արար, որ ամէն մարդ իմանա, թէ այնպիսի չար գործքն սոդոմացւոցն հրոյն են արժանի: Եւ թէ այժմ ոչ պատժէ Աստուած, մեծի աւուրն դատաստանին պահէ, որ ի հուրն յաւիտենից արկանէ: Թէ զամենայն մեղաւոր աստ պատժէ, վասն էր գա ի դատաստան: Վասն այդ պատճառ՝ սոդոմացիքն վասն արուազիտութեան եւ անողորմութեան այրեաց եւ զջրհեղացիք վասն պոռնկութեան՝ ջրով շնչեաց, որ պոռնկաց. եւ արուազիտաց օրինակ լիցի:

32/ Եւ մի ասասցեն մեղաւորք աւուրն դատաստանին, թէ՝ «Թող դու մեկ մեղաւոր պատժեալ էիր ի մարմնաւոր կարքն, որ մեր աչօքն տեսեալն, եւ հաւատացեալ էաք քո արդար դատաստանին»: Այլ ոչ կարեն հակառակ խօսել մեղաւորքն, զի ականչով աստուածային գրոց կոլ լսեն հանապազ. զարդարոց փառքն եւ մեղաւորաց տանջանքն: Եւ զօրինական աչօք կոլ տեսնուն[34] զազգի ազգի մեղաւորքն ազգի ազգի պատժօքն տանջեալ: Նոյնպէս կա արդար մարդ, որ այս կեանքս փարաւորեաց Աստուած, վասն իւր առաքինութեամբ եւ սրբութեամբ խոնարհութեան եւ համբերութեան, որպէս զՄովսէս, որպէս զԴալիք որ ի նմանի մարդիկք որ արդարոցս մեծ փառք եւ պսակ է պատրաստեալ Աստուած:

33/ Եւ կա շատ արդար, որ այս կեանքս ա / fol. 218r /աղքատացան, չարչարացն եւ տանջանացն, որպէս Ճգնաւորքն եւ մարտիրոսն, որ իմանան մարդիկք, որ այն կեանք է արդարոց բարի փոխարէն եւ հանգիստն եւ փառքն: Թէ զամենայն արդար աստ փառաւորէր Աստուած, այսպէս իմանային մարդիկք, թէ այն է փոխարէնն Ճգնութեանց եւ այլ ոչ ինչ է տալոց նոցա Աստուած: Այլ զոմանս արդարոց փառաւորէ, որ իմանա արդարութեան: Եւ արդար մարդն սիրական է եւ ընդունելի եւ բարեկամ Աստուծոյ եւ զոմանս արդարոց աղքատ պահէ եւ չարչարեալ եւ անարգեալ, զի անդի կեանքն յաւիտենից տա նոցա զփոխարէն զանմահ կեանքն եւ զանանց լոյսն եւ զանտրտում ուրախութիւն եւ զանցաւ եւ զանաշխատ կեանքն եւ զհան<գ>իստն:

Եւ Քրիստոսի փառք յաւիտեանս ամէն:

---

33. Read արիւն in both instances here as արուն "male" (GM).
34. Postclassical form.

Critical Apparatus

The lemma is M5571 and the variant is M2242 except where explicitly marked otherwise. Orthographic variants that do not affect the meaning are found throughout the manuscripts. As well as the unusual spellings noted in the "Introductory Remarks" above, M5571 also tends to have:

ա	for	այ
ու	for	ոյ
ո	for	օ
նկ	for	նզ, etc.
ոյ	for	ւոյ, etc.

Both manuscripts sometimes omit -յ in final position or in the middle position in a triphthong. The orthography of the text follows M5571. In the apparatus M5571 is cited as 5571 and M2242 as 2242. Translations of particularly significant variants are given.

Title/ omit
1/ Սոդինայեցոցն | գոմորասցոցն | ելեալ] իջեալ "will descend" | զի] om | կարծիս

2/ երէ | հաստատէր | դատաւորաց եւ թագաւորաց] ∞ | եւ ամենիմաստ] ու ամենազէտ | առանձ] առանց | հարցման եւ քննութեան] հարցաքննութեան | չէ] ոչ է | կարձէ] կարձեօք

3/ զմատնած | գշտարախոսա<ծ>] 2422 -աց 5571 | յատնել] յայտնի լիցի | տուկանելոյ] տուքանելոյէ | սպանելոյ] սպանելոյ | որք ստուզանեն] տուզանեն | ազատեն] ազատ անեն | դատապարտել] դատաւորաց | մեկից—մատնողին] որ ի մեկ հետէ օտար մատնողաց աատան | մատնութիւնն | սպանեն | թեպետ] թեպէթ | փոշիմանին | իւրոյ] որոյ | մեկից] որ մեկենց | մեկ | լսեն | մարդոյն] մարդոց | քննեն | ստոյգ | դատեն | արձանեցաց

4/ դատաւոր կամ թագաւոր | դատաստանին | նոյնպէս եւ] նոյնպէս | է] նորա է | եղեցի | իրաւամ<բ>ք] 2242 իրաւամբ 5571

5/ զրկերոց] զրկելոց | մարդի] մարդոյ | կայ | յատակ | թոզաւորաց | հոգեւոր] + եւ | պահապան | քաղաք<ի>] 2242 քաղաք 5571 | հրեշտակ<բ>] 2242 հրեշտակ 5571 | Աստուծոյ] առաջի Աստուծոյ | մին1°] մեկ | մնայ | մին2°] մեկ | առնու] + իրիկունն | զպա<հ>սն] ed զպասն 5571 զպահին 2242 | աղօթքն] եւ զաղօթքն | զարտաուքն | զողորմութիւնն | զբարեգորձ

6. SUPPLICATION ABOUT THE SODOMITES AND GOMORREANS 39

6/ յետ] հետ | լուսանալու | դուռն] + որ | զայր] զա | թաթափելին] թարթն | յօգնութիւն | յԱստուածոյ | բարի] բարի եւ | յողորմութիւն | աշողի] յաշողեն | զբարին

7/ յայնժամ | գնայ | Աստուծոյ] քո | կատէ այզէական դնէ] պահապան կու դնէ | տայ | այգոյ | զքեզ] քեզ

8/ զանկատն | տարեցը | ծանձրանան] 2242 ծանձանա 5571 | <զազը>ազգործ] 2242 զազըազգործ 5571 : corrupt | որպէս] զի որպէս | բերանց | նեղանայ | կամի] եւ կամի ի | յայնպիսեացն | բարձումն կենաց

9/ զանկատն | այնմ | զրկեալն | յականջս | այրին | աղքատն | շունեն] ոչ ունին | օգնական 1°-2°] om 2242: haplography | <ի վեր անցաէ>] 2242 վեր անձնէ 5571 | զրկողաց

10/ մարդ | om | ժամանակի | <հունծն>] 2242 ունծ 5571 | զվարձն | շարծեն] կուշարծեն | ասէՄովսէս | ∞ | զվարձավարձկա | արհինահեղձն | եղիցի | զվարձս | վարձն] վարձկանի | ընդ արհինահեղից | ընդ մարդասպանից | եւ] om | ընդ մարդասպանութեան] մարտասպանիս | պարտ է] վատ որոյ պարտ է | պահմանաւ | յօմանաւ | զվարձն | այն] որոյ | զերկինք] զրկեալն քանցի | մեծութեանն | զերկայնմտութիւն | թեպէթ | զրկելոց եւ հրէշտակացն | զԱստուած

11/ քաղաքիցն] քաղցր եւ : corrupt | եւ գշարիս | սողումայեցիոց | ասէ] այս է | լիութիւն | հացի | յղ<փ>ութիւն] ed յղութիւն 5571 յղբութիւն 2242 | զի յօրն յույն] զօրասնայր | որ հերն] եւ հերն | յաղքատ | ադայշ

12/ զայդ | որ դուն ես] դու ներես | զի մինն] զմէկդ | ամբարշտին

13/ սրբոյդ] սրբուտ | համար 1°] om | <մեղաւորաց պատժեն յանցանի>] 2242 մեղաց պատժեն 5571 | Տէր 2°] ասա] om եմ |] om | մոխիրս | արժանան] արժանի | յերք | այտպէս] 2242 այտես 5571 | էպազ | այն և. քաղաքէն] երկրով | զտանի | <այլոց>] 2242 այլ ոչ 5571 | մեղաւորացն] մեղացն

14/ եւ Լ] Լ | եւ մինչեւ | ամբարձակիմ] համարցակիմ | եւ մինչեւ | եւ թէ] եւ ասէ թէ | զՕ | <ըստ>] 2242 ընդ 5571 | զմարդիկ | դիակիր | կենսակիր | առնէ | շարժ<ի>] 2242 շարժ 5571 | զաբականեալ | Խե] + են | մարդն] om | յառաքինութիւն | արդարն | յապականութիւն | զանապականեալ | Խե] + են | որդեծնութեան] ոգեծնութեան | հասակին | Ի թիւն զինուորութեան] omit | զչորս թիւն | զԴ զի Դ թիւն | յանկատարն | ծածուկ է] ծածկէ | ազգն] զի ազգն | որդձն | կինն] + է | պասկեաց] պակասեաց

15/ յայտ | նցա 2°] om | աս] այս | յետ 2°] հետ | էն] էին | աղքատ] յաղքատս | ի դեմ] դեմ | հ<ու>ր] 2242 հիւր 5571 : perhaps orthographic | հետն | յԱստուծոյ | աղքատի եւ օտարականի | դուռն 2°] դուռ | փակի

| այնպիսեացն | աղքատ] յաղցատս | հետոն | յԱստուծոյ | չարէն | վաղնմահ] վաղամահ

16/ տանէն] իւր | տանովն | հանեցէք | հետ առաւօտու | տեղի] տեղ | սիրելեացն | խնայելով | յելանք] յեղականք

17/ եկն | հրեշտակքն | երեքի] է | խնայող | զպատուհասն | <երկուց>] 2242 բաց 5571: corrupt from ß.g | երեքի] է | զօրութեան | որ] + եւ | գործօյն | կոչի | եւ չար — չարի] om : hkt | անդրանկացն | տայ | հրեշտակն2°] հրեշտակքն | յայնժամն | խնդրէն | լուսու | իսկ] իսկ ի | ծագելոց

18/ իւրոյ | եր] om | <աշակերտի>] 2242 աշտարակի 5571 | նմա<նի> | 2242 նմա 5571 | յիւր | ոզհիւրընկալութիւն | աղքատ | զակն] om | զանկատար | վկայէք | ասէք | բռնադատէ | եւ նորա | վկայենք | ասենք | ունի | Ղովտ | չարագորձ | ջեմ տեսեալ] չէ մտեր | իմանան | այտ] այն | մեձարեց | իւր տունն] ի տունն իւր | եւ տարաւ] տարաւ | պատուել] պահել : perhaps preferable | ճամփու | ճանապարհաւ | քաղաքացոց] քաղաքացիքն | նախ] նմին իրի | յերկրի | սողոմայացւոց | զզերին | որում | ում | քանանացոց

19/ <Սողոմ>] 2242 աղամ 5571 | օտար<ատեացք>] 2242 օտարացաք 5571 | է] om | բռնեն] բեռն են | բաղարջ | ոչ] om | նկանակս | զոր] զիւր | խմոր | <ի>] 2242 om 5571 | թեպէտ

20/ էր] om | Ղովտայ | յերիտասարդաց | զձերս | թեպէտ | ծածկ<էլ>] 2242 ծածկեալ 5571 | հարցին | մատնեցին] + թէ | տուն] յայտե] յայնէ : և above line | անտկար | զենապիտի] զի՞նչ պիտի | զպղծութիւնն | հրեղէնսն | այլայլով] in marg p.m. 2242 | յառաջն

21/ եւ1°] om | յետին փակ] յետնփակ | որքիետեւ] որովհետեւ | դատաստան<աւ>] 2242 դատաստան 5571 | կամիս | եւ երկրի մերում] ասին եկիր ի մեջ մեզ | կուզես | իշխանաբար | առնես] անես | <դու — մեր>] 2242 om 5571 | անցուցցութ | ունիմ | նոցա | ձերէն | ընդ ձերէն եւ | եւ արանցն | տուն | զանունն

22/ յարուազիտութիւնն | նաեցին | ամենեւին | հացի] մարդ | աղի | ուտէին1°] ուտէ | եւ կամ] եւ | ուտէին2°] ուտէ | յարտօրէնն | խառնակութիւն

23/ հրեշտակ<ք>ն] 2242 հրեշտակն 5571 | զՂովտայ | յորում | զդունն եւ] + կալան : in margin p.m. | Խովտ | ժամայն | զտուն | արդարոյն | զգայութիւն | յապաշաւանս | մոլեզնութիւնն | այլ] om | գիշերոյն | թուլացան] չորացան

24/ գիտես] + թէ | ենք | այսպէս] ապա | ընտանի] 2242 ընդ տամբ 5571 | եհան] հան | ընկերլու | լինին կելոյ : corrupt | ելցեն եւ

6. SUPPLICATION ABOUT THE SODOMITES AND GOMORREANS

թէ | կ<ո>րիցեն] 2242 կերիցեն 5571 | զի] om | այս] այդմ | եւ եւ] եւ | առելոցն և above ln | յիմարութիւն

25/ աշխատեցար] աշխատ եղար | չգտեր | զոք] զքո | արժանին | եւ] եւ ի | ափշեցաւ | բաց] բայց | նմին] մին | կիննlº] om | եւ հանեալ | զնա] զնոսա | արտաքոյ | լուանա | արեկակն | ամենեվին | նախք | աղձան | սխտումեցի | <է ասեն>] 5571 ասէ 2242

26/ չհաւատաց | ընդանիս | ադե | ոչ է] չէ | առնել | թշնամոյն | վասն] եւ վասն | աղձան | փութով

27/ յեզր | ողորմած էք] ողորմեցէք | <ի>] 2242 om 5571 | սիրոյն համար] om | փրկի | սակաւ անմեղ] սակաւամեղ | զուին] զո ի նա | արդարք | երկրի | երկիր | ե1º] om | ե.] vacat in 2242 | այտ է] յայտ է | է] էր | բարելի : perhaps preferable

28/ արարած] արարաք | հրեշտակաց | ի 1º] om | հայերէն | ասած] եւ զածած | ծագեց | տեառնէ] յերկրէ | նման] om | հուրն է | եւ զո] ծնումք ոչ գոյ : perhaps preferable | անդ] + այլ յորժամ կամի Աստուած անգուն գոյանա | <կոտորեալ>] 2242 կոտորոտեալ 5571 | հրոյն | գզենոյր | տեղոյն | այլ] + եւ | անդաստանն | եւ գշար] իբրեւ գշար | ճրճիս | դաղարս] 2242 արդարս 5571 | նոցա] իւրեանց | այրեց | գղրախղ | սեւ] եւս | պատժոք | մէջ] մէկ | զմարդ | երեկ] երեւտ | զերկիր

29/ անցանի | զ<ե>տի] 2242 զիտի 5571 | ի զարնան | շուրշու] շուրք իր | ծուլուն | կրսւլի | ծուլի | <զրսւլ>] 2242 զզսւլ 5571 | այնպէս | վառ | աշխար<ի>ի] 2242 աշխարի 5571 | այսպէս] om | ի սոդոմայն | տանցանք | նշանս] նշան | չարար] ոչ արար | ստուցապէս | նշան | յաի | զՍոդոմ | առ] om | երեւեւ | յաի

30/ ցանկութիւն | տիրանց] տիրեց | արմատոյն եւ | գայսպիսի | չարար] ոչ արար | նոքա / որպէս] ∞ | արարչութեանն | կարքոյն] կարգացն | զկարքոյն] զկարգ | երկինք | զկարգ | իջոյց | կարքն] կարգ | զի] զի եւ | մարդիք | ծննանին | զա] զան | յաշխարիս | քանի որ] om | էր] om | աստուածային | եւ իւր] եւ հետ իւր | յետ] om | զմեղաց | այս] այտ | աստուածադիր] + աստուածային | եղեալ | կարգն | բնական | աճմանն | բաճման | նական | արուագիտութիւն | անասնագիտութիւն | արարչութեանն | եւ քան] քան | արտաքոյ | մեղեոք] om | եւ ոչ] ոչ | շուն] շուն է | մեղանչելն | շքանց | քան | հոր<ի>ացն] 2242 շնորաց 5571 | տուն | հաղորդել | <էզն — այլ>] 2242 om 5571 | <արուին>] 2242 օրին 5571 | էզին

31/ հիմա | Աստուած] om | սողոմայեցիք | չարագործքն | սողոմայեցոց | արկանէ] այրէ | պատժէ] + ապա | գայ | սոդոմայեցիքն | անողոր | այրեաց] հրով այրեաց | ջնջեաց

32/ մեղաւորքն] յաւուր] պատժեալ] պատժել] յաւուր] մէկ] om | կարքն] կեանքն | մեր] մէք | աշօր] տեսեալն] տեսեր էաք | հաւատացեր | խօսիլ | ականջով] ականջօր | յաստուածային | զազգի ազգի մեղաւորսն | պատժօր | զայ | յայս | փարաւորեց | զԱստուած | վասն] om | առաքինութեան | սրբութեան | որպէս զՄովսէս — որ] om | ի նման] իմանան : perhaps preferable | մարդիք | արդարոց | պատրաստել] պատրաստեր

33/ յայս | տանջանացն] տանջեցան | մարդիք | կեանքն | փոխարէնն | փարք | փոխարէն | յարդարոց | իմանաս] + որ | արդարութիւն | յանդի | տայ | զփոխարէնն | լոյսն | ուրախութիւնն | Քրիստոսի] + մարդասիրին

Translation

Title/ Supplication about the Sodomites and Gomorreans

1/ And the Lord said to Abraham, "The supplication of the Sodomites and the Gomorreans has come up before me. And now, going forth I shall see whether they will pay with their life, according to the supplication. If not, how shall I know?"[35] (Being) God, he does not stop with opinions, he who examines the heart and the reins.[36]

2/ And it is not that God did not know their evil, but he established the laws for judges and kings, first to examine and to establish the truth exactly and then to render the decision. For God who knows secrets and discerns everything, must not pass sentence without questioning and examination and pronouncing judgment. For humans' knowledge is limited (and) they do not know the tru(th).

3/ But[37] the treacherous and slanderous man must be bound in iron and imprisoned for thirty days until two or three witnesses come and reveal

---

35. See Gen 19:13 and compare further Gen 4:10 for the phrasing.

36. Standard expression, see Jer 11:20, 20:12, and Ps 7:9 (7:10).

37. From this point to the end of §4, there is an excursus about righteous judgment. This is part of the author's interest in wise government, noted in the introductory remarks above. The rule that a matter is established only by two witnesses is Pentateuchal, see Num 35:30: "if anyone kills another, the murderer shall be put to death on the evidence of witnesses; but no one shall be put to death on the testimony of a single witness." The passage shows interest in determining the reliability of evidence. This is most likely a response to an assumed question such as "Why does an omniscient Deity need go down to Abraham to verify the sinfulness of the people of Sodom?"

6. SUPPLICATION ABOUT THE SODOMITES AND GOMORREANS 43

the lie and the truth.[38] And then, if he is to pay compensation or be executed, those who exact compensation or execute (do so). And if he is sinless, they free (him). The princes in ten instances to one, must not condemn (based upon) believing an informer. Perhaps he informed for envy, and they would execute someone innocent. And even if they subsequently repent, they cannot revive (him) again, and (thus) they become murderers and guilty of innocent blood. Because of his great wisdom, not one of the judges or kings listens to a backbiting man, but examines precisely and then gives judgments according to the merits.

4/ For the judge or the king, when sitting on the throne, his throne must be like God's throne, not material but an action of judgment. And just as they decorate the throne and the king takes his seat, in the same way the one who is under that authority, will be adorned by justice.

5/ Then the supplication by the angels, or by the elements, or by the injured[39] took place. For every man has a guardian angel, the believers (have) two angels and the unbelievers, one (angel). And Christ is the guardian of kings, and of rulers, spiritual and bodily, archangels are guardians. And of a city and a land, classes of angels are guardians.[40] When a human is a good and fruitful tree, the angels go and praise God. And one angel remains and guards a human at night, lest a demon deceive or strangle a human. And one angel[41] takes the day's good deeds by a human, the fasts and prayers, the

---

38. That is, of the case.
39. Here I read զրկէիոց as զրկէլոց "deprived" in M2242.
40. The classes or ranks of angels are mentioned by texts published in Stone, *Angels and Biblical Heroes*, index s.v. "angels"; on guardian angels, see there Text 3.12 *Prayer to the Twelve Guardian Angels*. Hierarchy of angels paralleled by human and ecclesiastical ranks is laid out in detail, for example, in Stone, *Angels and Biblical Heroes*, 86–88. The general idea is present already in Ps 91(90):10–11, which is an apotropaic psalm. Alexander Kulik discusses guardian angels in some detail in *3 Baruch: Greek-Slavonic Apocalypse of Baruch*, CEJL (Berlin: de Gruyter, 2010), 349–51.
41. I.e., the other of the two guardian angels.

tears and the mercifulness, and like a gift he takes it (and) places it before God, [42] and praises the human's good deeds.[43]

6/ And after it becomes light on every morning, the gate of God's mercy is opened towards this world.[44] The angel came and in the blink of an eye came and helped the human. And he (the angel) carries God's good mercy and is a helper of the human and guards (him) from every evil, and makes the good prosper.

7/ But when a human is evil and barren of good deeds, then the guardian angel goes before God. He complains and supplicates, "That man is an evildoer and has no good fruit that I might bring before God. Remove him from life and set me as the guardian of another good and fruitful human.[45] (This is) just as if a king makes someone he hates[46] keeper of his vineyard, and the vineyard yields no fruit, he supplicates the king and says, 'Cut down that vineyard and make me guardian of a fruitful vineyard, so that I may bring you fruit and I should not be ashamed.'"[47]

8/ The second complaint and supplication is that of the elements, which are annoyed by homosexual and <licen>tious mankind. They grow disgusted and supplicate God, that they are so heavy a burden upon this world since they (humans) continually corrupt the earth with sins. Just as a man who is

---

42. Compare Greek *Apoc. Bar.* 12 where the angels carry baskets in before God, full of flowers which represent the prayers of the righteous. This is discussed in detail in Kulik, *3 Baruch*, 346–49. On the ancient sources and later developments of the idea of gates of heaven, see J. Edward Wright, *The Early History of Heaven* (New York: Oxford University Press, 2000). The heavenly gates are discussed in detail in his book, see the index s.v. "gates"; see further Kulik, *3 Baruch,* 128–29. Ancient Egyptians believed in heavenly gates that are opened in the morning, so that the sun is visible in the sky (Kulik, *3 Baruch*, 19–20), and let this one example stand for many. The concluding synagogue service for the Day of Atonement is constructed around the metaphor of the heavenly gates that open to admit the prayers of humans.

43. Literally: the good-doing.

44. The gates in heaven are a common theme, discussed by Kulik, *3 Baruch*, 128–29. See n. 42 above.

45. Compare the very similar description in *3 Apoc. Bar.* 12:1–13:7.

46. I take կատէ as կ' or կու + ատէ, so "hates." How this detail fits into the parable is unclear to me.

47. The use of parables comparing of human beings and angels with keepers of or workers in vineyards or orchards and their owners and keepers is quite common: some biblical sources are Song 1:6, 2:15, Isa 5:1–7, compare Matt 20:1–5 and parallels. The story is very like the story of the blind and the lame in Ps.-Ezekiel, see Benjamin G. Wright, David Satran, and Michael E. Stone, *The Apocryphal Ezekiel,* EJL 18 (Atlanta: Society of Biblical Literature, 2000), 9–19 and 61–68.

6. SUPPLICATION ABOUT THE SODOMITES AND GOMORREANS   45

afflicted by heavy burdens wished to cast (them) away, thus the elements too are afflicted by such things (acts) and supplicate God and seek release from this world.

9/ The third complaint and supplication is from the deprived, according to that (saying), "The ones deprived by you supplicated and the protest of the harvesters have reached the ears of the Lord of Hosts."[48] For the orphan, the widow and the poor are abandoned and have no helper. The father of orphans and the judge of men is God. When a faithless and merciless man renders them bereft, they do not have any helper with God. They supplicate and their supplication passes higher than the ranks of angels and enters before God. It moves God to anger against the merciless bereavers and (is) a protest of the reapers.

10/ When a man causes someone to <harvest> in summer, the time of the heat, and cuts off his wages, and they[49] supplicate God, they also move God to anger. Just as Moses says, "He who cuts off the wages of a wage-earner will be (considered) a shedder of blood."[50] If a man cuts down the wages of a wage<-earner> he is in the rank of the shedders of blood and of murder.[51] One should hire someone by a contract[52] and when the time is over[53] give the whole wages and to seek after justice. Because of this it says that God possesses the heavens according to his own greatness, with long-suffering. Although he knows everything, yet he forgives through mercy. But the supplication of the angels and the deprived moves God to anger.[54]

11/ Then Abraham stood before the cities and the terrible Judge,[55] who, by making known to him the evil of the Sodomites, moved him to intercession for those whom He accused. The prophet said, "Your injustice Sodom, (is) through fullness of bread and glu<tt>ony with wine, for on that day on

---

48. Jas 5:4.
49. I.e., the reapers. Such variation in number is not uncommon, and is typical in posing a hypothetical instance.
50. Lev 19:13.
51. This sanction is not found in Leviticus.
52. Reading պահման as an odd spelling of պայման (G. Muradyan).
53. The time for which he was hired. This section is another piece of legislation, comparable with the material discussed in n. 37. The structure of the immediately preceding argument, with enumeration of three complaints, has the character of a speech in a law court.
54. Part, at least, of these three sentences appears to be a quotation, but its source is unclear.
55. Gen 18:22.

which the poor did not hold out his hand[56] and those who make an offering to men are impious towards God."[57] Then Abraham supplicated not for the righteous but for the sinners, knowing that the righteous is saved without an intercessor.[58]

12/ And Abraham said[59] "Far be it from You, who judge the whole earth. Do not perform this judgment. The whole world is full of sins," he said, "and you are merciful, for in truth, you do not destroy anybody, unless you are extremely angered.[60] I ask of you," he said, "that you do not destroy the righteous with the wicked."[61] And Abraham wept before God.

13/ And the Lord God said to Abraham, "There are five cities on the earth.[62] If there will be found a righteous man in them, for love of you and for love of the righteous <I will stop punishment of the transgressions of the sinners>." And Abraham fell upon his face. He prostrated himself to God and said, "Lord, I am dust and ashes. You made me, this dust and ashes, worthy to speak with you. If you are of this s<o>rt, merciful and loving humans, if fifty righteous are found in the midst of those five cities, will you afflict (them) with the other sinners?" And the Lord said, "I will not destroy if fifty righteous are found in their midst."[63]

14/ And Abraham said, "Lord, if you are merciful, I shall venture yet more: if five lack?" And the Lord said, "Let it be forty-five!"[64] And he came to forty and thirty and twenty, down to ten.[65] And why did he seize upon the number fifty? Because the number fifty freed (them) according to the law; it

---

56. Not only is this sentence difficult to understand, but it is also a very periphrastic rendering of Ezek 16:49.

57. From this point, the citation of Ezekiel ceases. The source of the rest of this quotation remains unknown.

58. Compare *Pr. Man.* 8, Mark 2:17, and Luke 5:32. A similar idea occurs in *4 Ezra* 8:31–33.

59. The following address by Abraham is a mosaic of biblical verses, with some modifications and additions. The first phrase draws on Gen 18:25: "Far be it from thee! Shall not the Judge of all the world do right?"

60. This sentence is not from Genesis.

61. Gen 18:23: "Wilt thou indeed destroy the righteous with the wicked?" and compare 18:25. The last phrase is drawn from Gen 18:23.

62. The five cities are specified in Gen 14:2, the other narrative context in which the city of Sodom is mentioned.

63. This refers to incidents related in Gen 18:23–33.

64. Gen 18:28.

65. This sentence summarises Gen 18:29–32. In the biblical text, too, the argument breaks off at ten righteous.

6. SUPPLICATION ABOUT THE SODOMITES AND GOMORREANS 47

freed not only humans but also land and beasts, and made the corpse-eating mother bearer of living ones.[66]

By six[67] it includes the inquiry, through what is the movement of the body and man becomes corruptible, and by the six-fold movement, a human moves to virtue or to evil.[68] For the righteous can bring those corrupted by sins to incorruptibility. Forty-five for the begetting of first-born children, forty is the respiration of the male;[69] thirty is the perfection of humankind in age and wisdom;[70] twenty is the number for being a soldier; ten is for perfection, which it has as a foundation; the number four begets the ten.[71] With this, the incomplete was not worthy to pass away, and since love of family is hidden, the generations were four—Lot and his wife, and two daughters, and the fourth is the woman whom he married.[72]

15/ And it is known that, first, no righteous person was found among them. And what was their wickedness, that God was so angry with them? It says that they were homosexuals, male with male. They continually had

---

66. This strange formulation refers to the earth, which absorbs corpses, but in the fiftieth year, that is the jubilee year, is renewed. Likewise, in the creation stories in Genesis, the earth is said to bring forth living things, e.g., Gen 1:24. Here, this is a development of the idea of the jubilee year, which follows seven "weeks" of seven years; see Lev 25:1–38. That is combined with broader concepts of redemption in interpretations of Isa 61:1, which shares the phrase "proclaiming liberty" with Lev 25:10; compare also the development of this conjunction of phrases in 11QMelch 2:6–10.

67. Apparently, five was not taken for a sufficient number of righteous to save Sodom, since six was number of movements of human beings. Some parts of the rest of the section are unclear.

68. The rest of this section deals with possible symbolical or numerological aspects of the numbers that Abraham elicited from God. There are considered to be six movements: forward and back, right and left, up and down. On the six directions of movement that were distinguished, see Michael E. Stone and Manea E. Shirinian, eds., *Pseudo-Zeno, Anonymous Philosophical Treatise*, PhA 83 (Leiden: Brill, 2000), §4.3.4, p. 152. The six numbers that are here in the text are: 50, 45, 40, 30, 20, and 10.

69. The meaning of "respiration" here is unclear. The Armenian means literally, "the bringing of breath, inspiration."

70. On thirty as the ideal age of humans, see Stone, *Armenian Apocrypha Relating to Adam and Eve*, 92.

71. This probably harks back to the Pythagorean Tetraktys, which is particularly the set of four numbers $1 + 2 + 3 + 4 = 10$. The Tetraktys was regarded as the source of all things.

72. The remark about hidden generations may mean that the daughters are only mentioned, with no details. The list is drawn from Gen 19:12, "sons-in-law, sons, daughters, or anyone you have in the city." Instead of "anyone you have in the city," the text has the seeming duplicate, "woman whom he (apparently Lot) married."

intercourse with cattle and beasts. And second, that they were[73] without mercy and they did not stretch out their hand to the poor. They closed the door in the face of the poor and then they ate bread. He who encountered a foreign guest, instead of giving him honor and food, they seized him and then did wickedness. They were merciless on which account they found not God's mercy. Whatever man shuts the door in the face of the poor and the stranger, the gate of God's mercy is also closed in the face of such people and is no more opened. And because they were completely evil and had no portion of goodness, on that account they perished, for he who has no portion of the good, the wicked one, will soon be dead.

16/ And the Lord said to the two angels, "Go to Sodom and bring forth Lot, Abraham's nephew from his house, for the love of Abraham. For, after the shining of the sun in the morning, I will burn the five cities with fire."[74] And Abraham prostrated himself to God and went. And God departed from that place.[75] Because God is not in a place, but God is the grounds and he does not abandon his beloved ones but hides his increate self, by caring for the created beings.[76]

17/ And the two angels came to Sodom. When God does good, he appears between the two of them.[77] But the punishment <is> through two caring and punishing powers, whom people call good according to their action. And he sent evil punishment to them through an evil angel, such as the slaughterer of the firstborn of the Egyptians.[78] A good king gives good gifts with (his) hand, and killing is carried out by an executioner.[79]

And the two angels came to Sodom towards evening,[80] for at that hour visitors used to seek lodgings, but they came to Abraham in the middle of

---

73. Taking էն as էին.
74. On the five cities, see n. 62 above. This divine speech is introduced by the author, based on the events narrated in the rest of Gen 18.
75. Gen 18:32–33. The author tries to soften the anthropomorphic assertion that God was in that specific place by a semantic play in which the meaning of the plural տեղիք "places" is taken, as often, to be "reason for" or "grounds of."
76. The reading of the text, յելանըս is corrupt. Here the variant reading յեղականբ is introduced into the text (G. Muradyan).
77. That is, when the "three men" came to Abraham; see Gen 18:2. These are interpreted as two angels flanking God, or even sometimes as the three Persons of the Trinity. See Stone, *Abraham*, index s.v. "Three men."
78. Exod 12:12 says that it was God, not an angel, who passed through and killed the Egyptian first-born; compare Exod 12:23, Ps 78(77):51, etc.
79. Note the idea that divine punishment comes through an intermediary and is not executed directly by the Deity.
80. Gen 19:1: "The two angels came to Sodom in the evening."

6. SUPPLICATION ABOUT THE SODOMITES AND GOMORREANS

the day for Abraham was worthy of the Lord's light, but to Sodom towards evening for the sun would shine no more for them.

18/ And Lot was sitting by the gate of Sodom[81] like his teacher, Abraham. For just as it is impossible for a good <student> not to be in some measure li<ke> his teacher, just so he learned from his teacher Abraham, his father's brother, hospitality and the love of the poor.[82]

And he prostrated himself like the eye[83] of imperfect servants, and he seized (them) to bring (them) to his house, while doubting their wickedness. Because they were angels they appeared with a beautiful image. So we do when we see a handsome man, we give witness and say that they have an angelic form. Lot seeing that beauty of their appearance said to himself, "I have never seen a man as handsome as they in this city. If my evil-doing fellow-citizens learn of it, they will bring great evil on their heads."

On account of that he welcomed (them) to his house. And they said, "Not thus, but we shall repose here in this city center."[84] And Lot seized them, brought them to his house, saying, "For God's sake, enter my house and rest at my place." Lot wished to honor (them)[85] secretly and surreptitiously to set them on the way, so the evil-doing ones of the citizens would not learn of that very affair.

First, he brought the angels to Abraham, showing (them) what sort of good servants he has on the earth, who supplicated on account of the destruction of the Sodomites and brought back prisoners from there,[86] those whom he had sought in connection with the slaughter of the Canaanites, for He had promised the land to him.[87]

---

81. Gen 19:1: "and Lot was sitting in the gate of Sodom."
82. That Lot learned hospitality from Abraham is not in the Bible. The same theme occurs elsewhere in the Armenian Abraham saga; see Stone, *Abraham*: Abraham Text 2 *Story of Father Abraham*; Abraham Text 18 11.30, 35; Abraham Text 11 *Terah and Abraham* 30, 42; Abraham Text 15 *Sermon* 35–36.
83. The word ակն may mean "eye, expectation, look." The exact sense here is unclear. A. Terian suggests emending to զակնկալեալ "expected."
84. Gen 19:2, "No; we will spend the night in the street."
85. That is, offer them hospitality.
86. This refers to the incident related in Gen 14:16. "From there" means the persons taken captive from Sodom by the attackers.
87. Therefore, apparently, he was obligated to bring back the captives who were not of his own company.

19/ And then He sent the angels to <Sodom>, knowing how wicked they were and <haters> of strangers,[88] whom also justly he expels from that life, who seized the land.

And Lot prepared unleavened bread for the food, not modest round and sacramental loaves, which he placed as a symbol.[89] For he did not have any yeast, <due to> the evils of Sodom. And although he was sinless, yet he was not as wise as Abraham.

20/ And before the Sodomites had gone to sleep, they had surrounded Lot's house, from young to old.[90] And although Lot strove to hide them, they had seen (them) in the city and asked one another, "What happened to them?" And it was reported that Lot brought a strange man to his house.

And then it shows their ferocity,[91] for neither weak youth nor wrinkled old age stopped them from sinning. And the abomination went on for so long that they did not consider fiery things.[92] Perhaps they did not die[93] through fire, but by another sort of punishment. They surrounded the house in the front, lest he have them flee through a secret door.

21/ Then they said to Lot, "Where are the men who entered your place. Give (them) to us that we may know them."[94] And Lot went out to them and he commanded his household to close the door behind him.[95] And Lot said to them, "Because those men have entered under my roof,[96] do not do any wicked thing to them." And they said, "You entered to dwell as a sojourner, and you wish also to judge us by judgment. You are one foreign man. You took up your dwelling in our land. You wish by (by your own) authority to

---

88. There is a wordplay in the Armenian here: "hatred of strangers" and "expels from" both mean literally "makes strangers to."

89. This section, of course, is based on Gen 19:3 "and he made them a feast, and baked unleavened bread." Note the use of unleavened wafers in the sacrament of the Eucharist.

90. Gen 19:14: "But before they lay down, the men of the city, the men of Sodom, both young and old, all the people to the last man, surrounded the house." The author of our text has misunderstood the pronoun "they" in the biblical text, which he takes as referring to the Sodomites, while the apparent meaning of the biblical verse would take "they" as referring to the angels.

91. That is, the narrative.

92. That is, punishment by fire.

93. The sense is unclear.

94. Gen 19:5: "and they called to Lot, 'Where are the men who came to you tonight? Bring them out to us, that we may know them.'"

95. The biblical text simply says, "(he) shut the door after him" (Gen 19:6).

96. Literally, "the beams of my roof."

6. SUPPLICATION ABOUT THE SODOMITES AND GOMORREANS 51

hold a judgment against us. Are you our counsellor?[97] Give (them) to us," they said, "If you do not, you have made their bad things[98] pass onto your own head." And Lot again began to supplicate them and he said, "I have two marriageable daughters. I will give them to you. Do with them as you wish. Do not sin against those men be<cause> they entered my house."[99] And when he said the name(s) of his daughters,[100] they began to beat him.

22/ And thus they had become so accustomed to homosexuality that they did not look at a woman at all. (It was) as if instead of bread they ate dog turds, or instead of mutton, they ate dog flesh. Thus, they were burning with illegitimate intercourse instead of legal marriage.

23/ When the angel<s> learned of Lot's tribulation in which he was, they opened the door and seized the back of his neck and took Lot into the house.[101] And they blew into their[102] faces and at once they were blinded and they saved the house of the righteous one.[103] And they put the feeling of pain into their heart, to turn (them) to penitence. And he did not permit their usual mania, but they thought that the darkness was night. And groping about they sought the door, until having tired (of it), they left.[104]

24/ And the angels said to Lot, "Unthinking one! Do you know (that) we are bodily men? We are angels of God Almighty." Thus, they recalled Abraham's supplications and said to Lot, "Is there anyone here of yours in the house? Bring them hence. For if, being believers, they are worthy of living, let them come forth, and they will not p<e>rish." As indeed happened, for he had become captive of Sodom for that, so that they would not be worthy of that, but of this.[105]

---

97. Expanded from Gen 19:9, "This fellow came to sojourn, and he would play the judge!'"

98. That is, the bad things that will befall them will be because of you.

99. Gen 19:9: "Now we will deal worse with you than with them." The rest stems from the author.

100. Or: mentioned. This sentence is more or less lifted whole from Gen 19:8. Therefore, we have emended the senseless որով to որովհետեւ, which occurs in this position in Gen 19:8.

101. Gen 19:10.

102. That is, the Sodomites.

103. Gen 19:11. Blowing into the face, an act of magic, is not mentioned in the Bible. Moreover, the next clause of the text is part of the authorial editing, as is the aspiration to turn them into penitents. This gives the angelic act a laudable purpose in the eyes of the author.

104. Gen 19:11.

105. This sentence is not quite clear. The point seems to be that believing members of the household were saved on Lot's account. In the same way, earlier, Sodomite captives of

And Lot went forth and said to his sons-in-law, who were going to marry his daughters, and other members of his household and friends, and they did not believe, but laughed,[106] reckoning the matter as foolishness.[107]

25/ And when morning came, they said to Lot, "All this night you labored and did not find[108] anyone worthy. Arise with the few, and go forth." And by terrible fear he was distraught and astounded. They took them by the hand and led four people forth outside with him. They spoke with him, "Hasten," they said, "save yourself." They knew what the daughters were going to do.[109] And they brought his wife forth and put her outside the city. And they (the angels) said to them (Lot and his wife). "Go quickly, for when the sun rises and shines,[110] you (will) climb a high mountain. And on no account should you look back."

Lot's wife turned backwards and she became a pillar of salt.[111] Lot's wife was a Sodomite, whom the angels had ordered not to turn backwards, for that was a symbol of lack of faith.[112]

26/ He said, "Do not be of little faith as to what you heard. Either you disbelieved or the Lord would render other family members into salt, or He was angry that there was nobody worthy of God's acting (i.e., on their behalf). It says to those who are in existence at the time of the fall of the enemy not to rejoice because this one's becoming a pillar of salt, for it will melt and never

---

Chedorlaomer were returned by Abraham on account of Lot (Gen 14:14–16).

106. Or: mocked. The mockery is mentioned en passant in the last phrase of Gen 19:14.

107. By highlighting that the sons-in-law were fiancés of Lot's daughters (based on Gen 19:14), the author, like the Bible, avoids this section contradicting §21 where Lot says, "I have two marriageable daughters." The biblical verse, Gen 19:18 adds "who have not known man" which heightens the contradiction and enhances its resolution.

108. Here the infinitive չգտնել occurs, where an aorist 2nd pers. sing. would be expected.

109. The incident is related in Gen 19:30–36. Its mention here shows the idea that, even though the daughters were going to act wrongly, nonetheless the angels saved them from the city. Such a mention is in line with this text's consistent striving to provide answers in advance to critical questions about the biblical text and story.

110. See Gen 19:17. The sunrise is inferred from the beginning of Gen 19:15.

111. Gen 19:26.

112. The parsing of this story as a test of faith is notable. The theme was already introduced in §24 and it is developed here.

6. SUPPLICATION ABOUT THE SODOMITES AND GOMORREANS 53

be taken for service.[113] And Lot and his two daughters remained. And they went quickly and were unable to reach the mountain.[114]

27/ And there was a small city on the border of the land, named Zoar (Sek'ovr).[115] Lot asked the angels and said, "You are merciful to me. I can go on no longer. Let this small city be free, so that I may rest and be saved <in> it.[116] And it is not a small, but a great favor for me. On account of Abraham's prayers and for love (of him) save this city. For it was a little (more) sinless than the other cities, and there were ten righteous so that a memory remain of the fruitfulness of the earth. You (are one) for whom the earth is a mile[117] and you were able protect five kings.[118] This (i.e., fruitfulness) is that it was like a garden in summer, and in winter it does not lack good things and fruit.[119] And just as they (Adam and Eve or humans) could not inherit the Garden[120] on account of sins, so the Sodomites were deprived of such bounties from the earth because of their sins.

28/ And the angels said to him, "Behold, creations welcome your presence.[121] This matter is not of the angels, but of the Lord of angels, to escape in Zoar," which in Armenian means "small."[122]

The sun shone (rose) and Lot entered Zoar. And the Lord God rained fire from the Lord and heavenly brimstone like fire round about and there was there as if <destructive> fire, clothed with brimstone. And fiery rain fell. It burnt not only humans, but also the animals, the building(s) and the fields all together, so that the punishment of the enemies of the great king would be greater, and evil maggots (made greater) and frenzied beasts in their dens and their lairs.

They destroyed those who were befouled by their sins and burned them as their punishment. And thus fire and brimstone together poured over the

---

113. Perhaps meaning, "never be of use."
114. Gen 19:19. All but the last sentence of this section are due to the author and are not in the biblical narrative.
115. See Gen 19:20a.
116. See Gen 19:20b.
117. This means that the angel was so mighty that the whole earth was as if just a mile wide for him.
118. Again, this is a reference to Gen 14 and it asserts the angel's power.
119. Here the author refers to Gen 13:10. The connection that links these passages is the mention of Zoar.
120. The Garden of Eden is intended.
121. That is, by the fruitfulness of the place.
122. The etymology is from Aramaic z.'r meaning "small." Similarly in Syriac.

whole of the earth to the height of a man. And in the midst of the time,[123] he burnt up together humans and animals, gardens and vineyards. And then black water, as heavy as pitch came up from the depths and concealed the earth. And just as a dead man does not move, in the same way the sea is called "Dead."[124]

29/ And the Jordan passes through the midst. The river's water is not mixed with the sea, nor the sea's (water) with the river. And in spring time around the whole sea trees flower and bear fruit. And when they cut the fruit open, its inside is ashes from fire. And the fire that descended from heaven burns down to the bed of the sea, smoke goes forth and settles upon the sea like <mist> and fog. And thus, the fire remains burning until the end of the world. Thus, also when the last fire shall burn the earth, then the fire of the Sodomites shall be mixed (with it) and form the punishment for sinners.

If someone were to say that God judged mercilessly and did not give a sign first,[125] he did not give exactly this sign, but he made Sodom a sign for the whole earth. Also that to one he appears merciless, he will have mercy on all the earth by rebuking (with) dread and fear of a great calamity.

30/ Strange desire ruled over them; with strange fire coming down from above, they flamed up as a thorn uprooted burns on its roots, as a sign of the fearsome judgment of God,[126] which will be carried out by such deeds. For it is a great fear to fall into the hands of the living God.[127]

And they, just as they changed the divinely established order and broke down righteous marriage, and acted against God's creation and good order, in the same way the heavens changed their order and instead of rain, brought down fire from on high and burnt them. For every human who is born and who comes to this world must live as a virgin in holiness as much as a human can. And when he has become unable to withstand sins, he must take a legitimate wife according to the divine laws, and to satisfy the needs of the sin with his legitimate one.

This is the divinely established order and the natural law. As, from the beginning God made male and female for increase and begetting of children, both homosexuality and bestiality are contrary to God's good will and creation. And these are more hated by God than all sinners, they sin outside the

---

123. This probably means something like, "in the meanwhile."
124. Here the footprints of Question and Answer literature may be discerned. See excursus above, pp. 9–11.
125. At the time of the eschatological burning.
126. Heb 10:27. Language from Heb 10 has permeated this section.
127. The last sentence is drawn from Heb 10:31.

6. SUPPLICATION ABOUT THE SODOMITES AND GOMORREANS 55

law and (are) unpardonable in sins more abominable than the dog, and more promiscuous than the donkey. And of no living thing, does male go to male, neither the dog nor the ass. And those who go (thus) are more abominably promiscuous and impure than the dog and the ass. And they are deprived of God's grace.

And they are not worthy of entering into God's house, and of communicating in the holy communion. And just as it is an unpardonable sin that <female draws close to female>, that male goes to male, in the same way it is an unforgivable sin that <the female goes to the female>. But intercourse is commanded for the <male> and female and union through the divine law.

31/ And if a person asks, "Now many men are homosexual, why does God not burn (them) with fire? He burnt the Sodomites (and) made an example (of them) to the world so that every man would learn that such evil deeds as of the Sodomites are deserving of fire. And if God does not punish (them) now, for the great day of Judgment he preserves those so as to cast them into the fire. If he punished every sinner here (in this world), why would He come in judgment? Why did he burn the Sodomites for homosexuality and bestiality and he destroyed those of the Flood with water?[128] It was on account of licentiousness, so that it might be an example to prostitutes and homosexuals.

32/ And let the sinners not say on the Day of Judgment, "If you have punished one sinner in the bodily order, which we saw with our eyes, we too would have believed in your just judgment." But the sinners cannot speak against (this) for they continually hear the divine books with (their own) ears[129] and see with their eyes the glory of the righteous and the punishment of the sinners and the example of various sorts of sinners punished with various sorts of punishments. Likewise, there is a righteous man who glorified God in this life with virtue and sanctity on account of his humility and forbearing,[130] like Moses (and) like David, so that among the similar men, God prepared great glory and a crown for the righteous.

---

128. That is, the generation of the Flood. All this section is expansionary and it seems to be governed, as may be observed elsewhere in this work, by an agenda of preempting questions attacking the biblical text such as are found in the literature of Questions and Answers. It is very likely that the idea of two stelae, a widespread trope from Graeco-Roman times on, is also behind the drawing of the parallelism of the fire of Sodom with the Flood.

129. This is an intriguing reference to reading aloud, they will have *heard* Scripture and will see the execution of divine judgment.

130. Forbearing is the most prominent virtue of Joseph as he is depicted in the *Third Story of Joseph* in Stone, *Angels and Biblical Heroes*, 177–229.

33/ And there are many righteous men who in this life became poor, were objects of wrongdoing and suffering, such as the ascetics and martyrs, people who understood that the future life is a good recompense for the righteous, and rest, and glory. If God glorified every righteous person in this world, thus humans would learn that that (future) world is the recompense for the ascetics and that God will give them nothing more. But he glorifies certain of the righteous so that you may learn righteousness. And the righteous one is beloved and acceptable and a friend of God,[131] and he keeps certain of the righteous poor and suffering and humiliated so that in the world to come he might give them eternal life as recompense and undying life and light that does not pass away and gladness without despair, and the painless and non-working life and rest.

And eternal glory to Christ. Amen.

---

131. This is a title of Abraham's, see 2 Chr 20:7, Jas 2:23.

7. Brief History of Joshua Son of Nun

Introductory Remarks

In Armenian there exist a number of texts relating to the Ark of the Covenant and Joshua bin Nun. They focus on various aspects of Joshua's activities—partly referring to his succession, partly to the Ark of the Covenant, partly to the incident of Jericho and other, later events in the Book of Joshua. The Ark itself formed a special feature of these texts and was the subject both of learned comments and of narratives. Certain stories focus mainly on the Ark of the Covenant and overlap with the Joshua saga and naturally, the focus of these Ark stories differs somewhat from the purely Joshua material.

Joshua may have taken such a prominent role in the Armenian pseudepigrapha in part because he shared his name with Jesus. When the Joshua stories were read as the New Testament presaged in the Old, this similarity inevitably factored into the typological understanding of this document. So, as often in Armenian texts and the more so under the stimulus of the onomastic hint, the narrative of events is interspersed with hortatory and typological exegesis.

This pattern is to be observed frequently and, when the homiletic remarks are discounted, narrative coherence is quite clear, the incidents usually being strung together in the sequence of the biblical text. Below, we shall outline the narrative of the long Joshua text being published here, and its development and structure should be compared with the Armenian treatment of the Abraham saga.[1] The question may arise, but cannot yet be answered and, most likely will never be answered unambiguously, whether the homiletic sections are original to such documents, or whether they are added in at a somewhat later stage. It is quite evident, however, that an expanded, that is, retold and embellished, biblical narrative was current among the Armenians, what I have called elsewhere, an "embroidered Bible."[2]

---

1. See Stone, *Abraham*, 1–2.
2. See Stone, *Abraham*, 5 and "The Armenian Embroidered Bible," *JSP* forthcoming.

First, however, let us enumerate the relevant texts. So far there exist seven different texts that have come to light about Joshua and/or the Ark of the Covenant:

(1) *Brief History of Joshua son of Nun* in M4618 fols. 146v–148v, and M2168 fols. 310v–327r (the present document). The Joshua text in M6092 is yet another, incomplete copy of the same writing.[3] It too has been collated and its readings given in the critical apparatus following the text below.
(2) *The Short History of Joshua* in M6349.
(3) *The Story of the Ark of the Covenant* in M6340, fols. 55v–58r. This text is also published in the present volume as text no. 8. It also included another copy of part of it, under the title *Concerning the Ark of the Covenant* of the Israelites in an earlier publication, being drawn from an unknown manuscript in Erevan.[4]
(4) *Concerning the Ark of God* in M9100, being extracts from the preceding work.
(5) *Dimensions of the Ark* published from Galata 54 in Stone, *Abraham* and republished from further manuscripts in Stone, *Angels and Biblical Heroes*, 16–17.
(6) *Concerning the Story of the Ark of the Testaments* in LOB Egerton 708 published in Stone, "Two Stories."[5]
(7) *History of Joshua in Biblical Paraphrases* M3854 and M4231 published in Stone, *Patriarchs and Prophets*, 117–20.

The text in M6092 preserves parts of *Joshua Text (1) Brief History*. As I have noted above, the leaves of its exemplar were apparently displaced. The last two words on fol. 343v do not continue the preceding Abraham text, *Memorial of the Forefathers*, which I published from this manuscript and from M1665.[6] Instead, these words are from §58 of *Joshua Text (1)*. This Joshua text continues until halfway through §68 on fol. 350r. It then continues on fol. 350r with the last lines of §55 and continues until the rest of §68. Then text from *Short History of Elijah* commences and runs to the fourth line from the bottom of fol. 353r. The three bottom lines of that folio are the end of §68 of the Joshua

---

3. See below, "Note on M6092."
4. This is published in Michael E. Stone, "Two Stories about the Ark of the Covenant" in *Sion, Mère des Églises: Mélanges liturgiques offerts au Père Charles Athanase Renoux*, ed. Michael Daniel Findikyan, Daniel Galadza, and André Lossky, Semaines d'Études Liturgiques Saint-Serge 1 (Münster: Aschendorff, 2018), 237–71.
5. See Stone, "Two Stories."
6. See Stone, *Abraham*, 55–77.

text. None of these segments of text bears a title or any indication that a different document or a different section is starting, or that it does not continue the preceding writing.

The copying of M6092 is in a very informal *notrgir*. It has two distinctive spelling tendencies, neither carried through systematically. The diphthong ɯւ appears where seventeenth century spelling would normally have o. This variant is not recorded in the apparatus. The second variant of this sort is its tendency to write ҍ instead of ҍ. This is only noted in instances where it brings about a change in meaning. It is significant that this manuscript, though quite often corrupt, preserves a number of pieces of text that are lost from M4618, some of them quite long. These are usually instances of omission by homoeoteleuton or anablepsis.

In the table that follows, the texts are designated by the numbers in the list above. The section division is that of *Brief History*. Bold section numbers indicate major topics. Nonbolded section numbers are references to that topic in other sections or the wording of which resembles the other Joshua works.

Table of main incidents in texts 1, 3, 4, 6, and 7 of the list above[7]

topic no.	topic	sections	source	source	source	source
1	Joshua's origins and office	**1**	Text 1			
2	Joshua's dream	**2**	Text 1			
3	Joshua fasts awaiting Moses	**3**	Text 1			
4	Joshua's name changed; his qualities	**4–5**	Text 1			
5	Spying out Jericho	**6**	Text 1			
6	Joshua appointed Moses's disciple	**7–13**	Text 1			
7	Crossing of the Jordan	**14–16**	Text 1			
		24–33	Text 1			
	Miracles while the Ark crossed Jordan	4				Text 6
		10–11		Text 3	Text 4	
		8–9		Text 3		
		4			Text 4	

---

7. Not including Texts 2 and 5.

topic no.	topic	Sections	source	source	source	source
8	Dimensions of the Ark and its miracles	1–3			Text 4	Text 6
		2–3		Text 3		
		1.6				Text 7
		3–5		Text 3		
9	Rahab	17–23	Text 1			
		15		Text 3		
10	Renewal ceremonies	34–37	Text 1			
11	Joshua encounters an angel of God	38–41	Text 1			
12	Description of Jericho	42–43	Text 1			
		7		Text 3		
		6–7		Text 3		
		1–3			Text 4	
13	The attack on Jericho	44–47	Text 1			
		8–9, 12–14		Text 3		
		4–6				Text 6
		10–11		Text 3		
		5–6			Text 4	
14	The cursing of Jericho	48–51	Text 1			
15	Achan's disobedience	52–54	Text 1			
		55–56	Text 1			
16	Destruction of Ai	57–58	Text 1			
			Text 1			
17	Treaty with Gibeonites; war Canaanites	58–63	Text 1			
			Text 1			
		12–13		Text 3		
18	Conquest of Canaan	64	Text 1			
		65	Text 1			
19	Division of land among twelve tribes	65	Text 1			
20	Cities of refuge	66	Text 1			

7. BRIEF HISTORY OF JOSHUA SON OF NUN

topic no.	topic	Sections	source	source	source	source
21	Last days of Joshua	66–68	Text 1			
			Text 1			

From the table it is clear that Joshua Text (1) *Brief History* is the fullest of the Joshua stories. Joshua Text (3) *Story of the Ark* is briefer, not giving the details about the Ark of the Covenant at the start and shortening the narratives, especially about the Gibeonites and the war against the Canaanites. It does not include the allotment of the land and the narratives connected with Joshua's death. Joshua Text (4) *The Ark of God* deals with the river crossing and Jericho, but in less detail. It is also noteworthy, in contrast with the Abraham stories, that there is very little textual overlap between the different Joshua texts. Shared major narrative units not based on the biblical story are not to be found, though minor parallel exegetical developments exist. The material published here suffices to show that these two focuses, the Ark and Joshua, were powerful magnets for apocryphal embroidery among the Armenians.

Text[8]

M4618 Title/ Համառօտ Պատմութիւն Յեսուայ որդւոյ Նաւեայ։

1/ / fol. 146v / Յեսու որդին Նաւեայ էր յազգէն Եփրեմի՝ որդւոյն Յովսեփայ. եւ աշակերտ էր Մովսէսի։ Եւ իբրեւ զաարկաւագ պահէր զդուռն խորանին վկայութեան զամս ԽՑ (40) յանապատին եւ ոչ մեկնէր ի դրանէ խորանին, այլ պահօք եւ աղօթիւք պաշտէր զԱստուած՝ անհանգիստ ճգնաւորութեամբ։

2/ Եւ էր կուսան սուրբ եւ անարատ՝ նման անմարմին հրեշտակաց։ Եւ մի անգամ փորձեալ երազով, կամէր զինքն սպանանել։ Եւ հրեշտակ Տեառն ըմբռնեաց զձեռն եւ ասէ. «Մի՛ գործեր չար կամ վնաս անձին քում։ Յայսմհետէ անփորձ պահեցից զքեզ։ Այլ զի զիտասցես, թէ մարդ ես մարմնաւոր եւ ոչ անմարմին, վասն այնորիկ հանդիպեցաւ քեզ այն»։

3/ Եւ յորժամ պահեաց Մովսէս զառաջին քառասունն եւ էառ զպատուածագիր պատգամանն, սա արտաքոյն ամպոյն ԽՋ. (46) օր անհաց անջուր եւ անքուն եկաց ի վերայ ոտիցն, Մովսէսի մաշիկն ի ձեռն, զի յորժամ էլցէ, ձիգէ առաջի նորա։ Որ յոյժ զարմանալի էր, քան զՄովսէսին, ժուժկալութիւն նորա։ Զի նա ընդ Աստուծոյ խօսելով,

---

8. Down to §33, the text is drawn from M4618, fols. 146v–147r.

յԱստուծոյ մխիթարէր, եւ սա ոչ ինչ ունելով մխիթարութիւն զայն, քան աւուրս ժուժկալեաց։

4/ Եւ էր սա զօրավար Իսրայէլի՝ արի եւ քաջ ի պատերազմի եւ յաղթող թշնամեաց ազօթիւքն Մովսէսի։ Զառաջինն յաղթեաց Ամաղեկայ եւ ապա այլոց պատերազմացն, մինչեւ չրնչեաց զազգն Քանանացւոց, եւ բաժանեաց զերկիր նոցա որդւոցն Իսրայէլի։

5/ Առաջին անունն Ովսէ էր, եւ Մովսէս փոխեաց եւ Յեսու կոչեաց, զի Յեսուն փրկիչ թարգմանի։ Եւ նա փրկիչ լինելոց էր ժողովրդեանն ի մարմնաւոր թշնամեաց յօրինակ Քրիստոսի։ Եւ զի զիր մի պակաս է յանուն սորա, զի սա մարդ էր, եւ Յիսուս փրկիչն Աստուած մարդացեալ, եւ զի սորա փրկութիւնն մարմնաւոր էր անկատար, եւ Քրիստոսին կատարեալ եւ հոգեւոր փրկութիւն յաւիտենական։

6/ Եւ յորժամ առաքեաց Մովսէս ԲԺ.ան (12) լրտէս յերկիրն պարգեւաց, մինն սա էր ԲԺ.անիցս (12)։ Եւ յորժամ եկին յանապատ, Ժ.ունք (10) յանհաւատութիւն եւ յուսահատութիւն ձգեցին զժողովուրդն։ Իսկ Յեսու եւ Քաղէբ հաստատեցին զսիրտ ժողովրդեանն վասն այսորիկ. զՃՌ.էն (100,000), որ ելին յեգիպտոսէ, սրբա միայն մտին յերկիրն պարգեւաց՝ վասն հաւատոց իւրեանց։ Եւ այլքն յանապատին սատակեցան վասն անհաւատութեան իւրեանց։

7/ Եւ յորժամ եհաս վախճանն Մովսէսի, ասաց Մովսէս առ Աստուած. «Տեսցէ Արարիչն հոգոց եւ մարմնոց առաջնորդ ժողովրդեանս, եւ ապա մեռայցես,[9] զի մի մնասցէ ժողովուրդս իբրեւ զոչխար որոց ոչ իցէ հովիւ.»։[10]

8/ Եւ հրամայեաց Աստուած Մովսէսի զՅեսու կարգել առաջնորդ եւ իշխան ժողովրդեանն փոխանակ իւր։ Եւ ելին ի լեառն Նաբաւ ընդ Մօսէսի Յեսու / fol. 147r / եւ Եղիազար քահանայ եւ ԲԺ.ան իշխանքն։ Եւ ձեռադրեաց Մովսէս զՅեսու, եւ եդ զձեռն ի գլուխ նորա եւ աւրհնեաց զնա։ Եւ ձեռամբն իւր ի նա զիշխանութիւնն իւր, զոր ինքն յԱստուծոյ առեալ էր։

9/ Եւ զի մարդս հոգի եւ մարմին է, եւ Աստուած է հոգւոց եւ մարմնոց արարիչ եւ երկոցունց միապէս խնամք տանի Աստուած։ Վասն այն հոգեւոր եւ մարմնաւոր առաջնորդ եւ իշխան կարգեաց մեզ յաշխարհի, զի հոգեւոր առաջնորդքն հոգւով կարգաւորեն զմարդիկ ի հաւատք եւ յաստուածպաշտութիւն հաստատեն, եւ մարմնաւոր առաջնորդք մարմնով կարգաւորեն զաշխարհս՝ ի խաղաղութիւն,

---

9. A first person verb would be expected.
10. Citing Num 27:17.

7. BRIEF HISTORY OF JOSHUA SON OF NUN

ի սէր եւ ի միաբանութիւնն, իշխանութիւն եւ ի շինարարութիւն հաստատեն:

10/ Վասն այդ պատճառի Մովսէս մարմնաւոր առաջնորդ զՅեսու կարգեաց եւ հոգեւոր՝ զեղիազար քահանայ զորդին Ահարոնի: Եւ պատուիրեաց, զի միաբանութեամբ արասցեն զառաջնորդութիւն ժողովրեանն. եւ զի հոգեւոր եւ մարմնաւոր առաջնորդեաց դիտաւորութիւնն մի է, միթէ զի միապէս ջանալ պիտին, որ զմարդիկ ի մեղաց հեռասցեն, եւ յարդարութիւն եւ ի բարին հաստատեն: Վասն այն պատուիտեաց Մովսէս, զի միմեանց խորհրդով արասցեն զիշխանութիւնն:

11/ Եւ յետ վախճանելոյն Մովսէսի խօսեցաւ Տէր ընդ Յեսուայ պաշտօնէին Մովսէսի: Խոնարհութիւն է Յեսուայ, եւ ի ժամանակի, իբրեւ հաւասարեաց զնա Աստուած ընդ Մովսէսի, «որպէս եղէ ընդ Մովսէսի՝ նոյնպէս եղէց եւ ընդ քեզ»: Այլ նա ոչ հաւասարեաց զանձն՝ զոնէ թէ աշակերտ Մովսէսի, այլ թէ պաշտօնեայ Մովսէսի, որ է ծառայ Մովսէսի:

12/ «Անց», ասէ, «դու եւ ժողովուրդ քո ընդ Յորտանան. եւ ամենայն երկիր, զոր կոխեսցեն ոտք ձեր, ճիշտ հաւատեցէք, զի ձեր լիցի ժառանգութիւն: Եւ զոր օրինակ էի ընդ Մովսէսի, նոյնպէս եղէց եւ ընդ քեզ: Զօրացիր եւ քաջ լեր, զի ես ընդ քեզ եմ: Ոչ թողից զքեզ եւ ոչ անտես արարից յամենայն մարտս պատերազմի, մինչեւ ժառանգացուսցեն զերկիրն ժողովրդեանն, որպէս խոստացայ Աբրահամու, հարց դոցա:

13/ Բայց միայն զի պահեսջիք զպատուիրանս իմ, զոր պատուիրեաց ծառայն իմ Մովսէս, որպէս եւ ինքն պահեաց հաստատուն զպատուիրանս իմ»: Թէպէտ հաւասարեաց զնա Աստուած Մովսէսի, այլ նա զինքն ծառայ անուանէր Մովսէսի: Զի այսպէս խոնարհութեան սիրող են սուրբքն եւ ոչ կամին զանձինս այլոց հաւասարել, այլ քան զամենայն մարդ զիւրեանքն անարգ եւ անարժան եւ յետին համարեն:

14/ Ասէ Յեսու գժողովուրդն. «Պատրաստեցէք ձեզ պաշար իւրաքանչիւր ոք» եւ զինչ պիտոյ էր նոցա պատրաստութիւն: Զի մանանայն մինչեւ ցայնժամ ոչ էր արգելեալ ի նոցանէ: Այլ զի ընդ գետն անցանելոց էին, ետ նոցա հրաման աւուրք յառաջ պատրաստել եւ զպաշար ի մանանայէն, որպէս պարապորդ լիցին կեալ եւ տեսանել զթագստէլիս, որ լինելոց էր ի գետի անդ ի վայրին:

15/ Եւ զի յՌուբենի՝ եւ Կադայ՝ եւ կէս ձեղի Մանասէի մնացին յայնկոյս Յորդանանու, զի մի բեկցեն զսիրտս եղբարց իւրոց, վասն այսորիկ ընտրեցին ի նոցանէ ԽՌ. (40,000) վառեալ, զի լիցին առաջապահ եւ վերջապահ ժողովրդեանն:

16/ Վասն այսորիկ թողին զտունս եւ զախսու[11] իւրեանց յայնկոյս Յորդանանու եւ գնացին զհետ ժողովրդեանն, մինչեւ լարաբաձին արարին գերկիրն ի վերայ Ժ. (10) ազգին. եւ ապա դարձին ի տուն իւրեանց:

17/ Եւ ապա առաքեաց Բ.(2) արս իմաստունս եւ ճարտարս՝ ի լրտեսել զերիքով: Թէպէտ առ ի քաջալերել ժողովուրդն առաքեցին, այլ վասն Րախաբու պոռնկի, զի հաւատացելոց էր նա յԱստուած կենդանի: Եւ գնացեալ մտին ի տունն Րախաբու, զի նա բոզ եւ պոռնիկ էր, եւ բազումք մտանէին առ նա, զի մի ի կարծիս անկցին վասն արանցն մտելոց: Եւ իբրեւ իմացան քաղաքացիքն, եկին առ Րախաբ եւ ասեն. «Ո՞ւր են արքն, որ մտին առ քեզ»:

18/ Եւ նա յառաջ իմացաւ զխորհուրդը քաղաքին եւ, հանեալ զերկու արսն ի տանիսն, ծածկեաց վշով եւ ասաց. «Ոչ ոք եմուտ առ իս». Եւ նոքա ստիպէին ցուցանել զարսն. եւ նա ասաց, թէ ինքն բոզ է «եւ բազումք գան առ իս եւ գնան»: Վասն այդ խօսից թողին գնա ի բաց: Եւ ապա կոչեաց գնա Րախաբ եւ ասէ. «Գիտացաք, զի մատնեաց Տէր / fol. 147v /[12] զերկիրս քանանացոց ի ձեռս ձեր, քանզի լուաք, թէ բաժանեաց Տէր զջուրս Կարմիր ծովուն առաջի որդւոցն Իսրայէլի Խ. (40) ամէ, եւ այս երկիրս այլ ձեր է, եւ արդեօք զի ապաշխարեցուք, բնակեցաք մեք ի սմա մինչեւ ցայսօր: Այլ յօրէ, զի բաժանեաց Աստուծով[13] գծով, եւ կոտորեցան Բ. թագաւորքն ամուրհացւոցն, զարհուրեալ դողացան սիրտք մեր, եւ ոչ մնաց ի մեզ շունչ կենդան{ի}»:[14]

19/ «Արդ, Աստուածն ձեր, որ նա ինքն է դաստաւոր, որ իշոյց կարկուտ հրախառն ի վերայ եգիպտացւոց, նա տայցէ ձեզ գերկիրս այս, եւ ես հաւատամ յԱստուածն ձեր: Արդ, եկայք երդուարուք ինձ, զի մի՛ մոռասջիք գերախտիս իմ, այլ, որպէս ապրեցուցի ես գձեզ այսօր, ապրեցուցանէք դուք զիս եւ զտուն հօր իմոյ եւ զամենայն ազգականս իմ ի միջի ձերում, ի ձեռն կարմիր նշանին, զոր կապեմ եմ»:

20/ Ասեն գնա, թէ՝ «Այսօր ոչ հատուցանել քեզ զշնորհս երախտաց քոց, զոր արարէր մեզ ի ծածուկ, այլ յորժամ տացէ Տէր Աստուած գերկիրս քանանացոց ի ձեռս մեր, յայնժամ յայտնապէս հատուսցուք

---

11. An odd orthography of աղխս "furnishings, goods."
12. From this point the text was transcribed by Tat'ewik Manukean of the Department of Study and Description of Armenian Manuscripts at the Matenadaran in Erevan (Curator Dr. Gēorg Tēr-Vardanean). I thank her here for her careful work.
13. The elided subject is apparently Moses.
14. Կենդանւոյ would be expected.

7. BRIEF HISTORY OF JOSHUA SON OF NUN

զփոխարէնն երախտաց քոց յանդիման արեզականն։ Բայց միայն կապեսջիր կարմիր նշան ի պատուհանի քում, եւ զգուշացուցին, թէ որ ելցէ ի տանէն, որ կապել է կարմիր նշանն, արիւն նորա ի զլուխ իւր»:[15]

21/ Եւ ապա պարանով իջոյց զնոսա ընդ պարիսպ քաղաքին, եւ եկեալ պատմեցին ժողովրդեանն եւ հաստատեցին զսիրտս նոցա եւ ասացին, թէ՝ «Քանանացիքն զարհուրեալ են ի մէնջ եւ կան ի դողման վերեւաց մերոց»: Եւ զի Րախաբ օրինակ էր եկեղեցւոյ, որպէս նա Բ. (2) լրտեսաց պատճառաւն հետագաւ ի կրապաշտութենէ եւ յամենայն մեղաց, նոյնպէս եկեղեցի ի ձեռն ԲԺ.ան (12) առաքելոց քարոզութեանն հետագաւ ի կրապաշտութենէ եւ յամենայն մեղաց։

22/ Եւ ապա այն, որ վանդակաւ իջոյց զղոսա ի պարսպէն, զխորհուրդ եկեղեցւոյ նշանակէր՝ այն, որ զՊօղոս առաքեալն վանդակաւ իջուցին ընդ պարիսպն[16] Դամասկոսի եւ ազատեցին ի սպանմանէ: Եւ զի կարմիր նշան եւ ոչ այլ գոյն զխորհուրդ խաչին քարոզէր, եւ որպէս կարմիր զոունվն փրկեցաւ տունն Րախաբու, նոյնպէս արեամբն Քրիստոսի փրկեցաւ տունն Ադամայ ի ձեռաց սատանայի: Եւ այն, որ հաւատաց կարմիր նշանին, ի ժամ կորձանման պարսպին ոչ երկնչէր նա, նոյնպէս որ ի խաչն հաւատոյ, որ ներկեցաւ կարմիր արեամբն Քրիստոսի, ի ժամանակի յորժամ քակտին եւ լուծանին արարածք, ոչ զարհուրի եւ ոչ դողայ ի ժամուն, եւ զի կապեր զնշանն ի փայտի, նշ խորհուրդ ժողովրդեանն, որ կախելոց էին զորդին Աստուծոյ զխայտ, զայն նկարէր նա:

23/ Ոյ Րախաբ, դուստր հեթանոսաց, զի մտանելովն իւրով գրէր, նկարէր զայն զելանելն այնոցիկ, առ որս երթայր, զի խաչին Քրիստոսի հրէից ազգն ելին եւ հետագան յաստուածապաշտութենէ, եւ հեթանոսք մտին յաստուածապաշտութիւն: Իբրեւ մերձեցաւ ձեռն նորա ի կարմիր նշանն, հետագաւ նա յամենայն կռոց եւ սպասեր տեսութեանն Յեսուայ կուսանի: Եւ եկեղեցի՝ յորժամ հաւատաց ի խաչն, հետագաւ ի կրապաշտութենէ, եւ սպասէ զալստեան միածնին անմահ թազաւորին:

24/ Եւ իբրեւ պատմեցին լրտեսքն զերկիւղ ժողովրդեանն քանանացւոց, չու արարին ժողովուրդն եւ եկին, բանակեցան յեզր Յորդանան գետոյ գերիս աւուրս, զի գուցէ լուիցեն բնակիչքն Երիքովի, երկիցեն եւ խնդրեսցեն զաշ խաղաղութեան Յեսուայ եւ հաւատասցեն յԱստուած կենդանին եւ յաւելցին ի հաւատացեալս, եւ

---

15. Josh 2:16–19.
16. Phrasing from 2 Cor 11:32.

ածզէ Աստուած զահ եւ զերկիւղ յամենայն ազգս հեթանոսաց, զի մի՛ եկեսցեն մարտնչիլ ընդ զօրութեանն, որ բաժանեաց զճովն Կարմիր ի ձեռն Մովսէսի, յաւել դարձեալ՝ բաժանեաց զգետն Յորդանան առաջի Յեսուայ որդւոյ Նաւեայ, զի գիտասցեն եւ ծանիցեն, զի թէ զան եւ մարտնչին ընդ զօրութեանն, որ բաժանեաց զՅորդանան առաջի Յեսուայ որդւոյ Նաւեա, ի ձեռն նորա կոտորեսցէ զնոսա, որպէս զամուրհացին, զօրութիւնն այն, որ բաժանեաց զճովն առաջի Մովսէսի:

25/ Եւ զի հանդերձեալ էր բառնալ ի նոցանէ ամպն եւ տինս հանդերձ մանանայիս, եզոյց թէ այսուհետեւ տապանակն կտակարանաց երթալոց էր առաջի նոցա: Ետ նոցա հրաման / 148r / հեռանալ ի տապանակէն ԲՌ. (2000) կանգնաւ, զի մեծաշուք արասցէ յայտ նոցա, վասն զի մեծաւ պատուով փառաւորեսցի սուրբ զօրութիւնն, որ բնակեալ է ի նմա: Նոյնպես պարտ է յեկեղեցւոյ եւ ի սրբութեանց հեռու կենալ յաշխարհականաց Խ. (40) կանգուն, զի մի՛ հեռասցի սրբութիւնն վասն անարժանից մերձաւորութեանն:

26/ Եւ զի առաւել փառաւորեսցի սրբութիւնն, եւ ահարկու երեւի յայս ռամիկ ժողովրդեանն, հրամայեաց նոցա սրբել զանձինս իւրեանց Գ. (3) աւուրբք յառաջ, զի արժանի լինիցին տեսլեան սքանչելեացն, որ լինելոց էր Յորդանան գետ, զի նշանակեսցէ զխորհուրդն սրբութեան, որ ի ձեռն ճշմարտին Յիսուսի տարածելոց ընդ ամենայն ազգս ազգաց խորիրդով սուրբ Երրորդութեանն երեքլուսեան մեծութեանն: Այսպէս պարտ է ամենայն հաւատացելոց նախ սրբել զանձինս յամենայն մեղաց՝ եւ ապա արժանանալ աստուածային սուրբ խորհրդոյն՝ եւ տէրունական տոնից կատարման:

27/ Եւ այս խորհրդովս եղեալ է Գ. (3) յիսնակս՝ նախ պահօք եւ աղօթիւք սրբել զանձինս, եւ ապա արժանանալ աստուածային տոնից կատարմանն՝ Ծննդեան, Զատկին եւ Վարդավառին: Եւ զի զարնանային էր ժամանակն, եւ Յորդանան զայր դարիւ դարիւ, եւ ասէ Յեսու, եթէ՝ «Ձիս Աստուած արժան համարի առաջնորդ ժողովրդեանս նման Մովսէսի, նա որպէս Մովսէսի ձեռօքն զճովն պատառեաց, իմ ձեռօքս զգետս պատարեսցէ»:

28/ Եւ ասէ Տէր ցՅեսու. «Արարից ըստ կամաց քոց եւ փառաւորեցից զքեզ յայս ժողովրդեան քո, զի գիտասցեն, թէ որպէս էի ընդ Մովսէսի ի բաժանիլ ծովուն, նոյնպէս եղից աստ ընդ քեզ ի բաժանել գետոյդ»: Արդ, Է. (7) քահանայք բարձեալ էին զտապանակն, եւ հրամայեաց Յեսու քահանայից մտանել տապանակաւն ի գետն: Եւ իբրեւ հասին ոտք քահանայից ի ջուրն, նոյնժամայն բաժանեցաւ գետն եւ դարձաւ յակն իւր Է. (7) աւուր ճանապարհի:

7. BRIEF HISTORY OF JOSHUA SON OF NUN

29/ Եւ ներքին ջուրն մտաւ ի ծովն արեւմտից, որ է աղի ծովն Սոդոմայ, եւ մեծ սքանչելիք էր այն, զի ոչ դիզացաւ եւ կուտակեցաւ ջուր գետոյն, այլ դարձաւ յակն իւր, զի մի՛ ի դառնալն հեղեղատեցէ զչինուածս յեզր գետոյն։ Եւ այնցափ կանգնեցան քահանայքն տապանակաւն ի մէջ չրոյն, մինչեւ էանց ժողովուրդն ամենայն, զի մի՛ երկնչիցին ի դառնալոյ չրոյն։ Եւ ապա հանին երկոտասան վէմն ի գետոյն եւ եդին ի ցամաքի եւ ԲԺ.ան (12) վէմ ի ցամաքէն եդին ի մէջ գետոյն, <եւ յորժամ ելին քահանայքն տապանակաւն> ապա դարձաւ ջուրն եւ գնաց զճանապարհս իւր, որպէս յերէկն եւ յեռանդն։

30/ Եւ թէ զի՞նչ խորհուրդ ունէր, զի Յեսու օրինակ էր Քրիստոսի, եւ տապանակն սրբոյ խաչին, եւ որպէս տապանակաւն դարձաւ ջուր գետոյն յակն իւր, նոյնպէս զալստեամբն Քրիստոսի եւ խաչին դարձաւ մարդկային բնութիւնս յառաջին փառս իւր։ Եւ ներքին ջուրն օրինակ անհաւատողն, որք ոչ եկին ի ծովէ մեղաց ուռկանու աւետարանին, այլ մնացին յառաջին անհաւատութիւնն եւ ընկղմեցան մեղօք ի խորս անդնդոց։ Նոյնպէս ԲԺ.ան (12) վէմն, որ հանին ի գետոյն, օրինակ եւ խորհուրդ ԲԺ.ան (12) ազգաց հաւատացելոց, որ ի ձեռն քարոզութեան ԲԺ.ան (12) առաքելոցն ելին ի ջուրց մեղաց եւ ցանկութեանց։

31/ Եւ գերկոտասան վէմն որ եհան, շինեաց սեղան Աստուծոյ եւ գրեաց ի վերայ նորա գերկրորդ օրէնքն վասն հեթանոսաց ի յանցս Ցորդանանու, զի եւ հեթանոսք վայելեցցին ի փչրանաց հոգեւոր սեղանոյ աստուածային օրինացն, եւ մի՛ մնասցեն կոյր եւ տգէտ կամացն Աստուծոյ՝ խաւարեալ մտօք։ Նոյնպէս եւ այն օրինակ հաւատացելոց էր, որ զսիրտս իւրեանց կազմեցին սեղան սրբութեան եւ մատուցին բանական պատարագ զաղօթս իւրեանց եւ եդեն տեղիք պատգամացն Աստուծոյ՝ գրեալ զօրէնս Աստուծոյ ի սիրտս իւրեանց։

32/ Եւ ԲԺ.ան (12) վէմն, որ եդին ի ցամաքէն ի ջուրն, օրինակ անհաւատ ԲԺ.ան (12) ազգին հրէից եւ ամենայն անհաւատող, որք ոչ հաւատացին ի Քրիստոս, այլ ծանրացան մեղօք, իբրեւ զվէմ կապարող, եւ իջին ի խորս դժոխոց։ Այս խորհուրդն է, թող ըստ ճառին, զի ԲԺ.ան (12) վիմովն, որ հանին ի գետոյն, ի նշան փառացն Աստուծոյ, զի անմոռաց յիշատակի սքանչէ|148բ|լիքն Աստուծոյ մինչեւ ի կատարած աշխարհի։

33/ Եւ ջուր գետոյն, զի բաժանեցան վասն քանանացւոցն, զի լուիցեն եւ երկիցեն եւ հաւատասցեն յԱստուած կենդանին, եւ մի՛ մաշեսցին ի սուր սուսերին Յեսուայ։ Այլ որպէս յորժամ բաժանեցան ջուրք ծովուն, եւ ո՛չ երկեան ամուրհացիքն, այլ եկին պատերազմիլ ընդ ժողովրդեանն եւ սատակեցան, նոյնպէս եւ աստ քանանացիքն ո՛չ հաւատացին եւ ո՛չ երկեան յԱստուծոյ, այլ եկին պատերազմիլ ընդ Յեսուայ եւ սատակեցան:

34/ Արդ, ...

Here the text of M4618 breaks off. The following is drawn from M2168, starting on line 4 of fol. 317r

34/ Արդ ի ամին այսմ ժամանակի՝ հրաման թղթատութեան, որ խափանեալ էր յանապատին ցամս Խ. (40): Եւ դարձեալ նորոգեցաց զնա ի ձեռն Յեսուա, իբրեւ մտանէ ի խառնակել ընդ ազգս հեթանոսաց, զի այնու նշանաւ բաժանեցին յանհաւատիցն: Թղթատեաց Յեսու զանթղթատսն, որ ծնան յանապատին, վասն զի անթղթատութիւն պահեաց զնոսա յանապատին: Ի ժամանակին, զի մահն իշխեալ տիրէր ի վերայ թղթատութեան գՃՌ.ին (100,000): Եւ հրամայեաց թղթատել նոցա, զայլախազիւ, վասն զի դիւրին է հարուած նորա եւ երագազգյունք են առ ի բժշկել, քան զվերս երկաթոյ:

35/ Եւ դարձեալ ամենայն մարդոյ պատրաստ առ ի գտանել, զի ոչ առաւ ի պաշտօն կռոց: Եւ զի ի ձեռն զայլախազին արտաքին անդամս նոցա դրոշմ էր, զի սիրտք նոցա զայլախազեա կակղացին: Եւ օրէնաւքն Աստուծոյ զանթղթատութիւն սրտից իւրոց թղթատեցէ: Եւ արար Յեսու դանակ զայլախազեա եւ թղթատեաց զժողովուրդն ի Գաղգաղեա յեզր Յորդանան գետոյ, որ / fol. 317v /թարգմանի բոլորակ թղթատութեան՝ ի նշան հաւատելոց, օրինակ մկրտութեանն Յիսուսի, որ է Ը. (8) օրն մկրտին Քրիստոսի հաւատացեալքս եւ խաչին նշանաւ բաժանին յանհաւատից: Այլ եւ յետ եւթն դարու կենցաղոյս, ի մուտս Ը. (8) դարին յորն դատաստանին բաժանին հաւատացեալքն յանհաւատիցն: Հաւատացեալք հետ Քրիստոսի վերանան յարքայութիւնն, եւ անհաւատքն հետ սատանայի իջանեն յատակս դժոխոց:

36/ Արարին զՁատիկն, եւ արգելու մանանայն, զի ցուցէ թէ փոխանակեցին հարք նոցա յանապատին ընդ տփին եւ ընդ սխտորին, արհամարհեցեն յայս որդոցն յերկիրն պարգեւաց, յորժամ տեսանեն զերկիր ժառանգութեան իւրեանց՝ լի ամենայն բարութեամբ, եւ իբրեւ թղթատեցաւ ժողովուրդն եւ նստան իւրաքանչիւր տեղիս անխիղճ, մինչ զի բաժանեցան:

37/ Ասէ Տէրն, թէ՝ «Այսօր անցուցի զնախատինս եգիպտացոց ի ձենձ»,[17] քանզի թղթատեալ էին եւ չէր ոք, որ հալածեր զթղթատութիւնն իբրեւ զտղայսն յեգիպտոս: Չի վասն թղթատութեան ընկենային

---

17. Sic!

7. BRIEF HISTORY OF JOSHUA SON OF NUN

զնոսա ի գետն, կամ զի յայնժամ պանտխտութեամբ նստէին ի մէջ եգիպտացոցն եւ այսօր կոխեցեն ի վերայ այլազգեաց:

38/ Եւ / fol. 318r / մինչդեռ նստէին նոքա, երեւեցաւ այր մի Յեսուա, զի կայր ընդ յերկինս եւ ընդ երկիր եւ ունէր սուսեր մերկ ի ձեռին իւրում: Եւ զի մի զարհուրեցոյց ժողովուրդն, միայն Յեսուա երեւեցաւ, զի յայտ լիցի Յեսուա, թէ հրեշտակ Տեառն երթա առաջի նոցա կոտորեալ զքշնամիս նոցա: Եւ ապա նուաւ ազդ եղեւ ամենայն ժողովրդեանն: Բայց իբրեւ ետես Յեսու զայրն, համարեցաւ,[18] թէ ումն ի դիմացն հեթանոսաց ժպրհեցաւ նմա ի ձեռն սուսերին, զի արկցէ ի վերայ նոցա զահ եւ երկիւղ:

39/ Վասն այնորիկ եհարց գնա եւ ասէ. «Դու ի մեռոց ես, թէ յօտարաց»: Չի թէ գիտացեալ էր, թէ նա է զօրագլուխ զօրաց Տեառն, ոչ հարցանէր գնա, այլ խոնարհութեամբ երկիր պագանէր եւ հնազանդէր կամացն նորա: Եւ յորժամ եհարց գնա, եւ ասէ. «Մի՛ երկնչիր. ես զօրագլուխ եմ զօրու Տեառն եւ արդ եկի օգնել քեզ», զի ուսուցէ, թէ հրեշտակն երկնաւոր եկեալ է յօգնութիւն մանկանց ժողովրդեան նորա: Եւ զի ասաց, թէ՝ «այժմ եկի, յայտ արարի, թէ որչափ յանապատին էիք առանց պատերազմի եւ կայիք անհոգս, ոչ եկի ես. բայց այժմ զի սկսայք տալ պատերազմ ընդ քանանացիքն, / fol. 318v / եկի ի թիկունս յօգնութիւն ձերոյ»:

40/ Եւ ասաց նմա. «լոյծ զկոշիկս յոտից քոց». այս ընկեր է այնմ որ զաւսերն եգոյց նմա. այսպէս Տէրն էր ընդ հրեշտակին եւ ասէ. «լոյծ զկոշիկս յոտից քոց ի կոխել զքշնամիս, իբրեւ զինձան ի ձեռն այդովատիկ սուսերիս, որ ցուցի քեզ դիաթաւալ, զի տեղիք յորում կաս դու. սուրբ է». զի ցուցցէ թէ ուր կայր նա առաջի.

41/ Չի զոր օրինակ այն, որ[19] բնակեալ էր ի մորենին, Աստուած էր եւ ի ձեռն հրեշտակին խօսէր ընդ Մովսիսի, թէ՝ «Լոյծ զկոշիկս յոտիս քոց առ ի կոխել զեգիպտացիսն», նոյնպէս եւ ասդ Տէրն է, որ ի ձեռն զօրագլուխ հրեշտակին հրամայէ լուծանել զկոշիկս՝ ելանել, հարկանել, կոխել եւ սպատակել զքանանացիսն: Բայց զաւարքն սուրբ անուանեցան, յայտ եղեն վասն աստուածութեանն, որ ի մորենին եւ ի զօրագլուխ: Անդ բնակեր, զի յերկիր, որ կենդանի Աստուծոյ պաշտի, երկիր կենդանեաց եւ սուրբ անուանի: Յորժամ ոչ երկեան քանանացիքն եւ ոչ հաւատացին յԱստուած կենդանին:

42/ Ապա եկն Յեսու ժողովրդեամբն, եւ շրջապատեցին զքաղաքն Երիքով, որ նման էր / fol. 319r / դժոխոց: Եւ թէ ով շինեաց գնա: Չի

---

18. ր above line between h and ա.
19. In margin p.m.

Քուակ որդոցն Քամա ունէր Գ. (3) որդի՝ Գայի եւ Գադ եւ Երիքով: Եւ Գայի եւ Գադ շինեցին ըստ անսան իւրեանց զԳայի եւ զԳադգադ: Յետոյ Երիքով լիր անուն շինեաց զԵրիքով, որպէս յետոյ սատանայ շինեաց եւ զմահ եւ զդժոխք: Չի Աստուած զմահ ոչ արար. «նախանձու բանսարկուին եմուտ մահ յաշխարհի»:

43/ Եւ ունէր Երիքով է. (7) տակ պարիսպ ի մազլնիտ քարէ անգործելի յերկաթոյ, անյաղթ եւ անառիկ: Եւ թէ երկաթ ոչ գործի, առանց երկաթոյ որպէս էր շինեալ: Այսպէս ասեն, թէ զպղինձն եւ զկլայեկն լիրապ խառնեն եւ գործիք կազմեն եւ այդու արեամբ մխեն եւ այնու տաշեն զքարն քայս: Վկա քեզ ալմասն, որ երկաթն ոչ յաղթէ եւ արճճով կոտրի եւ փշրի` յօրինակ կակղութեան եւ խոնարհութեան, զի խոնարհութեամբ յաղթէ մարդ ամենայն չարի, եւ նովաւ խափանի ամենայն չար:

44/ Եկին շրջապատեցին զքաղաքն: Երկաթով ոչ կարէին մօտն երթալ, զի քարն այն յինքն քարշէր զերկաթն եւ ի մէջ գրեհին ջարդէր եւ փշրէ / fol. 319v / զուկերքս մարդոյն: Եւ առանց երկաթի ոչ կարէին մերձենալ, զի ի վերուստ ի պարսպէն սպանանէին: Եւ այնպէս անառիկ էր. միայն Աստուծոյ զօրութեանն էր գործ քակել եւ կործանել զնա:

45/ Եւ հրամայեաց Տէր Յեսուա, եւ բարձին է. (7) քահանայ զտա<պա>նակն յուսս իւրեանց եւ է. (7) փող ի ձեռս իւրեանց, եւ ԽՌ. (40,000) մարդ յառաջ եւ ԽՌ. (40,000) յետոյ տապանակին, զի մի ելցեն քահանայքն եւ զերեցան զտապանակն: Եւ Ձ. (6) օր Ձ. (6) անգամ շուրջ եկին զքաղաքաւն, եւ քահանայքն զփողն հարկանէին, եւ ժողովուրդն ամենայն առ հասարակ «Տէր ողորմեա» ասէին ցած: Եւ յաւուր շաբաթու կարծեցին, թէ պահեցեն եբրայեցիքն զշաբաթն, ելին ի պարիսպն եւ նայէին եւ կատակէին զնոսա:

46/ Եւ նոքա ոչ պահեցին զշաբաթն, եւ է. (7) օրն, որ էր շաբաթ, է. (7) անգամ շուրջ եկին ըշտապով, Ձ. (6) անգամն ցած «Տէր ողորմեա» ասելով եւ է. (7) անգամն բարձր աղաղակել եւ գոչել առ Աստուած: Եւ նոյնժամ պարիսպն Երիքովի հալեցաւ որպէս եւ զջուր, եմուտ եւ իջաւ ի հողն, որպէս հալեալ կապար: Բայց միայն / fol. 320r / պարիսպն այն ոչ կործանեցաւ, յորում Ռախաբ նստէր. վասն հաւատոց իւրոց ապրեցաւ ինքն եւ տունն հօր իւրոյ: Եւ արք ելին ի պարիսպն յաւուր շաբաթու. ըստ կործանման պարսպին յանդունդս ընկղմեցան, զի մի աշխատեսցեն կոտորել զեբրայեցիսն:

47/ Եւ այն զօրութիւնն, որ կործանեաց զաշտարակն բարձր եւ անյաղթ, նոյն աստուածային զօրութիւնն պահեաց զմահարձանն եւ զպարիսպն, յորում Ռախաբ նստէր՝ խորհրդով կարմիր նշանին, որով ազատեցաւ տունն Ռախաբու: Նոյնպէս խորհրդով արեամբն Յիսուսի

7. BRIEF HISTORY OF JOSHUA SON OF NUN

ազատեցաւ եւ ապրեցաւ տունն Ադամա ի կործանմանէ, մահու եւ դժոխոցն։ Եւ ապա հանին գտունն Բախարու յԵրիքովէ եւ տարան ի մէջ իւրեանց. սրբեցաւ եւ խառնեցաւ յազգն Յուդա։

48/ Յայնմ աւուր անէծ Յեսու գերիքով եւ զշինողս նորա։ Եւ անդր ասաց, թէ ոք շինեսցէ զքաղաքս զայս, անդրանիկ որդովն հիմն դիցէ եւ կրսերան զդունն։ Ազան Բեթելացի հրամանաւ Աքայարու շինեաց զերիքով եւ, զի / fol. 320v / քամահեաց Աքայեաք գՅեսու, թէ ոչ գոյ զօրութիւն յանէծս նորա, Աբիրոն անդր անկաւ։ Եղ զհիմն պարսպին Ազան բեթելացին եւ կրսերան Սերազալ կանգնեաց զդունն։ Եւ բնակչաց քաղաքին սերմանիքն ոչ բուսանէին եւ անասունքն ոչ յղանային։ Եւ թէ ոչ էր հասեալ աւրհնութիւն Եղիայի մարգարէին, բնաչինչ լինէին։ Եւ թէ վասն չէր յանէծ Յեսու գերիքով եւ զշինողս նորա։ Զի Երիքով օրինակ էր դժոխոց. որպէս նա է. (7) տակ պարիսպ ունէր անարիկ եւ մարդ ոչ կարէր բակել զնա, այլ Աստուծոյ զօրութեամբն կործանեցաւ, նոյնպէս սատանայ զդժոխքն շինեաց եւ է. (7) ջափ մահու մեղօք պարսպեաց ի ներքս աշխարհիս, եւ մարդ ոչ կարէր զնալ անդր եւ բակել զնա, այլ Աստուծոյ զօրութիւնն կարօտացաւ, որ քակէր զնա։

49/ Վասն այդ պատճառի միածինն անմահ թազաւորն խաչի չարչարանաւքն իջաւ ի դժոխքն եւ բակեաց զնա եւ ազերեալ հոգիքն ազատեաց։ Եւ որպէս Յեսու բակեաց գերիքով եւ անէծ զշինողս նորա, նոյնպէս Քրիստոս զմեր բաժին դժոխքն բակեցու եւ զայն մարդն / fol. 321r / անիծեաց, որ այլ նոր մեղք գործէ, իւր հոգւոյն դժոխք շինէ։ Այլ մեր բաժին դժոխքն բակեցաւ, եւ սատանայի բաժինն մնաց։ Եւ թէ մարդիք ամենայն ի Քրիստոս էին հաւատացեալ եւ Քրիստոսի էին կամարար, նա Ադամայ որդոցս այլ ոչ կայր դժոխք։ Այլ զի բազումք անհաւատ մնացին եւ սատանայի եղեն կամարար, վասն այն զնան ի հուրն, որ պատրաստեալ է սատանայի եւ կամարարաց նորա։

50/ Եւ դարձեալ վասն այն անէծ զնա, զի ժպրհեցաւ յետ բաժանմանն Յորդանանու եւ զի է. (5) օր երկայնամբրտեաց Աստուած եւ նորա անհաւատ եւ անզէղջ մնացին։ Եւ ոչ կամեցան զկէանս իւրեանց եւ ոչ խնդրեցին զաչ խաղաղութեան Յեսուա։ Վասն այն անէծ եւ ոգովեաց զնոսա, եւ կորտրեցին զբնակիչս քաղաքին։ Եւ զէ. (5) թազաւորս ձերբակալ արարին, եւ երիկունն երկճղի փայտէ կախեցան։ Եւ գտունն Բախարու հանին. եւ է. (7) օր նստան եւ արտաքս բնակեցան, եւ մինչեւ թլփատեցան արք նոցա, եւ ապա խառնեցան յարիւնեալ ազգն Յուդա։

51/ Եւ ասաց Յեսու, թէ՝ «Անիծեալ եղիցի մարդ, որ ացցէ յածից Երիքովի, այլ զամենայն հրահալելի նիւթ յատաջք ի խորանն

Աստուծոյ բաժին»: Եւ զայլ ամենայն ինչս եւ զայլն ամենայն կորուսին՝ հրով եւ սրով մա/ fol. 321v /ծեցին: Եւ զոսկին եւ զարծաթն, զպղինձ եւ զերկաթն ի խորանն առին: Եւ դարձեալ խորհրդով կործանումն Երիքովի եղեալ է կանունագլուխն՝ զվեց զուբդյան ցածեն եւ զէ-ն (7). բարձրաձայնիւ եւ գյետին անկումն՝ բարձր աղաղակել, որ կործանի պարիսպ մեղաց, զոր էած սատանայ եւ[20] զօրութեամբ խաչին Քրիստոսի, որում օրինակ էր տապանակն:

52/ Եւ զղացաւ Աքար <Գ>արմեա[21] որդի ի նծովեցն Երիքովի՝ ոսկեզործ խալիշա մի, որ եղեալ էր ի ներքո կոցն, եւ արծաթէ թաս մի, եւ ոսկի լեզու մի կոցն բերանոյն էատ եւ տարաւ ետ ի կինն իւր ծածկաբար: Մեծ եւ անթողելի մեղք էր այն Աքարայ. մի՛[22] զի տասանորդ էր եւ Աստուծոյ բաժին ինչն Երիքովի Ժ. (10) ազգէն քանանացոց, զԱստուծոյ բաժինն զղացաւ. եւ Բ. (2)՝ զի անց եւ կոխեաց զհրաման Յեսուա եւ եմուտ ի ներքո նզովից նորա վասն ագահութեան: Եւ զհրաման նորա անարգելով զԱստուած անարգեաց:

53/ Եւ յետ կործանմանն Երիքովի եկին շրջապատեցին զփոքր քաղաքն զԳային: Եկին քաղաքացիքն եւ սպանին Լ. (30) այր ի / fol. 322r / ժողովրդենէն, եւ այլքն փախեան եւ եղեն յահէն որպէս զմում, որ հալի ի հրոյ: Եւ իբրեւ լուաւ Յեսու, պատառեաց զհանդերձս իւր, եւ ԺԲ. (12) իշխանքն ընդ նմա, եւ անկան ի վերայ երեսաց իւրեանց մինչեւ յերեկոյ: Եւ ասէ Յեսու ցՏէր. «Անցուցեր զմեզ ընդ Յորդանան մատնել ի ձեռս ամուրհացոց: Եւ դու զի՞նչ արասցես զմեծ անուն քո: Չի երդուար առնել զմեզ քեզ ժողովուրդ սեփհական»: Բայց ոչ կամեցաւ Աստուած լսել Յեսուա եւ ծերակոյտ ժողովրդեանն, զի թերեւս երկիցէ Աքար եւ խոստովանեսցի զմեղս իւր եւ անցուսցէ զբարկութիւնն յանձանէ եւ լրնտանեաց եւ ի ժողովրդենէ իւրմէ:

54/ Եւ Յեսու աղերս էր եւ աղաղակէր առ Աստուած եւ ոչ գիտեր խիղճ զանձնէ իւրմէ. եւ ասէ. «Այժմ լուիցեն քանանացիքն, թէ տկարացաք մեք: Գան միաբան եւ ջնջեն զմեզ: Եւ դու զի՞նչ արասցես զամենազօր անուն քո, որ յամենայն տեղիս յաղթող ցուցաւ ի յեզիպտոս եւ յամուրհացիս»: Եւ ապա վաղիւն ասէ Տէր ցՅեսու, զի «Անկեալ կեաս ի վերայ երեսաց քոց զօժիս, անօրինեցաւ[23] ժողովուրդն եւ անցին զնզովիւքն քո եւ զղացան / fol. 322v / յրնչից Երիքովի: Արդ մի կարասցեն կալ ի պատերազմի եւ յաղթել թշնամեաց, եթէ ոչ

---

20. Above line p.m.
21. Emended from Զարմեա, which is clearly a graphic corruption. His father is named Carmi in Josh 7:1.
22. Above line p.m.
23. ան above line p.m.

7. BRIEF HISTORY OF JOSHUA SON OF NUN 73

բառնայք գշարն ի միջոյ ձերմէ»։ Եւ իբրեւ լուաւ զայս Յեսու եւ գիտաց զպատճառս բարկութեանն Աստուծոյ, ասաց ժողովուրդեանն. «Առ որում որ գտցի գողութիւն, ազգաւ եւ ազխիւք ընծքեցցի»։

55/ Զայս ասաց, զի երկիցէ Աքար եւ խոստաւանեցցի զմեղս իւր եւ ապաշխարեցէ։ Եւ ապա հրամանաւ Աստուծոյ արկ վիճակ ի վերայ ԲԺ.ան (12) ազգին Յուդա եւ զազգն Յուդա դարձեալ բաժանեաց ԲԺ.ան (12) մասուն եւ արկ մարզարէական հոգով վիճակ. եւ անկաւ վիճակն ի վերայ տանն Աքարու։ Եւ ասէ Յեսու ցԱքար. «Տուր փառս Աստուծոյ եւ խոստավանեա ճշմարիտ»։ Եւ նա ոչ կամեցաւ, եւ ապա հրամայեաց Յեսու բարկոծել զԱքար տամբ իւրով։ Եւ յորժամ տարան զԱքար ի բարկոծումն, ապա յակամա խոստավանեցաւ եւ ոչ գտաւ թողութիւն։ Եւ գնացեալ ի տունն նորա, գտան զգողութիւնն զխալիշան ի ներքո կնճ նորա եւ զոսկի լեզուն եւ զարծաթի թասն թաղեալ ի ներքոյ գըցի վրանին։ Եւ բերին / fol. 323r / առ Յեսու, եւ ամենեքեան թքին գերեսն Աքարու եւ, տարեալ զինքն[24] եւ զնտանիքն եւ զամենայն ստացուածս եւ զանասունս, լցին ի ձոր մի եւ քարկոծեցին։ Եւ արարին այնպէս եւ կուտեցին մեծ հողաբլուր ի վերայ նորա։ Եւ ապա էանց բարկութիւն <Աստուծոյ>։

56/ Եւ զնտանիքն վասն էր քարկոծեցին։ Զի գիտակ էին նորա մեղացն եւ ոչ խոստավանեցան, վասն այն ընդ Աքարա պատժեցան։ Եւ զանասունս եւ զստացուածսն վասն այն պատճառի, զի գիտասցէ ժողովուրդն, թէ չէր աղքատ եւ ոչ վասն աղքատութեան գողացաւ, <այլ վասն ագահութեան>։ Վասն այն կուտեցին հողաբլուր, թէ ամենայն իրացվդ չի կիշտացար գնա հողովդ կշտացիր։ Վասն այն ասեն, թէ ագահ մարդն Ա. (1) աք հողով կշտանա, եւ աչքն լցվի։ Եւ այսպէս, սպաննելով զգողն, <անցուցին զբարկութիւն եւ զԱստուած հաշտեցուցին եւ> ապա ելին ի վերայ Գայեա։

57/ Եւ հրամայեաց Յեսու դարանամուտ լինել իմաստուն զօրացն եւ ինքն եկեալ եցոյց զինքն քաղաքին, եւ քաղաքացիքն մտին զհետ նոցա։ Եւ իբրեւ հեռացուցին զբնակիչս քաղաքին, եւ ելին դարանամուտքն եւ հրով վառեցին զքաղաքն։ Եւ իբրեւ յետս / fol. 323v / նայեցան եւ տեսին, զի ելաներ ծուխն քաղաքին յերկրէ յերկինս, եւ թուլացան եւ յերկիր կործանեցան։ Եւ յԲ. (2) կողմանց ի մէջ առեալ եւ կոտորեցին զնոսա։

58/ Եւ ձգեաց Յեսու <զգայիսունն> ի վերայ Գայեա, եւ կապեցաւ <գայիսունն> յօդա։ Եւ ոչ իշոյց Յեսու զձեռն իւր, այլ կացբացկատարած յաղօթս, որպէս Մովսէս ընդդէմ Ամաղէկա, մինչեւ բնաջինճ արարին

---

24. The text in M6092 starts here.

զքաղաքն եւ կուտեցին եւ արարին հողաբլուր։ Եւ ապա իջոյց զձեռն յաղօթից։ Եւ իջաւ <գայիսոնն> ի վերայ ձեռացն Յեսուա։ Եւ շինեաց Յեսու սեղան Աստուծոյ եւ մատոյց զաղօթս իւր առաջի Աստուծոյ սեղանոյն։ Եւ հրամայեաց կարգել զօրէսս ի լուր ժողովրդեանն²⁵ եւ զօրհնութիւնս եւ զանէծս, զի երկիցեն յանիծիցն եւ մի լիցին որպէս զԱքար անցող պատուիրանացն Աստուծոյ, որ գողացաւ ի նզովիցն եւ մնաց անեղծ։ Եւ յետոյ անդէպ ժամանակի «մեղա» ասաց եւ ոչ զտաւ²⁶ թողութիւն, զի անցեալ էր <ապաշխարութեան> ժամանակն։ Եւ զի ոչ կամաւ զղջացաւ, վասն այն ոչ եզիտ թողութիւն Աքար զարմեան։ Եւ / fol. 324r / Սալուր Կիսեան եւ Յուդա Սիմոնեան «մեղա» ասելով ոչ արդարացան վասն ասացեալ պատճառացդ։ Ժամ եղին, ասա արարին միմեանց քանանացիքն գալ միաբան պատերազմիլ ընդ Յեսու<այ> եւ ժողովրդեանն։

59/ Իսկ զաբաւոնացիքն ոչ միաբանեցան ընդ նոսա, վասն զի զարհուրեցան ի դիպուածոց Երիքովի եւ Գայեա։ Չի լուան նորա զասելն Մովսէսի, որ ասաց. «Մի դիցես ուխտ ընդ քանանացիսն. այլ անխնա կոտորեսջիք զնոսա բայց որք հեռաւորք իցեն եւ հնազանդեցին եւ հարկատու լիցին ձեզ, խնայեսջիք ի նոսա։ Իսկ որք մօտաւորք իցեն, անխնա կոռոտեսջիք, զի մի բնակելով ընդ անհաւատս մոլորեցուցեն զձեզ ի կռապաշտութիւն, որպէս ասէ մարգարէն. «Խառնակեցան ընդ հեթանոսս եւ ուսան զգործս նոցա»։ Չայս պատուէրս Մովսէսի լուան զաբաւոնացիք եւ հնարս իմացան եւ զգեցան հին ոտնաման եւ պաշար հնացեալ ճճակեր եւ եկին առ Յեսուա եւ ասեն, թէ. «Լուաք զլուր զօրութեանն Աստուծոյ ձերոյ եւ եկաք ի հեռաստանէ ի հնազանդութիւն ձեզ, զի դիցես ընդ մեզ / fol. 324v / ուխտ եւ ապրեցուսցես զմեզ։ Եւ մեք հաւատամք յԱստուածն ձեր եւ ձեզ ծառայ լինիմք հարկատու, զի հեռի տեղաց եկեալ եմք։ Եւ վկայ է պաշարս եւ ի տան նոր եփեցաք, եւ երկայնութեամբ ճանապարհին հնացաւ եւ ցեցակեր եղեւ, եւ ոտնաման նոր զգեցաք, եւ այժմ մաշեցեալ է»։

60/ Եւ հաւատացին բանից խաբէութեան նոցա եւ երդուան եւ ուխտ եղին, զի ապրեցուսցեն զնոսա, եւ լինիցին ծառայք խորանին փայտակիր եւ ջրակիր քահանայիցն։ Իբրեւ լուան թագաւորք քանանացոց, բարկացան ի վերայ զաբաւոնացոցն եւ ելին միաբան ի վերայ Գաբաւոնի կոտորել եւ ջնջել զնոսա։

---

25. The following text commences in M6902 with the last three words on fol 344v.
26. Postclassical form.

7. BRIEF HISTORY OF JOSHUA SON OF NUN

61/ Ազդ արարին զաքաւոնացիքն Յեսուա, զի հասցէ ի թիկունս յօգնականութիւն նոցա։ Եկն Յեսու ընդ լուսանալ առաւօտուն. եւ սկսան կոտորել։ Եւ զի անթիւ էր ազգն քանանացոցն եւ ոչ կոտորելով սպառել զնոսա, զի ազգն քանանացոցն բոլոր անդ էին ժողովել եւ ի ժամ ահագին պատերազմին։ Էարկ Աստուած ի վերուստ կարկուտ քարեա, եւ բազում էին սպանեալքն ի քարէ կարկտին, զոր Էարկ Տէր / fol. 325r / Աստուած ի վերայ քանանացոցն, քան զսպանեալքն իսրայէլացոցն։ Եւ իբրեւ ետես Յեսու, թէ մտանէ յարեզական, եւ ոչ կարեն առ հասարակ կոտորել զնոսա, եւ մնան թշնամիքն կենդանի, եւ լինին հակարակք ժողովրդեանն, եւ յայլում աւուր աշխատ առնեն զնոսա պատերազմաւ։

62/ Զայն ետ եւ խօսեցաւ Յեսու առաջի Տեառն եւ առաջի գնդին իսրայէլացոցն եւ ասէ. «Կացցէ արեզական ի Գաբաուոն, եւ լու<ս>ինն ի վերայ ձորոյն Իլիոնի»։ Եւ նոյնժամայն կապեցան եւ կանգնեցան աւուր միոյ չափ ԲԺ.ան (12) ժամ, զի զարնանային էր ժամանակն, եւ տիւն եւ գիշերն <հաւասար> էր։ Արգել զարեզական եւ զլուսինն, զի թշնամիքն չնչեցին եւ սպանողքն տեսցեն զտկարութիւնն պաշտելեաց նոցա եւ մի մոլորեսցին ընդ նոսա կռապաշտութեամբ, որք զլուսաւորս պաշտէին։ Արդ զդիս հեթանոսաց եւ զհեթանոսս առ հասարակ յաղթեաց Յեսու, զի միայն բանիւ եւ հրամանաւ հնազանդեցոյց զդիս։ Օրինակ եւ խորհուրդ էր Քրիստոսի, որ հանդերձեալ էր յաղթել զամենայն զդիս եւ զդիականս հեթանոսաց զօրութեամբ եւ ինքրիրդով խաչին իւրոյ։ «Կացցէ», ասէ, «արեզական ի Գաբաուոն եւ լուսին ի դաշտն / fol. 325v / Եյլիոնի»։

63/ Արդ նոքա կանգնեցան ըստ բանին Յեսուա եւ ոչ եթէ երկինքն շրջէին. <զի եթէ երկինքն շրջէին>, ոչ հրամայէր նա կեալ եւ գտեղին առնուլ լուաւորացն, զի սաստիկ շրջածն երկնից արզել նա։ Եւ վկայ է այնմ, որ բանիւ գերկիսա եւ լուսաւորս արար։ Որպէս Արարիչն բանիւ արար, նոյնպէս եւ սա բանիւ եւ հրամանաւ Արարչին արզել զնոսա։

Չի ԲԺ.ն (12) կենդանակերպքն կան յերկինս, եւ կենդանակերպք ի կենդանակերպք Լ. (30) աւուր ճանապարհի է արեգական։ Չի կենդանակերպքն բարձր են ի հաստատութեան յերկինքն, եւ արեգական է. (7) գօտեացն մէջն միջին գօտովն դեմ կենդանակերպիցն անցանէ։ Լ. (30) աւուրք ճանապարհին կենդանակերպք ի կենդանակերպ, եւ ՅԿ. (360) օր վճարէ զերկոտասան կենդանակերպսա։ Եւ Ե. (5) օրն արարչութեան աւուրքն ի Ե. (5) աստեղքն մնան որ են այտքիկ լոյծ, եղջիւրի, կծաւրի, փառանձնոտի, արտախոյր։ Չի թէ արեգական կանգնեալ էր եւ երկինքն շրջեալ, յայլ տեղի աժեր զկենդանակերպքն, եւ խանգարումն եւ խախտումն լինէր արեգական ճանապարհին եւ աստուածադիր կարգին: / fol. 326r / Վասն այս պատճառի երկինքն այլ կանգնեցաւ ընդ արեգականն: Այսպէս վկայէ սուրբն Եփրեմ: Եւ մեծ փառք է, որ Ա. (1) հողածին մարդոյ հրամանաւ արեգակն կանգնի, եւ երկնից շրջագայութիւնն դադարի: Իսկ զԲ. (2) օրն, q<ո>ր[27] արար Յեսու Ա. (1) օր, օրինակ եւ խորհուրդ էր Քրիստոսի, որ զմի օրն Բ. (2) արար յաւուր խաչելութեան իւրոյ:

64/ Եւ այսպէս կոտորեաց զթշնամիսն եւ հարուանեաց զաշխարհս նոցա ի սմպակս երիվարացն, եւ ոչ ապրեցաւ քաղաք կամ գիւղ, այլ առ հասարակ մաշեցան ի սուր սուսերի: Յորժամ անցին զպատուիրանան Աստուծոյ, բնակիչքն փոքր քաղաքին Գայիա սպանին ի նոցանէ ԼԲ. (32) այր: Իսկ յորժամ պահեցին զպատուիրանս Աստուծոյ, այնպէս զօրացան նախախնամութեամբն եւ օգնականութեամբն Աստուծոյ, որ զէ. (7) ազգն քանանացոցն ջնջեցին եւ զԼԲ. (32) թագաւորս սպանին, եւ մի այր ի նոցանէ ոչ պակասեաց: Չի այսպէս յամենայն ժամանակի օրինապահացն պահապան եւ օգնական լինի Աստուած, եւ նովաւ զօրանան ի պատերազմի եւ յաղթեն հոգեւոր եւ մարմնաւոր թշնամեաց: Թագաւորք եւ իշխանք ամենայն հաւատացեալք եւ որք հետեւական / fol. 326v / յօրինաց եւ ոչ պահեն զպատուիրանս Աստուծոյ, թողու զնոսա Աստուած ի ձեռաց եւ վասն մեղաց իւրեանց տկարանան եւ կորեան լինին եւ մատնին ի ձեռս երեւելի եւ աներեւոյթ թշնամեաց: Եւ ջնջին եւ կորձանին թագաւորութիւնն ազգին այնմիկ:

65/ Յետ այնորիկ կոտորեաց զհսկայազունս եւ զղենայինս ի Քեփրոնի եւ ի լեռնէ Յուդա եւ Իսրայէլի: Եւ ոչ ոք մնաց անդր ազգէն քանանացոց: Եւ ապա լարաբաժին արարին զերկիրն ի վերայ ԲԺ.ն (12) ազգին, եւ ոչ ետ բաժին յազգին Ղեւեա, այլ ԽԸ. (48) քաղաք ապաստանի ընտրեաց յերկոտասան ազգէն եւ ետ քահանայից: <Եւ զազգն քահանայից> իբրեւ զաղ գրուեցաւ ի մէջ ԲԺ.ն (12) ազգին, զի ի մէջ նոցա բնակեցեն, յաստուածային օրինօքն խրատեցեն զնոսա եւ որպէս <զաղ, անհամութիւն> նոցա համբերիցեն: Եւ այս է քաղաքն ապաստանի, զի յակամա սպանօղքն անկանէին ի նոսա եւ անդ մնային մինչեւ մեռանել մեծ քահանայապետին: Եւ յորժամ մեռաներ քահանայապետն, եւ ապա <ազատ էր> յակամա սպանօղն. ուր կամէր երթայր:

66/ Օրինակ մեծ պահոցն քառասնորդացն, որ յակամա / fol. 327r / մեղաւորքն եւ սպանօղքն հոգոց իւրեանց անկանին ի պա<հ>քն մեծ եւ ապաշխարեն, մինչեւ ի մեռանել մեծ քահանայապետին Քրիստոսի

---

27. Apparently զոր became զոր by contamination.

7. BRIEF HISTORY OF JOSHUA SON OF NUN

ի վերայ խաչին յաւագ ուրբաթ օրն։ Եւ ապա ազատին ի պարտուց մեղաց եւ ի սպանմանէ հոգոց[28] իւրեանց։

Եւ մերձեցան աւուրք Յեսուա մեռնելոյ. ժողովեցան ԲԺ.ն (12) ազգն, եւ պատուիրեաց նոցա եւ ասէ. «Զգուշ կացէք եւ մի առնէք խնամութիւն ընդ մնացորդս քանանացոց»։ ‹Եւ աւէ ցնոսա. «Զճշմարիտն ասէք ինձ. ահաւաիկ ես մեռանիմ, եւ դուք զո՞ր Աստուած պաշտէք. զԱստուածն, զոր հարքն ձեր պաշտեցին յայնկոյս գետոյն յարածանց, եթէ զաստուածն քանանացւոց›, որ ոչ կարացին փրկել զպաշտօնեայս իւրեանց, այլ ես եւ տուն հօր իմո զՏէր կենդանին պաշտեմք»։ Ուխտս եդին եւ դաշինս կռեցին եւ ասեն. «զՏէր կենդանին պաշտեմք եւ զպատուիրանս նորա պահեմք»։

67/ Եւ ասէ Յեսու, թէ՛ «Դժուարին է աստուածպաշտութիւնն, զի ձեզնէ սրբութիւն, արդարութիւն, առաքինութիւն խնդրէ։ Եւ ես գիտեմ, զի յետ մահուան իմոյ երթայք զհետ աստուածոց օտարաց»։ Եւ ասեն. «Ոչ այդպէս, այլ զՏէր պաշտեցուք եւ ճայնի նորա լուիցուք։ Որպէս յանապատին ուխտեցին հայրքն[29] առաջի Մովսէսի պահել զպատու/fol. 327v/իրանս նորա, նոյնպէս եւ աստ երկրորդին զուխտ»։ Առ ի հանգուցանել զկեանս Յեսու եւ կացոյց Յեսու մինչնորդ զուխտ կտակարանացն եւ կանգնեաց արձան մեծ եւ գրեաց զուխտս նոցա. եւ ասէ. «Ահա վէմ եդիցի վկա, զի դուք ուխտ եդիք ինքնին պաշտել զՏէր»։ Եւ նորա ասեն. «Այսպէս եդիցի»։

68/ Եւ վախճանեցաւ Յեսու ՃԾ. (150) ամաց, եւ թաղեցին զնա ի բաժնի[30] ժառանգութեան իւրոյ եւ եդին ընդ նմա զսուրն գայլախազեա, որով թլպատեաց զորդիսն Իսրայէլի։

Եւ Քրիստոսի մարդասիրին փառք յաւիտեանս յաւիտենից, ամէն։

Critical Apparatus

These collations cover §§1–33 and 55–67. From the beginning and as far as the word Արդ in §34 the text is drawn from M4618. There the witness of M4618 breaks off, and thence the text is drawn from M2168. For §§55 to the end a second witness, M6092 also exists and its variants are recorded below.

For §§1–33 the lemma is M4618 and the variant is M2168.

Title/ Պատմութիւն Յեսուա որդոյ Նաւեա համառօտ
1/ ազգէն | Յովսեփա | եւ ոչ — խորանին] om : hmt

---

28. Vertical line precedes.
29. Strange form.
30. M6092 fol 350r ends here.

2/ կուսան] կոյս | յերազով | ասէ] ասաց | պահեցից զքեզ անփորձ

3/ քաղասունքն | պատգամն | արտարոյ | ԽՁ] զի | անհաց եւ անջուր | մաշիկն] մաշային | ելցէ] + մարգարէ | դիցէ] դիպէ

4/ ամադէկա | պատերազմաց | ջնջեաց | գերկիրն | նոցա] om

5/ առաջի | յովսէ | եւ նա] զի նա | ի 1°] եւ ի | թշնամեաց] ժողովուրդ | սորա | նորա | Քրիստոսի] Յիսուսի | անուն

6/ պարզեւացն | սայ | յերկոտասանիցն | Ժ.ունքն | իսկ Յեսու] եւ Յեսու | զԾՌ.էն] զԾՌ.էին

7/ վաղձան

8/ ձեռնադրեաց | ի գլխոյ] ի վերայ գլխոյ

9/ hոգի] + է | է] om | երկուցունցն | եւ իշխան] om | մեջ յաշխարհի] աշխարհիս + ի խաղաղութիւն ի սէր : dtg | առաջնորդքն | զմարդիկք | ի1°] om | աստուածապաշտութիւն | կարգաւորէն] առաջնորդեցեն | ի խաղաղութիւն / ի սէր] ~ | միաբանութիւն եւ

10/ եւ 1°] om | քահանայն | միաբամութիւն | դիտաւորութիւն | զի] միթէ] om | պիտին պարտին | մարդիք

11/ վաղձանելոյն | Մովսէսի 1° — Մովսէսի 2°] om : hmt | Յեսուա | եւ ի ժամանակի] զի ի ժամանակին | հաասարեաց] հաւարեաց | Մովսէսի] + ասաց նմա | աշակերտ] + ընդ | Մովսէսի 5°] om

12/ ոտքն | ձիշտ—ձեր] om | էի] է | եւ 3°] om | խոստացա

13/ զիւրեանք | համարին

14/ ցայնժամն | եւ 2°] om | կեալ] կալ | զաքանչելիսն

15/ կաթայ | ձեղին | Մանասէին | Յորդանանու] գետոյն | բեկցեն] M2168 բերկցեն M4618 | այնորիկ | յառաջապահ

16/ այնորիկ | տուն] տունս

17/ զժողովուրդն առաքեցան | պորնկին | աստուած | մտանելոց | առ2°] om

18/ ինքն բոզ է] ես բոզ եմ | զնա] զնոսա | եւ 4°] above line p.m. M2168 | ապա] + Ռախաբ | զնա] զնոսա | քանանացից | որդոց | Խ. ամէ] om | այսր | այլ] այս | յօրէ] + մինչեւ | բաժանեցաւ | ամուրհացոց | կենդանոյ

19/ նայ | հրախառն] om | եկիպտացոցն | ապրեցուցանէք | իմ

20/ երախտեաց | արար | գերկիրն | քանանացող | զփոխարէն | երախտեաց | միայն] + զի | կարմիր2°] om | նշան

21/ զնոսա] զնա : corrupt | պատձառ | մեղաց1° — մեղաց2°] om : dtg

22/ որ1°] օրն | եկեղեցոյ] եկեղեցոյ | Քրիստոսի] Յիսուսի | Ադամա | ի ժամանակի | այնմ ժամանակի | յորժամ] որ | արարածք] + նա | դոդա | ոյ] ի | եկարէր

7. BRIEF HISTORY OF JOSHUA SON OF NUN

23/ ն՛ | աստուածապաշտութենէ | տեսութեան | Յեսուա

24/ եւ 1°] om | քանանացոց | ժողովուրդնն : ն above line p.m. | յեզրն | յորդանանու | զխորհուրդ | մեծութեանն] աստուածութեանն | գետոյն] om | լուիցէ | աչ խաղաղութեան] զխաղաղութիւնն | Յեսուա | հաւատացեալս] + իւրեանց with erasure mark | մատչել | զօրութեան | յաւել] + եւ | Յեսուա | որդլոյ] om | յառաջի

25/ տիւնն | տապանակն] տապանն | հեռու կենալ] հեռանալ | յաշխարհականաց] om

26/ յաջս | տեսլեանն | տարածելոց] + էր | երկրորդղութեան

27/ կատարման | ծնընդդեան | ձեռքն | ձեռս

28/ բաժանել | բաժանիլ — բաժանել] om : hkt | ծովուն] գետոյդ

29/ Սողոմա | եւ 3°] + ոչ | կուտեցաւ | երկնչիցեն | եղին] եդ | <եւ — տապանականն>] M2168 om M4618 : hmt | զճանապարհն

30/ եւ 2°] om | սրբոյ] սուրբ | եւ3°] om | քրիստոսի] Յիսուսի | անհաւատիցն | եկին] ելին | ուրկանաւ | յանհաւատութիւնն | ցանկութեան

31/ վայելեցեն | փշրեսնաց | սեղանյն

32 / հրէիցն | անհաւատից | կապարեա

33/ քանանցն | քահանայիցն] + աւր | պատերազմել | Յիսուս | մաշեցեն | Յեսուա | պատերազմել1° | պատերազմել2° | Յեսուա

Collations of M6092

From §55 on, the text is M2168 and the variant is M6092, unless otherwise stated.

55/[31] զրնստանիքն | ըստագցուածս | ձոր] փոր | <Աստուծոյ>] M6092 om M2168

56/ զրնստանիքն | եր | Աքարայ | եւ3°] om | զանասուն | զրստացուածքն | գիտասցի | <այլ վասն ագահութեան>] M6092 om M2168 | չի կիշտացիր] չկշտացիր | զնայ | ափ | կշտանայ | լցուի | ըսպանանելով | <անցուցի — հաշտեցուցին եւ>] M6092 om M2168 | Գայեա

57/ հրամաեաց | դարմանամնուտ | եւ5°] om | յետոս] յէտոես | նաեցան | եւ7°] om | ելաներ | ծուխն] ծուխ ի | յերկրէ] om | եւ յերկիր] երկիր | | եւ8°] om | յԲ] Բ | եւ կոտորեցին] կոտորին

58/ <զզայիսունն>] 6092 զզայիսունն 2168 | Գայեաց | կապեցաւ] կապ եղաւ | <զզայիսունն>] 6092 զզայիսունն 2168 | Գայիս | իշուց

---

31. M6092 fol 350v, top.

| Ամադեկայ | բնաջինչ | ապայ | <զայիսունն>] 6092 զայիսոն 2168 | Յեսուա | Աստուծոյ2°] om | հրամաեաց | կարքել | յանիծիցս] յանեծ | լիցին] լցին | անցող] ձանցող | <ապաշխարութիւն>] ed ապաշխարութեան M6092 om M2168 | էզիտ | զարմեան] զամենայն : corrupt | Յուդա Սիմոնեան] յուշայի սիմանրեան : corrupt | մեղայ | ոչ զարդարացան] դաթարեցան : corrupt | պատճառեաց | աստ] այզդ | պատերազմել | Յեսու<այ>] ed Յեսու M2168 Յեսոայ M6092 | ժողովրրդեանն

59/ զազաունացիքն | դիպուածցըն | Գայեաց | քանանացիս | հեռոսր լիցին] լիցից : corrupt | մոտաուրք | մարզարէն] + թէ | զաքաուննացիքն | զզեցան] + եւ | հնացեալ ճճակեր եւ | ճակեր | զզօրութեանն] զօրհնութեանն | եկայք | զօրութեանն] զօրհնութեանն | Յեսու | Աստուածն | հեռի] ի հեռուստ | ենք : postclassical form | ապրեցուցեա | Աստուածն | զվկայ | եւ ի տանն] զի ի տան | յերկարութեամբ | ճանապարհիս | եղաւ : postclassical form

60/ հաւատացին] նոքա հաւատից | բանից | խաբէութեանց | եւ2°] om | քանանացոց | կորուսել

61/ յոջնականութեան | ընդ] ի | առաուտուն | կոտորել] + զնոսա : perhaps preferable | եւ զի1°] զի | քանանացոցն | ոչ] + կարէին | քանանացոցն2°] քանանացոց | էարկ] արկ | սպանեալքն] սպարեալ | կարկուտէն | արեզակն : perhaps preferable | առ] om | զդիս] դիս | կոտրել | հակառակ32 | այլում | աուր] եւ այլ ամենայն օր

62/ ձայն ետ] ձաներ | առաջի2°] առաջին | զնդին | իսրայելացոց | կանկեցան | միոյ չափի | միաչափի | ԲԺ.ան] Բ տիսան | տիին] եւ տիին | <հաւասար>] M6092 հասարակ M2168 | զարեզակն | սպանեալքն | զտկարութիւնն | կրայպաշտութեամբ | զլուսաուրսն | հեթանոս | զդիս1°] զի դիս նոցա | զդհայկունս | խորհրդով] խորի | լուսինն

63/ նոքայ | կանկեցան] կարքեց | Յեսուայ | <զի եթէ երկինքն շրշէին>] M6092 om M2168 : hmt | զտեղի | նա2°] նայ | ոզերկինս | լուսաուրս | լուսօր | սայ | կենդանակերպքն1°] կենդանակերպաս | կենդանակերպքն2°] կենդանակերպն | երկինքն | զատեաց | մեջն միջին] մեջին ի միջեն | զոտովն | աուր | 34] ի 34 | ալրն | կենդանակերպակ | կերպ | եւ է (5)] եւ է (7)33 | օրն | աուրն | արարչութեան] + արարչութիւն | է (5)] է (7) | մնայ | լուծ | ձկաուրի | փարազնոտի | կանկնեալ] եալ : corrupt | այլ | եւ խախտումն] om | աստուածայդիր | այս] այիս | արեզական | մարդոյ] արեզական |

---

32. Stone and Hillel, "Index of Variants," no. 333.
33. See Stone and Hillel, "Index of Variants," no. 222. Another instance occurs further on in the verse.

7. BRIEF HISTORY OF JOSHUA SON OF NUN

կանկնի | շրջայկայութիւն | q<ո>բ] M6092 զոր M2168 | արար] ար | յալուր] ալր

64/ այսպէս] + ի սպառ | սմպակս] ամբազս | զպատուիրանցն | Աստուծոյ 1° — Աստուծոյ 3°] om : hmt | ջնջեցին ի] շրջեցին | թազաւորսն | ըսպանին | յամենայն] ամենայնի | ժամանակի | նմանակից : corrupt | պահպյպան | յաղթեն հոզեւոր եւ] om | իշխանք] + եւ | հաւատացեալ | թազաւորութիւն

65/ այտրիկ | կձակոտորեաց : dtg | զհսկազունայ | լեռնայսինս | Քեբրոնէ | լեռնեն | Յուդայ | յազզեն | Դեւեայ | ազզեն] ազզին | ի մէջ ԲԺ] յԲԺ | զի] եւ | քահանայիցն <եւ զազզն քահանայից>] M6092 om M4618 : hmt | եւ յաստուածային] զաստուածային | <զաղ անհամութիւն>] M6092 զանհամութիւն M2168 | ի համբերեցեն | ակամայ | սպանողքն | մինչեւ] + ի | եւ ապա] ապա | <ազատ էր>] M6092 om M2168 | ակամա | սպանաւղն | յուր

66/ յարինակ | ակամայ | մեղաւորքն եւ] մեղաւք | պա<հ>քն] M6092 պաքն M4618 | եւ 2°] om | Յեսուա | ժողովեաց | զԺԲ | ազզին | <եւ ասէ — քանանացոց 2°>] M6092 om M4816 : anablepsis | պաշտոնեայս | այլ եւս եւոյն] այլ ես եւ տուն | իմոյ | ուխտ

67/ աստուածպաշտութիւն | ի ձեզանէ | արդարութիւն] + եւ | ես] ասէ | յետ] հետ | իմոյ | + եւ | լուիցէուք | որպէս — առաջի] աջին | զպատուիրանան | երկրորդին] երրորդին | զուխտն] զխունկն | զկեանսն | Յեսուլ°] Յեսուեայ | զուխտն | կանկնեաց | ապայ | վէմս այս | վկայ | ուխտ եղիք ինքնին] ի ներքին ուխտիք | նորայ | եղիցի այսպէս

68/ ՃԾ. (150)] Ճ եւ Ժ. (110) | զնա] զնոսայ[34] | բաժին

On fol. 353r, three lines from §68 continue directly from the text on fol. 350r and conclude the document in M6092 with the same doxology as in M4618. There happen to be no variants in this piece of text.

Translation

Title/ Short Story of Joshua son of Nun

1/ Joshua son of Nun was of the tribe of Ephraim, son of Joseph.[35] And he was Moses's disciple.[36] And like a servant he guarded the door of the Tent of Witness for forty years in the desert, and he did not separate himself from

---

34. Stone and Hillel, "Index of Variants," no. 393.
35. Num 13:8 on the tribal affiliation of Joshua, who was previously called Hoshea, concerning which, see Num 13:16 where Moses changes his name to Joshua.
36. Josh 1:1.

the door of the tent,[37] but through fasts and prayers he worshipped God with untiring ascesis.[38]

2/ And he was a holy virgin and immaculate, like the bodiless angels.[39] And on one occasion being tested by a dream he wished to kill himself. And an angel of the Lord seized his hand and said, "Do no evil or damage to yourself. Henceforth, I will keep you not tested. But, you should know that you are a bodily human and not a bodiless one. For that reason, you encountered that."[40]

3/ And when Moses observed the first forty-day fast,[41] and received the divinely written commandments,[42] he (Joshua) was forty-six days[43] outside the cloud, without food, water, and sleep. He[44] stood on his feet holding Moses's shoes in his hand,[45] so that when he (Moses) came forth, he might

---

37. Exod 33:11; there Joshua is said to have not left the tent, but there is no mention of guarding of the door.

38. This statement is permeated with Christian monastic ideals. Compare the Rabbinic characterization of Joshua as continually busied with Torah study, for instance Mishnah Aboth 1:1 which says, "Moses received the Torah and transmitted it to Joshua." On this Rashi remarks, "And why did he transmit it to Joshua and not to Eleazar and Phinhas, and not to the seventy elders who were prophesying in the camp?" (see Num 11:25). He responds to his own question, "Since he did not wish to transmit it except to one who, from his youth, totally devoted himself (lit: killed himself) in the tents of wisdom and thus got a good name in the world. That is Joshua, for it says of him: Joshua the son of Nun, a young man, did not depart from the tent." This is a striking illustration of differences in perspective of the Jewish and Christian sources.

39. A common theme of Armenian Christian thought. On the concept of the "angelic life" see K. Suso Frank, *ΑΓΓΕΛΙΚΟΣ ΒΙΟΣ: Begriffsanalytische und begriffsgeschichtliche Untersuchung zum "Engelgeleichen Leben" im frühen Mönchtum*, BGAMB (Münster: Aschendorf, 1964) *non vidi*; James E. Goehring, *Ascetics, Society, and the Desert: Studies in Early Egyptian Monasticism*, SAC (Harrisburg, PA: Trinity Press International, 1999).

40. I.e., trial. This tradition of Joshua's wet dream has no biblical basis.

41. Referring to Exod 24:18. "The forty days' fast" is also an Armenian name for Lent. The implication is clear here.

42. Rabbinic traditions speak of God's words being recorded in "fire black on white fire" (y. *Shelamim* 6:1, 49d). *4 Ezra* 14 explains how Ezra, being inspired, wrote Scriptures with the assistance of five scribes; see *4 Ezra* 14:37–42. Ezra's role in chap. 14 is to be a new Moses.

43. Three days' preparation for the revelation of Sinai are mentioned in Exod 19:11. However, this does not explain the number forty-six. In Exod 24:16 it is said that a divine cloud covered the mountain for six days and on the seventh day Moses went up into the cloud. This is most likely the explanation for the "extra" six days.

44. The context seems to point at Joshua as the only one who followed Moses onto Mount Sinai: Exod 24:13.

45. Presumably inferred from Exod 3:5.

7. BRIEF HISTORY OF JOSHUA SON OF NUN

place (them) before him. His (Joshua's) abstinence was much more wondrous than Moses's. For he (Moses), by speaking with God, was comforted by God, and he (Joshua) had no part of that comfort, that[46] he was abstinent for <forty-six>[47] days.

4/ And he was a commander of Israel, brave and valorous in battle, and victorious over enemies by Moses's prayer.[48] First of all, he overcame Amalek,[49] and then in the other battles, until he annihilated the people of the Canaanites, and he divided their land to the children of Israel.[50]

5/ His former name was Hosea and Moses changed (it) and called him Joshua for Joshua is translated "savior."[51] And he was to be the savior of the people from bodily enemies in the pattern of Christ. And that one letter of his name is missing[52] is because he was human and the savior Jesus was incarnated God and because his salvation was bodily and imperfect, and Christ's (was) a perfect and an eternal spiritual salvation.

6/ And when Moses sent twelve spies to the promised land he was one of the twelve.[53] And when they came to the desert,[54] ten of them cast the people into disbelief and despair,[55] but Joshua and Caleb encouraged[56] the people. On account of this, of the hundred thousand[57] who came forth from

---

46. Perhaps բան "than," translated here "that" is actually part of բանզի "because," and the զի has been lost.
47. Or: <forty>. The number is not found in the Armenian text, though it is obviously missing. We restored forty-six; see n. 44 on this text, above.
48. Exod 17:9–13.
49. Exod 17:13.
50. Josh 19:51.
51. The change of name is recorded in Num 13:16. Note the use of onomastic explanations as a exegetical technique in the Armenian apocryphal stories. The meaning proffered here is known in Armenian onomastic lists; see Franz Xavier Wutz, *Onomastica Sacra: Untersuchungen zum Liber Interpretationis Nominum Hebraeorum des Hl. Hieronymous*, TU 41.2 (Leipzig: Hinrichs, 1915), 921, 983; Michael E. Stone, *Signs of the Judgment, Onomastica Sacra and the Generations from Adam*, UPATS 3 (Chico, CA: Scholars Press, 1981), 144.
52. Perhaps the final "s" of "Jesus." The name Joshua adds a single letter at the beginning of Hosea in the Hebrew forms of these names.
53. See Num 13:3–16.
54. I.e., returned from their mission.
55. Num 14:1–4.
56. Literally: "made the people's heart firm." Num 14:7–9.
57. According to Exod 12:37 and Num 2:11, 600,000 left Egypt. Exodus 38:26 offers 600 and 3,550. The figure of 100,000 does not occur in the Book of Joshua nor does that book give any other figure. However, the same figure is given in §34 below.

Egypt, they alone entered the promised land,[58] on account of their faith. And the others were killed in the desert on account of their faithlessness.

7/ And when Moses's end came, Moses said to God, "May the Maker of souls and bodies see a leader for this people, and then {you}[59] might die, lest this people be left as sheep without a shepherd."[60]

8/ And God commanded Moses to appoint[61] Joshua as leader and prince of the people,[62] in his place, and Joshua and Eleazar the priest and the twelve princes[63] went forth to the mount Nebo with Moses.[64] And Moses consecrated Joshua and laid his hand on his head and blessed him.[65] And through his hand[66] he gave him the authority that he himself had received from God.

9/ And because this human is soul and body and God is the maker of souls and bodies, God supports them both equally with care. Therefore he appointed a spiritual and a bodily leader and prince in the land. For the spiritual leaders regulate men spiritually in faith and arrange the worship of God and the bodily leaders regulate this world through the body, for peace, for love, and for unity they strengthen rule and building.[67]

10/ For that reason Moses appointed Joshua as a bodily leader and Eleazar the priest, the son of Aaron, as spiritual (leader).[68] And he commanded that they lead[69] the people in harmony. And because the spiritual and bodily

---

58. Num 14:30, 26:65, 32:12.
59. The context demands a first-person verb.
60. Num 27:17 is quoted here: "... that the congregation of the LORD may not be as sheep which have no shepherd." The incident related is based on that passage.
61. Literally: "to appoint, to range."
62. Deut 3:28, 31:7, 34:9. The Bible says Joshua was appointed leader, but not prince, but in fact, իշխան has both meanings.
63. That is, the heads of the twelve tribes.
64. The incident of Moses's ascent of Mt. Nebo, prior to his death, is related in Deut 32:48–52. Joshua may be included here, because he is mentioned just before this in Deut 32:44. However, the presence of Eleazar the priest at the Mt. Nebo incident is not related in Deuteronomy, nor that of the twelve princes of the tribes.
65. The laying on of hands is mentioned in Deut 34:9, but no blessing is recorded.
66. His hand that was laid upon Joshua.
67. This passage makes a pattern of rule explicit. The author adds this to the biblical narrative, reflecting his own ideal polity, ruled by a king and a Catholicos or other religious leader.
68. See Num 32:28, 34:17, Deut 3:32, 20:28, 31:23, etc.
69. Literally: "do the leadership." The appointment of Eleazar together with Joshua is not mentioned in the Bible. In various places in the Book of Joshua, they are mentioned as acting together; see Josh 14:1, 17:4, 19:51, and 21:1. This is dominantly so when the division of the land is under discussion.

leaders have one purpose, for they must strive together to distance humans from sin, and establish (them) in righteousness and good, for that reason Moses commanded that with mutual counsel they carry out the(ir) rule.

11/ And after Moses's death, the Lord spoke with Joshua, Moses's officer.[70] Joshua was humble[71] and in time God made him as an equal to Moses, "As I was with Moses, thus I shall be with you."[72] But he did not make himself equal (to him), (but saw himself) only as a disciple of Moses or as Moses's officer, who was Moses's servant.[73]

12/ "Cross the Jordan," he (God) said, "you and your people, and all the land on which your feet tread, truly believe that it will be yours as an inheritance.[74] And, just as I was with Moses, thus I will be with you. Be strong and of good courage, for I am with you. I will not abandon you[75] and I will not neglect you in all the battles of the war[76] until you have the people inherit the land, as I promised to Abraham, their fathers.[77]

13/ "But only keep my commandments which my servant Moses commanded, as he firmly kept my commandments." Although God made him equal to Moses, yet he designated himself as Moses's servant. For the saints love this sort of humbleness, and do not wish to make themselves equal to others but they consider themselves lower and more unworthy and least worthy of all people.

14/ Joshua said to the people, "Each of you, prepare provisions for yourself," and whatever preparation was needful for them. For the manna was not withheld from them up to that point. But because they were going to cross the river, he gave them an order to prepare days in advance a provision of manna, so that they would have leisure to live and see the wonders which were going to take place in the river on the morrow.[78]

---

70. Or: servant, official. See Deut 31:23, Josh 1:1.
71. Literally: humility.
72. Quotation taken from Josh 3:7; compare 1:17.
73. Josh 11:15, 23.
74. Josh 1:3, 14:9; compare Deut 11:23.
75. Deut 31:6, 31:23, compare 1 Chr 32:7 for the phrasing here.
76. See Josh 10:25 for the enemies.
77. Deut 31:7. Our author adds "Abraham" but he has "fathers," in the plural. Were Isaac and Jacob also mentioned here originally? In Stone, *Abraham*, 15–16, in the analysis of the Abraham saga, I pointed out that promises made to Abraham of the gift of the land are omitted from all the texts. For the alternation of singular and plural, see nn. 78, 103, 134, 187, 221.
78. Joshua 5:11–12 speaks of the cessation of the manna. In Josh 1:11 we read that Joshua said, "Prepare your provisions; for within three days you are to pass over this

15/ And since Reuben[79] and Gad and half of the tribe of Manasseh remained on the other side of the Jordan[80]—so that they should not break the hearts of their brothers,[81] for this reason they chose forty thousand armed men from them to be a vanguard and a rearguard for the people.

16/ On account of this they left their homes and goods on the other side of the Jordan and followed the people until the land was allotted to the ten tribes and then they returned to their home.[82]

17/ And then he sent two wise and ingenious men to spy out Jericho.[83] Although they were sent[84] to encourage the people, yet (it was also) for the sake of Rahab the prostitute. For she was going to believe in the living[85] God. And they went and entered Rahab's house, for she was a harlot and prostitute and many went to her place. Thus, it would not be noticeable[86] that the men entered. And when the people of the city learned (this),[87] they came to Rahab and said, "Where are the men who entered into your place?"[88]

18/ And she realized in advance the city's intent,[89] and bringing the two men out onto the roof, concealed (them) with flax.[90] And she said, "No one came to me." And they were constraining (her) to point out the men, and she said that she was a prostitute "and many come in to me and leave."[91] Because of this statement they left her outside (the matter). And then Rahab called

---

Jordan, to go in to take possession of the land which the Lord your God gives you to possess." Our text apparently combines these two verses, assuming that the "provisions" of 1:11 are manna, the cessation of which is announced in Josh 5:11–12.

79. The meaning of հ (յ-) with the locative here is unclear.

80. Num 32:33–34 and Josh 4:12, 18:7.

81. I.e., lest their brothers become afraid.

82. The division of the land is described in Josh 18–21:45. The departure of Reuben, Gad and half of Manasseh is related in Josh 22:1–6.

83. Joshua 2:1, but the characterization of the two men is not biblical.

84. The verb has an active ending, but must be passive in meaning.

85. This attribute of God is used elsewhere in this text. In the Bible it occurs quite often; see, e.g., Deut 5:26, Josh 3:10, 1 Kgs 17:26, 36, 2 Kgs 19:16. See here §§33, 41, 67, and 68.

86. Literally: fall into attention.

87. Josh 2:2.

88. Josh 2:3.

89. Or plan; that is, to capture the spies.

90. Josh 2:6.

91. The incident is related in Josh 2. Rahab's statement there is somewhat different, see Josh 2:4.

him[92] and said, "We know that the Lord has given over[93] this land of the Canaanites into your hands, because we heard that the Lord split the waters of the Red Sea before the Children of Israel, forty years ago. And this land, henceforth is yours, and indeed because we repented, we have lived in it up to this day. But from the day that he split the sea through God's help and the two kings of the Amorites were cut down, our hearts were astounded (and) trembled, and the breath of life remained not in us."[94]

19/ "Now, your God, who himself is judge, who brought down hail mixed with fire on the Egyptians,[95] He will give this land to you, and I believe in your God. Now, come swear to me that you will not forget my service (to you) but, just as I saved you today, you (will) save me and my father's house and all my relatives in your midst, through that red sign which I tie on."[96]

20/ They said to her, "Today you will not be recompensed[97] for the kindness of your service, which you did secretly for us, but when the Lord God gives this land of the Canaanites into our hands, then we shall openly repay you the recompense of your service, in the light of day.[98] But only tie a red sign on your window, and they will be careful. If anyone comes out of the house on which the red sign is tied, his blood will be on his (own) head."[99]

21/ And then she lowered them by a rope below the city wall. They came and told the people and strengthened their hearts and said, "The Canaanites are afraid of us and are shivering before us."[100] And Rahab is a type[101] of the church and just as for reason of the two spies she distanced herself from idolatry and from all sin, thus the church, by means of the twelve Apostles' preaching, distances itself from idolatry and all sin.

---

92. A plural would be expected; see n. 78 above.
93. Josh 2:9.
94. Josh 2:10–11.
95. Exod 9:23–24.
96. Josh 2:12–13. The red sign is mentioned only in Josh 2:18 and there it is Joshua and Caleb who propose this signal to Rahab.
97. The use of the infinitive "to recompense" is unusual and it is not reflected in the translation.
98. Literally: opposite the sun. The contrast of Rahab's secret help and the Israelites' open recompense is added to the biblical text.
99. I.e., he should remain in the house: Josh 2:19.
100. Literally: from our faces: Josh 2:24.
101. Or: symbol. A homiletic section starts with this phrase and continues until §29. There the narrative resumes.

22/ And then that she lowered him[102] from the wall in a basket symbolized the mystery of the church, that they lowered the apostle Paul <due to> the wall of Damascus in a basket[103] and freed him from execution. And that the sign (was) red and not another color preaches the mystery of the cross; and just as Rahab's house was saved by the color red, thus the house of Adam was saved from Satan's hands by the blood of Christ. And that, that she believed in the red sign, at the time of the destruction of the wall she was not afraid, thus he who believes in the cross, which was painted red with the blood of Christ, at a time when creations are dissolved and undone, he is not afraid and does not shiver in that hour. And that she bound the sign to wood, O! symbol of the people who were to hang the Son of God from the wood, that (is what) it represents.

23/ Oh! Rahab, daughter of heathen! For through her entry, she wrote (and) she represented that going forth of those to whom she went.[104] For through the cross of Christ, the nation of the Jews went forth and became distant from worship of God and the heathen entered into the worship of God. When her hand drew near to the red sign, she distanced herself from all idols and awaited the sight of virginal Joshua. And when the church believed in the cross it distanced itself from idolatry; and they await the coming of the only-begotten, immortal King.

24/ And when the spies related the fear of the people of the Canaanites, the people commenced their journey and came, camped on the banks of the River Jordan for three days, so that perchance the inhabitants of Jericho would hear, would fear and would seek Joshua's right hand of peace, and believe in the living God,[105] and add themselves to the believers. And God would bring fear and dread on all the heathen peoples, lest they come to fight with the Power, who split the Red Sea at Moses's hand. Again moreover, He split the river Jordan before Joshua son of Nun, so that they might apprehend and know that if they come and fight with that Power who split the Jordan before Joshua son of Nun, he will cut them down at the hand of Him who split the sea before Moses, like the Amorites.

---

102. Presumably this should be plural, perhaps due to a corruption reading զնա for զնսա (= զնոսա). On similar variation of number, see nn. 78 and 93 above.

103. 2 Cor 11:32.

104. So proposed to me by G. Muradyan.

105. The author favors this divine name and attribute. See p. 54 n. 127 above.

25/ And because he was going to remove from them the cloud and the day[106] together with the manna, he showed that henceforth the Ark of the Testaments was going to go before them. He commanded them to distance themselves two thousand cubits from the Ark, to make it look magnificent before their eyes, so that the holy power that dwelt in it might be glorified with great honor. In the same way, it is necessary for the church and for the holy things to remain forty cubits distant from the profane ones,[107] lest the sanctity grow distant on account of its proximity to unworthy things.[108]

26/ And so that the sanctity be further glorified and look awesome in the eyes of the populace of the people, he commanded them to purify themselves for three days in advance, so that they might become worthy of the sight of the wonders that were going to take place at the River Jordan.[109] (This was) so that it would signify the mystery of sanctity[110] which at the hand of the true Jesus[111] was going to spread through all generations of the nations,[112] by the mystery of the thrice-luminous greatness of the holy Trinity. Thus, it is necessary for all believers first to purify themselves from all sins, and then to become worthy of the divine holy Mystery and the celebration of the dominical festivals.

27/ And through this mystery three fifties were set, first to purify the soul by fasts and prayers, and then to become worthy to celebrate the divine feasts—Nativity, Easter, and Transfiguration. And because it was springtime and the Jordan flowed in surges, and Joshua said, "God reckons me a worthy leader of this people, like Moses. Just as He split the sea through Moses's hands, He will split this river through my hands."

28/ And[113] the Lord said to Joshua, "I will do according to your wish and I will glorify you in the eyes of your people, so that they might know that just as I was with Moses in the splitting of the sea, so I will be here with you in the splitting of this river." Now seven priests[114] raised the Ark and Joshua

---

106. աւիւն, "the day" is perhaps a graphic corruption of սիւն, "pillar," i.e., of fire: compare Exod 13:21–22.

107. See 1 Kgs 6:17, Ezek 41:2.

108. Compare Josh 3:4 about the need to stay distant from the Ark.

109. Josh 1:11.

110. I.e., the Eucharist.

111. The name is the same as Joshua, so the writer contrasts Joshua with "the true Jesus."

112. Or: generations of generations, i.e., forever.

113. Having finished his homiletic remarks, the author here returns to the narrative.

114. It is not thus in Joshua. Seven priests with ram's horn trumpets figure prominently in the Jericho story in Joshua chapter 6.

commanded the priests to enter the river with the Ark. And when the feet of the priests reached the water, at that very time the river was split and turned back seven days' travel,[115] towards its source.

29/ And the lower water entered the Sea of the West,[116] which is the salt sea of Sodom,[117] and that was a great wonder for the water of the river was not heaped up and not accumulated, but turned back to its source, so that in its turning back, the water of the river would not submerge the buildings on the river bank.[118] The priests with the Ark stood in the midst of the water until the whole people crossed, lest they be afraid of the return of the water. And then they brought twelve stones from the river and placed them on the dry land, and twelve stones from the dry land and put them in the midst of the river.[119] And when the priests came out with the Ark, then the river again ran in its bed[120] as yesterday and the day before.[121]

30/ And[122] which symbol(ic meaning) did it have? That Joshua was a type of Christ; and the Ark, of the holy cross. And just as through[123] the Ark the water of the river returned to its source, in the same way through the coming of Christ and through the cross, this human nature[124] returned to its pristine glory. And the lower water (is) the type of the unbelievers, who did not come out of the sea of sins through the net of the Gospel, but remained in their former unbelief[125] and were drowned by sin in the depths of the abyss. In the

---

115. I.e., the distance of seven day's travel.

116. The "Sea of the West" is mentioned in the Josh 5:1, 23:4, compare Ezek 47:20. Here the author displays ignorance of the geography of the Land of Israel.

117. "The Sea of Sodom" is the Dead Sea; see Josh 3:16. The "Sea of the West" should designate the Mediterranean Sea, called "Sea of the West" in the Bible; see Josh 23:4. Such geographical anomalies appear not rarely in Armenian apocryphal texts, and witness to the authors' lack of direct knowledge of the geography of the Holy Land.

118. This sentence transmits the author's understanding of the mechanics of the miraculous splitting of the river. The Bible, in Josh 3:16 is much more succinct.

119. The book of Joshua is quite clear that only one set of twelve stones was made into a cairn and they were stones taken from the river and placed on the dry land; see Josh 4:3 and 4:8.

120. Literally: way.

121. I.e., as previously.

122. From here to the end of §33 there is another series typological exegeses of events narrated.

123. I.e., by means of.

124. բնութիւն "nature" in such contexts often means "body." Here the reference is clearly to Adam's garment of glory, which he lost when he sinned. See Agathangelos 3 etc. and Stone, *Adam and Eve in the Armenian Tradition*, 22, 56 and numerous other places.

125. Անհաւատութիւն "unbelief": a locative case would be expected.

same way, the twelve rocks which they brought from the river are a type and symbol of the twelve believing nations, who by means of the preaching of the twelve Apostles went forth from the waters of sin and desires.[126]

31/ And (with) the twelve rocks which they brought,[127] he built the altar of God and wrote the second law[128] on it for the sake of the heathen, in the crossing of the Jordan so that the heathen too would benefit from the crumbs of the spiritual table (altar)[129] of the divine law, and not remain blind and ignorant of the will of God, with benighted minds. In the same way, that type was going to believe, who formed their hearts into an altar of holiness and who offered their prayers as a rational sacrifice, and they became a cause of God's commands, having written the law of God on their hearts.

32/ And the twelve rocks[130] which they placed from the dry land into the water are a symbol of the unbelieving twelve tribes of the Jews and of all disbelievers, who did not believe in Christ, but were weighed down by sins like a rock of lead and went down to the depths of Hell. This is the mystery, may it be[131] according to the discourse, that by the twelve rocks which they brought forth from the river, (were) for a symbol of the glory of God, for (they were) an unforgettable memorial, a divine wonder, until the end of the world.[132]

33/ And the water of the river that were divided[133] (was) because of the Canaanites, so that they might hear and fear and believe in the living God and not be destroyed on Joshua's sharp sword. But, just as when the waters of the sea were divided and the Amorites did not fear but came to fight with the people and were killed,[134] in the same way also here the Canaanites did not believe and did not fear God, but came to fight with Joshua and were killed.

34/ Now. ...
Here the text of M4618 breaks off. The following is drawn from M2168, starting on line 4 of fol. 317r and continuing to the end of the work.

---

126. This list of twelve nations is inferred from the number of the Apostles.
127. That is, from the water.
128. This is also the Armenian name of Deuteronomy.
129. The Armenian word means both "table" and "altar."
130. These twelve rocks, taken from land to water, are an addition of our text to the biblical narrative.
131. ցնդ means "Let! Permit!" and in later Armenian marks a verb as a cohortative, "Let ..." whatever it is happen!
132. See Josh 4:21–24.
133. That is, the waters. There is a confusion of number here, see n. 78 above.
134. This is a combination of Josh 5:1 with the destruction of the Amorite kings related in Joshua chapter 10. Alternatively, note that the links between the Amorites and the splitting of the Red Sea were seen as great signs; see §§18 and 24 above.

34/ Now in that very same time the commandment of circumcision (was implemented). This had been prevented in the desert for forty years. And He again reinstituted it at the hand of Joshua when he entered into mixing among heathen peoples,[135] for by that sign they were separated[136] from the unbelievers. Joshua circumcised those who were uncircumcised, who were born in the desert, because uncircumcision preserved them in the desert.[137] At the time, death gained authority over the circumcision of the one hundred thousand.[138] And He commanded to circumcise them with a flint because its incision is easier than a wound (caused by) iron, and heals more quickly than the wound of iron.[139]

35/ And again every man (must be) prepared to find that he is not taken[140] to idol worship. For, through the flint[141] this external organ of theirs is a seal that their flinty hearts[142] will be softened and through God's laws, He will circumcise their hearts' uncircumcision. And Joshua made a knife of flint and he circumcised the people in Gilgal, on the banks of the Jordan River.[143] This[144] is translated "circle of circumcision" as a sign of the faithful after the fashion of the baptism of Jesus, which is that those believers in Christ are baptized on the eighth day and by the sign of the cross are separated from

---

135. That is, when the Israelites entered the land, they lived among other peoples and circumcision distinguished the Israelites from those other peoples.

136. Here the verb is active, but it is translated here *ad sensum*, as a middle/passive.

137. Presumably, from the danger of the procedure in the conditions in the desert.

138. See n. 58 above.

139. This explanation seems *prima facie* implausible. The author is faced with flint in the biblical text and knows iron knives, and has to find an explanation for the command to use flint. For the use of flint for circumcision, see, in addition to Josh 5:2–3, also Exod 4:25. Later Jewish practice is to use a metal knife, and the flint is presumably a memory of an archaic custom.

140. I.e., drawn.

141. I.e., through circumcision with a flint knife.

142. "Flinty hearts" is not a biblical expression. Circumcision of the heart, mentioned in the next sentence, is used metaphorically in Deut 10:16, 30:6, and Jer 4:4 to express repentance. In different contexts, in Job 41:24 and Ezek 36:26, "heart of stone" is evoked, and this literary figure is developed in 2 Cor 3:3. So, "heart of flint, flinty heart" here could well emerge from the association of the two images, facilitated by the shared word "heart."

143. Joshua 5:3 says that the circumcision took place at Gibeath-ha'aralot, which name means, "hill of the foreskins."

144. I.e., Gilgal. Josh 5:9 gives the etymology as "rolled away." The same basic etymology is found in Wutz, *Onomastica Sacra*, 876–77, 966–67, compare *gałgałay* in Stone, *Signs of the Judgment*, 129.

the unbelievers. But also after the seventh era[145] of this life, at the inception of the eighth era, on the day of the judgment, the believers are separated from the unbelievers. The believers ascend (to be) with Christ, to the kingdom, and the unbelievers descend with Satan to the foundations of Hell.

36/ They celebrated Passover[146] and the manna was withheld, for perhaps if their fathers would have exchanged (it) in the desert for onion and for garlic, they would have debased the promised land in the eyes of (their) sons[147] when they saw the land of their inheritance full of every good thing, and when the people was circumcised and each reached this faultless place, before they separated from one another.

37/ The Lord said, "This day I have removed the reproach of the Egyptians from you," because they were circumcised and there was no one who would persecute circumcision like the boys in Egypt.[148] Because of circumcision they drowned them in the river, or because then through sojourning they were reduced in number[149] among the Egyptians and today they will trample upon Gentiles."

38/ And while they were seated, a man appeared to Joshua standing between heaven and earth[150] and he held a naked sword in his hand. And so that the people would not be astounded,[151] he appeared only to Joshua, so that it would be known to Joshua that the angel of the Lord was going before them to cut down their enemies. And then it was announced to all the people by him. But when Joshua saw that man, he thought[152] that over against him

---

145. Or "millennium" in both instances here. For the idea that judgment follows the seventh millennium of the world, see Stone, *Angels and Biblical Heroes*, 34–36 and Michael E. Stone, *Ancient Judaism: New Visions and Views* (Grand Rapids, MI: Eerdmans, 2011), 71–75.

146. Josh 5:10.

147. Josh 5:12 speaks of the manna stopping.

148. A reference to the Egyptians finding the male children and drowning them; see Exod 1:16.

149. հունէլ is literally "to prune, lop." A common graphic alternation produced the text's հնարէլ.

150. See Josh 5:12, though the dimensions of the angels are not mentioned there. In his article "Le Couple de l'ange divin et de l'ésprit: Traditions juives et chrétiens," *RB* 88 (1981), 42–61, Gedaliyahu G. Stroumsa has a very interesting discussion of revelatory figures of enormous dimensions. Though not quite relevant here, nonetheless this article illustrates how gigantic in size was a sign of heavenly beings.

151. Or: startled.

152. Armenian համարեցաւ. There is a raised miniature letter ր above the beginning of this word. However, there is no verb հրամարեմ, or the like. So it seems to be an error, perhaps of the scribe in the course of proof reading the text, when he mistakenly read

one of the heathen dared him, with a sword in his hand, so that he might cast fear and fright upon them.[153]

39/ For that reason he asked him and said, "Are you one of ours or of the strangers?" For, had he known that he was commander[154] of the Lord's hosts,[155] he would not have asked him, but would have humbly done obeisance and submitted to his will. And when he asked him, he said, "Fear not. I am the commander of the Lord's host, and now I have come to help you," so that he might learn that the heavenly angel had come to help the warriors of his people. And because he said that "I have come and I have revealed that, as long as you were in the desert without war and you remained free of care, I did not come, but now that you are beginning to wage war against the Canaanites, I have come to help, to back you up."

40/ And he said to him, "Take your shoes off your feet." This (angel) is a companion of that one who showed him the sword.[156] Thus, the Lord was with the angel and he says, "Take your shoes off your feet to trample the enemies underfoot like the harvest by means of this steel sword, (that enemy) which I showed you dead. For the place on which you stand is holy."[157] For he showed him where he stood formerly.[158]

41/ For just as God was he who dwelt in the thorn bush[159] and he spoke with Moses by agency of an angel, "Take your shoes off your feet in order to trample the Egyptians underfoot,"[160] just so here too it is the Lord who, by agency of the angelic commander, commands to remove the shoes, to go

---

this word as deriving from հրամայեմ "to command." The incident is described in Josh 5:13 and thence continues to 6:5 where Joshua received instructions about vanquishing Jericho. The enormous size of the angel is not mentioned in the biblical text.

153. See Josh 5:13.

154. See Josh 5:14, 15.

155. The title appears in Josh 5:14. There Rashi identifies him as the angel Michael. Michael also bears this title elsewhere, see, e.g., *T. Ab.* A chaps. 1, 2, 3, etc.

156. No reason has been found for the introduction of this second angel.

157. Exod 3:5 where both removal of shoes and this pronouncement figure.

158. It appears that this section, which is somewhat unclear, tells of two angels. The angel mentioned in Josh 5:15 is distinguished from that mentioned in 5:13. This is because the command, "Put off your shoes etc." is strange coming in the middle of the angelophany. That phrase, of course, also occurs in a similar context in Exod 3:5, and there was the first element of a theophany. Here, moreover, a symbolic meaning of the removal of shoes is inferred, evoking the idea of trampling the enemy. This is an addition by the author to the biblical narrative.

159. Here the writer continues to draw on Exod 3 and makes the relationship explicit.

160. "In order … underfoot" is an addition of the author, paralleled in the next part of the sentence.

7. BRIEF HISTORY OF JOSHUA SON OF NUN

forth, to smite, to trample underfoot and to slaughter the Canaanites. But the regions were called holy; they revealed concerning the divinity who (was) in the thorn bush and in the commander.[161] He dwelt there, for the land in which the living God is worshipped is called the land of the living and holy.[162] At that time[163] the Canaanites did not fear and did not believe in the living God.

42/ Then Joshua came with the people, and they surrounded the city of Jericho which was like Hell.[164] And who built it? For Anak[165] of the sons of Ham had three sons, Ai and Gał and Jericho.[166] And Ai and Gał built (cities) in their own names, Ai and Gilgal. Afterwards Jericho built Jericho in his own name, just as Satan afterwards[167] built both death and Hell. For God did not make death, "by the envy of the Devil death entered the world."[168]

43/ And Jericho had sevenfold walls of magnetic stone,[169] unworkable by iron,[170] invincible and impregnable. And if the tool was not iron, how

---

161. In the Bible, of course, there is no hint that the speaker either in the Exodus theophany or in the Joshua one was an angel. In the two instances in our text, an intermediary angel is mentioned. In both, the case usage is unusual and an oblique case would be expected.

162. See Isa 38:11, Ps 116(114):9, and 142:5 (141:6).

163. Literally: at which time.

164. This typology is developed further on in the text; see §§42, 48, and 49.

165. Armenian *Kʻuak*, compare Josh 15:14 where, of Hebron, it says, "And Caleb drove out from there the three sons of Anak, Sheshai and Ahiman and Talmai, the descendants of Anak." Our text has moved this tradition to Jericho and made Anak, son of Arba according to Josh 15:13, into a descendant of Ham. Canaan and the Canaanites are descendants of Ham according to Gen 10:6, 15–20. Jericho son of Anak does not figure in those passages, but the Hamite ancestry of the Canaanites is clear. At this point it has displaced the tradition about Anak's origins as we have remarked.

166. These are the names of three cities taken by Joshua and the Israelites, Gał is presumably Gilgal. This has no direct biblical source.

167. This implies a strange chronography, that Satan built Hell several generations after the Flood.

168. This is a citation of *Wis* 2:24 in an explanatory gloss by the author.

169. I.e., lodestone.

170. See Michael J. Curley, *Physiologus* (Austin, TX: University of Texas Press, 1979). On p. 62 the adamant stone is discussed and the magnet stone on pp. 61–62. Neither of these sections is found in Gohar Muradyan, *Physiologus: The Greek and Armenian Versions with a Study of Translation Technique*, trans. Aram Topchyan, HUAS 6 (Leuven: Peeters, 2005). The chief point shared by our text and *Physiologus* is that iron cannot prevail against magnetic stone (lodestone). The other details present in our text are not in *Physiologus*. Curley translated the Latin and Muradyan the Armenian. Thus, the traditions that were shared are quite limited. Our section must have had a different source.

was it built without iron? They say thus: that they alloy copper and tin with one another and made tools, and they temper them in goat's blood and with that they work that stone. Adamant is a witness to you, which iron does not overcome and is cut and pulverized by lead. (This is) after the fashion of gentleness and humility, for by humility a person overcomes all evil, and by it he prevents all evil.

44/ They came and circumambulated the city. They were not able to go near (it) with[171] iron, for that stone attracts iron to itself. And inside armor it shatters and pulverises men's bones, and without iron they were unable to approach, for from above, from the wall, they were killed. And it was so impregnable that it was only the work[172] of God's power to break down and destroy it.

45/ And the Lord commanded Joshua and seven priests lifted up the A<r>k onto their shoulders and there were seven trumpets in their hands and (there were) forty thousand men before and forty thousand after the Ark,[173] so that the priests should not go forth, the Ark should not be captured. And on six days they went around the city six times, and the priests sounded the trumpets and all the people together said quietly,[174] "Lord have mercy." And on the Sabbath day they[175] thought that the Hebrews would observe the Sabbath. They went forth on the wall and looked and mocked them.[176]

46/ And they did not observe the Sabbath and on the seventh day, which was the Sabbath, they circumambulated seven times diligently[177] saying six times quietly, "Lord, have mercy" and on the seventh time, they beseeched loudly and cried out to God. And at that very time the wall of Jericho melted like water and it entered and went down to the ground, just like molten lead.

---

171. I.e., carrying.
172. Conceivably the word գործ "work" has lost a final letter ի, which turns it into the word "tool." This would fit admirably here.
173. According to Josh 6:9, some men went before the Ark and some after it, but no numbers are given.
174. Or: humbly. The Bible does not specify what they cried out: Josh 6:20.
175. The people of Jericho.
176. This story about the Sabbath is an expansion by the author. The idea of not fighting on the Sabbath is to be found in 1 Macc 2:34, 40 and 2 Macc 5:25 and 8:26. These books of Maccabees were firmly established in the Armenian Bible. The decision to fight on the Sabbath related in 1 Macc 2:41 may have been in the author's mind here. The Book of Joshua mentions the seven circumambulations but does not discuss how they fit with Sabbath laws. The observation here might derive from an elenchic text; see the excursus above, pp. 9–11.
177. Or "hastily."

But, only that wall in which Rahab sat (dwelt) was not destroyed.[178] On account of (her) faith she and her father's house were saved. Men climbed the wall on the Sabbath day; at the destruction of the wall they were engulfed in the abyss lest they labor to cut down the Hebrews.

47/ And that power which destroyed the high and unvanquished Tower,[179] the same divine power preserved the death monument,[180] and the wall in which Rahab sat (dwelt) through the secret of the red sign, by which Rahab's house was delivered. In the same way, by the secret,[181] by Jesus's blood, the house of Adam was freed and delivered from the destruction of death and from Hell.[182] And then they brought Rahab's house forth from Jericho and brought (Rahab's house) into their midst. It[183] was purified and became mixed with the tribe of Judah.[184]

48/ On that day, Joshua cursed Jericho and its builders.[185] And there he said that he who builds this city[186] will lay the foundation by means of his first-born son, and its gate by means of his younger (son).[187] Azan of Bethel built Jericho at Ahab's[188] command and since Ahab scorned Joshua, (considering) that there was no power in his curse, Abiron fell there. Azan of Bethel

---

178. In Josh 6:23–26 Rahab and her family are taken out of Jericho, but nothing is said about the wall being saved. Is it because Armenian տուն can mean both "house" and "household"?

179. I.e., the Tower of Babel. The Bible does not say that the Tower was destroyed, see Gen 11:8. The Armenian apocryphon, *Biblical Paraphrases* §9 says that the builders destroyed the Tower, and "the earth split open and swallowed up the city and the Tower": Stone, *Patriarchs and Prophets*, 92. In *Concerning the Tower 2* §3 it is said to have been destroyed by an earthquake; see Stone, *Angels and Biblical Heroes*, 115.

180. The meaning of this phrase is unclear. I have given a literal translation. քման is an orthographic variant of քմահն.

181. Or "mystery."

182. See §22, above.

183. I.e., Rahab's family. The purification means circumcision, see §50.

184. Thus, explaining Rahab's role in the genealogy in Matt 1:5.

185. Josh 6:26.

186. "He" refers to the builder of Jericho. The use of singular and plural wavers on many occasions in this document.

187. See Josh 6:26: "Joshua then pronounced this oath, saying, 'Cursed before the Lord be anyone who tries to build this city—this Jericho! At the cost of his firstborn he shall lay its foundation, and at the cost of his youngest he shall set up its gates!'" This is not quoted litteratim in the text but is reformulated.

188. This incident, the fulfillment of Joshua's curse, is related in 1 Kgs 16:34. The builder is Hiel of Bethel, which name becomes Azan in our text for no clear reason. The king was Ahab; the older son was Abiram and the younger Segub. Only the change of Hiel = Greek 'Αχιηλ = Armenian Bible Աբիէլ (*Ak'iēl*), to Azan remains unexplained.

laid the foundation of the wall, and by means of his younger (son) Serag, he set up the gate. And the seeds of the inhabitants of the city did not sprout and the beasts did not conceive.[189] And if the blessing of the prophet Elijah had not arrived, they would have been annihilated.[190] And on what account did Joshua curse Jericho and its builders? Because Jericho was a type of Hell.[191] Just as it had seven impregnable foundation walls and no human could break it down, except it was destroyed by God's power. In the same way Satan built Hell and walled it around with seven measures of death through sin beneath this world, and no human could go there and break it down, unless God's power[192] desired that he break it down.

49/ For this reason the only-begotten, immortal king through the sufferings of the cross, descended to Hell and broke it down and freed[193] the captive souls.[194] And just as Joshua broke down Jericho and cursed its builders, in the same way Christ broke down our division of Hell and cursed that man who does other new sins; he builds Hell for his own soul. But our division of Hell was broken down and Satan's division remained.[195] And if all humans had believed in Christ and were doers of Christ's will, behold there would no longer be Hell for Adam's children. But since many unbelievers remained and became doers of Satan's will, for this reason they go to the fire which is prepared for Satan and doers of his will.[196]

50/ And again, he cursed it[197] on account of this, that they dared, after the splitting of the Jordan and God being long-suffering for five days, and they remained unbelieving and impenitent. And they did not want[198] their

---

189. This sentence broadens the range of the curse and is not in the Bible.

190. See 2 Kgs 2:19–22.

191. This is foreshadowed in §§47 and 48 above, but is not said in the Bible.

192. This personification or hypostasis of God's power may be observed elsewhere in the present document.

193. Or: saved. This verb is often used in connection with the descent of Christ to Hell. See, e.g., *Ques. Ezra* B12.

194. Note the verb "to capture" used of Satan's gaining control of souls; see the Armenian of *Ques. Ezra* A31, B7, and in other sources.

195. If this statement is not just figurative, but implies a specific "geography" of the netherworld, its views are unusual. The two divisions might have been: one for the fallen angels and one for the wicked humans, as is clear from this paragraph. The divisions of Hell figure in Jewish apocryphal and rabbinic traditions from *1 En.* 22 on. On the "*nekuia*" traditions of descent to Hell, see Martha Himmelfarb, *Tours of Hell: An Apocalyptic Form in Jewish and Christian Literature* (Philadelphia: University of Pennsylvania Press, 1983).

196. Observe this idea of the eventual destruction of Hell by fire.

197. Jericho.

198. I.e., want to save.

own lives and did not seek Joshua's peaceful right hand.[199] On account of that he cursed and imprecated upon them and they cut down the inhabitants of the city. And they took the five kings captive and in the evening they hanged (them) from a forked tree.[200] And they brought forth Rahab's house and for seven days they sat and lived outside until their menfolk were circumcised. And then they were mixed with the blessed tribe of Judah.[201]

51/ And Joshua said, "Cursed be the person who takes any of Jericho's goods, but all flammable material are first a portion for the altar of God.[202] And they destroyed all the other things, they wasted everything else[203] by fire and the sword. And they took the gold and silver, the bronze and iron to the altar. And again according to the pattern[204]<of> the destruction of Jericho the canons (of the Psalter) were set down, six *gublas*[205] they say in a low voice and the seventh with a loud voice. And at the last, falling they beseech loudly that the wall of sins that Satan brought perish by power of the cross of Christ, the type of which was the Ark.

52/ And Achan[206] son of <C>armi took of the cursed things[207] of Jericho, a carpet worked with gold that was placed beneath idols, and a silver cup, and a golden tongue from the mouth of idols. He took and brought (them) and gave (them) to his wife secretly.[208] That was a great, unforgivable sin of

---

199. I.e., did not seek to make peace with Joshua. This expression, "seek the right hand" does not occur in the Bible and is an Armenian idiom. It presumably reflects a social convention current among the Armenians. See §24.

200. This is the fate of the king of Ai in Josh 8:29.

201. Josh 6:23, 25. There the saving of Rahab's house is described. However the text in Joshua says nothing about their circumcision or assimilation into the tribe of Judah. This is derived from the genealogy at the beginning of Matthew, see 1:5. See also §47 above.

202. I.e., are set apart. In Josh 6:19 it is ""the treasury of the Lord," and not the altar.

203. Literally: made thin, worn away.

204. One would expect կործանումն to be in the genitive case, not the nominative-accusative.

205. A subdivision of the Canons of the Armenian Psalter.

206. Armenian Akʻar, following the Septuagint Ἀχαρ. The story of Achan is told in Josh 7.

207. I.e., those things devoted to God, for the theft of which a curse ensues. See Josh 7:1. This incident, related in Josh 7:18–26 is also mentioned in a short text published in Michael E. Stone, "Three Apocryphal Fragments from Armenian Manuscripts," in *A Teacher for All Generations: Essays in Honor of James C. VanderKam*, ed. Eric F. Mason et al. (Leiden: Brill, 2012), 939–46: "Akʻar having taken the coat secretly from Joshua, | He was stoned by rocks in the valley of Akʻor."

208. This list is based upon, but not identical with the biblical text which reads, "a beautiful mantle from Shinar, and two hundred shekels of silver, and a bar of gold weighing fifty shekels, then I coveted them, and took them; and behold, they are hidden in the earth

Achan's, first because the goods from Jericho were a tithe from ten peoples of the Canaanites[209] (so) he stole God's portion; second, because he transgressed and trampled on Joshua's command and entered under the curse because of his greed. And by despising his commandment he despised God.

53/ And after the destruction of Jericho they came and surrounded the small city of Ai.[210] The citizens came and killed thirty men of the people[211] and the rest fled and from fear they became like wax, which is melted by fire.[212] And when Joshua heard, he rent his garments and the twelve princes with him, and they fell upon their faces until the evening.[213] And Joshua said to the Lord, "Did you bring us across the Jordan to deliver (us) into the hands of the Amorites?[214] And you, how will you make your name great?[215] For you swore to make us your own people." But God did not wish to hearken to Joshua and the elders of the people, for perhaps Achan would become afraid and confess his sins[216] and make the anger pass away from himself, his family and his people.

54/ And Joshua pleaded with and beseeched God and knew no doubt concerning himself, and said, "Now, the Canaanites will hear that we have been bested. They (will) come in concert and destroy us. And you, what will you do for your omnipotent name, which was shown to be victorious in every place, in Egypt and among the Amorites?"[217] And then on the next day the Lord said to Joshua, "You remain fallen upon your face,[218] this serpent,[219]

---

inside my tent, with the silver underneath" (Josh 7:21). The "bar" is the word translated "tongue" here based on the LXX γλῶσσαν.

209. Tithes are not mentioned in Josh 7. Their introduction is an interpretation of the consecrated spoils.

210. See Josh 7:3 which implies that Ai is a small city.

211. I.e., of Israel. In Josh 7:5 it is thirty-six men that are killed.

212. "Melted like water," Josh 7:5.

213. Josh 7:6. There the princes are called "the elders."

214. Josh 7:7. The rest of this question is developed from Josh 7:9.

215. Literally: will you make your great name?

216. The same strategy is used in the case of the similar conflict with divine omniscience in Gen 3:9, and elsewhere too. Thus, Armenian texts often comment on God's footsteps in Gen 3:3 along these lines; see Stone, *Adam and Eve in the Armenian Tradition*, 34, 74, 120, 151–52, etc.

217. Josh 7:9. "which is shown ... Amorites" is an addition by the author. In general, he associates "Amorites" with "Canaanites," which nation is not mentioned here.

218. This is the reverse of Josh 7:10, where he is told to rise up.

219. The form of this word, being a locative of օձ with prefixed զ-, seems to make little sense. If it were զի օձս one might translate "for the/this serpent." Օձիր means "collar," but that does not make sense either.

7. BRIEF HISTORY OF JOSHUA SON OF NUN

the people has acted lawlessly and have[220] transgressed your curses and have stolen from the goods of Jericho. Now, they will be unable to overcome in war and vanquish their enemies if you do not remove the evil from your midst."[221] And when Joshua heard this and apprehended this reason for God's anger, he said to the people, "Whomsoever the stolen goods are found with will perish with his family and chattels."[222]

55/ He said this so that Achan would fear and confess[223] his sins and repent. And then, at God's behest he cast a lot among the twelve[224] (tribes, and it fell) on the tribe of Judah. And again, he divided the tribe of Judah into twelve parts, and cast the lot by means of the prophetic spirit, and the lot fell upon the house of Achan.[225] And Joshua said to Achan, "Give glory to God and confess truly." And he was unwilling and then Joshua commanded to stone Achan with his house. And when they brought Achan to the stoning, then unwillingly he confessed and found no forgiveness.[226] And they went to his house and they found the stolen goods, the carpet underneath his wife[227] and the gold tongue and the silver cup were buried beneath the tent-peg. And they brought (them) to Joshua[228] and everybody spat in Achan's face and they brought him[229] and his family and all (his) possessions and beasts. They filled a valley (with them) and stoned (them). And they did thus and heaped up a great mound of earth over him.[230] And then <God's> anger passed away.

56/ And why did they stone his family?[231] Because they knew of the sin and did not confess it, therefore, they were punished with Achan. And his

---

220. Note once more the fluidity of singular and plural.
221. Josh 7:12.
222. Josh 7:15. The punishment there is specified to be burning.
223. This verb, in the text, is first person and not third person. Observe the same motive for God's action in §53.
224. I.e., tribes.
225. Josh 7:16–18. Here the casting of lots is specified, while the Bible has an unspecified "taking."
226. A first enquiry and refusal to confess are added, presumably to justify the stoning, for in the biblical story Achan both confesses and is executed: Josh 7:20.
227. Note the similarity of this scene, as rewritten by the Armenian narrator, to that of Rachel and the *terafim* in Gen 31:44.
228. This incident is related in Josh 7:22–23.
229. The text preserved in M6092 commences here.
230. Basically this is in line with Josh 7:24–26. The burning is omitted here and the stoning is extended back into Joshua's speech in 7:25. The heap, according to Josh 7:26, is of stones, not earth. The following section is one of those passages we suggested may go back to an elenchic document.
231. See Josh 7:25.

cattle and his possessions (were destroyed) for that reason, so that the people should know that he was not poor and he did not steal because of poverty <but on account of greed>. Because of that, they heaped up an earthen mound, so that you who were unsated by all possessions, be sated with earth![232] On that account they say that a greedy man is satisfied with one handful of earth and his eyes are filled.[233] And by thus killing the thief <they caused the anger to pass and conciliated God>. And then they went forth against Ai.[234]

57/ And Joshua commanded his skilled forces to surprise (them)[235] and he came and showed himself to the city and the citizens followed[236] them.[237] And when they had drawn the inhabitants of the city far away, the surprise forces went forth and burned the city with fire.[238] And when they (the Ai-ites) looked back, they saw that the smoke of the city was climbing from the earth to the heavens, they were weakened and were destroyed down to the ground. And they[239] caught them from two directions and cut them down.[240]

58/ And Joshua stretched out the javelin over against the Ai-ites and the <javelin> was bound to the air.[241] And Joshua did not bring his hand down but remained with his arm extended at prayer just like Moses against Amalek,[242] until they annihilated the city and heaped up and made a mound of earth. And then he brought down his hand from prayer. And the javelin went down upon Joshua's hands. And Joshua built an altar to God and

---

232. Josh 7:26.

233. This section answers potential questions that could be posed arising from the story of Achan. Such series of questions and the answers to them sometimes constituted independent works. See the excursus above, pp. 9–11.

234. Josh 8:3.

235. A summary of Josh 8:3b–6.

236. Literally: "entered after." Here Joshua's setting of his trap is described, which is given at length in Josh 8:10–13.

237. I.e., him and his forces. That is, he drew the inhabitants out of the city; see Josh 8:14–17.

238. Josh 8:19 describes the springing of the trap and 8:20 the burning of the city.

239. Joshua's forces.

240. Josh 8:22.

241. In Josh 8:18 God commands Joshua to hold out "the javelin that is in your hand toward Ai." Joshua 8:26 relates that "Joshua did not draw back his hand," until the destruction of all inhabitants of Ai. This strongly evokes Moses's holding up his hands at the time of Israel's battle with the Amalekites (Exod 17:11). This is perhaps the meaning being unclearly (to us) conveyed in the first sentence of this section.

242. Exod 17:11.

offered his prayers before God's altar.²⁴³ And he commanded to ordain the laws in the people's hearing, and the blessings and curses, so that they would be afraid of the curses and they would not be like Achan,²⁴⁴ transgressors of God's commandments. He stole from the cursed things and remained impenitent. And after, at an unfitting time he said, "<I have sinned>." And he did not find forgiveness, for the time <of penitence> had passed. And because he did not repent willingly, therefore Achan's seed did not find forgiveness. And Saul son of Kish, and Judah son of Simon were not justified by saying, "I sinned,"²⁴⁵ because of these stated reasons. The Canaanites fixed a time; they informed one another to come as one to fight with Joshua and the people.²⁴⁶

59/ Then the Gibeonites did not unite with them, because they were affrighted by the events at Jericho and Ai.²⁴⁷ For they heard what Moses said, he who said, "Make not a treaty with the Canaanites, but pitilessly cut them down.²⁴⁸ But those who are distant and submit and pay tribute to you, have pity on them,²⁴⁹ But cut down those who are nearby pitilessly, lest by dwelling with unbelievers, they lead you astray into idolatry,²⁵⁰ just as the prophet says, 'They were mixed with the heathen and learned their ways.'"²⁵¹ The Gibeonites heard this commandment of Moses and thought of a stratagem. They put on old footwear and (took) old, moldy, weevily provisions²⁵² and came to Joshua and said, "We heard the report of the power of your God and we have come from afar to submit to you, so that you may make a covenant with us and let us live.²⁵³ And we believe in your God and we will be tributary servants for you, for we have come from a far place. And these provisions are witness to that, which we baked freshly at home and they have grown

---

243. Josh 8:30–35 is another replay of earlier Israelite history. Then there is a repromulgation of the law of Moses, blessings and curses, the people passing between Mounts Ebal and Gerizim. This passage, of course, takes up the prescriptions of Deut 11:29 and chaps. 28–29.
244. In the Book of Joshua, Achan is not mentioned at this juncture. Here the author takes the opportunity for another homiletic intervention.
245. Saul: 1 Sam 15:24. Judas son of Simon Iscariot repented, see Matt 27:3,
246. Josh 9:1–2.
247. Josh 9:3.
248. The commandment is in Deut 20:16–17.
249. This is to be found in Deut 20:10–15.
250. Deut 20:18. All these verses based on Deut 20 are allusions and not citations.
251. Ps 106(105):35. "The prophet" then, is David and these details are an anachronistic embroidery of the biblical narrative.
252. Josh 9:3–5.
253. Josh 9:12–15.

stale because of the length of the journey and have become weevily, and we put on new footwear and now they are worn out."[254]

60/ And they[255] believed their deceitful words and swore and made a covenant that they would let them live and they would be servants of the altar, bringing wood and bringing water for the priests.[256] When the kings of the Canaanites heard, they were wrath against the Gibeonites and sallied forth together against Gibeon to cut down and annihilate them.[257]

61/ The Gibeonites informed Joshua so that he might come[258] to back up their rear.[259] Joshua came when morning dawned and they began to cut (them) down. And because the people of the Canaanites were innumerable, it was also impossible to reduce them to nothing by cutting (them) down, because the whole people of the Canaanites had assembled there at the time of that fearsome war. God cast from on high a hail of stone.[260] And those killed by the hail of stone, which the Lord God cast down upon the Canaanites, were more numerous than those killed by the Israelites.[261] And when Joshua saw that the sun was setting and they were unable to cut them all[262] down, and enemies remained alive, and they (would) become opponents of the people. And they strive[263] with them in battle on the next day.[264]

62/ Joshua gave voice and spoke before the Lord and before the company of the Israelites and said, "Let the sun stand still in Gibeon and the moon over the Vale of Aijalon."[265] And at that same moment they were held back[266] and stood still for the measure of one day, twelve hours, for it was

---

254. Josh 9:6–13.
255. I.e., the Israelites.
256. In Josh 9:21–23.
257. This section is a summary of Josh 10:1–6.
258. The verb form is singular.
259. This actually differs from the text of Joshua, in which the Gibeonites summon Joshua to help them. See Josh 10:6.
260. The preceding about the Canaanite enemies is an addition to the biblical text, in which the stones from heaven do appear: Josh 10:11. That verse also relates that the stones killed more men that the Israelites.
261. This sentence is very close to Josh 10:11.
262. We have thus translated առ հասարակ usually meaning "in common, generally."
263. I.e., will strive.
264. The preceding two sentences, painting the background for the sun standing still, are not in the biblical narrative.
265. Josh 10:12.
266. Literally: bound. This term is regularly used in magical texts of laying a spell or a compulsion on someone or something.

spring-time and day and night were <equal>.²⁶⁷ And he held back the sun and moon (from moving) so that they might annihilate the enemies and the killers might see the puniness of those who worshipped them,²⁶⁸ and not be led astray with them through the idolatry of those who served the luminaries. Now Joshua vanquished the gods of the heathen together with the heathen.²⁶⁹ For by mere speech and command he subjected the gods. This was a type and a symbol of Christ who was destined to vanquish all the gods and the corpses of the heathen by power and by the mystery of his cross. "Let the sun stand," he said, "in Gibeon and the moon in the valley of Aijalon."²⁷⁰

63/ Now they stood still according to Joshua's word. For it is not that the heavens were rotating. <For if the heavens were rotating>, would he not command them²⁷¹ to stand still and the luminaries (would) hold (their) position,²⁷² since he stopped the enormous turning of the heavens? And it is a witness to that, that He made the earth and the luminaries by word. Just as the Creator made (them) by word, he²⁷³ did this in the same fashion, he too by the word and command of the Creator stopped them.

For there are twelve constellations in the heavens and the sun travels for thirty days from constellation to constellation. For the constellations are high in the firmament in the heaven.²⁷⁴ And the sun passes in the middle zone of the seven zones over against the constellations, thirty days travel from constellation to constellation. And in 360 days it completes the twelve constellations.²⁷⁵ And on the fifth day of creation five stars remain²⁷⁶ which are these: the Yoke, of Horn, of … , … , ….²⁷⁷ For if the sun had stood still and

---

267. This sentence presages the coming discussion of the cosmic aspects of the stopping of the sun and moon in the world, as the author understood it.

268. I.e., the sun and the moon.

269. Observe the author's concern for combatting idolatry, which is not present in this context in his source material in Joshua.

270. Josh 10:12. The preceding homiletic passage has no correspondence with the book of Joshua.

271. That is, the heavens.

272. I.e., a fixed position, meaning that they too cease to move.

273. That is, Joshua.

274. The grammatical form is anomalous.

275. For a brief discussion of this calendar reckoning, see Michael E. Stone, "The Months of the Hebrews," *Le Muséon* 101 (1988): 5–12.

276. For the sun and moon were created on the fourth day, see Gen 1:14–19. Inexplicably, the preposition հ precedes this word.

277. What the first two names represent is unclear, though the Yoke and Horn are the meanings of the words. The three remaining names are not familiar, though they occur elsewhere in Armenian calendary texts. This remark in the text apparently reflects the

the heavens had moved, it would have brought the constellations to another place, and there would be disturbance and displacement of the sun's[278] path and of the divinely established order. On account of that reason, the heavens as well stood still with the sun. Thus, St. Ephrem bears witness. And it is most glorious that at the command of one earthborn man the sun stood still and the turning of the heavens ceased.[279] Indeed the two days th<a>t Joshua made into one day (were) a symbol and a mystery of Christ who made one day into two on the day of his crucifixion.

64/ And thus he cut down (his) enemies. And he passed quickly[280] over their land on the hooves of horses and city or village were not saved. Rather they were destroyed together[281] by the sharp sword. When they[282] transgressed God's commandment, the inhabitants of the small city of Ai killed thirty-two[283] of their men. But when they observed God's commandments they became so strong through God's providence and help that they annihilated the seven nations of the Canaanites and killed thirty-two kings and not one man of them was missing. For thus in all the time of observance of the Law, God is a guardian and helper and through Him they predominate in war and they vanquished spiritual and bodily enemies. All (un)faithful[284] kings and princes and those who were distant from the law and do not observe God's commandments, God abandons them from (his) power,[285] and they are weakened on account of their sins and are trampled down and delivered

---

idea of seven spheres surrounding the earth, with the "movable stars," which are seven in number including the sun and the moon and five planets. Compare the following passage: Իսկ արարչութեան աւուրցն աստեղք այս են՝ Լուծ, Եղջիւրու, Ծկրատրի, Փարազնտի, Արտախոյր, "And the stars of the days of the creation are the following: Luc [Mercury?], Eljeru [Venus?], Ckrawori [Moon?], Pʻaranjnoti [Mars?], Artaxoyr [Jupiter?]," in *The Ancient Armenian Calendar (7th–15th cc.)*, bilingual Classical Armenian-English edition, Classical Armenian text edited by Juliet Eynatyan, translated by Gohar Muradyan and Aram Topchyan (Erevan: Magaghat, 2002), 144–45.

278. A genitive, արեգականն, would be expected.
279. Both verbs are in the present tense, but style in English demands a past.
280. Reading հարեւանեաց.
281. Or: thoroughly.
282. The Israelites.
283. Previously our text had thirty as the number of Israelites killed, while the Bible has thirty-six. See §53 above and Josh 7:5.
284. One wonders whether a privative prefix might have been lost by haplography with the preceding abbreviated form of ամենայն, i.e., ամ.
285. Literally: hands. Does this excursus reflect contemporary conditions? In this respect, it might be compared with text no. 6, *Sodomites*, 1–4.

7. BRIEF HISTORY OF JOSHUA SON OF NUN

over into the power of visible and invisible enemies. And the kingdom of that people is annihilated and destroyed.[286]

65/ After that, he cut down the giants[287] and the mountain people in Hebron and from the mountains of Judah and Israel. And not a one remained there of the nation of the Canaanites. And then they made an allotment of the land[288] to the twelve tribes. And he did not give an allotment to the tribe of Levi, but he chose forty-eight[289] cities of refuge from the twelve tribes and gave them to the priests.[290] <And the tribe of the priests> he scattered like salt among the twelve tribes, so that they might dwell in them, to instruct them according to the divine law, and just like <salt>, they might endure their <tastelessness>.[291] And this is the city of refuge so that unwitting killers might escape into them and remain there until the death of the great high priest.[292] And when the high priest died, then the unintentional killer <was freed>; he might go wherever he wished.

66/ (It is) a type of the Lenten fast[293] so that the unintentional sinners and killers escape with their souls on the great f<a>st and repent until the death of the great high priest, Christ, on the cross on Good Friday. And then

---

286. The verbs are actually plural. See n. 77.
287. The word in the text, զհսկմցոյն, is not found in dictionaries but is derived from հսկայ "giant" and ազգ "nation, generation." The following word is the equally unknown զլեռնայինս, which must derive from լեառն, and so mean "mountain dwellers," vel sim.; see Josh 11:21–22. In the Armenian Bible, we read զԵնակիմսն ի լեռնակողմն Քեբրոնի, where "Anakim" is transliterated, while it is translated in our text. The LXX also transliterates it: τοὺς Ενακιμ ἐκ τῆς ὀρεινῆς, ἐκ Χεβρων.
288. I.e., they surveyed the land, measured it and divided it up.
289. Josh 21:4–8; the cities of refuge are discussed in Josh 21:13–40.
290. On the cities of the Levites, see Lev 25:32–34. Num 35:6–7 legislates for six cities of refuge and forty-two other cities, all belonging to the Levites. The idea that all forty-eight cities are of refuge is mentioned only in *b. Mak.* 10a and later, by Maimonides in *Mishneh Torah*, Laws of Murder, 8.5.
291. The exact formulation of the last clause is unclear. For the idea that priests scattered among the tribes are like salt, giving flavor, compare Job 6:6. Matt 5:13, Mark 9:50, Luke 14:34, and Col 4:6. See the same legislation in Josh 20:2–6. The distribution of these cities is set forth in the rest of Josh 20–21. In Josh 21:40 the sum total of the Levites' cities is said to be forty-eight, without a distinction being made between the cities of refuge and the other cities for habitation. It is this reading that our text follows, but it explicitly considers all forty-eight cities to be cities of refuge. Even though this is also the view of some Jewish authorities, I consider it unlikely that this agreement is more than a coincidence.
292. This provision is made in Num 35:28, Josh 20:6.
293. Literally: the great forty-day fast.

they are freed from the debts of sins[294] and from the killing of their own souls.

And the days of Joshua's death grew near. The twelve tribes of the people assembled and he commanded them and said, "Take care, and do not have pity on the remnants of the Canaanites." And he said to them, "Speak the truth to me. Behold I am dying and you, which God do you worship?—the God whom your fathers worshipped in the pasture-land on the other side of the river, or the gods of the Canaanites> who were unable to save their own worshippers.[295] But I and my father's house worship the living Lord."[296] They made this covenant and forged this agreement and said, "We worship the living Lord and we keep his commandments."[297]

67/ And Joshua said, "The service of God is difficult, for of you he asks sanctity, righteousness, virtue. And I know that after my death, you will go after foreign gods."[298] And they said, "No so, but we shall serve the Lord and hearken to his voice. As our fathers covenanted in the desert before Moses, to observe his commandments, so here too (is) the covenant for a second (time)."[299] Before the laying to rest of Joshua's life, Joshua the intermediary set up this covenant of the testaments.[300] And he raised a great pillar and wrote this covenant of theirs and said, "Behold, let this rock be a witness that you yourselves have made a covenant to serve the Lord."[301] And they said, "Thus, let it be."

68/ And Joshua died aged 150 and they buried him in the portion of his inheritance.[302] And they put with him the flint knife with which he circumcised the children of Israel.

And to Christ, lover of humans, glory forever and ever. Amen.

---

294. Cf. Col 2:14.

295. Joshua 23 relates Joshua's death. His final exhortation is not to mix with the other nations (Josh 23:7), from which our author infers that a small number of Canaanites must have survived the conquest.

296. This is an epitome of Josh 24:14–15. The word "living" is not in the biblical text.

297. See Josh 24:21, 24 for the people's acceptance of the covenant.

298. This sentence corresponds to Josh 24:19–20, but differs somewhat from it.

299. We will covenant to obey. See Josh 24:16–18, 21–22.

300. Josh 24:25.

301. Josh 24:26–27.

302. Josh 24:29–30. The length of his life in the Bible is 110 years, both in the Hebrew and in the versions. The burial of the flint knife with him is our author's addition.

8. The Story of the Ark of the Covenant

Introductory Remarks

This text occurs in M6340, fols. 55v–58r. The manuscript, a *čařentir* (*Collection of Homilies*) was copied in Łazvin in 1651.[1] The document preserved in M6340 is a second and fuller copy of a text that I published in 2016.[2] In that publication I gave an edition and a translation of a manuscript text bearing the title *Concerning the Ark*, from a long-hand copy made many years ago in Erevan. The shelf number of the manuscript was missing from the copy and attempts made to identify it were unsuccessful.[3]

It was with considerable satisfaction, therefore, that I discovered in M6340 a full copy of the same text, and I publish it here. It has some differences from the unidentified manuscript, which I have dubbed X. First, I give a variant form of the beginning of the material, which is preserved in X. Then the twenty-five extant sections of M6340 followed by an apparatus of the variants between the two manuscripts where both are extant in §§ 2b–12.[4]

At the end of the document published here, that is at §25, the text of M6340 stops. The next page of manuscript M6340, fol. 57r starts with a new text, but not at its beginning, and a page has apparently been lost. The content of the subsequent pages is quite different, being a disquisition on the priesthood.

The present document is one of a number of works dealing with the Ark of the Covenant and Joshua's conquest. All those unpublished and currently available to me are given in this section of the present book. They are discussed in the introductory remarks to text no. 7, *Brief History of Joshua*.[5] The

---

1. *Short Catalogue* 2, 298–99.
2. Stone, "Two Stories," 257–71.
3. See Stone, "Two Stories," 258.
4. The methodology used in the apparatus is set forth at its beginning. The section numbering previously used in "Two Stories" has been replaced in the present edition.
5. See above, p. 58.

-109-

present document deals with the construction of the Ark and its contents, the prophetic and other powers inherent in the Ark, and the conquest of Jericho which was executed due to the power integral to the Ark.

Text

First Section of Manuscript X

MS X / p. 369 / 2/ Եւ եղեւ իբրեւ միւս անգամ խնդրեաց Մովսէս ի տեսութեան Աստուծոյ, եւ խնդրեաց ի Տեառնէ զխնդիր ժողովրդեան:
3/ Եւ հրամայեաց Տէր Մովսիսի ...

2/ And it came to pass when Moses sought again in a vision of God and he besought from the Lord the people's request[6]
3/ and the Lord commanded Moses.

M6340

M6340 Title/ / fol. 55v / [Ա]յս է [Պ]ատմութիւն [S]ապանակի [Ո]ւխտին[7]
1/ Ի[...]ոցժողովուրդնասացին Մովսէսի թէ. «Դու աստուածախաւս մարգարէ եղար վասն մեր: Զի հանապազ խաւսիս ընդ Աստուծոյ եւ զաղաւթս մեր մատուցանես <Աստուծոյ>: Եւ զԱստուծոյ աղհնութիւնն եւ զ[պատ]գամս ի մեզ բերես եւ զզալացո[8] բանն պատմես մ[եզ]:
2/ «Զի զայ ժամանակ, որ [ոչ] գտանէ մարգարէ իբրեւ զքեզ եւ ոչ խոսի Աստուած մարդկան: Այլ ով պատմէ զբանն Աստուծոյ»:[9] Եւ եղեւ ի[բրեւ մի]ւս անգամ գնաց Մովսէս [խօ]սել ընդ Աստուծոյ եւ խնդրէ ի Տեառնէ զխնդիրս ժողովրդ[ան]: / fol. 56r /
3/ Եւ հրամայեաց Տէր Մովսիսի շինել զտապանակ անփուտ փայտէ: Եւ ոսկով ծածկեաց զերեսս անփուտ տապանակին: Չքարեղէն տախտակն եւ գաւփորն ոսկեղէն լի մանանայիւ եւ բուրվառն ոսկեղէն ետ ի մէջ տապանակին. եւ այն եղեւ տապանակ ուխտին:

---

6. Exod 25:15–18. Note the verb of seeing in Exod 24:10.
7. The continuation of the title is illegible on the images.
8. No sense could be made of this word. One might speculate that it was derived somehow from գալոց, a future participle of գամ "I come." If so, it would mean "that which is to come": compare §4 which says of the Ark եւ զամենայն գալոցն պատմէ⊠ "and it told all coming things." However, this is uncertain.
9. MS X continues from this point.

8. THE STORY OF THE ARK OF THE COVENANT 111

4/ Չի որբ խնդիրս ինչ ունեին, գնային ուխտիւք եւ ընծայիւք, երկիր պագանէին տապանակին: Ուխտ կատարէին եւ խնդիրք առնէին: Իսկ յետ Մովսէսի[10] աստուածախոսութիւն ի նմանէ լինէր: Չի որբ մարգարէ լինէին կամ քահանայ, երբ գնային ի դուռն տապանակին, խնկարկէին եւ երկիր պագանէին: Աստուածախաւսութիւն լինէր ի նմանէ, եւ զամենայն զայլոցն պատմէր:

5/ Իսկ մարգարէք նովաւ մարգարէանային եւ զզայլոցն պատմէին: Թէ պատուհաս[11] գային վասն մեղաց, գային առ ոտն տապանակին, պաղատէին, փրկէին ի պատուհասէն: Եւ թէ թշնամի կամ թազաւոր կայր ի վերայ Իսրայէլի, առնէին զտապանակ ուխտին եւ գնային եւ չարդէին եւ ջնջէին զնոսա:

6/ Եւ կայր Երիքով բերդ մի, անդամանդեա քարէ պարիսպ նորա: Եւ ի վերայ պարրսպացն կանգացուցանեալ էին պատկերք կռոց եւ աստուածպաշտէին զնայ:[12] Կայր ի մէջ բերդին ԼՌ . (30,000) / fol. 56v / այր պատերազմող:[13] Եղանէին հանապազ, աւար հարկանէին եւ կոտորէին զազգն Իսրայէլի եւ բազում վնաս առնէին:

7/ Իսկ իսրայէլացոց հետեւն բազում էին: Մինչ իմանալ իսրայէլացոցն աւար հարկանէին շուրջ զԵրուսաղէմի, դառնային[14] եւ մտանէին ի բերդն Երիքովի: Բազում անգամ գնացին իսրայէլացիքն ի վերայ բերդին Երիքովի եւ ոչ կարացան առնուլ զնա:

8/ Իսկ միւս անգամ Յեսու որդին Նաւեայ գլուխ եղեւ հետեւին Իսրայէլի, եւ առեալ ընդ իւր տապանակ ուխտին, եւ գնային ի վերայ Երիքովի: Իբրեւ հասին ի Յորդանան գետ, ԺԲ. (12) քահանայք սպասորք կային տապանակին: Իբրեւ մտին քահանայքն ի գետն, ճանապարհի արարեալ[15] յետ դարձո գետն եւ ցամաք անցին[16] քահանայքն եւ տապանակն:

9/ Իբրեւ [ան]ցին անդ, ԺԲ. (12) քարս մեծամեծս կանգնեցին ի տեղի ոտնատեղաց քահանայիցն: Եւ կա[յ] մինչեւ ցայսաւր վկայ սքանչելեաց տապանակին եւ արդար քահանայիցն: Եւ անուանեցին անուն տեղուն[17] Գաղգաղա, որ ասի տեղ սքանչելեացն:

---

10. There is damage to the paper between ս and ի, but no letters are lost.
11. A plural would be expected.
12. A plural would be expected.
13. ող above line p.m.
14. This refers to the men of Jericho.
15. Erasure of գետն.
16. Two unclear letters precede անցին.
17. Middle Armenian form.

10/ Իբրեւ հասին երիքով, աղ[օթ]ս արարին եւ է. (7) անգամ շո[ւր]ջ պատեցին զերիքովի բե[ր]դովն։ Հայր զվյուրիսպ իբրեւ զմու: Եւ ժողովուրդն միաբան քաջցրաձայն գՏէրն [ա]ղաչէին, եւ քահանայքն «կեցո Տէ[ր], Տէր ողորմեա» ձայնէին, մինչ[եւ]¹⁸ հայեցաւ զպարիսպն ամենայն։

11/ Առին զբերդն երիքովի, / fol. 57r / սրահար արարին եւ մի ի նոցանէ ոչ պահեցին։ Կոտորեցին զամենայն կենդանիսն, զայրս եւ զկանայսն եւ զմանկունսն եւ իրք մի աւար ոչ բերին։ Այրեցին հրով զամենայն ինչս նոցա։ Բայց պոռնիկն զՌահապ իւր ազգովն ոչ սպանին, զի հաւատացեալ էր Աստուած:

12/ Դարձեալ միւս անգամ Գ. (3) թագաւորք եկին ի վերայ Իսրայելի։ Իսկ որդին Նաւեայ Յեսուայ առեալ զժողովուրդն Իսրայելի եւ զոսպանական ուխտին եւ քահանայք ընդ նոսա։ Մինչ գնային ի ճանապարհին, թեքվեցաւ տապանակն. քահանայ մի դեմ կացաւ տապանակին։ Նոյնժամայն այրեցո ի մէջ շրջառին, եւ շրջառն ոչ այրեցաւ։

13/ Իբրեւ հասին ի տեղի պատերազմին, կոխեցին զթշնամին զաւրութեամբ տապանակին։ Չի ի ժամ պատերազմին հողմ եկաւ ի տապանակէն, առեալ զհող եւ զմոխիր, եւ ցանեաց ի յաչաց նոցա եւ կուրացոց զնոսա։ Չի յարեւն ի մուտս էր, եւ աղաչեաց¹⁹ Յեսու զԱստուած եւ զտապանակ ուխտին։ Յոտնակապ արար զարեգակն, մինչեւ վանեալ խորտակեաց զթշնամին իւր։

14/ Եւ Գ. (3) թագւորքն բռնեցին եւ կապեալ բերին երուսաղէմ, զի հանապազ սպանչելիս առնէր տապանակ ուխտին։ Չի իսրայելացոց ազգին²⁰ թագաւոր ոչ ունէին, եւ նոցա թագաւորն Աստուած էր, եւ դատաստան առնողն քահանայ լինէր կամ մարգարէ։ Չինչ թշնամի որ կայր ի վերայ նոցա, Աստուած յայտնէր նոցա տապանակաւն. զոր ինչ ասէր, այնպէս առնէ/ fol. 57v /ին եւ հարկ տային թագաւորաց։

15/ երբ զայր թշնամի ի վերայ նոցա, զամենայն²¹ միաբան {միաբան}²² ելանէին պատերազմել ընդ թշամոյն, մինչ ի ժամանակս Սօուղ թագաւորին։ Եւ ժամանակ մի քահանայ եղեւ Հեղի եւ դատեաց

---

18. Reading uncertain.
19. եաց above line p.m.
20. The use oblique case is perhaps reflected also in the similar construction in vernacular East Armenian, e.g., ինձ (Dat.) ունեմ, "I have."
21. The q- appears to be superfluous.
22. միաբան2° corrupt by dittography. The q on զամենայն is superfluous: compare the preceding note.

8. THE STORY OF THE ARK OF THE COVENANT 113

գխսրայէլ Ի. (20) տարի: Եւ ծառայէր տապանակին, եւ Բ. (2) որդիք նորա՝ Ովնի եւ Փենէհէս, քահանայացան:

16/ Զի ուխտաւորք բազում զային եւ ուխտ կատարէին: Իսկ որդիքն Հեղիայի՝ Ովնի եւ Փենէհէս, չարացան եւ որսային զզեղեցիկ աղջկունս եւ զիարան ուխտաւորաց եւ շնանային: Իմացան ժողովուրդն եւ զանգատեցին Հեղի քահանային: Իսկ նա խրատեաց զորդիքն, եւ ոչ հաւանեցան խարտու հաւրն, այլ գործեցին գշ[ա]րութիւն:

Իսկ բարկացաւ Տէր ի վերայ նոցա եւ յարոյց գթշնամի ի վերայ նոցա: Իբրեւ եկին իսրայէլացիքն ի վերայ նոցա, ԼՌ . (34,000) [.]: Քանզի անպատրաստ էին, իբրեւ պատերազմեցան²³, ԼՌ. (30,000) հոգի մեռաւ Իսրայէլաց²⁴ ազգի:

17/ Զի առաջնորդք նոցա չար քահանայքն էին՝ Ովնի եւ Բենէհէս, ի մուտս արեւուն էր, որ պատերազմեցան եւ կոխեցան: Եւ գիշերին առաքեցին եւ բերին զտապանակ ուխտին, կարծելով թէ տապանակաւն յաղթել կարեն գթշնամին: Ոչ գիտէին՝ տապանակ Աստուծոյ խռովեալ էր վասն անօրէն քահանային մեղացն: Իբրեւ լուսացաւ, մտին կրկիւ պատերազմեցան թշնամիքն/ fol. 58r / եւ կոտորեցին ԼՌ. (30,000) մարդն Իսրայէլի: Եւ մին մարդ պրծաւ իսրայէլացի, փախեաւ եւ գնայր առ Հեղի քահանային, դէմ երթայր եւ դէմ հողն գլխովն տայր:

18/ Եւ Հեղի քահանայն ի վերայ բարձր բլրի մի կանգնեալ էր եւ հայէր ընդ ճանապարհին, զի տեսցէ, թէ որպէս լինի զկատարածն պատերազմին: Իբրեւ եկն այրն, որ հողն ի գլխովն տայր, վայ տայր եւ ասէր. «Պարտեցաւ գխսրայէլ, եւ ես միայն պրծայ: Սպանին Բ. (2) որդիքն քոյ Ովնի եւ Փենէհէս»,

19/ ասէ Հեղի. «Զի՞նչ եղաւ տապանակ ուխտին»: Ասէ այրն. «Գերի տարան»: Իսկ Հեղի իբրեւ լուաւ զգերութիւն տապանակին, եւ զլուին ի քարովն ետ, անկաւ, եւ մէջքն²⁵ կոտրաւ, եւ մեռաւ:

Իսկ վասն Բ. (2) բռնիկ քահանայից մեղաց ԼՌԴ. (34,000) մարդ մեռօ, եւ տապանակն գերի գնաց:

20/ Իսկ որ երկիր որ տարան զտապանակն, մահ անկաւ, սով անկաւ, մորեխ անկաւ, եւ մուկն եռաց. այսպէս սպանչելիք առնէր: Զի ոչ ոք կարէր վնաս առնել տապանակ ուխտին, զի զաւրութիւն բազում լիներ ի նմանէ, իբրեւ զԱստուած պաշտէին: Եւ յետ Ի. (20) ի²⁶ . սրուն լծեցին Բ. (2) երինջք, եւ տապանակն սայլին կապեցին եւ թողին: Բ.

---

23. ա 2° over ի.
24. This word appears to be apocopated.
25. The Armenian Bible has ողն, literally "vertebra," while our text has մէջքն "back."
26. The letter ի is quite clear, but the first letter of the next word is unclear.

(2) մարդ ընկեր դրին եւ ասացին, թէ՝ «3ետեւ տապանակին գնացէք եւ տեսէք, թէ յոր աշխարհի կամի գնալ»։ Եւ արարին այսպէս։

21/ Առին զտապանակն / fol. 58v / երինջքն եւ եկին ի յերուսաղէմ. ի ժամանակս հնձոցն էր։ Իբրեւ տեսին հնձողքն, զի գայր տապանակ ուխտին, գնացին ընդդէմ նորա եւ բերին ի տեղին իւր առաջին։ Եւ դարձին պահապանքն, որ եկեալ էին ընդ տապանակին։

22/ Իսկ ամենայն յերուսաղէմ եւ ամենայն իսրայէլացիք գնացին ընդդէմ տապանակին, ուրախացան եւ խնդացին վասն զալստեան տապանակին։ Այնով զիտացին, որ Աստուած հաշտեցաւ ընդ նոսա, բայց ոչ առներ տապանակն սքանչելիս, իբրեւ զառաջինն։

23/ Եւ յետոյ տեսիլ երեւեցաւ հրեշտակի, եւ յծեցին զտապանն²⁷ եւ թողին։ Եւ տարաւ զնա ի լեռն Սինեայ, եւ է անդ մինչեւ գայսաւր։ 3երեկն ամպ հովանի է շուրջ զլերամբն, եւ ոչ ոք կարէ զտանել զնա, եւ զզիշերն լոյս հրո ծագէ ի վերայ նորա։ Չի կա անդ անտես ի մարդկանէ մինչեւ ի ժամանակս վերջին։

24/ Իսկ տապանակն աւրինակ էր եկեղեցոյ։ Չի որպէս յայն ժամանակին աստուածախաւսութիւն լինէր ի նմանէ, իսկ այժմ աստուածախաւսութիւն լինի յեկեղեցին օետարանաւ եւ սուրբ գրովք։

25/ Չի որպէս յայն ժամանակին քարեղէն տախտական խրատէր, զի այժմ գրովք մարգարէիւքն²⁸ խրատէ եկեղեցին։ Չի որպէս ի տապանակէն սուրբ սափորի մանանային ճաշակէին, իսկ յեկեղեցոյն հաղորդին ճաշակեմք։

CRITICAL APPARATUS

These collations show the variants of the unidentified manuscript, here called X,²⁹ from the text of M6340. X is incomplete. It differs from M6340 at the beginning, and breaks off in §12. In comparison with M6340, we note that its text tends to be somewhat shorter, with a number of instances of homoeoarchton and homeoteleuton. I have not introduced into the text those of its variants that I consider superior, because I am not certain of the transcription of manuscript X and, at this remove, do not know whether is was carefully verified or not. Such instances are marked, therefore, with the word "preferable" in the apparatus. This rule does not apply in the few instances in which M6340 is illegible or lacunose and the reading of X is clearly appropriate. Such read-

---

27. A different word տապանն is used here than in all the preceding instances. Below, the use of տապանակ is resumed.

28. p above line p.m.

29. See the introductory remarks, above.

8. THE STORY OF THE ARK OF THE COVENANT   115

ings have been introduced into the text and marked with pointed brackets: <>. Unless otherwise noted, the lemma is M6340 and the variant is X.

1/ totum] om

2/ Աստուծոյ] manuscript X commences after this word | ի[բրեւ մի] u] X lacuna M6340 | գնաց] խնդրեաց | [խօ]սել ընդ] ի տեսութեան | խնդրէ] խնդրեաց | զխնդիր

3/ գտապանակն | անփուտ 1°] անփոյթ | զերես | անփուտ 2°] om | ոսկեղէն] ոսկողն | լի] om | մանանային | բուրվառն ոսկեղէն] ∞ | եւս] եղ | տապանակին — տապանակ] om : hkt

4/ որ | ուխտիւ | պազանէին | ուխտ] ուխտին | խնդիրքն | առնէին] om | Մովսիսի | ի նման̃է / լինէր] ∞ | զի որք — պատմէր] om : major omission

5/ մարգարէք] մարգարէ<ի>ն | մարգարէանային] մարգարէք լինէին | զային] զայր : preferable | պաղատէին] + եւ | կայր] զայր | գնային] + ի վերայ թշնամոյն | չարդէին] կոտորէին | գնաա] om

6/ յերիքովի | անդամանդեա] խանդամանդ | եւ ի վերայ— կանգացուցանեալ էին] կանգեալ and precedes ի վերայ | գնա | ԼՌ. (34,000)] Չ. (6) | հանապազ աւար] հանապազաւր | առնէին] հարկանէին

7/ խրայելացոց | հեծեալն | էին] + եւ անթիւ բայց | յերիքովի1° | յերիքովլի 1° — յերիքովի 2°] om X : hmt | կարացին

8/ Նաւայ | յերիքովի | ԺԲ. (12)] om | քահանայքն / ի գետն] ∞ | Ճանապարհն—տապանակն] դարձաւ գետն եւ ցամաքեցաւ եւ ճանապարհի արար տապանակին

9/ քահանայից | զանուն | Գաղքաղայ զանուն | ասի] om | տեղ] տեղոյն : preferable

10/ յերիքով | եւ 1°] + տապանակին | է. (7)] Գ. (3) | շրջապատեցին | հալէն | զպարիսպն | կեցո | Տէր որոդմեա] եւ ողորմեա | ճայնէն] ասէին | մինչ<եւ> | հալեցան | ամենայն պարիսպն

11/ սրահար] սրահուտ | եւ 1°] + կոտորեցին եւ | ոչ] եւ ոչ | կոտորեցին — իրք մի] om | ոչ 2°] om | բերցին այլ | զՐահաբ | ազգով

12/ Նաւա | Եսուն | տապանակն | քահանայքն | կեցաւ | տապանակին] om | եւ նոյն | ապրեցաւ] MS X ends here

TRANSLATION

[T]his is the [S]tory of the [A]rk of the [C]ovenant.

1/ In [...] the people said to Moses, "You were a prophet, speaking with God on our account. For you always talk with God and offer up our prayers to God. And you bring God's blessing and command to us and [coming]³⁰ matters you related to u[s].

2/ "For a time is coming (in) which he will not find prophet like you and God does not speak with humans;³¹ who else will relate God's word?" And it came to pass when Moses went to [sp]eak with God for a [sec]ond time and he asked the people's question of God.

3/ And the Lord commanded Moses to build the Ark of wood³² that does not rot. And he covered the surface of the unrotting Ark with gold. He set the stone tablet and the golden urn full of manna and the golden censer inside the Ark; and that became the Ark of the Covenant.³³

4/ For those who had any requests would go with oath³⁴ and gifts to prostrate themselves to the Ark.³⁵ They would carry out their oath and pose questions. Then, afterwards, Moses's speech with God took place through it.³⁶ For when those persons who were prophets or priests came to the door of the Ark,³⁷ they would cense and worship. There was divine speech from it and it related all coming things.³⁸

5/ Indeed, prophets used to prophesy by means of it and (fore)tell the coming things. If punishment was coming on account of sins,³⁹ they would

---

30. That is, future.
31. Contrast Exod 33:61.
32. This is the answer to the preceding question: when Moses will not be able to speak with God, i.e., to act as an oracle, then they will have the Ark of the Covenant to fill this role.
33. A similar form of the list of furnishings and details of construction of the Ark occurs in a number of texts in Armenian; see the introductory remarks to text no. 7, *Brief History of Joshua*, and Stone, *Angels and Biblical Heroes*, 16–17. This subject comes up once more on pp. 259–60, 267–68 of Stone, "Two Stories."
34. Here "oath" means, it seems, the promise of an offering to God, such as a sacrifice. The procedure of eliciting an oracular response from the Ark is set forth in this section.
35. This is based on Exod 33:7 "And every one who sought the LORD would go out to the tent of meeting, which was outside the camp." Here the features there attributed to the Tent of Meeting are transferred to the Ark of the Covenant.
36. Exod 25:22, Num 7:89.
37. Apparently, this means "the doorway of the Tent of Meeting where the Ark was."
38. That is, the Ark. This view, highlighting the Ark's oracular function as God's mouthpiece, is not in the biblical text, though Exod 25:22 makes it clear that the Ark was the place used for communication with the Divine. So it reads, "There I will meet with you, and from above the mercy seat, from between the two cherubim that are upon the ark of the testimony, I will speak with you of all that I will give you in commandment for the people of Israel." Compare also Num 7:89.
39. In n. 38, we remarked on the oracular function of the Ark. This is implied not only by the statement that God spoke with Moses before the Ark, but also by such verses as

8. THE STORY OF THE ARK OF THE COVENANT

come to the foot (base) of the Ark, supplicate, (and) they were delivered from the punishment. And if an enemy or a king attacked Israel, they would take[40] the Ark of the Covenant and they would go (i.e., to battle) and would slaughter and annihilate them.[41]

6/ And Jericho was a fortress, its walls (were) of adamantine stone and they had set up images of pagan gods upon the walls and they would worship them.[42] In the fortress were 30,000 warriors.[43] They sallied forth continuously, took plunder, and cut down the nation of Israel, and they did much damage.[44]

7/ But the cavalry of the Israelites were very numerous.[45] When[46] the Israelites learned that they were plundering around Jerusalem, they (the Jericho-ites) would turn back and go into the fortress of Jericho. The Israelites frequently attacked the fortress of Jericho and were unable to take it.

8/ Then, on another occasion, Joshua the son of Nun was at the head of the Israelite cavalry. He took the Ark of the Covenant with him and they attacked Jericho.[47] When they reached the River Jordan, twelve priests were servants of the Ark. When the priests entered the river, they made a way; the river turned back and the priests and the Ark crossed on dry land.[48]

9/ When they had [cro]ssed, there they set up twelve very large stones on the place over which the priests' feet had walked.[49] And that is a witness

---

Judg 20:27–28. It is related to its function as guaranteeing victory in battle (n. 41).

40. Reading առնէին as if it were from առնուլ, or from postclassical առնէլ.

41. This function of the Ark is deeply rooted in biblical tradition; see Num 10:35 and 1 Sam 4:4–5.

42. These two observations, the strength of Jericho's walls, and the setting up of idols on them are additional to the biblical narrative in Josh 6.

43. The number of soldiers in Jericho is not mentioned in the Bible. The figure of 30,000 is mentioned as the size of an army repeatedly in the Books of Joshua and Samuel; see Josh 8:3, 1 Sam 4:10, 11:8, 2 Sam 6:1.

44. These incidents are not mentioned in the Bible.

45. The role given to the cavalry here is not featured in the Bible, and presumably derives from the author's contemporary context.

46. Literally: while.

47. Josh 6:6–13. In the Bible this attack follows the crossing of the Jordan, while here the crossing of the Jordan happened during the attack.

48. The story of the Ark's crossing of the Jordan and the setting up of twelve stones is related in Josh 3:11–4:7.

49. Josh 4:3, 9.

unto this day to the wonders of the Ark and to the righteous priests.[50] And they called the name of the place Gilgal, which means, "place of wonders."[51]

10/ When they reached Jericho, they prayed and circled the fortress of Jericho seven times. He[52] melted the wall like wax.[53] And all the people together melodiously beseeched the Lord, and the priests declaimed, "Live! O Lord. Lord have mercy," until the whole wall melted.

11/ They took the fortress of Jericho and put (it) to the sword and did not spare (even) one of them. They cut down all living things, men and women and children.[54] And they did not carry off a single thing as plunder. They burned all their possessions with fire. But they did not kill Rahab the harlot with her family, for she was faithful to God.[55]

12/ Again, on another occasion, three kings attacked Israel.[56] Then the son of Nun, Joshua, took the people of Israel and the Ark of the Covenant and priests with them. While they were going along the road, the Ark slipped downwards; a priest stood in the Ark's way.[57] At that very time he was burned amidst his surroundings, and the surroundings were not burned.[58]

13/ When they reached the site of the battle, they trampled the enemy underfoot by the power of the Ark. For, at the hour of battle a wind issued

---

50. This is based on Josh 4:7.

51. The Book of Joshua provides a name midrash for Gilgal: Josh 5:9 "And the LORD said to Joshua, 'This day I have rolled away the reproach of Egypt from you.' And so the name of that place is called Gilgal to this day." *Story of the Ark* draws upon a different onomastic tradition; see Wutz, *Onomastica Sacra*, 876-77. In addition to "rolling" (from the root *glgl*) his texts offer "revelation" from the root *gly*. Subsequently, "revelation" may well have been taken as "wonder." So, the present text offers an instance of an etymology taken in a special direction so as to suit the immediate context. Armenian apocryphal retellings often use onomastic traditions, as I observed earlier and this literary technique remains notable.

52. Apparently, God; alternatively, "it," i.e., the Ark. "melt like wax" is of course a common simile in poetic diction in the Hebrew Bible, see: Ps 22:14, 68:2, 97:5, Mic 1:4. The Book of Joshua does not use the wax image here, but speaks of the walls "falling down flat" (Josh 6:20; compare Heb 11:30). In Joshua, moreover, the circling of Jericho is much more elaborate.

53. In text no. 7, *Brief History of Joshua* §46 (p. 96 above) the wall melts like water and is absorbed by the ground like molten lead.

54. Josh 6:17-18, 21.

55. This seems to be the meaning, with Աստուած in a strange case. Alternatively, it could be translated, "for God was faithful, trustworthy," but that seems odd in context.

56. Perhaps the basis of this statement is to be found in Josh 10:3.

57. Here the text refers to the danger inherent in a venerated object as exemplified by the incident in David's time recounted in 2 Sam 6:6-7.

58. The fate of the surroundings does not feature in 2 Sam 6.

8. THE STORY OF THE ARK OF THE COVENANT

forth from the Ark, took up earth and ashes and scattered them into their eyes and blinded them.[59] Because the sun was in the West, Joshua[60] beseeched God and the Ark of the Covenant. He[61] halted the progress of the sun; while it delayed, he crushed his enemies.[62]

14/ And they seized the three kings and brought (them) bound to Jerusalem. For the Ark of the Covenant was always doing wonders. Since the people of the Israelites did not have a king and God was their king,[63] also the one who administered judgment was a priest or a prophet. Through the Ark God would reveal to them whichever enemy was attacking them. Whatever it (the Ark) would say, thus they would act. And they would pay tribute to kings.[64]

15/ When an enemy attacked them, all would issue forth in concert to fight with the enemy, up to the times of king Saul.[65] And one time Eli was priest and he judged Israel for twenty years.[66] And he served the Ark and his two sons Hophni and Pinhas became priests.[67]

16/ For many pilgrims would come and would fulfill their vows. Then the sons of Eli, Hophni and Pinhas, acted wickedly and hunted the beautiful girls and the brides of the pilgrims and acted adulterously.[68] The people

---

59. This is not related in Josh 10.
60. Literally: and Joshua.
61. Either God or the Ark.
62. The context is Joshua's war on behalf of Gibeon, in the course of which Joshua called (10:12–13): "Sun, stand thou still at Gibeon…." The Ark is not even mentioned in Josh 10, so its introduction here is an embroidery serving the author's overall aim of glorifying the Ark, by treating it as an oracle. See moreover, the first part of the next section. The incident with the dust and ashes earlier in §13 is another expression of this tendency of the text.
63. See Samuel's words in 1 Sam 12:12, "when the Lord your God was your king."
64. The second part of this section is an expansion, serving the author's goal of aggrandizing the Ark. The meaning of "they paid tribute to kings" is not clear in context; perhaps it means kings of Israel.
65. This seems to imply that there was a change in the Ark's activity corresponding to Saul's becoming a human king, instead of the kingship of God; see 1 Sam 12:12, which was already cited in the preceding section in n. 63.
66. According to 1 Sam 4:18 in MT he judged Israel for forty years. The Septuagint and the Armenian Bible have twenty years, while the Vulgate has forty.
67. Observe that the author does not seem familiar with the idea of hereditary priesthood, which is perhaps a reflection of his Christian concept of a priest.
68. In 1 Sam 2:12 they are described as "worthless men" and in the continuation of that passage their wickedness is described as taking the choice portions of sacrifices for themselves; 1 Sam 2:13–17. Their promiscuity is mentioned in the biblical text in 1 Sam 2:22.

learned (of this) and complained to Eli the priest. Then he rebuked his sons and they did not accede to their father's rebuke but acted wickedly.[69]

Then the Lord was angry with them and raised up an enemy against them. When the Israelites went forth against them, (they were) 34,000. Because they were unprepared when they battled, 30,000 men of the people of Israel died.[70]

17/ Since their leaders were the wicked priests Hophni and Pinhas, it was at sunset that they fought and were trampled underfoot. And in the night they sent and brought the Ark of the Covenant, reckoning that through the Ark they could vanquish the enemies.[71] They did not know that the God's Ark was disturbed on account of the sins of the lawless priests.[72] When it became light, the enemies engaged (and) fought and they cut down 30,000 men of Israel.[73] And one Israelite man escaped, fled, and came to Eli the priest. He went before[74] him and put earth on his head.[75]

18/ And Eli the priest had taken a stand on a high hill and was watching the road, so that he might see what the nature of the end of the battle might be. When the man who had put earth on his head came, he[76] cried, "Alas!" and said, "Israel is overcome and I alone escaped. Your two sons Hophni and Pinhas were killed."[77]

---

69. Eli's rebuke is described in 1 Sam 2:23-25.

70. In 1 Sam 4:2, about 4,000 men are said to have died in battle against the Philistines. That is, of course, the difference between the two figures given in our text. Then 1 Sam 4:10 speaks of 30,000 casualties which, together with 4:7 makes 34,000. Note that §16 implies that the Philistines' war against Israel was because of Eli's sons' conduct. This is not stated in the Bible.

71. 1 Sam 4:3.

72. This explanatory sentence does not correspond to anything in 1 Sam 4. However, it is in accord with the author's almost magical understanding of the functioning of the Ark.

73. First Samuel 4:10 relates this incident. The nighttime arrival of the Ark and the dawn attack by the Philistines are not specified in First Samuel.

74. Or: to meet.

75. See 1 Sam 4:12.

76. That is, the man.

77. This is related in 1 Sam 4:16-17. There it is said that the Ark is of great concern to Eli, while it is not mentioned at this point in the retelling, but is highlighted in the next section.

8. THE STORY OF THE ARK OF THE COVENANT

19/ Eli said, "What happened to the Ark of the Covenant?" The man said, "They have taken it captive." Then when Eli heard of the capture of the Ark, he hit[78] his head against a stone, fell, broke his back and died.[79]

Indeed, because of the sins of two concupiscent priests 34,000 men died and the Ark went into captivity.

20/ Then,[80] upon whichever land to which they took the Ark, there befell death, there befell famine, there befell locusts, and mice swarmed. Thus, did it do marvels. For no one could harm the Ark of the Covenant for there was great power from[81] it when they worshipped God. And after twenty to [*indecipherable*],[82] they yoked two heifers. And they tied the Ark to a wagon and let (it) go. They set two men as companions and they said, "Go behind the Ark and see to which land it wishes to go." And they did thus.

21/ The heifers took the Ark and came to Jerusalem; it was in the time of the harvest. When the reapers saw the Ark of the Covenant coming, they went to meet it and brought (it) into its former place. And the guards who had come with the Ark returned.

22/ Then all in Jerusalem and all the Israelites went to meet the Ark. They were happy and rejoiced on account of the coming of the Ark. Through that they realized that God was reconciled with them. But the Ark did not do wonders as formerly.[83]

23/ And afterwards a vision of an angel was seen, and they yoked the Ark and departed. And he brought it to Mt. Sinai and it is there up to this day. By day a cloud is shelter around the mountain and no one can find it, and at night, a fiery light shines over it. For it is there invisible to men until the last times.[84]

---

78. Literally: gave.

79. The expression հ պարոցու, i.e., the preposition հ with an instrumental case, is bizarre. The incident is recounted in 1 Sam 4:12–18. There he is sitting by the gate watching the road, and not standing on a high hill. 1 Samuel does not have the stone as the instrument of Eli's death. His stance on a high hill recalls Moses's location in a similar situation according to Exod 17:9–11.

80. The incidents related from here to the end of §22 are included in text 1 in Stone, "Two Stories."

81. Or: through.

82. Presumably a word meaning "cart." The other texts have սայլ, which does not accord with the letters surviving here. The story of the captured Ark is the main subject of *Joshua Text (5), Ark of Testaments*.

83. There is no biblical basis for §§22–25.

84. There is a complex tradition of the hiding of the Temple vessels after the destruction. The idea that the Tent of Meeting and the Ark of the Covenant were hidden in a cave

24/ Indeed, the Ark was a symbol of the church. For just as at that time divine speech took place through it, so now in the church divine speech takes place through the Gospel and the Scripture.

25/ For, just as in that time he counseled through the stone tablet, now the church gives counsels through Scripture, through the Prophets.

For just as from the Ark they ate manna from the holy urn, thus from the church we eat the communion.

---

on Mt. Sinai is already developed in 2 Macc 2:4–5. Its eschatological manifestation is a commonplace.

9. Concerning the Ark of God

Introductory Remarks

Maštocʻ Matenadaran manuscript M9100 is a *Miscellany* and it was copied by the priest Markos in 1686. Its 382 folios contain various pseudepigraphical and other relevant works. In addition to the composition presented here, these include *Book of Esdras*, an Armenian version of the Vulgate of *2 Esdras*,[1] *Story of Gog and Magog, Adam Story 1* and *Adam Story 2*,[2] *Names of the Gems*,[3] *Question*,[4] *Names of the Forefathers* and *Names of the Apostles*,[5] *Concerning Six Millennia*,[6] *The Eleven Periods*,[7] *Names of the Jewels of Aaron's Ephod*,[8] and *Concerning the Periods*.[9] The *Infancy Gospel* follows the text about the Ark on fol. 37r.

Concerning the Ark of God in M6340, 55v–58r is an excerpted form of the beginning and end of a longer Ark text, *Joshua Text (5), Concerning the Story of the Ark of the Testament,* which is preserved in LOB (British Library) MS Egerton 708.[10] Indeed, in my publication of *Concerning the Ark of the Testament* from Egerton 708, variants drawn from M9100 were given. Nonetheless, in view of the numerous texts about the Ark published in this present volume, it seemed worthwhile to give it *in extenso*.[11] However, because quite

---

1. See Michael E. Stone, "The Book of Esdras," *JSAS* 4 (1988): 209–12.
2. Stone, *Armenian Apocrypha Relating to Adam and Eve*, 101–8; 109–13.
3. Michael E. Stone, "An Armenian Epitome of Epiphanius's *De Gemmis*," *HTR* 82 (1982): 467–76.
4. Stone, *Armenian Apocrypha Relating to Adam and Eve*, 109–13; Michael E. Stone, "The Document Called 'Question,'" in *La diffusione dell'eredità classica nell'età tardoantica e medievale: Il "Romanzo di Alessandro" e altri scritti*, ed. Rosa Bianca Finazzi and Alfredo Valvo (Alessandria: Orso, 1999), 295–300.
5. See *Short Catalogue 2*, 869–70.
6. Stone, *Angels and Biblical Heroes*, 34–38.
7. Stone, *Angels and Biblical Heroes*, 38–41.
8. Stone, *Angels and Biblical Heroes*, 22–24.
9. Stone, *Angels and Biblical Heroes*, 38–41.
10. See the list of Ark and Joshua texts given on p. 58.
11. See publication of *Story of the Ark of the Testaments* in Stone, "Two Stories," 257–71.

copious notes on the contents of this work are given in that publication, here I remark briefly only on the most striking traditions. The section numbers of *Joshua Text (5) Ark of Testaments* are given in parentheses following the section numbers assigned to this text, except where they are identical.

The main focus of this document is upon the Ark as repository of supernatural power. The main points of the narrative are:

§§1–2 The construction of the Ark and its contents.

§3 The Ark as a mediator of divine speech.

§§4–5 Wonders of the Ark in the days of Joshua Son of Nun.

§§6–7 The Ark in the days of Eli the High Priest and its vanquishing of the idol Dagon.

§8–10 The Ark in Beth Shemesh. David took it from Kiriath Jearim and brought it to Zion; Solomon placed it in the Temple beneath the altar. Divine speech issued from it.

§11–12 On the Assyrian destruction of the Temple, Jeremiah hid it on Mt. Sinai where it is sheltered by a cloud by day and light by night.

§13 The antichrist will take it from there, open it to taste the manna, and then fire will issue forth and burn him up.

Text

M9100 Title/ Վասն տապանակին Աստուծոյ

/ fol. 35r / 1/ Մովսէս աստուածախօս մարգարէն խրատովն Աստուծոյ արար զտապանակն սուրբ, անփոյթ փայտից Բ. (2) կանկուն երկայն եւ կանկուն ու[12] կէս լայն, եւ կանկուն ու կէս բարձրութիւն տապանակին:

2/ Եւ պատեաց զնա ոսկով սրբով ներքոյ եւ արտաքոյ, / fol. 35v / եւ եդ ի ներքս ի տապանակին զքարեա տախտակոն պատգամացն Աստուծոյ եւ զգաւազանն Ահարոնի, որ ծաղկեաց կանանչ տերեւով եւ Գ. (3) ընկուզով, եւ սափորն ոսկի՛ լի մանանայիւ, եւ բուրվառն պղնձի, որ դարձաւ ոսկի ի ձեռն Ահարոնի:

3/ Եւ եդ Մովսէս զտապանակն ի խորան ժամուն. եւ անդ լինէր Աստուածախօսութիւն ի տապանակէն սրբոյ:

4/ Եւ Յեսու որդին Նաւեա տապանական ցամաքեցոյց զՅորդանան՛ ի խրախոյս ժողովրդեանն Իսրայէլի եւ յահ եւ երկիւղ եւ ի սասանումն քանանացոցն:

---

12. Nonclassical form.

9. CONCERNING THE ARK OF GOD 125

5// fol. 36r / Ի տիպ դարձ ի բնութեանս ի դրախտին եւ ի կորուստ չարեցաւ զաստանայի[13] եւ ամբարիշտ մարդկան: Տապանական էառ Յեսու զերիքով եւ կործտեաց զԼԲ. (32) թագաւորսն: Եւ ամենայն զօրութիւն Իսրայելի ազգին ի հինն:

6/ տապանական լինէր ի յօրինակ խաչին Քրիստոսի, զի Յեսու պատկեր էր Ճշմարտին Յիսուսի եւ սուրբ տապանակն սրբոյ խաչին, Երիքով` դժոխոցն, եւ բռնացեալ թագաւորն ի նմա՛ սատանա:

7/ Եւ յաւուրս Հեղեա քահանային վասն չարեաց որդոց նորա զերեցաւ տապանակն սուրբ այլազգացն, եւ տարան Ազովտոս եւ եդին առ Դագոնայ չաստուածոցն իւրեանց:

8/ Եւ ի վաղիւն տեսին զԴագոն կործանեալ ի վերայ երեսաց իւրոց յերկիր` առաջի տապանակին՝ այլ տեղին գլուխ, եւ այլ տեղի / fol. 36v / զոտսն, եւ այլ տեղի զձեռսն: Եւ մնացեալ էր միայն ողնա[շ]արն Դագոնա, եւ այլ անդամքն ամենայն գրուեալ էին ընդ գետնամէջսն: Վ...պոկ տնա մէջսն:

9 (20b) / Եւ եկաց տապանակն Աստուծոյ ի Բեթսամիւս. {մ}եհար ի ժողովրդենէն Իսրայելի հարուածս մեծամեծս եւ սպան Իսրայելէ ԵՌ. եւ Հ. (5,070) այր:

10 (21) / Իսկ Դաւիթ, յորժամ էառ զերուսաղէմ յերուսացոցն եւ շինեաց զտուրբ Սիոն, եւ եհան զտապանակն ի Կարիաթարիմ եւ բերեալ եդ ի սուրբն Սիոն: Եւ յորժամ Սողոմոն զտապանակն շինեաց, ապա փոխեաց զտապանակ ու<խ>տին[14] Տեառն եւ եդ ի ներքոյ սուրբ սեղանոյն, / fol. 37r / ուր աստուածախօսութիւն լինէր:

11 (22)/ Եւ ի զերեալն Ասորոց զերուսաղէմ, առեալ մարգարէն Երեմիա զտապանակն ուխտին եւ, տարեալ ի Սինեա, եդ ի վէմն ի մէջ երկուց լերանց:

12 / Եւ ի տուրնչեան լինէր ամբ հովանի, եւ լոյս` ի գիշերի: Եւ ոչ ոք գիտէ զտեղին, եւ ոչ ոք տեսանէ զտապանակն, մինչեւ յայտնեցցի ի ժամանակս Ներինն, զոր ինքն առեալ բերէ եւ բանայ առ ի յուտել զմաննային:

13/ Եւ անտի ի տապանակէն ելանէ հուր եւ այրէ զՆեռն. եւ այնու սատակի մարդն անօրէնութեան՝ որդին կորուստեան, ի փառս սատանայի:

---

13. u above q which was apparently written erroneously.
14. Ed. M9100 has, corruptly, ուստին.

Translation

1/ Moses,[15] the prophet who talked with God, by God's counsel made the Ark of pure, imperishable wood. (It was) two cubits long, a cubit and a half wide, and the height of the Ark was a cubit and a half.[16]

2/ And he covered it with pure[17] gold, inside and outside. And he set inside the Ark the stone tablets of the commandments of God, and Aaron's staff which flowered with a green leaf and three nuts, and the golden pitcher full of manna,[18] and the bronze censer which turned into gold in Aaron's hands.

3/ And Moses placed the Ark in the Tent of Meeting.[19] And there, there was divine speech from the holy Ark.

4/ And Joshua the son of Nun dried up the Jordan by means of the Ark to encourage the Children of Israel and for the fear and terror and trembling of the Canaanites.

5/ It turned[20] into the form of their nature[21] in the Garden and into destruction of Satan's wicked ones and of impious men. By means of the Ark Joshua took Jericho and decimated the thirty-two kings. And all the power of the people of Israel is in the old (Ark).

6/ Through the Ark there was a symbol of the cross of Christ. For Joshua was the image of the true Jesus and the holy Ark of the holy cross, Jericho of Hell, and the king captured in it, of Satan.[22]

---

15. This passage also occurs in Galata MS 54 in the Armenian Patriarchate of Constantinople; see Stone, *Abraham*, 12, 80, 84.

16. The dimensions are drawn from Exod 25:10 and 37:1.

17. Or: sacred.

18. On the jar of manna, see the note on this passage in *Joshua Text (5) Ark of Testaments*.

19. Armenian ժամ means "hour, occasion." Here it occurs where Greek has ἡ σκηνὴ τοῦ μαρτυρίου which understands Hebrew מועד to be taken from the stem meaning "witness." The Syriac *zbn'* and the Targum's *zmn'* here are the words for "time," and the Armenian translator has used this meaning; see, for example, Exod 27:21. What is even more significant is that the Armenian Bible has վկայութեան, "of witness." This seems to indicate a Syriac source of this stereotypical translation.

20. That is, humans, through the divine commandment.

21. բնութիւն means basically "nature," but often indicates the body. Here the assertion is that humans' Edenic body is represented through the Ark, and the commandments that it contains.

22. Doubtless the tradition of the Descent into Limbo is referred to here.

7/ And in the days of Eli the priest, on account of his evil sons the holy Ark was taken captive to the Gentiles and they brought it to Azotos (Ashdod). And they placed it by Dagon their god.

8/ And on the next morning they saw Dagon destroyed upon his face on the ground in front of the Ark. His head was in one place, his feet in another, and his hands in one place and only Dagon's backbone remained and all his other limbs were scattered over the center of the floor. *Illegible section title.*

9 (20b)/ And the Ark of God was in Beth Shemesh. It smote great blows upon the children of Israel, and killed 5,070 men.

10 (21)/ Then David, when he took Jerusalem from the Jebusites and built holy Zion, brought the Ark forth from Kiriath Jearim and having brought it, put it in holy Zion. And[23] when Solomon built the {Ark}[24] he moved the Ark of the Lord's covenant there and put it beneath the holy altar, where the speech with God took place.

11 (22)/ And when the Assyrians captured Jerusalem, the prophet Jeremiah took the Ark of the covenant and brought (it) to Sinai, and placed (it) between two mountains.[25]

12/ And by day a cloud was its shade and light by night. And no one knows the place and no one will see the Ark until the times of the antichrist,[26] who will take it and bring it and open it in order to eat the manna.

12 (23)/ And then fire will come forth from the Ark and burn the antichrist. And by that the man of lawlessness, son of destruction will be killed, for the glory of Satan.

---

23. *1 Ark of the Testaments* §21b.

24. This appears to be a corruption, of տաճար "temple" to տապանակ "Ark," probably caused by the latter word's dominance in this text.

25. Jeremiah's role in this matter is already to be found in two ancient works, both extant in Armenian. First, 2 Macc 2:4–6 relates that Jeremiah hid the Temple's furnishings on Mt. Sinai. Second, *Paralipomena Ieremiou* 3:10, 18–19 tells that Jeremiah and Baruch hid the Temple furnishings in the earth.

26. Armenian Ներն *Nern* < *Nero* as the archetypical antichrist figure.

10. Concerning Solomon and the Building of the Temple

Introductory Remarks

This document is preserved on fols. 83v–84v of manuscript M10986, a rich *Miscellany*, copied in the seventeenth century by Xačʻatur *erēcʻ* of unknown provenance. A second copy of it is found in BnF 128, fols. 91v–93.[1] That manuscript was also written by Xačʻatur *erēcʻ* in the seventeenth century. It is likely but not certain that the scribe was the same person. The writing of the two manuscripts is very similar, but not completely identical. They might have been copied at different times of the scribe's life. The writing on M10986 is more restrained in its ascenders and descenders. In addition to *King Solomon and the Temple*, as we shall call it, M10986 contains some other texts of interest,[2] including *Concerning the Prophet Jeremiah* (fols. 27r–31r).

The manuscript is well preserved and inscribed in clear *notrgir* script. The decorated initial letter Ե of the document was not painted in, though an outline was prepared. In addition, last letters of words, or last words of a line are often spaced so as to produce justification up against the vertical right ruling of the columns. Another Solomon text entitled Սքանչելիք տաճարին Սողոմոնի (*Wonders of Solomon's Temple*) is noted in the description of M6617.[3] This does not seem to be the same writing though it might be another copy of *Signs and Wonders of the Temple*, published here from M10945. The corpus of Armenian Solomon texts is large enough to

---

1. Raymond H. Kévorkian et al., *Manuscrits arméniens de la Bibliothèque nationale de France: Catalogue* (Paris: Bibliothèque Nationale and Calouste Gulbenkian Foundation: 1998), 459–64.
2. See *Short Catalogue* 3, 280–82 for a concise description of it. Unfortunately, the images of BnF 128 reached me too late to include its readings here.
3. *Short Catalogue* 2, 358. This additional Temple document is published below on pp. 137–42.

require a monographic treatment, but for the moment, we publish those texts presently available to us.

The building of the Temple by King Solomon as well as his wisdom attracted the attention of Jewish exegetes and storytellers as would be expected, but its significance did not stop there. In Christian and particularly in Moslem circles this king and his feats were also the subject of much speculation and he became the hero of a number of literary works, sometimes connected with the building of the Temple.[4] In Armenian chronological texts the building of Solomon's Temple served as a pivotal happening, marking the end of one historical age and the beginning of another.[5] It was seen as one of those central events that constituted the structure of world history.

The text being presented is made public here for the first time. In addition to it and to the second Temple text published below, in this volume we publish some other texts about King Solomon, his penitence, his magical ring, and his communication with distant lands and with birds. These stories indicate a major emphasis of the role that he played for the Armenians—and it was not solely a paradigmatic one, but was enveloped by an atmosphere of storytelling, wonders, and wisdom sayings. It will be worth considering how such tales of King Solomon may have been influenced by the extensive Solomon legends that developed in Islamic contexts, in addition to the Jewish and Christian traditions.[6]

In Jewish legend, Solomon's building of the Temple became surrounded by an atmosphere of wonderworking, demonology, and miracles.[7] This wonderworking and stress on demons are already evident in the apocryphal work *Testament of Solomon*.[8] The present text, however, is not part of this legendary literature.

---

4. On the figure of Solomon, see Torijano, *Solomon the Esoteric King*.

5. See Stone, *Angels and Biblical Heroes*, 32, 36, etc. Consult the index there s.v. "Solomon" for further examples.

6. Many Solomon stories are gathered in St. John Drelinc Seymour, *Tales of King Solomon* (London: Oxford University Press, 1924).

7. See *JE* 11:438–39. See also Ginzberg, *Legends of the Jews*, 4.125–76, 6.277–303.

8. P. S. Alexander, "Incantations and Books of Magic," in *The History of the Jewish People in the Age of Jesus Christ*, ed. Géza Vermès, Fergus Millar, Martin Goodman, and Emil Schürer (Edinburgh: T&T Clark, 1986), 3.1:342–79; Chester Charlton McCown, *The Testament of Solomon* (Leipzig: Hinrichs, 1922); and Dennis C. Duling, "The Testament of Solomon: Retrospect and Prospect," *JSP* 2 (1988): 87–112. A rich corpus of medieval Solomon legends and traditions was early assembled by Johann A. Fabricius, *Codex Pseudepigraphus Veteris Testamenti* (Hamburg: Liebezeit, 1713), 1.1013–72.

Indeed, it should be remarked that the text I publish here is principally a mosaic of scriptural phrases and verses. Most of these verses are related to King Solomon, either mentioning his name explicitly, or being drawn from works attributed to him. They are sometimes adapted by the author, but often are *literatim* quotations of the Armenian biblical text. The variants from the text of the Armenian Bible have no text-critical significance. The text does not expatiate on the marvellous aspects of Solomon's construction, but rather condenses the more pragmatic biblical record of it. Moreover, the document has a homiletic character. The transition from narrative to homiletic is accomplished, not by treating Solomon paradigmatically, a technique often used, but by developing ideas present in the biblical books of Solomon.

Text

/ fol. 83v / Title/ Վասն Սողոմոնի եւ տաճարի շինութեանն

1/ Եւ արդ ասեցէք, ո՞ որ ի մէնջ կարող[9] է մեծանալ իբրեւ զարքայն Սողոմոն՝ այն, որ զ.Խ. (40) ամ թագաւորեաց ի վերայ Իսրայէլի, Սողոմոն, որ զամենայն թագաւորս հարկատու արար անձին իւրում եւ ընծաբեր:

2/ Սողոմոն, որ ընդ ամենայն երկիր ել համբաւ մեծութեան {բ}[10] նորա եւ իմաստութեան, որ եւ գրեալ է յաւետարանին, «դշխոյն հարաւոյ», ասէ փրկիչն, «եկն ի ծագաց երկրէ՛ լսել զիմաստութիւն Սողոմոնի»:

3/ Եւ դարձեալ ասէ. «Նայեցարուք ընդ շուշանն վայրենի. ասեմ ձեզ եւ ոչ Սողոմոն յամենայն փառս իւր զգեցաւ իբրեւ զմի ի նոցանէ»[11]: Եւ ինքն իսկ ի գիրս իւր ասէ. «Գահաւորակս արար իւր արքայն Սողոմոն ի փայտիցն Լիբանանու:

4/ «Ձիւնն նորա արծաթիս եւ գկունք նորա ոսկիս եւ գձողունս նորա ծիրանիս եւ զմէջն ականակապ տարածեալ»[12]: Եւ յետ այնորիկ ասէ. «Դստերք յերուսաղեմի,[13] ելէք տեսէք զարքայն Սողոմոն եւ

---

9. The manuscript has կարողէ, which we interpret as կարող {ղ} է.

10. The բ, the addition of which would indicate an instrumental ending rather than the genitive we give, is anomalous here. There is a space between it and the end of the word in the manuscript.

11. The text of Armenian Matt 6:28 for this phrase reads: հայեցարուք ի շուշան վայրկենի, i.e., with minor variants.

12. Variant readings in Arm Song 3:10: սիւնս, գձեղունս, ծիրանիս. The -u on գձեղունս and ծիրանիս must have arisen by attraction from արծաթիս.

13. The superfluous յ of յերուսաղեմի makes no sense, and has no biblical support.

10. SOLOMON AND THE BUILDING OF THE TEMPLE   131

զպսակն, որով պսակեաց զնայ մայր իւր յաւուր փեսայութեան իւրոյ
եւ յաւուր յուրախութեան սրտի յիւրոյ»:[14]

5/ Եւ դարձեալ, եթէ կամիս գառաւելությիւն փառաց նորա / fol.
84r / իմանալ, լո՛ւր, պատմեցից քեզ, զոր վասն տաճարին շինութեան,
քան[15] յորժամ սկիզբն արար շինել գտաճարն մեծ եւ զարմանալի,
զան[16] յօրինուածով կացոյց վերակացոյս գործոյն արս երիս հազարք
եւ բարահատա ՁՌս. (80,000), եւ որք զփայտոն հատանէին ի լերինն
Լիբանանու ՃՌ. (100,000), եւ գրաստ բեռնակիրս ՀՌս. (70,000):

6/ Եւ կարգեաց ԲԺ.ան (12) իշխանս ի վերայ երկոտասան ցեղիցն
Իսրայէլի, որպէ{ա}ս գործոյն անպակաս մատակարարէին: Իսկ
կերակուր Սողոմոնի յամենայն յաւուր Հ. (70) քոր նաշի, որ է ամէն
մէկ քոր մոթ քառասուն, եւ արոտական ընտիր իշանց եզինք Ժ. (10)
եւ կովս Ի. (20) եւ ոչճարս[17] Ճ.(100), թող զեղջիւրու եւ զեզունս, եւ զայլ
ազգ եւ ազգ որսերուցք եւ թռչնոց, եւ կամ այլ զանազան խորտիկ, որ
սովոր են առնել մեծատանց, զորս եւ ոչ կարացին պատմագրողքն[18]
ի համար բերել:

7/ Արդ սա, որ այսքան մեծացաւ եւ իմաստնացաւ, տեսեալ հոգով
աշող զիւրաքաւալ կենցաղս եւ զինքն ընդ մահուամբ գրաւեալ, վասն
որոյ գրեալ է այսպէս. «Ունայնութիւն ունայնութեանց, ամենայն ինչ
սնոտի է, եւ ի զուր տանջեցաւ նախատանօք անձն իմ.

8/ Եւ թէ ատից զամենայն արարս իմ, վասն զի թողլոց եմ այժմ,
որ ոչ գիտիցիմ, եւ ոչ գիտիցէ, եթէ իմաստուն լինիցի, եթէ անմիտ, որ
ժառանգելոց է զկնի իմ»:

9/ Եւ արդ որովհետեւ յառաջնոցն եւ վերջնոյն ծանեաք
զունայնութիւն կենցաղոյս, մի յապաղեսցուք դառնալ ի մեղաց եւ
ընթանալ ի ճանապարհս արդարութեան եւ մի խնայեցցուք յինչս
անցաւոր տալ ի ձեռս / fol. 84v / բժշկաց եւ ընդունել ի նոցանէ
պատոռճութիւն հոգոց:

This variant is commonplace. In Song 3:11, the main source of this verse, we read Սիոնի
"of Zion."

14. Variants from the Armenian Bible, Song 3:11: տեսէք] հայեցարուք, յարքայ
and ի պսակն (change engendered by replacement of verb). On the superfluous յ on
յուրախութեան and յիւրոյ, see preceding note.

15. քան may be taken with the Middle Armenian sense of քանզի "when" and քան
յորժամ simply means "when."

16. Read as զայն.

17. Note the sometimes bizarre spelling variants of this manuscript. Earlier in the
present section we find որպէաս for որպէս and here ոչճարս for ոչխարս.

18. ն above line, p.m.

10/ Եւ ո՞յք են բժիշկ: Հոյլք աղքատացն եւ դասք սրբոց եւ այրեացն, վասն զի նոքա զանբժշկելի ախտ եւ զհիւանդութիւն հոգւոց մերոց բժշկեն, նոքա առանց երկիւղի անցուցանեն ընդ խաւարային իշխանութիւնն:

11/ Սոքա զանշիջանելի հուրն, յորում, թէ դարձցուք, այրելոց եմք, շիջուցանեն. նոքա զանմահ որդունսն, որ զմեզ խածատելոց են, մեռուցանեն նոքա զլալ աչացն եւ կրճտել ատամանցն խափանին:

12/ Նոքա բանան մեզ զդուռն դրախտին, զոր մեղօք եւ անհնազանդութեամբ փակեցաք, նոքա զուարթ եւ առանց ամօթոյ կացուցանեն զմեզ առաջի թագաւորին:

13/ Նոքա տան լսելի զերանական բարբառն, երէ՝ «Եկայք, աւրհնեալք հօր իմոյ, զի քաղցեայ եւ ետուք ինձ ուտել, ծարաւեցի եւ արբուցէք ինձ, օտար էի եւ ժողովեցէք զիս, մերկ էի եւ զգեցուցէք ինձ, հիւանդ էի եւ ի բանտի եւ ողորմեցաւորուք ինձ»: Եւ երթիցեն ի կեանսն յաւիտենից:

14/ Ուստի փախուցեալ են ցաւք եւ տրտմութիւնք եւ հեծութիւնք, միշտ յարազուարճ բերկրելով ընդ ամենայն սուրբս եւ տարփողելով քաղցրածայն եղանակաւ զեռահիւսակ սրբասացութիւն երանակի տերութեան եւ միասնական Աստուածութեան, որում փառք իշխանութիւն եւ պատիւ այժմ եւ միշտ եւ յաւիտեանս յաւիտենից. ամէն:

Translation

Title/ Concerning Solomon and the Building of the Temple

1/ And now, say, which of us can be magnified like King Solomon, him who was king of Israel for forty years, Solomon who made all kings pay tribute and bring gifts to him.[19]

2/ Solomon, the renown of whose greatness and wisdom went forth through the whole earth, (concerning) whom it is also written in the Gospel that the Savior said, "The Queen of the South came from the ends of the earth to hear the wisdom of Solomon."[20]

---

19. I.e., to himself.
20. The expression "Queen of the South" occurs in Matt 12:42, Luke 11:31. In the Bible the Armenian word դշխոյն "Queen," and indeed the phrase դշխոյն հարաւոյ "Queen of the South" occur only in those two verses. The "Queen" of Sheba, mentioned in 1 Kgs 10:1 is translated տիկինն. դշխոյս is also the term found in *Questions of the Queen and Answers of King Solomon*, a wisdom work published by Yovsēpʻianc̔, *Uncanonical Books*, 229–32; translation by Jacques Issaverdens (*The Uncanonical Writings of the Old Testament Found in the Armenian Mss. of the Library of St. Lazarus* [Venice: Mekhitarist

10. SOLOMON AND THE BUILDING OF THE TEMPLE

3/ And again it says, "Regard the lily of the field. I say to you, not even Solomon in all his glory was garbed like one of these,"[21] and he himself[22] says in his book, "King Solomon made himself a palanquin from the wood of Lebanon.

4/ "Its pillar<s> are silver and its basin is of gold and its beams are purple and its inside is bejewelled."[23] And after those things he said, "Daughters of Jerusalem,[24] go forth and see King Solomon and the crown with which his mother crowned him on the day of his marriage and on the day of his heart's rejoicing."[25]

5/ And again, if you wish to apprehend his excessive glory, listen! I shall tell you about the building of the Temple, for[26] when he began to build the great and wondrous Temple, having organized it, he set up overseers of the work, 3,000 men, and 80,000 stonecutters,[27] and 100,000 woodcutters in Mount Lebanon, and 70,000 beasts of burden.[28]

Press, 1901], 163–66). On the Syriac text of *Questions of the Queen and Answers of King Solomon*, see Sebastian P. Brock, "The Queen of Sheba's Questions to Solomon. A Syriac Version," *Le Muséon* 92 (1979): 331–45.

Strictly speaking, the Armenian is ambiguous and either "the Savior" or "the Queen of the South" could be the subject of the verb. The context seems to imply taking it as I have here. The hearing about Solomon's wisdom is clearly drawn from 1 Kgs 10:6–8, compare 1 Kgs 4:34 (5:14).

21. An abbreviated form of Matt 6:28–29: "And why are you anxious about clothing? Consider the lilies of the field, how they grow; they neither toil nor spin; yet I tell you, even Solomon in all his glory was not arrayed like one of these."

22. I.e., Solomon.

23. Song 3:10. The text reflects the Armenian version of Song with slight variants: զահատրակ արար իւր Սողոմոն ի փայտից Լիբանանու:

24. This vocative occurs six times in Song of Songs. The continuation of the sentence is taken from Song 3:11 and, indeed, the passage Song 3:9–11 deeply influenced the text here.

25. Song 3:11.

26. Taking քան "than" as corrupt for քանզի "because, for."

27. 1 Kgs 5:15(29).

28. Compare 1 Kgs 5:15(29) "Solomon also had 70,000 burden-bearers and 80,000 hewers of stone in the hill country, 5:16(30) besides Solomon's 3,300 chief officers who were over the work, who had charge of the people who carried on the work." In the MT these numbers are in 5:29 and 5:30. Thus, except for the hewers of wood and the overseers, the numbers of craftsmen accord with those in First Kings. The author of our text understood the "burden bearers" to be beasts of burden, while the biblical text seems to mean human porters.

6/ And he set in order twelve princes over the twelve tribes of Israel[29] so that they might manage the work with nothing lacking.[30] As for Solomon's food: on every day seventy[31] kors of fine flour, and each kor is forty modii.[32] And ten choice oxen from the pasture,[33] and twenty heifers, and one hundred <sheep>[34] besides the deer and the oxen, and other various sorts of venison and fowls, or other various sorts of viands which the grandees were accustomed to prepare,[35] which the historians[36] were unable to reckon.

7/ Now he who became so great and wise, saw[37] with the eyes of the spirit, how easily life is reversed,[38] and that it was taken under the power of death, therefore he wrote thus, "Vanity of vanities, all is in vain[39] and for nothing my soul was tortured with insults."

8/ "And if all the works of my hands will be hated because I am going to abandon (them) now, so that I shall not be known; and who will know whether he who will inherit after me is wise or senseless?"[40]

---

29. 1 Kgs 4:7.
30. 1 Kgs 4:27.
31. Here MT 1 Kgs 4:22(5:2) has "thirty cors of fine flour, and sixty cors of meal." In the Armenian version of 1 Kgs 4:22 it is thirty cors of fine flour and forty cors of meal. In the text being published here these two types of cereal are combined into seventy cors of fine flour, following the Armenian of 1 Kings.
32. The measure kor is biblical, and one kor is forty modii according to Anania of Širak, *On Measures* VII.16; see Michael E. Stone and Roberta R. Ervine, *The Armenian Texts of Epiphanius of Salamis: de mensuris et ponderibus*, CSCO 583 (Leuven: Peeters, 2000), 105 and table 5 on p. 36. The word մոբ does not occur in the dictionaries but there is մոդ "modius" in the published text of Anania. Thus, in the present context մոբ also clearly means "modius."
33. The phrase is ընտիր իշաց եզինք ժ, literally "ten choice oxen of asses"; see n. 35, below.
34. Reading ոչճար as ոչխար "sheep."
35. This list is taken, with some adaptation, from 1 Kgs 4:22–23(5:2-3). The phrase ընտիր իշաց եզինք is obscure, particularly the word իշաց. The word means "ass, donkey, herd of donkeys." The biblical text does not have this word and I can venture no speculation as to its meaning in this context.
36. First Kings does not give the numbers of the creatures mentioned in the latter part of this list.
37. Literally: having seen.
38. Literally: life's easy-turning/reversing, i.e., how easily one's fortune or life may be reversed.
39. Adapted from Qoh 1:2, etc. The latter part of this statement appears in Qoh 2:12, 18–21.
40. Qoh 2:12–13.

9/ And now,[41] because from the beginnings and to the last we have recognized the vanity of this life, do not delay turning away from sins and running in the paths of righteousness and do not have care for transient things, giving (yourselves) into the hands of doctors[42] and receiving from them the health of the soul."

10/ And who are doctors?[43] The crowds of the poor and ranks of saints and of widows are (doctors) because they heal the incurable illness and sickness of our souls.[44] They cause them[45] to pass fearlessly through the dominion of darkness.[46]

11/ If we repent, these extinguish the inextinguishable fire in which we were to be burnt;[47] they kill the undying worms which nibble us; they kill the weeping of eyes and prevent the gnashing of teeth.[48]

12/ They open the gate of the Garden to us, which we shut through sins and disobedience:[49] They set us standing joyous and unshamed before the King.

13/ They make heard the blissful word, "Come, you (who are) blessed by my Father. For I was hungry and you gave me to eat, I was thirsty and you gave me to drink, I was a stranger and you gathered me in, I was naked and you clothed me, I was sick and in prison and you were merciful to me."[50] And they will go to eternal life.

---

41. At this point the author turns away from Solomon, using his example to make a homiletic point about repentance.
42. Metaphorical usage of spiritual leaders as doctors of the soul.
43. I.e., by supplying the needs of the poor, the saints and the widows, humans can live righteously and achieve redemption.
44. I.e., sin.
45. That is, our souls.
46. Compare Col 1:13 which speaks of God delivering humans from the kingdom of darkness. The text here attributes that deliverance to the poor, the saints, and the widows.
47. The syntax is very clumsy here, but this seems to be the meaning. The unquenchable fire and the undying worm are fixed features of Hell, deriving from Isa 66:24, the last verse of the Book of Isaiah.
48. Weeping and gnashing of teeth are a common pair in the Matthew; see Matt 8:12, 13:42, 13:50, 22:13, 24:51 and 25:30. This pair also occurs in Luke 13:28.
49. Adam's sin and disobedience are intended which caused the closing of the gates of the Garden of Eden before Adam and Eve (Gen 3:24).
50. See Matt 25:34–36 is the source of this passage.

14/ From it[51] pains and sadness and wailing have fled, always through glad rejoicing[52] with all the saints and celebrate with sweet voiced tune the threefold sanctification (i.e., the Trishagion) of the Three Person Lordship and unified Deity to whom glory, power, and honor, now and always and forever and ever. Amen.

---

51. I.e., eternal life.
52. The preceding sentence is adapted from Isa 35:10 and 51:11, which both have the words "everlasting joy shall be upon their heads; / they shall obtain joy and gladness, / and sorrow and sighing shall flee away."

11. Signs and Wonders of the Temple

Introductory Remarks

This short text is a list of wondrous aspects of the Temple in Jerusalem and miracles that took place in it. It occurs in two recensions. One is in manuscript M5933, fols. 27r–27v. The manuscript is a *Miscellany* of the fourteenth century. According to the titles of works listed in the *Catalogue*, this appears to be the only text found in it of possible interest for the present volume.[1]

A second recension of this text occurs in M1495, fol. 137r, col. ii. This manuscript is described in *General Catalogue* 4:1431–42. It, too, is a *Miscellany* copied in Constantinople in 1684. The manuscript contains several parts and this document occurs in a corpus of various texts. The text, numbered 8 in the catalogue, occurs on fol. 137r. Its text differs in many respects from that in M5933, being more expansive. However, the enumeration of the wonders is in the same order in both manuscripts. M1495's wording is further from the Hebrew source than M5933 and at no point does it seem to be more original. I have elected to give separate editions of these two text forms.

The list of wonders in M5933 is followed by a concluding section that connects the signs and wonders listed to the Second Temple, adding a prooftext drawn from Psalms at its end. I judge it possible that this final passage was added to the list by the Armenian tradent. This view is based on literary grounds and there is nothing in the text of this additional passage to indicate the language or authorship of its original.

In Rabbinic literature, indeed, there are texts referring to wonders that took place in the Temple. One of the best known occurs in the Mishnaic treatise 'Abot 5:7,[2] where a list of ten miracles that took place in the Temple is set forth. Of eight miracles included in the Armenian list, seven are identical with miracles enumerated in the list in *m. 'Abot* 5:7. Moreover, the Armenian

---

1. *Short Catalogue* 2, 214.
2. "'Abot" means "fathers." This treatise is also called *Ethics of the Fathers*, and occurs in the Jewish prayer book, since a chapter is read each Sabbath afternoon in the summer.

text does not enumerate the miracles in a random order nor does it follow *m. 'Abot* line for line. Instead the miracles occur in three groups within each of which the sequence is the same as the Mishnah's. Immediately below I give a translation of the Mishnaic list, indicating the place of the corresponding miracle in the Armenian text by a number in parentheses, thus "(=N)." Moreover, though the seventh Armenian miracle is unparalleled in *m. 'Abot* it is not an invention of the Armenian tradition but instead is to be found in the allied Rabbinic treatise, *'Abot de Rabbi Nathan (ARN)*. Finally, it should be observed that the concluding passage attributes these wonders to the Second Temple although the Rabbinic tradition is not specific as to their attribution.

The mishnaic text reads:[3]

Ten miracles were wrought for our fathers in the Temple:

1. no woman miscarried from the scent of the holy flesh;
2. (= 1) the holy flesh never became putrid;
3. (= 2) no fly was seen in the slaughter house;
4. no unclean accident ever befell the High Priest on the Day of Atonement;
5. (= 6) the rain never quenched the fire of the wood-pile on the altar;
6. (= 7) neither did the wind overcome the column of smoke that arose therefrom;
7. (= 3) nor was there ever found any disqualifying defect on the omer, or in the two loaves (on Shavuot), or in the showbread;
8. though the people stood closely pressed together, they found ample space to prostrate themselves;
9. (= 4) never did a serpent or scorpion injure anyone in Jerusalem;
10. (= 5) nor did any man say to his fellow, The place is too narrow for me to lodge overnight in Jerusalem.

Clearly the Armenian text is based on the Mishnah's list or on a closely allied form of it.[4] As to content, the list recorded both in M5933 and M1495 enumerates only eight wonders, while *m. 'Abot* includes two further items. Both the omitted items deal with bodily functions: miscarriage and involuntary seminal emission. Only one of the eight wonders, no. 8 in the Armenian list, does not occur in *m. 'Abot* 5:7. As noted above, that wonder is not an Armenian invention and it occurs and is paralleled in *'Abot de Rabbi Nathan*

---

3. I introduce numbers for the miracles to facilitate the discussion.
4. Judah Goldin, *The Fathers according to Rabbi Nathan*, YJS 10 (New Haven: Yale University Press, 1955).

(*ARN*), which is another recension of the material included in *m. 'Abot*.[5] This eighth wonder reads, "when an earthenware vessel broke, the fragments disappeared on the spot."[6]

This document is, therefore, an Armenian translation of a rabbinic source and it is the second such text to come to light.[7] The different form in M1495 indicates that it has had a literary history in Armenian.

The question arises of how this material reached the Armenians. Its origins must lie in Jewish Hebrew sources. Since *m. 'Abot* is included in the Jewish prayer book, it was readily available wherever Jews and Armenians resided side by side. Although the knowledge of *m. 'Abot*'s list may have been easily accessible, familiarity with *ARN* was far less so. In 1970 I argued that the translated *Baraitha* passage from the Babylonian Talmud might have been transmitted by a direct oral translation,[8] but this does not seem likely in the present instance. As distinct from the Baraitha, the close rendering in M5933 gives the impression of being a literary translation from an unknown source very similar to but not identical with either *m. 'Abot* or *ARN*.

It remains only to add here that the inscriptions in the medieval Jewish cemetery in Ełegis show that at least one community of knowledgeable Jews did exist in medieval Armenia.[9] Of course, outside Armenia, Armenian and Jewish diasporas were widespread in the lands around the Mediterranean. The interest in and preservation of this list are another instance of the affinity of Armenian scholasticism for lists associated with the contents of the Bible. Its significance for both tradition history and the history of Jewish-Armenian relations must await further detailed investigation.[10]

The last, concluding passage in M5933 in this text is not paralleled in either *'Abot* or *'Abot de Rabbi Nathan*, and it is impossible to tell on internal grounds whether it is of Jewish or Armenian origin. It is noteworthy, though, that it refers to the Second Temple. On the other hand, the text in M1495 mentions Solomon's Temple in its heading and so affiliates this small text

---

5. See Goldin, *Fathers*, xviii–xx.

6. Goldin, *Fathers*, 146. In n. 21 he suggests that this avoided cluttering the Sanctuary.

7. Michael E. Stone, "An Armenian Translation of a Baraitha in the Babylonian Talmud," *HTR* 63 (1970): 151–54.

8. I published this passage in Stone, "An Armenian Translation of a Baraitha," 151–54.

9. Michael E. Stone and David Amit, "Report on the Survey of a Medieval Jewish Cemetery in Eghegis, Vayots Dzor Region, Armenia," *JJS* 53 (2002): 66–106; Stone and Amit, "The Second and Third Seasons of Research at the Medieval Jewish Cemetery in Eghegis, Vayots Dzor Region, Armenia," *JJS* 57 (2006): 99–135.

10. Observe that the two wonders relating to subjects of impurity and bodily functions are omitted from the Armenian list: wonders nos. 1 and 4 of the list in *'Abot*.

140 ARMENIAN APOCRYPHA RELATING TO BIBLICAL HEROES

with the quite extensive Solomon literature, discussed in the present volume in connection with texts 10 and 12.

Text

M5933, fol. 83v	M1495, fol. 137r
Title/ Իսկ նշանք[11] եւ սքանչելիք տաճարին էին այսորիկ։	Վասն սքանչելեաց Սողոմոնի տաճարին.
Ա.[12] Առաջին. զի մին ոչ բնաւ հոտէր անդ։	Ա. Առաջին որ մին մատաղացն ոչ հոտէր.
Բ. Եւ ոչ երբեք երեւեցաւ ճանճ, թէպէտ հեղեալ լինէր[13] այնչափ արիւնն։	Բ. Երկրորդ. որ ճանճ եւ մժիխ ոչ լինէր անդ. որչափ որ արիւն թափէր.
Գ. Եւ ոչ ապականէր հացն առաջաւորութեան։	Գ. Երրորդ. զի հաց սեղանոյն անապական մնայր. որքան եւ մնայր անդ.
Դ. Եւ ոչ երբեք փասեաց ատճ եւ կարիճ յերուսաղէմ։	Դ. Չորրորդ. զի օձ եւ կարիճ ոչ երեւէր անդ. ոչ ի մէջ տաճարին. եւ ոչ ի յերուսաղէմ քաղաքի.
Ե. Եւ ոչ ոք ասաց, թէ՛ «նեղ է ինձ տեղիս յերուսաղէմ»։	Ե. Հինգերորդ. զի ոչ ոք ասէր թէ նեղ է տեղ իմ ի մէջ տաճարին. եւ թէ որքան մարդ որ լինէր անդ.
Զ. Եւ ոչ երբեք շիջուցին անձրեւք զհուրն, որ այրէր ի տուէ եւ ի գիշերի։	Զ. Վեցերորդ. զի հուր տաճարին էր անշիջելի. ոչ անձրեւ եւ ոչ ճիւն կարէր զնա շիջուցանել տիւ եւ գիշեր.
Է. Եւ ոչ յաղթեաց հողմն զճուխն, որ իբրեւ զսիւն ելանէր ի հրոյն։	Է. Եօթներորդ. ծուխն դիզացեալ վերանայր յերկինս իբրեւ զսիւն. եւ ոչ կարաց գրուել զնա բռնութիւն հողմոյ.
Ը.[14] Եւ զփշրեալ անօթս կաւեղէնս կլանէր երկիր։	Ը. Ութերորդ. փշխրանք անօթիցն երկիր կլանէր.
Այս ամենայն նշանքս դադարեցան խ. (40) ամ յառաջ քան զաւերումն տաճարին եւ բա/ fol. 27v /դարին ի ձեռն Տիտոսի եւ Վասպանոսի ըստ սաղմոսին, որ ասէ. «Նշանս մեք ինչ ոչ տեսաք»։	

---

11. Erased եւ follows.
12. These numbers are repeated in the outer margin.
13. ր above line, p.m.
14. The number Ը is not in the margin, but in the text.

11. SIGNS AND WONDERS OF THE TEMPLE

Translation

A M5933, fol. 83v	B M1495, fol. 137r
The miracles[15] and wonders of the Temple were these:	Concerning the wonders of Solomon's Temple:
1. The meat there was never putrid.	1. First, that the meat of the sacrifices was not putrid.
2. And no fly was ever seen, even though so much blood was poured out.	2. Second, that there was no fly or gnat there however much blood flowed.
3. And the show-bread did not become moldy.[16]	3. Third, that the bread of the altar remained without mold, however long it remained there.
4. And no snake or scorpion ever did harm in Jerusalem.	4. Fourth, that no snake or scorpion was seen there, neither within the Temple, nor in the city of Jerusalem.
5. And nobody said, "This place is narrow for me in Jerusalem."	5. Fifth, that nobody said, "My place is narrow in the Temple," however many people were there.
6. And rains never extinguished the fire that burned day and night.[17]	6. Sixth, that the fire of the Temple was inextinguishable; neither rain nor snow was able to extinguish it by day or by night.
7. And the wind never overcame the smoke which ascended from the fire like a pillar.	7. Seventh, the smoke having accumulated, rose to the heavens like a pillar and the might of the wind could not scatter it.
8. And the earth swallowed up broken pottery vessels.	8. Eighth, the earth swallowed up the sherds of vessels.
All these wonders stopped forty years before the destruction of the Temple and the city by Titus and Vespasian, in accordance with the Psalm which says, "We did not see any of our wonders."[18]	

When the texts of A and B are compared against the text of the Mishnah (=M), it becomes clear that while A has certain small glosses that are not present in M, such as in 6 = M 5 where "day and night," B further glosses A, but none of its additions to A have the support of M. So, in the same sign 6, it interpolates

---

15. So I translate the Armenian նշան which basically means "sign."
16. This sign is more complex in *m. 'Abot*.
17. "on the altar" *m. 'Abot*.
18. Ps 74(73):9. The phrase is drawn *literatim* from the Armenian Psalter.

a repititous first clause "that the fire of the Temple was inextinguishable" and in the second clause it adds "nor snow" to "rain."

In two signs B interpolates "the Temple" where it is in neither A nor M. So in sign 4 it adds the Temple to "Jerusalem" and in sign 5, it replaces Jerusalem with the Temple.

12. King Solomon: Four Short Texts

Introductory Remarks

In his collection of Armenian pseudepigrapha published in 1896, Sargis Yovsēpʻianc̒ presents three short texts concerning King Solomon.[1] He dubbed the first of these *Concerning King Solomon*, the second he named *Concerning the Writings of Solomon I* and the third short Solomon text he called *Concerning the Writings of Solomon II*. The Armenian Solomonic corpus known to date is wider than this and also includes a sapiential work, *Questions of the Queen and the Answers of King Solomon*,[2] which was also published by Yovsēpʻianc̒ and translated by Issaverdens.[3] Since their days, the Syriac original from which *Questions of the Queen* was translated into Armenian has been discovered and edited.[4] Thus, the total number of Solomon texts published by Yovsēpʻianc̒ is actually four.[5]

I republished part of Yovsēpʻianc̒'s Solomonic corpus in 1978 based on the oldest witness available to me, thirteenth-century manuscript M1500, and adding collations of several more copies.[6] During the years since, I have come across a number of further copies of certain of these documents, as well as the titles of Solomonic works whose exact contents are still unknown, but which seem likely also to belong to this body of texts. M10986 preserves text

---

1. *Concerning King Solomon* is in Yovsēpʻianc̒, *Uncanonical Books*, 228–29 and *Paralipomena* under the title *Concerning the Writings of Solomon* occurs in Yovsēpʻianc̒, 232–33 and *Concerning the Writings of Solomon II* in Yovsēpʻianc̒, 233–34. Issaverdens (*Uncanonical Writings*) translates them on pp. 161–62, 167–68, and 169–70 respectively.
2. On question and answer texts, see the excursus above p. 9–11.
3. Yovsēpʻianc̒, *Uncanonical Books*, 229–32; Issaverdens, *Uncanonical Writings*, 163–66.
4. Brock, "Queen of Sheba's Questions," 331–45.
5. In their various copies, texts 1, 2 and 3 add or omit small units of text. The fluidity of these compositions is noteworthy. Stone, "Penitence of Solomon," reprinted in Stone, *Selected Studies*, 58–76. On this authorial tendency, see Stone, *Ancient Judaism*, 151–71.
6. Stone, "Concerning the Penitence," 1–19.

no. 10 published above which is entitled *Concerning Solomon and the Building of the Temple*. That text is made public in the present volume and adds a fifth member to the published Armenian Solomonic corpus.[7]

On fols. 132r–133r of manuscript M4618, which contains many apocryphal texts,[8] there occurs a group of four short texts concerning King Solomon. Two of them, the first, *Concerning King Solomon* and the second, *Concerning the Writings of Solomon I* (under the title *Paralipomena*) are copies of the first two of the short texts initially published by Sarkis Yovsēpʻianc'.[9] Manuscript M4618 does not include Yovsēpʻianc''s third short Solomon text, titled *Concerning the Writings of Solomon II*. In addition to these two writings, M4618 also preserves two further short Solomon texts which I publish here for the first time. They constitute the sixth and seventh works of Armenian Solomon pseudepigrapha. In addition, in this section I present here a second recension of Text 1 taken from manuscript M1500 which, having been copied before 1281 CE[10] is notable for its relative antiquity.

The Armenian Solomon Works and Their Publication to Date

With this background in mind, I choose to refer to these works as Solomon Texts 1–7, in accordance with the following list:

(1) *Concerning King Solomon* in two recensions : 1 in M4618 first published here and 1.1 in M1500[11]
(2) *Concerning the Writings of Solomon I*
(3) *Concerning the Writings of Solomon II* or *Paralipomena* (Yovsēpʻianc')
(4) *Questions of the Queen and Answers of King Solomon* (Yovsēpʻianc')
(5) *Concerning Solomon and the Building of the Temple* (M10986 published above)
(6) *King Solomon's Ring* (M4618 published here)
(7) *Solomon and the Bubu Bird* (M4618 published here)

Allied with this tradition is text no. 11, *Signs and Wonders of the Temple*, published here.

---

7. See pp. 128–36 above.
8. For a more detailed discussion of this manuscript, see pp. 7–8 above.
9. *Concerning King Solomon* is in Yovsēpʻianc', *Uncanonical Books*, 228–29 and *Paralipomena* under the title *Concerning the Writings of Solomon* occurs in Yovsēpʻianc', 232–33; Issaverdens (*Uncanonical Writings*) translates them on pp. 161–62 and 167–68 respectively.
10. This is given here in full, because the layout of my 1978 article is confusing.
11. The references given here are to the chief witness in each case.

More works may well exist in manuscripts.¹² The legendary stories about the building of the Temple are discussed in connection with *Solomon Text 5* (M10986), which is published above in the present book; see text no. 10, *Concerning Solomon and the Building of the Temple*.¹³ Following, in the introductory remarks to *Solomon Texts 6 and 7* (M4816), I discuss briefly the legendary, exorcistic, and apotropaic features of the Solomon tradition. The further study of Armenian Solomon literature would be a substantial project in its own right. It would involve publishing and investigating the development of all the Solomon texts and traditions surviving in Armenian as well as material on Solomon embedded in magical, apotropaic, hymnic, exegetical, and homiletic writings, and in iconography, as far as such as exists.

The three short documents, Solomon Texts 1–3, published by Yovsēpʻianc' are the following. English translations of these three texts are to be found in Issaverdens¹⁴ and in my article of 1978.¹⁵

Text 1, First Recension: Վասն Սողոմոնի Արքային (Concerning King Solomon):

Yovsēpʻianc', *Uncanonical Books*, 228–29. He did not have the old copy of the text of *Concerning the Writings of Solomon I* preserved in M1500 (before 1282) at his disposal where it is called *Paralipomena* "Things Left Out." Norayr Bogharian published another copy of this work drawn from J2558, fols. 184r–v. MS J2558 is a Bible written in Mokkʻ and Van in 1615.¹⁶

---

12. Text 2 occurs in J1455, perhaps in J1761, in M43 42v–43, M10561 *Short Catalogue* 3, 116: Յաղագս գրեանցն Սողոմոնի Երանելոյն Եփրեմ ասէ այսպէս ..., "Concerning the Writings of the Blessed Solomon. Ephrem says thus...." There are also connections with St. Ephrem in text no. 7, *Brief History of Joshua*, §63, text no. 12, *King Solomon, Text 2*, and text no. 17, *The Ninevehites* (pp. 204–6). See also, Stone, *Armenian Apocrypha Relating to Adam and Eve*, 153–54: *Abel and Other Pieces* 3.1 concerning the Harrowing of Hell, 5.4 on the sign of Cain. See also Stone, "Penitence of Solomon," 4–5.

13. *Short Catalogue* 3, 280–82 briefly describes this manuscript.

14. Issaverdens, *Uncanonical Writings*, 158.

15. Stone, "Penitence of Solomon," 1–19.

16. See Norayr Bogharian, Մայր ցուցակ ձեռագրաց Սրբոց Յակոբեանց (*Grand Catalogue of St. James Manuscripts*) (Jerusalem: St. James Press, 1973), 5:253–54; Chahé Adjémian (Ajamian), *Grand Catalogue des manuscrits arméniens de la Bible*, Bibliothèque arménienne de la Fondation Calouste Gulbenkian (Lisbon: Gulbenkian Foundation, 1992), 644.

Text 1.1, Second Recension: Ի մեկնութենէ Մնացորդաց (From the Commentary of the Paralipomena)

This text, a differing recension of Solomon Text 1 from that published by Yovsēpʻianc‛, is preserved in Matenadaran M1500, fol. 359v and I first published it in 1978.[17] M1500 is an important codex that often preserves very significant textual witnesses to the Bible and Apocrypha.[18] The manuscript is described in detail by Adjémian (Ajamian),[19] and by A. Kēoškeryan and Y. Kʻeōsēyan.[20]

The Armenian word մնացորդ here translated "Paralipomenon" means literally "remainder, something left out."[21] In the plural it is the translation of παραλειπόμενα as in the Greek title of the Book of Chronicles. The Canon List assembled by Mxitʻar Ayrivanecʻi (1222–1307) includes a book named 3 Paralipomena.[22]

Mxitʻar Ayrivanecʻi was the copyist of M1500 (1271–1288), a great *Miscellany* that contains, *inter alia*, a whole Bible. Mxitʻar wrote this copy of the Bible to accord his Canon List mentioned above. In his copy of the Bible some short works occur following 2 Paralipomena (that is, 2 Chronicles) in the position of "3 Paralipomena" in his Canon List. One is titled "Things left out of the Paralipomena," that is, "historical" items not included in the Book of Chronicles. That work is composed of 2 Chr 36:1–23 and the *From the Commentary on the Paralipomena* that is, the present Solomonic text.[23] In addition, the word "Paralipomena" recurs in the titles found in various manuscript copies of the first two of the three Solomonic works published by Yovsēpʻianc‛, that is, Solomon Texts 1 and 2.[24]

---

17. Stone, "Penitence of Solomon," 8–10.
18. This is evident, for example, in the editions of *4 Ezra* and *Testaments of the Twelve Patriarchs*. See the discussions in Michael E. Stone, *The Armenian Version of IV Ezra*, UPATS 1 (Missoula, MT: Scholars Press, 1979), 10–15 and Stone and Hillel, *Armenian Version of the Testaments of the Twelve Patriarchs*, 13–27.
19. Adjémian, *Grand Catalogue des manuscrits*, 63–70.
20. *General Catalogue* 4, 1449–62.
21. As, of course, does its Greek original, παραλειπόμενον.
22. Michael E. Stone, "Armenian Canon Lists III: The Lists of Mechitar of Ayrivankʻ (c. 1285)," *HTR* 69 (1976): 289–300.
23. On this issue see Stone, "Penitence of Solomon," 1–2.
24. Stone, "Penitence of Solomon," 3–4.

The word "Paralipomena" is also found in the titles other apocryphal texts.²⁵ Thus, for example, the first verse of the Adam apocryphon, *Death of Adam*, reads: "but in the history/narrative of the Paralipomena of the Greeks it is found to be written thus concerning the Protoplasts."²⁶ In Yovsēpʻianc'ʼs collection, the title of Solomon Text 3 reads "From the Books of the Paralipomena which I found in the books of the Greeks,"²⁷ resembling the title of *Death of Adam*. In J2558, fol. 182r the title of *Solomon Text 2* is: Ի մնացորդաց մնացորդէն զոր բազմաջան յուզմամբ հազիւ կարացի գտանել, "From the Paralipomenon of the Paralipomena, which I was barely able to find with laborious trouble."²⁸ These titles seem to imply the existence of some *Palaea*-like document from which these apocryphal narratives were taken, though there is no proof of that nor have Greek originals of such a document come to light.²⁹

Solomon Texts 1 and 1.1 are reproduced here in a synoptic edition. The translations of all documents given here are new.

Solomon Text 2: Վասն գրեանցն Սողոմոնի (Concerning the Writings of Solomon I)

This is the title of *Solomon Text 2* published by Yovsēpʻianc' on pp. 232–33.³⁰ The same text, entitled "*Paralipomena*" also appears in M4618, and that copy is transcribed and translated here. We also have noted a copy in J2558, a

---

25. Note the use of this term in the title of the Greek apocryphal work, Paraleipomena Ieremiou (= *4 Baruch*). In M1500 the title of *Paralipomena Ieremiou* is Ի մնացորդաց զոր գտի ի զիրս Հոռոմոց *From the Paralipomena which I found in the Book(s) of the Greeks*. See Michael E. Stone, "Some Observations on the Armenian Version of the Paralipomena of Jeremiah," *CBQ* 35 (1973): 47–59, reprinted in Michael E. Stone, ed., *Selected Studies in the Pseudepigrapha with Special Reference to the Armenian Tradition*, SVTP 9 (Leiden: Brill, 1991), 77–89. These repeated references made in Mxitʻar's Bible make it plausible that he thought that a Greek *Paralipomena* (distinct from biblical Chronicles) existed.

26. Michael E. Stone, "The Death of Adam: An Armenian Adam Book," *HTR* 59 (1966): 283–91 and "Concerning the Death of Adam," in Stone, *Patriarchs and Prophets*, 15–31.

27. See Stone, *Patriarchs and Prophets*, 19.

28. Bogharian, *Grand Catalogue*, 8:253–54.

29. One wonders also about the attribution of copies of certain of these texts to St. Ephrem, the most famous Syriac Church Father; see n. 12 above.

30. An English translation is given in Issaverdens, *Uncanonical Writings*, 167–68.

Bible, written in Mokkʻ and Van in 1615[31] and another in J562, p. 490, *Epistles of N. Šnorhali*.[32]

Text 3: Յաղագս գրեանցն Սողոմոնի (Concerning the Writings of Solomon II):

This text, under the title *Concerning the Writings of Solomon II* is a variant form of *Solomon Text 2* in our list above. To minimize confusion, we preserve the name given by Issaverdens.[33]

Solomon Text 3 was published by Yovsēpʻiancʻ, 233–34 from Venice V57, a religious miscellany. See also Bogharian who printed the text from J1455, *Poetic Collection*, 1622, fol. 122v;[34] and it occurs in M10561 of the seventeenth century fols. 90a–91a.[35] It is not included in M4618, which is being presented here and so no new edition is given. It also occurs in J2558, Bible, Mokkʻ and Van, 1615;[36] and also in J562, *Epistles of S. N. Šnorhali*, p. 491.[37]

The Present Edition

Maštocʻ Matenadaran manuscript M4618 is a *Miscellany*, composed of parts of several manuscripts of the late sixteenth and seventeenth centuries.[38] It preserves the texts of a number of apocryphal works, certain of which have already been published, while others are included in the present volume for the first time. These include: text no. 3, *The Construction of Noah's Ark* and the manuscript is discussed in the introductory remarks to that text; text no. 5, *Abraham and the Idols*; and text no. 7, *Brief History of Joshua*. In the present section, I give an edition and translation of the group of Solomonic texts in M4618, and notes on them. The texts of the two Solomon documents, which are copies of works in Yovsēpʻiancʻ's collection and have been discussed in my

---

31. Bogharian transcribed it in *Grand Catalogue*, 8:254; see further Adjémian, *Grand Catalogue des manuscrits*, 644. Late in the day, a copy of *Appendix* I in M10561, fols. 90–91 came to my attention.

32. Bogharian, *Grand Catalogue* 3:71.

33. Issaverdens, *Uncanonical Writings*, 169.

34. Bogharian, *Grand Catalogue*, 5:14.

35. Malkhasyan, *Catalogue*, 3.116.

36. Bogharian, *Grand Catalogue* 8:254; Adjémian, *Grand Catalogue des manuscrits*, 644.

37. Bogharian, *Grand Catalogue* 3:76.

38. See for a fuller description of this manuscript, the introductory remarks to text no. 3 *Construction*.

own older study, will be presented diplomatically. I note only major divergences from the published texts. Any changes I introduce into the text are signalled by pointed brackets.

The third text in M4618 is entitled *Solomon's Ring* and the fourth, *Solomon and the Bubu Bird*. Both are narratives showing King Solomon's powers. They are discussed in the introductory remarks below.

Solomon Texts 1 and 2

The section division introduced into Solomon Text 1 follows that in Stone, "Concerning the Penitence" and I have treated the other documents similarly.[39] Of the textual material found there, manuscript M4618 contains sections 3/ to 12/. As noted in my study of 1978, the texts that deal with Solomon's sin and repentance are often composed of different combinations of very similar or identical literary or tradition units, especially at the start and end. This appears to be an example of a textual cluster, a phenomenon that has been discussed recently.[40] Though the documents share much text, there seems no way of establishing clear directions of literary relations between them. This is one of the signal characteristics of textual clusters.

These documents deal with the apparent tension between the proverbially wise King Solomon and his marriage to an unconscionable number of wives and concubines, which led him to idolatry.[41] This conundrum is resolved by constructing a repentance story that, as we shall see, is not completely clear. Apparently, this story also aims to reconcile the biblical record that Solomon wrote three thousand proverbs[42] with the fact that we have only three biblical books surviving attributed to king Solomon.[43]

Solomon Text 2 (Yovsēpʻianc̣, *Uncanonical Books*, 232–33) also deals with Solomon's many wives and concubines, but more compactly than Text 1. It then proceeds to resolve the same issue raised by 1 Kgs 4:32, which speaks of Solomon writing three thousand proverbs, chiefly about natural phenomena, and the contrast between this large number and the three surviving books

---

39. Yovsēpʻianc̣, *Uncanonical Books*, 228 gives no division into sections for Solomon Texts 1–3. I introduced such for ease of reference.
40. Stone, *Ancient Judaism*, 151–71.
41. Solomon's idolatry in the context of his wives is related in 1 Kgs 11:4. The theme of wives leading a man into idolatry is also picked up in *Hezekiah and Manasseh,* text no. 15 in this volume, §§ 8–12.
42. 1 Kgs 4:32.
43. A fourth Solomonic work in the Armenian Bible is *Wisdom of Solomon*. On Solomon writings, see Torijano, *Solomon the Esoteric King*.

attributed to Solomon, Proverbs, Song of Songs, and Ecclesiastes.[44] Unlike some Rabbinic treatments of Solomon's writings, it does not remark explicitly on the three protocanonical Solomonic works. Moreover, it treats the question that could arise from Prov 25:1, which speaks of Solomon's proverbs copied by the companions of Hezekiah. These were, *Solomon Text 2* claims, part of the three thousand proverbs that were not burnt by his chamberlain and were hidden.

There are number of other works related to Solomon noted in manuscript catalogues, but their exact identification among Solomon Texts 1–3 is unclear. The chief difficulty in identifying texts that I have not autopsied is that the titles of these closely connected works are often very similar and, barring cases where a catalogue gives *incipits* and not always then, it is impossible to distinguish between them using the information included in catalogue records. For that reason, I doubt the wisdom of giving here any detailed information additional to that which I published in 1978.

Here I provide the following texts:

(1) A normalized transcription of Solomon Text 1.1 from M1500 in a synoptic edition with Yovsēpʻeancʻ's text.
(2) A diplomatic edition of the four texts in M4618 with some of which a number of other manuscripts are collated, all rather later than M1500.
(3) Critical apparatuses for Solomon Texts 1 and 2, and translations and notes.

Following Texts 1–2, there are two other documents included in M4618, and they are transcribed and published here for the first time. Each is furnished with some introductory remarks and comments.

Text 1.1: Concerning King Solomon

M4618 and M1500—Synoptic Edition
Manuscripts: Yovsēpʻiancʻ's text is drawn, so Issaverdens says, from V280/10, Bible, 1418–1422, Xlatʻ[45] and from V1260/1095 *Epistles of Nersēs*

---

44. Or four, counting *Wisdom of Solomon*. Shahé Ananyan, "La Figure de Salomon et les livres sapientiaux dans la tradition arménienne," *REArm* 34 (2012): 29–39 discusses the theme of Solomon's repentance in a number of varied sources.

45. See Issaverdens, *Uncanonical Writings*, 158 for details.

12. KING SOLOMON: FOUR SHORT TEXTS

Šnorhali;[46] Text 1 is also to be found in J652, *Epistles of Nersēs Šnorhali*, on p. 490;[47] and most of text 1 occurs in M4618, 132a and that text from M4618 is published below. This double occurrence seems to indicate that there is some connection between this text and Nersēs Šnorhali's epistolary, at least in its transmission.

The consistent orthographic peculiarities of manuscript M4618, which are listed in *Sodomites: Construction*, are normalized in the present edition.[48] We present *King Solomon Text 1* in two columns. M1500 is closer to Yovsēpʻianc‘'s text of §§1–2 and to M4618's text in §§3–11. Although the italicized plusses in the translation are not many, there are rather a lot of other lesser variations between the manuscripts not reflected in the English. The synoptic presentation enables these to be seen clearly. Mxit‘ar of Ayrivank‘ (Gełard) being a learned man, he also transmitted a second form of part of this document which he found "elsewhere," presumably in a manuscript other than his exemplar. This text is given after the end of §11 below.

Manuscript M1500 always uses the following orthographies, which are not recorded in the critical apparatus, and which I regularized in the text I print below:

— ե for եա
— ե for է
— ա for այ
— n for նյ
— ւ for ու preceding a vowel

in nouns ending in ի, the declined forms end in –նյ, –նյք, etc. and are regularized to –ւնյ, –ւնյք, etc.

---

46. Barseł Sarghissian, vol. 1 of *Grand Catalogue des manuscrits arméniens de la bibliothèque des Pp. Mekhitaristes de Saint-Lazare* (Venice: Mekhitarist Press, 1914), Bible 10/MS 280 (1418–1422) described in cols. 99–116. The Solomon text is discussed on col. 105 and there Sarghissian suggests that it was known to Grigor Narekac‘i (tenth century) and cited in *Narek* 48:6. This seems to quite possible, especially in the reference to his tears filling his palace, though that section of Narek evidences other traditions as well.

This manuscript is Venice no. 10 and Ajémian no. 258; note that V1260 is *Catalogue* no. 1095, and in the description of that manuscript in the *Catalogue*, nothing is said about these Solomonic fragments. We have not been able to autopsy these manuscripts, and the occurrence of these short fragments from them is not necessarily disproved by the absence of a catalogue listing.

47. Bogharian, *Grand Catalogue*, 3:76.
48. See p. 7–9 of this volume.

Synoptic Text

Section division is maintained consistently throughout.

M1500	M4618
Title/ Ի մեկնութենէ Մնացորդաց	Title / / fol. 132r / Վասն Սողոմոնի արքայի որդւոյ Դաւթի:
	In margin/ վասն Սողոմոնի, որ շատ մեղաւ, եւ յետոյ շատ զղջացաւ:
	§§1–2 are not in *MS M4618*; the text of these sections printed here is taken from Yovsēp'ianc', 228.
1.1/ Վասն զի գրեաց Մուսէս. «Մի առնուցուս[49] զուստր նորա դստեր քո եւ մի տացես զաւակի քո փեսայանալ նոցա, զի մի մոլորեցուցանիցեն զկնի իւրեանց, այլ զբագինս նոցա հրով այրիցես եւ զդիսն նորա խորտակիցես եւ մի դնիցես ընդ նոսա ուխտ»:	1.1/ Վասն զի գրեաց Մովսէս, թէ «Մի առնուցուս զուստր նորա դստեր քում, եւ մի տացես զաւակի քում փեսայանալ նոցա, զի մի մոլորեցուցանիցեն զնոսա զկնի դիցն իւրեանց, այլ զբագինս նոցա հրով այրեցաս եւ զդիս նորա խորտակեցաս եւ մի դնիցես ընդ նոսա ուխտ»:
1.2/ Զի ոչ կամեցան ձեռն տալ ժողովրդեանն, որպէս Գաբաւոնացիքն եւ տունն Րահարու՝ Հ. (70) ոգւք:	1.2/ Զի ոչ կամեցան նորա ձեռն տալ ժողովրդեանն, որպէս Գաբաւոնացիքն եւ որպէս տունն Ռահաբու եօթանասուն հոգւով:
	Here MS M4618 commences
1.3/ Իսկ Սողոմոնն արար իւր կանայս բազումս՝ Չ. (700)։ Եւ զի ոչ հանդարտեաց այսմիկ, այլ դիմեաց ի վերայ հեթանոսաց եւ առ հարճս Յ. (300) ի պեղծ հեթանոսաց անդի՝ զդստերս թագաւորացն եւ իշխանացն:	1.3/ Իսկ Սողոմոնն արար իւր կանայս բազմութեան՝ Չ. (700), եւ զի ոչ շատացաւ այսուիկ, այլ դիմեաց նա ի վերայ հեթանոսաց, եւ էառ հարճ .Յ. (300) պիծս ի քանանացւոց անդի՝ զդստերս թագաւորաց եւ իշխանաց:
1.4/ Ի զայթակղութիւն անձին իւրոյ եւ յարհամարհութիւն բազմութեան սուրբ կանանց իւրոց, որք ժողովեցան առ նա վասն զարմանալի գիտութեան նորա:	1.4/ Ի զայթակղութիւն անձին իւրոյ եւ արհամարութիւն բազմութեան կանանց իւրոց, որք ժողովեցան առ նա վասն զարմանալի գիտութեան իւրոյ:

---

49. կին occurs here, but is deleted.

12. KING SOLOMON: FOUR SHORT TEXTS

1.5/ Որպէս իմաստուն կինն, որ եկն ի յեթովպացւոց[50] անդի վասն աւրհնութեան առնն իմաստնոյ եւ գիտել գիմաստութիւն նորա, զոր լուաւ ի վաճառականաց անդ՝ ի Քիրամայ արքայի։	1.5/ Որպէս իմաստուն կինն, որ եկն յեթովպացոց վասն աւրհնութեան առն իմաստնոյ ի գիտել գիմաստութիւն նորա, զոր լուաւ ի վաճառականաց անդի ի Քիրամա արքայէ։
1.6/ Այլ առ նա զկանայս իւր առեալս ի Բաղամա ի գայթակղութիւն որդւոցն Իսրայէլի ոչ միայն խառնակիլ, այլ եւ հաղորդիլ պաշտամամն գայթկղութեանն։	1.6/ Այլ էառ նա զկանայս ազատեալս ի բազում գայթկղութեանց որդւոցն Իսրայէլի ոչ միայն պղոնկեալն, այլ եւ հաղորդ պաշտման գայթակղութեէն։
1.7/ Չի խաբեցաւ ի պատճառս իմաստութեան իւրոյ եւ թոյլ ետ խորհրդող իւրոց զնալ ի ճանապարհս կանանցն, որք խորիեցան միաբանութեամբ ի լուծումա անձին նորա,	1.7/ Չի խաբեցաւ նա ի պատճառս իմաստութեան իւրոյ, թոյլ ետ խորհրդոցն զնալ ի ճանապարհս կանանց, որք խորհեցան միաբանութեամբ գլուծումն անձին նորա։
1.8/ մինչեւ կանգնեաց պատկերս ի վերայ լերանց եւ յայտնապէս պոռնկեցաւ դէմ յանդիման տաճարին եւ թշնամեացն իւրոց։	1.8/ մինչեւ կանգնեաց զպատկերս ի վերայ լերանց եւ յայտնապէս պոռնկեցաւ դէմ յանդիման տաճարին սրբութեան եւ թշնամեաց իւրոց։
	Here Yovsēpʻianc'ʻs text ends.
1.9/ Բայց եղեւ նմա ժամ պարապոյ ի սենեկի իւրոյ, խորհեցաւ ի միտս իւր յիշել զպատուէր հաւր իւրոյ Դաւթի. «գնալ քեզ», ասէ, «ի ճանապարհս Տեառն եւ յարդէնս Մովսիսի ծառայի նորա»։	1.9/ Բայց զի եղեւ նմա ժամանակ պարապոյ ի սենեկի իւրում, եւ խորհեցաւ ի միտս իւր յիշել զպատուէր հօրն իւրոյ. «գնալ քեզ ի ճանապարհս Տեառն եւ յօրէնս Մովսէսի ծառային Տեառն»։
1.10/ Իբրեւ յիշեաց զպատուէրս հաւր իւրոյ եւ զժամ մահուն Դաւթի, ելաց նա ի խորոց սրտէ իւրմէ, մինչեւ ողողանել զսենեակն եւ զմահիճս իւր ի տան ձմերոցաց արքայութեան իւրոյ։	1.10/ Եւ յիշեաց նա զպատուէր հօր իւրոյ եւ զժամ մահուն Դաւթի: Ելաց նա ի խորոց սրտէ իւրմէ, մինչեւ յողոզեալ նա զսենեակն եւ զմահիճս իւր ի տան ձմերոց արքայութեան իւրոյ։

---

50. In the manuscript, որ եկն յ- has been written unclearly above the line, but the text given here seems accurate.

1.11/ Եւ եղ սահման ապաշխարութեան անձին իւրոյ՝ գղուրս սենեկի իւրոյ ինքնին բանալ առանց բացողի, զի Դաւիթ ելաց զամենայն գիշերս, եւ սա հեղիղեաց զմահիճս իւր։	1.11/ Զդուրս սենեկին ինքն ձգեալ առանց ձգողի, զի Դաւիթ ելաց զամենայն գիշերս, եւ Սողոմոն հեղեղեաց ի սենեակն իւր։

Translation

M1500	M4618
Pluses of a manuscript are italicized in the translation. §§1–2 are not in MS M4618; and for these sections the text translated here is taken from Yovsēpʻianc‛, 228.	
Title / From the Commentary of the Paralipomena	Title / Concerning King Solomon, Son of David
	In margin/ Concerning Solomon who sinned greatly and subsequently repented greatly.
1.1/ Because Moses wrote, "You shall not take *his son for* your daughter and you shall not give your seed to marry them,[51] lest they turn them astray after *them*, but you shall burn their temples with fire and you shall destroy their idols and you shall not make a covenant with them."[52]	1.1/ Because Moses wrote, "You shall not take his daughter *to you* and you shall not give your seed to marry them, lest they turn them astray after *their idols*, but you shall burn their temples with fire and you shall destroy their idols and you shall not make a covenant with them."
2/ For they did not wish to give a hand to the people,[53] as did the Gibeonites and the house of Rahab, seventy souls.[54]	1.2/ For they did not wish to give a hand to the people, as did the Gibeonites and *as did* the house of Rahab, seventy souls.
1.3/ Then Solomon made for himself *many* wives, seven hundred.[55] And because he was not *pleased* by these, he had recourse, moreover, to the heathens and took three hundred abominable concubines from the *heathens*, daughters of kings and princes.	1.3/ Then Solomon made for himself *numerous* wives, seven hundred. And because he was not satisfied by these, he had recourse, moreover, to the heathens and took three hundred abominable concubines from the *Canaanites*, daughters of kings and princes.

---

51. The command is found in Deut 7:3 and Neh 13:25–26, with the latter referring explicitly to Solomon. The wording of both recensions of the apocryphal text differs from those biblical verses.

52. Deut 7:3, cf. 3–5.

53. I.e., "to aid." See *Joshua Text 1 Brief History of Joshua*, §24, which speaks of the "right hand of peace."

54. Compare the size of Jacob's household in Gen 46:27, Exod 1:5, and Deut 10:22.

55. 1 Kgs 11:3.

12. KING SOLOMON: FOUR SHORT TEXTS

1.4/ To a scandal to himself[56] and *to the contempt of the multitude of his pure wives*, who had gathered to him on account of his wondrous wisdom.	1.4/ To a scandal to himself[57] and the contempt of the multitude of his wives, who had gathered to him on account of his wondrous wisdom.
1.5/ Such as the wise woman who (came) from the Ethiopians on account of the blessing of *the* wise man and to know his wisdom, of which she had heard from the merchants *there*, from King Hiram.[58]	1.5/ Such as the wise woman who came from the Ethiopians on account of the blessing of a wise man, to know his wisdom, of which she had heard from the merchants, from King Hiram.
1.6/ But he took *the hated women of Balaam*[59] to the scandal of the children of Israel, not only being promiscuous but also a participator in the worship *of the scandalous (object)*.	1.6/ But he took the *freed women* to the *great* scandal of the children of Israel, not only being promiscuous but also a participator in the worship scandalously.
1.7/ For he was deceived because of his wisdom, he permitted his thoughts to go in the ways of *the* women who planned together the dissolution of his soul,	1.7/ For he was deceived because of his wisdom, he permitted his thoughts to go in the ways of women who planned together the dissolution of his soul,
1.8/ until he set up images upon mountains and was openly promiscuous over against the temple and his enemies.	1.8/ until he set up images upon mountains and was openly promiscuous over against the *holy* temple and his enemies.
1.9/ But he had leisure time in his room, he thought in his mind to remember his father *David's* command, "that you should go in the ways of the Lord and in the Law of Moses, the Lord's servant."[60]	1.9/ But *because* he had leisure time in his room, he *also* thought in his mind to remember his father's command, "that you should go in the ways of the Lord and in the Law of Moses, the Lord's servant."
1.10/ And *when* he recalled his father's command*s* and the hour of David's death, he wept from the depths of his heart until he irrigated the room and his bed in his kingdom's winter house.	1.10/ And he recalled his father's command and the hour of David's death. He wept from the depths of his heart until he irrigated the room and his bed in his kingdom's winter house.

---

56. Or: of his soul.

57. Or: of his soul.

58. King Hiram of Tyre is mentioned often in Jewish writings in connection with Solomon, but not usually in connection with the Queen of Sheba.

59. The text here differs from Stone, "Penitence of Solomon," which reads ատեալ ի բաղղու "hateful (wives) from {the Baal}" which does not make much sense. M1500 seems to have Balaam and that is equally problematic. The "freed women" of M4618 is also difficult.

60. Josh 22:5; compare Neh 10:29 in both recensions. Furthermore, similar commands specific to Solomon are to be found in 1 Kgs 2:1–4 and 11:6.

156 ARMENIAN APOCRYPHA RELATING TO BIBLICAL HEROES

1.11/ *And he set a limit of his own penitence.*[61] *He himself* opening the doors of his room without a doorman, for David wept the whole night and he (i.e., Solomon) inundated his bed.[62]	1.11/ Himself opening the doors of his room, without a doorman, for David wept the whole night and Solomon released floods (i.e., of tears) in his room.

Additional Passage in M1500

An additional passage is found in M1500. It is headed "According to another (copy), thus." This scholarly remark shows that probably Mxit'ar (or his exemplar) consulted more than one copy. This, in turn, underlines the complexity of the textual tradition. As I remarked above, such textual clusters are constructed in various ways from similar units of textual material. The range of this material, and which parts of it might be original, if that is to be determined, can be clarified only after the assembly of the complete surviving textual evidence.[63]

Text

Ըստ այլում այսպէս:

Իսկ Սողոմոն ի վերայ այսքան յանցանաց ի մէջի տրտմութեան եղեալ անյուսութեամբ, կոչեաց սենեկապետ իւր եւ հրամայեաց այրել զբազմութիւն գրոց իւրոց, զոր էր խաւսել ի շնորհաց հոգոյն: Եւ նորա արարեալ զհրամանն: Ապա հարցեալ Սողոմոնի, եթէ՝ «Զի՞նչ տեսեր», եւ նա ասէ. «Լոյս անբաւ ընդ բոցոյն վերացաւ յերկինս»: Եւ նա վասն այնր ելաց ի խորոց սրտէ իւրմէ:

Translation

According to another (i.e., exemplar), thus:

Then Solomon in deep grief over so many transgressions, fell into despair. He called his chamberlain and commanded that the multitude of his books be burned, which he had pronounced through grace of the Spirit. And he carried out the command. Then Solomon asked, "What did you see?" And he said, "Boundless light rose with the flame to the heavens." And he wept from the depth of his heart on account of that.

---

61. He ceased his penitence.
62. Both recensions are based on Ps 6:6, but there of David's tears.
63. For further examples of this, see Stone, "Concerning the Penitence," 59.

12. KING SOLOMON: FOUR SHORT TEXTS

Apparatus to Text 1

Although M1500 constitutes column 1 of the synoptic text above, for convenience, I have also included its variants in the apparatus. Thus, the base of collation is Recension 2, which is Yovsēp'ianc' for §§1–2 and M4618 for the rest. Yovsēp'ianc''s text ends at the conclusion of §8.

Sigla and Collation

M = M4618
Z = M1500
Y = Yovsēp'ianc'
J = Jerusalem J652, pp. 490–91[64]
B = Jerusalem 2558 in Bogharian's edition.[65]

These sigla are used throughout this section of the book.

§§1–2 are missing from M. For these two sections the text is Yovsēp'ianc' = Y and variants are from Z and J. For the rest of the text, the lemma is M and the variants are drawn from Z Y and J and so marked. From §9 to the end, the text is missing from Y, and the apparatus is adjusted accordingly. Only the incipit and a long explicit of MS B were printed by Bogharian. These are collated and variants included in the apparatus. It seems that it shares a number of readings with MS Z, the important codex M1500, though it does not share the additional passage presented above. This procedure makes §1 and §§8–11 available in this way from MS B.

Critical Apparatus

Title/ որդոյ Դավթի] om M ի մնացորդաց յաղագս Սողոմոն J ի մնացորդացն մնացուրդաց վասն Սողոմոնի արքային B
1. 1/ Մովսէս թէ] Մովսէս J | քում 1° and 2°] M քո Z | մոլորեցուցանիցեն զնոսա] մոլորեցուցանիցէք J | զնոսա] om Z | դիցն] om Z | բակինս J | այրիցեն Z այրելոց են J | խորտակիցէս Z
1.2/ եւ1°] om J | որպէս] եւ որպէս J | Րախաբու Z | զգուվք Z hոգով J
From this point the lemma is M and the variants are those of Z Y J.
1.3/ Սողովմոն Y | բազումա Z ըստ բազմութեան Y բազմութեան J | շատացաւ] հանդարտեաց Z | այսուիկ] այսմիկ Z | նա] om Z | էառ] առ Z Y | հարձ] հարձս Z Y յարձու J | պետծ Z J | քանանացւոց]

---

64. This is collated from a longhand copy prepared at my request several decades ago.
65. Bogharian, *Grand Catalogue*, 8:253–54.

հեթանոսաց Z | անդի Z | թագաւորացն Z | ի՞խանաց] ի՞խանացն Z + նոսա Y

1.4/ յարհամարհութիւն Z Y J | կանանց] սուրբ կանանց Z | իւրոց] իւրոյ J

1.5/ որ եկն յ-] above line p.m. Z | զիտութեանն Y J | յեթովացոց անդի յեթովացւոց անտի Y | յեթովկացւոց անտի J | իւրոյ] նորա Z | ի զիտել] եւ զիտել Z Y | զիմաստութիւնն Y J | ի Քիրամայ] Քիրամայ Y J | անտի] անդ Z | արքայի Y J

1.6/ էառ] առ Z | ազատեալս] իւր ատեալս Z զատեալս Y J | զայթակղութիւն Z Y J | պորնկեյն Y J | հաղորդեան Y հաղորդին J | պաշտաման Z Y J | զայթակղութեանն J

1.7/ խաբեցաւ] + նա Y | թոյլ] եւ թոյլն Z Y ընդ այլ J | խորհրդոց իւրոց Z | կանանցն Z Y J | որ] որք Z J | խորհեցան] խոնարհեցան J | ի լուծումն Z

1.8/ կանկնեաց Y | պատկերս Z | յայտնապէս] B resumes here | սրբութեան] om Z | թշնամեացն Z

1.9/ զի] om Z | ժամանակ] ժամ Z B | իւրոյ Z | եւ1°] om Z | հաւր Z հօր B | իւրոյ] + Դաւիթ Z | քեզ] + ասէ Z նմա B | յօրէնսն J | Մուսիսի Z Մովսէսի J | ծառայի J Z B | Տեառն2°] նորա J B | եւ զնալ] զնալ Z J

1.10/ յիշեաց] + նա Z B | զպատուէրս Z B | հօրն B | եւ ելաց B | որդզեալ] յորզանել Z J առզանել B | զեենեակն Z | մահիճն J | ձմերոց] ձմերցաց Z J B

1.11/ inc } + եւ եղ սահման ապաշխարութեան իւրոյ Z | սենեկին] սենեկի իւրոյ Z J B | ձզեալ ... ձզողի] բանալ ... բանողի Z ձզեաց ... ձզողի B | Սողոմոն] սա Z | հեղիլեաց Z | ի սենեակն իւր B | ինքն] ինքնին | զսենեակ Z

Text 2: The Writings of Solomon I

Manuscripts: Yovsēpʻianc' published Text 2 from a Venice Mekhitarist manuscript V1260/1095 of the *Epistles of Nersēs Šnorhali*, discussed above (Y).[66] This is the second work included in M4618, fols. 132r–132v (M). It also occurs in J652, another copy of the *Epistles of Nersēs Šnorhali*, pp. 491–92 (J).[67] Parts of this document are also published by Bogharian from J2558, Bible,

---

66. This is all the information given by Issaverdens, *Uncanonical Writings,* 158–60. See Yovsēpʻianc', *Uncanonical Books,* 232–33; Stone, "Concerning the Penitence," 60–61.
67. On pp. 491–92 of the manuscript. See Bogharian, *Grand Catalogue,* 3:76.

12. KING SOLOMON: FOUR SHORT TEXTS

Mokkʻ and Van, 1615 (B).[68] The text published here follows M4618 down to the end of §8; Yovsēpʻianc̒ and J652 continue with §9; and J652 alone has §10. Textually Y and J are very close indeed, with almost no variants between them.

Text

Manuscript M
M4618 Title/ fol. 132r /   Մնացորդաց:
in marg: Մեղանքն Սողոմոնի ընդդէմ Աստուծոյ:
2.1/ Յորժամ յարոյց Աստուած սատանայ Սողոմոնի զԱդրիազար արքայ Եդովմայ, եւ նա բազում անգամ կռփահարեալ եւ վանեալ ի նմանէ, ծանեաւ, թէ ձեռն Տեառն դարձաւ ի թշնամեաց ի վերայ իւր: Եւ եղեւ զորավիգ եւ ոխ թշնամեաց նորա, զի բարկացոյց զԱստուած մոլորութեամբն խորհրդոյն:
2.2/ Նախ՝ խաբանեաց զորէնսն, որ յառաջագոյն գրեալ էր ի ձեռն Մօսէսի, թէ «Մի՛ արասցես խնամութիւն, որ շուրջ զքեւ ազգ[69] իցեն»:
2.3/ Երկրորդ՝ վասն շինելոյ զտուն Տեառն ի մայրից Լիբանանու եւ զտուն դստեր փարաւոնի / fol. 132v / ոսկւոյ կեփազոյ եւ ոսկերաց փողաց:
2.4/ Երրորդ՝ զի խոտորեցաւ սիրտն նորա զհետ Աստարտայ՝ զարշելոյն Սիդոնայ:
2.5/ Եւ իբրեւ մերձեցաւ յոգնականութենէ Տեառն, հրամայեաց սենեկապետին իւրոյ հրկէզ առնել զիւր գրեանսն, որք էին հոգւով գիտութեան՝ ԳՌ. Առակաց, ի մայրիցն Լիբանանու մինչեւ զզոբրայն, որ յորմն ելանէ, եւ ի թռչնոց եւ ի զազանաց եւ ի սողունց: Բայց առեալ մասն ինչ թագուցանէր, զոր եւ յետոյ իսկ գրեցին բարեկամքն Եզեկիայի:
2.6/ Եւ իբրեւ հարցանէր Սողոմոն վասն պատուիրանաց հրկիզութեանն, թէ «Արդարեւ կիզեցա՞ն ամենայն գրեանքն, եւ զի՞նչ նշան եղեւ ի կիզին»,
2.7/ պատասխանի ետ սենեկապետն եւ ասէ. «Բորբոքեալ հուր եւ բոց ելանէր յերկինս»:
2.8/ Եւ ասէ Սողոմոն. «Այն հոգին սուրբ էր, որ ազդեալ էր ինձ ի խօսիլ զնա»: Եւ եղեւ յարտասուս եւ զղջացեալ ելաց դառնապէս, եւ համարեցաւ նմա Աստուած յապաշխարութիւն:

---

68. Bogharian, *Grand Catalogue* 5:254; and see also concerning the manuscript, Adjémian, *Grand Catalogue des manuscrits*, 644.
69. For the variation of կ and կը, see Stone and Hillel, "Index of Variants," no. 333.

M *and J continue:*
2.8A/ Եւ զայս եւս ի նոյն երանելի վարդապետի գրոցն գրեցի:
M ends and J adds:
2.9/ Պատասխանեալ Սողոմոնն ասէ. «Այն հոգին սուրբ էր, որ ազդեալ էր ինձ խոսել զնոսա»: Եւ եղեալ յարտասուս զչացեալ ելաց դառնապէս: Եւ համարեցաւ նմա Աստուած յապաշխարութիւն:
J adds:
2.10/ Եւ զայս եւս ի նոյն երանելի վարդապետին գրոցն գրեցի, զոր եւ յերիանոսի գիրսն գեղեցիկ յիշատակ է վասն Սողոմոնի:

Apparatus to Text 2

Lemma is M4618 and variants are drawn from:
Y = Yovsēpʻianc‘
J=Jerusalem 652

Title ի մնացորդաց մնացորդ են զոր բազմաջան յուզմամբ հազիւ կարացի գտանել J
2.1/ սատանան Y | Սողոմոնի Y J | Աղրազար Y զԱղրազար J | Եղովմայ Y Եղովմայ J | վանեալ] վատնեալ Y J | եթէ Y J | թշնամեաց] թշնամութիւն Y J | ի վերայ իւր] նորա Y | զօրավիք եւ ոխ] զօրավիգն Y J | մոլորութեամբն] երեք մոլորութեամբ Y J | խորհրդոց Y J
2.2/ խաբանեաց] խափանեաց Y J | Մովսիսի Y Մովսէսի J | թէ] om Y J | ազգ] ազգք Y J[70]
2.3/ գտունն Y J | դստերն Y J | յոսկերոյ Y J յոսկոյ Y | կեփազեայ Y J | յոսկերաց Y
2.4/ սիրտ Y սիրդ J | Սիտոնայ Y J
2.5/ մերձեցաւ] + նա Y J | իւր Y | գրեանն որ Y J | գիտութեամբ Y J | գրեանն J | որք] որ J | գզուպայ Y գզուպայն J
2.6/ Սողոմոնն Y | պատուիրանանցն Y J | հրկիզութեան Y J | թէ] om Y | ամենայն գրեանքն] բոլոր գրեանն Y J | նշան] + հայեցածն Y J | ամեն այր] պոլոր Y J | եղեւ] ցուցանէր YJ
2.7/ պատասխանեալ Y J | եւ1°] om Y | հուր եւ բոց] բոցոյն՝ հուր Y J | ելանէր յերկինս] կիզանող վերացեալ մտանէր ընդ երկնիւք YJ
2.8/ եւ ասէ Սողոմոն] պատասխանեալ Սողոմոն Y J պատասխանեալ J | Սողոմոն Y | եւ ասաց Աստուած եւ Y J | ինձ ի] ինձ Y J | խոսել Y J | զնա] զնոսա Y J | եղեալ Y J | եւ2°] om Y
2.9/ Սողոմոնն J

---

70. On this variant, see Stone and Hillel, "Index of Variants," no. 333.

12. KING SOLOMON: FOUR SHORT TEXTS

Translation

Title/ Paralipomena

in marg/ The Sins of Solomon against God

2.1/ When God raised up as a satan for Solomon, Adriazar, king of Edom[71] and he, having been smitten and chased away[72] by him, realized that the Lord's hand had turned from (his) enemies against him. He (God) became a supporter and a vengeance of his (Solomon's) enemies, for he had angered God through the error of his intention.

2.2/ First, he annulled[73] the Law, which had formerly been written by Moses's hand, "You shall not pity the people who are around you."[74]

2.3/ Second, on account of the house of the Lord (built) from the cedars of Lebanon[75] and the house of the daughter of Pharaoh from finest gold[76] and from ivory.[77]

2.4 / Third, since his heart was perverted (to go) after Astarte, the abomination of Sidon.[78]

2.5/ And when he was distanced from the Lord's assistance, he commanded his chamberlain to burn his writings which were (written) with

---

71. This phrase is cited from the Armenian of 1 Kgs 11:14 "And the Lord raised up an adversary against Solomon, Hadad the Edomite." "Adversary" appears as "satan" in our text, drawing on the Armenian Bible. In our text Hadad has been identified with another individual, whose name, "Hadad the Edomite" (1 Kgs 11:14) is combined with Hadadezer of 1 Kgs 11:23.

72. This, the reading of M, is clearly preferable. վատնեալ of Y J means "spend, squander."

73. Reading խափանել with Y J.

74. Deut 7:2. This law plays a considerable role also in text no. 7, *Brief History of Joshua*, §59.

75. First Kings 6 describes the use of cedar wood in Solomon's royal constructions, including the Temple. See Michael E. Stone, "The Cedar in Jewish Antiquity," in *The Archaeology and Material Culture of the Babylonian Talmud*, ed. Markham J. Geller, IJS Studies in Judaica 16 (Leiden: Brill, 2015), 66–82.

76. This word, meaning "finest gold" occurs once in the Bible, in Song 5:11. Issaverdens, *Uncanonical Writings*, 167 also translates "fine gold."

77. The Armenian means, literally, "from the bones of elephants." First Kings 7:8 relates the building of a house for Pharaoh's daughter, after the pattern of his own palace. This building is also mentioned in 1 Kgs 9:24.

78. Compare Judg 10:6: "the Ashtaroth, the gods of Syria, the gods of Sidon." Ashtoreth as goddess of the Sidonians is connected with Solomon in 1 Kgs 11:5, and 2 Kgs 23:13 says Solomon had built high places "for Ashtoreth the abomination of the Sidonians." These verses are probably the source of the text here.

the spirit of knowledge, three thousand of proverbs,[79] from the cedars of Lebanon to the hyssop which grows from the wall,[80] and from birds and from beasts and from reptiles. But he[81] took a part (of them) and hid (them), which afterwards the companions of Hezekiah wrote down.[82]

2.6/ And when Solomon asked about the orders to burn,[83] "Indeed were all the writings burnt? And what sign took place at the burning?"

2.7/ The chamberlain answered and said, "The fire flared up and a flame climbed to the heavens."

2.8/ And Solomon said, "That was the Holy Spirit, which influenced me when I spoke that." And he was in tears and repented. He wept bitterly and God reckoned it as penitence for him.

Y omits: M and J continue:

2.8A/ And this also I wrote from the book(s) of the same doctor.

M ends here; J adds:

2.9/[84] And Solomon answering, said, "That was the Holy Spirit which influenced me to speak them." And tearfully he wept bitterly, repenting. And God reckoned this to him as a penitence.

2.10 / And this also I wrote from the book(s) of the same blessed doctor, which is also a beautiful memorial concerning Solomon also in the books of Ierianos.[85]

Text 6. King Solomon's Ring

This text, though sharing the theme of Solomon's penitence, is rather different from the group of closely related passages we have noted above. The idea of the sanctity and special powers of Solomon's ring, though not explained here,

---

79. This narrative resolves the question of what happened to the 3,000 proverbs that 1 Kgs 4:32–33 attributes to King Solomon: "He also uttered 3,000 proverbs; and his songs were a 1,005. He spoke of trees, from the cedar that is in Lebanon to the hyssop that grows out of the wall; he spoke also of beasts, and of birds, and of reptiles, and of fish."

80. First Kings 4:33 is cited here. The next phrase is rewritten but has three elements. It has գանասանց եւ զթռչնոց եւ զձկանց, "the animals and the birds and the fish," omitting the reptiles of 1 Kgs 4:33.

81. I.e., the chamberlain.

82. See Prov 25:1 which verse reads, "These also are proverbs of Solomon which the men of Hezekiah king of Judah copied." Again, the text resolves an exegetical problem, arising from the attempt to harmonize all biblical statements about Solomon's writing.

83. Literally: of burning.

84. §2.8 in MS J = §2.8 immediately above, with a few differences.

85. This seems preferable to regarding §10 as the title of the next work.

is found elsewhere. Thus, in the Greek *Testament of Solomon*, Solomon's ring was granted him "from the Lord Sabaoth through the Archangel Michael, a ring which has a seal engraved on precious stone," and he is told that with it "you shall imprison all the demons … and with their help you shall build Jerusalem when you bear this seal of God" (*T. Sol.* 1:6–7). Indeed, the theme of Solomon's magic ring is widespread and as old as Josephus, or older.[86] The theme of a valued or powerful ring being thrown in the water and recovered from the belly of a fish is widespread. An example from ancient Greece is found in Herodotus, Book 3.40–43 in the story of Polycrates who threw away a valued ring and received it back in the belly of a fish.

A ring inscribed with Solomon's name is used in exorcism, described by Josephus in *A.J.* 8.46–48. To this ring material a further, widely known element is added. This is that a demon succeeded in replacing Solomon on his throne and he was only restored to it by means of a magical ring, or some other such instrumentality.[87]

Solomon played a very considerable role later in Armenian magical and apotropaic prayers.[88]

Text

M4618 in marg above: Սողոմոնի գիրշն առ Աստուած

in marg alongside: Վասն հպարտութեան. տե՛ս, թէ Սողոմոն իմաստուն ինչ բաշեց

6.1// fol. 132v / Գեղեցիկ յիշատակ Սողոմոնի:

6.2/ Սողոմոնի սահման կայր, որ երբ ի մարմնոյ կարիս լինէր եւ կամ չրհեր, նա զիւր թագաւորական մատանին տայր յիւր հրեշտակն, որ պահէր:

6.3/ Եւ դարձեալ առնոյր, նստէր յաթոռն: Վասն այն պահէր սրբութեամբ, զի տէր թագաւորութեան իւրոյ այն մատանին էր, եւ

---

86. See for a detailed discussion, Torijano, "Solomon, Exorcism and the Magic Ring," in *Solomon the Esoteric King*, 76–86.

87. This is widespread in Rabbinic and later Jewish sources. See the excellent summary by Kaufman Kohler and Louis Ginzberg in *JE* 5:217–20, s.v. "Asmodeus." The matter is also discussed in detail in Ginzberg, *Legends of the Jews* 4:171–72. The Jewish legend also relates that the ring was discovered later in the belly of a fish. See also Seymour, *Tales of King Solomon*, 172–73.

88. See "Solomon," in the index to Sargis Harut'yunyan, *Հայ հմայական և ժողովրդական աղօթքներ* (*Armenian Incantations and Folk Prayers*) (Erevan: Erevan University Press, 2006).

այն այլ իմաստութիւն էր, զի առաջինքն սրբութեամբ պատուէին զապիկին եւ զափորն, եւ նա զիւր մատանին պատուէր:

6.4/ Հանդիպեցաւ ի ջրեղն գնալ: Ետդ զմատանին ցցեն եւ զիտաց, թէ հրեշտակն էր: Չի միտքն եւ խելքն գնաց վասն հպարտութեան եւ յոլովութեան մեղաց, եւ ոչ զիտաց, թէ դեւ է, զի հրեշտակապետ էր կերպարանեալ դեւն, ետդ ի նա զմատանին եւ գնաց:

6.5/ Եւ դեւն եղիր զմատանին ի ձեռոսն եւ նստաւ յաթոռն թագաւորութեան, եւ տեսանէին որպէս զՍողոմոն:

6.6/ Եկն Սողոմոն եւ տեսաւ յաթոռ թագաւորութեան նստեալ՝ այլ զարհուրելի քան զինքն, ափշեցաւ եւ ի վայր մնաց:

Ասէ Սողոմոն ի միտս իւր. «Թէ ասեմ՝ ես եմ Սողոմոն, դա դեւ է, վախեմ, թէ ջիաւատան: Ասեն թէ դու ես Սողոմոն, ապա սա ո՞վ է, զան ի վերաս եւ զիս սպանանեն»:

6.7/ Մարդոյ իրք չուաց, ելաւ ու գնաց, ուր մարդ չգիտաց: Սյա էր եղաւ հանց: Վասն այն, զի ամենայն մարդ գիտասցէ, թէ Աստուծով լինի թագաւորութիւնն. զով պիտի, նստուցանէ յաթոռ, եւ զով չպիտի, իջուցանէ յաթոռոյ, ըստ այնմ թէ՝ «Տէր աղքատուցէ եւ Տէր մեծամեծանայ»:

6.8/ Եւ վասն առաւել հպարտութեան Սողոմոնի արար Աստուած, որ խոնարհի, եւ այլ ոչ առնէ զայն անպատեհ բանն: Գնաց Սողոմոն խեղճ եւ դառն եւ ոչ զիտեր, թէ զինչ առնէր: Հասաւ ի գետեզր մի, ետես, զի ձկնորաք ձուկն որսային, եւ մտաւ[89] նոցա մօտն[90] մշակ, եւ տային աւուրն հաց մի եւ ձուկն մի կերակուր նմա:

6.9/ Խ. օր նստաւ դեւն յաթոռն Սողոմոնի, եւ արար թագաւորութիւն. /fol. 133r/ յետ Խ աւուրն տարաւ ձգեց զմատանին ի գետն, եւ ձկնորսերն[91] կալան զձուկն, որ կլեալ էր զմատանին:

6.10/ Եւ Աստուծոյ հրամանաւ տուալ այն ձուկն եւ հաց մի Սողոմոնի: Էառ զհացն կերաւ եւ երեք զձուկին, զի ուտիցէ, եւ գտաւ զմատանին ի փոր ձկանն: Ուրախացաւ եւ գոհացաւ զԱստուծոյ, եղեւ թագաւոր եւ նստաւ յաթոռն իւր եւ արար զիւր թագաւորութիւնն հաստատուն:

6.11/ Ո՛վ եղբարք, մեք էլ հանց եմք: Գայ ժամանակ, որ ի փառաց ձգէ զմեզ Աստուածն, եւ զայ ժամանակ, որ պատուէ զմեզ, քանի քո ընչիցն եւ ապրանացն տէր ես եւ պարոն ես:

6.12/ Ջանա, որ ի քո տունն առնես քեզ վճար, եւ լինիս բաժին արքայութեան: Մի՛ հպարտ կենայք, տե՛ս, թէ զՍողոմոն ինչպէս

---

89. Middle Armenian form.
90. Written over մօշն.
91. Postclassical form. Compare զտաւ in §3.9.

խոնարհեցոյց Աստուած վասն հպարտութեան եւ անօրէն գործոյն։ Այս փորձանք է եւ մեզ խրատ, որ մեք խրատինք եւ ի պատուիրանն Աստուծոյ կենանք։

Translation

in marg above: Solomon's penitence to God.
in marg alongside: Concerning pride: see how Solomon the wise suffered.

6.1/ A beautiful memorial of Solomon.[92]

6.2/ Solomon set a boundary,[93] that when it became necessary (to excrete) through his body or (there was) urine, he would give his royal ring to his angel to guard it.[94]

6.3/ And[95] returning, he took it and sat on the throne. For this reason he kept it pure, for that ring was lord of his kingdom, and it was also wisdom, for the former people honored the jar and the urn[96] with purity and he honored his ring (thus).

6.4/ He happened to go to urinate. He gave the ring to the demon and apprehended[97] that it was an angel. For his mind and intelligence had departed because of (his) pride and the multitude of (his) sins, and he did not know that it (was) a demon, for the demon had taken on the form of an archangel.[98] He gave the ring to it and went.

6.5/ And the demon put the ring on its hand and sat on the royal throne and it looked like Solomon.[99]

6.6/ Solomon came and saw (it) sitting on the royal throne, but more frightening than he. He was astounded and remained upon the spot.[100]

---

92. This phrase also occurs in *Solomon Text (2) Concerning the Writings of Solomon I* §10 in the preceding section.
93. Or: a rule, limit. See *Solomon Text (1) Concerning King Solomon* §11 for the same phrase in a different context.
94. Thus, he avoided bringing the royal ring into contact with impurity. The idea of guardian angels is a prominent theme in the texts edited by Matilda Koen-Sarano in *King Solomon and the Golden Fish: Tales from the Sephardic Tradition* (Detroit: Wayne State University Press, 2004), 127.
95. I.e., when the danger had passed.
96. Apparently the urn of the manna which was, according to the New Testament, of gold; see Heb 9:4.
97. That is, thought.
98. Compare the disguise of Satan in the *Pen. Adam* 44.17.1.
99. Literally: "they saw as if Solomon."
100. That is, froze on the spot, did not move.

Solomon said to himself,[101] "If I say, 'I am Solomon; that is a demon,' I fear lest they believe me not. They (will) say, 'If you are Solomon, then who is that?' They (will) attack me and kill me."

6.7/ He set out (from) the things of men,[102] he went forth and proceeded (to a place) where no man knew (him). Why did such a thing happen? For the following reason: that every man might come to know that kingship is through God. He seats one worthy on the throne and the one who is unworthy he makes descend from the throne. This is in accordance with (the verse), "The Lord makes poor and the Lord enriches."[103]

6.8/ And on account of Solomon's exceeding pride God humbled him and he no longer did this unfitting thing. Solomon went away unfortunate and bitter. And he did not know what to do. He reached the bank of a river, he saw that fishermen were fishing. And a farmer came near and they were each given daily one (loaf of) bread and a fish as food.

6.9/ For forty days the demon sat on Solomon's throne and ruled as king. After forty days he took and cast the ring into the river and the fishermen caught the fish that had swallowed the ring.[104]

6.10/ And by God's command that fish and a (loaf of) bread were given to Solomon. He took the bread (and) ate (it). He split the fish so as to eat it and found the ring in the fish's belly. He rejoiced and praised God. He became king and sat on his throne and made his kingdom secure.

6.11/ Oh, brothers, we also are likewise. A time comes when God casts us down from our glory and a time comes when he honors us, while you are lord and master of your possessions and palaces.

6.12/ Strive that in your house you make a reward for yourself, and yours will be a portion of the kingdom.[105] Be not proud. See how God humbled Solomon because of pride and lawless deeds. This is a misfortune and a counsel for us, to that we might be admonished and live in God's commandment.

---

101. Literally: "in his mind."
102. Translation of this phrase is uncertain.
103. The wording is drawn from 1 Sam 2:7 Տէր աղքատացուցանէ եւ մեծացուցա նէ and compare Job 1:21(22).
104. No explanation is given of why the demon threw the ring into the river. On the story, see the introductory remarks.
105. Literally: and you will become/be a portion of kingdom.

12. KING SOLOMON: FOUR SHORT TEXTS

TEXT 7. SOLOMON AND THE BUBU BIRD

Introductory Remarks

This text occurs only in M4618, following directly on Text 6. It has a legendary character and is associated with the stories of the wondrous powers of King Solomon. In Rabbinic literature there are also such tales of wonder and of Solomon's ability to talk with birds and animals.[106] A very similar narrative is referred to by Ginzberg, with the elements of the absence of a bird, its bringing news of a far country, the beautiful woman (identified as the Queen of Sheba, but not in our text) and the hairy legs which become white.[107] They are often linked with the statements in 1 Kgs 4:29–33, where great wisdom and, almost explicitly, wonderworking are attributed to King Solomon. No parallels to the story of Solomon and the bubu bird are familiar to me in Armenian but they are known in Muslim literature. Thus, in the third book of al-Tabari's *History*, concerning the Children of Israel, stories about King Solomon are found that have numerous points in common with our text.[108] Al-Tabari's work has Solomon texts including the following features: The birds provided shade (Solomon Text (7) *Solomon and the Bubu Bird* §1, Tabari 156–57); a bird was missing (Solomon Text (7) *Solomon and the Bubu Bird* §1, Tabari 157); beauty of a foreign land seen by bird (Solomon Text (7) *Solomon and the Bubu Bird* §§2–3, Tabari 158); bird saw wondrous woman (Solomon Text (7) *Solomon and the Bubu Bird* §4, Tabari 158); Solomon sent a letter to the woman by means of the bird (Solomon Text (7) *Solomon and the Bubu Bird* §§4–6, Tabari 159); the woman has hairy legs (Solomon Text (7) *Solomon and the Bubu Bird* §7, Tabari 162–65). The woman is Biqlis, the Queen of Sheba, though not identified as such in the Armenian. The Armenian text is shorter, less circumstantial, and differs at many points from Tabari's story. It is clearly an independent telling of this tale.[109] Nonetheless, it seems clear that the Armenian text is a reworking of some Islamic Solomon writing.

---

106. Ginzberg, *Legends of the Jews*, 6:289.
107. Ginzberg, *Legends of the Jews*, 4.142–45 and 6.288–89.
108. See William M. Brinner, *The Children of Israel*, vol. 3 of *The History of Al-Tabari* (*Tar'arik al-Rusul wal-Muluk* (Albany: State University of New York Press, 1991), 158–63.
109. See the discussion of this story in Max Grünbaum, *Neue Beiträge zur Semitischen Sagenkunde* (Leiden: Brill, 1893), 216–20. Earlier it was retold in great detail by Gustav Weil, *Biblische Legenden der Muselmäner* (Frankfurt am Main: Literarische Anstalt, 1845), 243–50, 255–64.

Text[110]

M4618 7.1/ Յորժամ աղօթեր Սողոմն ի դուրս ի սրահին, եւ լինէր շող, նա զային հաւերն եւ շուք առնէին ի վերան, որ արեգական ջերմութիւնն զինքն չի տաքցնէր: Օր մի մեկ հաւն չերեկ, արեգական ի վերայ իջաւ, նայեցաւ ի վեր. այս հաւս, որ բուբու կասեն, չէր եկեր:

7.2/ Արեգական ի վրեն իջաւ, նայեցաւ ի վեր. այս հաւս, որ բուբու կասեն, չէր եկեր: Եհարց Սողոմն, թէ «Այս հաւս էր չէ եկեր»: Ասացին. «Հետ հաւի օտարի գնաց, որ եկեալ էր յոտար յաշխարհէ, որ չեր[111] այս երեւելի աշխարհէս: Գնաց այն հաւն ու տեսաւ քան զմեր աշխարհն այլ գեղեցիկ ամենայն իրօք»:

7.3/ Բարկացաւ Սողոմն հաւին, թէ՝ «Էր օտար աշխարհի գնացեր: Թէ գայ, սպաննեմ[112] զնա»: Երեկ հաւն, ասաց. «Ուստի՞ գաս»: Ասաց. «Բ. (2) հաւ եկեալ էին յոտար յաշխարհէ, զիս տարան իւրեանց աշխարհն: Գնացի, տեսայ քան զմեր աշխարհն այլ գեղեցիկ ամենայն իրօք:

7.4/ Եւ կայր կին մի հանց գեղեցիկ, որ մարդ այլ չէ տեսել»: Ասաց Սողոմն. «Ես գիտեմ, թէ ամենայնի թագաւոր եմ, ու այլ աշխարհի չկայ, քան զմեր աշխարհն, ու իմ հրամանքս են մարդ, եւ թռչուն, եւ ամենայն կենդանի, եւ դեւք: Այլ դու կասես, թէ այլ կայ»:

7.5/ Երետ հաւ մի հետ այդ հաւին, թէ՝ «Գնացէք, տեսէք՝ ըղորդ է, թէ սուտ»: Գնացին, եկին, ասացին, թէ «Հղորդ է»: Ասաց Սողոմն, թէ՝ «Ո՞վ երթայ զայն կինն բերէ»: Ասաց մեկ դեւն. «Ես երթամ, շուտով բերեմ»: Գրեց գիր եւ երետ ի հաւն. եւ իւրն նայիպ մի կայր ի հետ, տարաւ հաւն ու զգիրն ի վերան ձգեց:

7.6/ Երեկ ամպն ու աստեղ ու անձրեւ էած, եւ ի հետ անձրեւին մարգարտ երեկ: Եկաւ այն կինն, կու տեսնուր զմարգարատն: Ամպն ի յինքն ժողովեցաւ, եւ քամին ի ներքեն մտաւ: Էառ զայն կինն քամին եւ մօտ ի Սողոմն տարաւ: Տեսաւ Սողոմն եւ էառ զինքն:

7.7/ Եւ ասացեալ էին Սողոմնի թէ ոտքն միայն զէշ է՝ զի մազոտ է, եւ այլ ամենայն մարմինքն լաւ է: Վասն այն, երբ ի ջուրն կանցանէր, տեսաւ, որ ոսն այլ էր ջերմակ: Խիստ սիրեաց զայն կինն եւ էառ իւրն, եւ եղեւ ի նմանէ տղայ:

---

110. I express my thanks to my learned friend, Prof. Abraham Terian, who suggested a number of improvements to the edition of Text 7.

111. Read as չէր.

112. Note the late loss of interconsonantal -a-.

Translation

7.1/ When Solomon was praying outside his chamber and a ray shone.[113] Behold, birds came and made a shadow above (him), so that the warmth of the sun did not warm him. One day, one bird did not come. The sun came (shone) down upon him.[114] He looked up, this bird which they call Bubu[115] had not come.

7.2/ The sun descended from on high. He looked up; this bird which they call Bubu did not come.[116] Solomon asked, "Why has this bird not come?" They said, "It went with a foreign bird, which had come from a foreign land, which was not from this visible world. That bird went and saw that in everything it was more beautiful than our land."

7.3/ Solomon grew angry with the bird, saying,[117] "Why did you go to a foreign land? If it comes I will kill it." The bird came. He said, "Whence do you come?" It said, "Two birds came from a foreign land. They led me to their land. I went (and) I saw that in everything it was more beautiful than our land.

7.4/ "And there was a woman so beautiful that no man has seen (one more beautiful)." Solomon said. "I know that I am king of everything, and there is no other world than our world, and (at) my commands are humans, birds and all creatures, and demons.[118] But you say that there is another (world)."

7.5/ He sent[119] a bird with that bird, saying, "Go, see whether it is true or false." They went, they came (back), they said, "It is true." Solomon said, "Who will go to bring that woman?" A demon said, "I will go, I will bring (her) quickly." He wrote a letter and gave it to the bird, and one of his deputies was present took the bird with the letter and released (it).

7.6/ A cloud came and a star and it brought rain and after the rain came a pearl. That woman came and saw the pearl. The cloud gathered (her) into itself and the wind entered underneath (her). The wind took that woman and brought (her) to Solomon. Solomon saw (her) and took her.

---

113. Literally: became, came into being.
114. I.e., went down on him.
115. Բու is the word for "owl" in Armenian. Here the name is բուպու and the bird is diurnal, which would weigh against its being an owl.
116. This sentence is a doublet of the last sentence of §1.
117. So I have translated բէ in this context.
118. The magical Solomon figure, introduced already in Text 3, here is not bested by a demon, but is ruler of them. This is a well-known theme, perhaps hinted at in *Wis* 7:20 and predominant in *Testament of Solomon*.
119. Literally: gave.

7.7/ And they told Solomon that her feet only are bad, for they are hairy, and all (the rest of her) body is good. For that reason, when she was crossing water, he saw that the feet too were white. He loved that woman very much and he took her and a boy was born of her.

13. Praise of the Prophets

Introductory Remarks

This document is composed of short characterizations of various biblical figures. It mentions a number of features of each, and often gives a brief typical phrase from their book. In the case of Isaiah, the citation is drawn from Psalms, which is odd. These figures are designated as prophets since they are the ostensible authors of biblical books.

M5531 is a *Miscellany* of religious texts of the eighteenth century. It is short, having only sixty-seven folios, and *Praise of the Prophets* occurs on fols. 66r–67r. There survive a number of documents dealing with the prophets, sometimes just lists of names and sometimes containing a series of paragraphs, written apparently in imitation of the *Vitae Prophetarum* or in response to the practice of list-making that was so prevalent in medieval Armenian scholastic literature. I list here a number of such works that have been published, omitting longer narrative texts dealing with a single prophet.[1]

(1) *Vitae Prophetarum*: The Armenian translation of this widespread text dealing with the four major and twelve minor prophets is published in Yovsēpʻianc', *Uncanonical Books*, 207–24 and the English translation of these in Issaverdens, *Uncanonical Writings*, 142–54.[2] In addition to those authors of biblical books, Armenian lives of Nathan, Elijah, Elisha, Zechariah (1), Eli, and Joad were published with translations in Stone, *Patriarchs and Prophets*, 136–55. Furthermore, see pp. 154–57 there for three lives known only in Armenian, those of

---

1. For examples of such longer texts, see the works on Hezekiah and Manasseh and on Elijah, below.
2. Material of this type relevant to Ezekiel is published in Wright, Satran, and Stone, *The Apocryphal Ezekiel*, 69–91.

Moses,[3] the Three Children[4] and Zechariah (2).

(2) *The Names, Works, and Deaths of the Holy Prophets*, a translation from Latin was published in Stone, *Patriarchs and Prophets*, 158–73.

(3) *Lists of Prophets' Names* were published in Stone, *Patriarchs and Prophets*, 174–75, from M533, V176, and M1500.

(4) Sarghissian, in his study of the *Vitae Prophetarum*, also quotes long sections from manuscript V176 of the twelfth century, which contain another document of narratives about prophets, like but not identical with *Vitae Prophetarum*[5]

Texts and Translations

M5531 Սողոմոն

Աստուածեղէն հանճարովն առատացել և զխորս իմաստից տեղակացեալ, խրատն աշխարհի և քարոզն ամենայն հասակի, մեծն իմաստնացեալ յԱստուծոյ Սողոմոն հրամայէ «Ի բանս իմում ասեմ»-ով:

Մանուկն դիող և ծերացեալ մտոք՝ հոգոյն սրբոյ ընդունարանն, իմաստնացեալն յԱստուծոյ սրբական և մեծ Սողոմոն հրամայէ ասելով:

Solomon

He was enriched[6] with divine discernment and was informed of the depths of wisdom, the counsel of the world and the sermon for every age, the great Solomon having been made wise by God, commanded by, "In my words, I say."[7]

---

3. Cognate material is included in Michael E. Stone, "Three Armenian Accounts of the Death of Moses," in *Studies on the Testament of Moses: Seminar Papers,* ed. G. W. E. Nickelsburg, SBLSCS 4 (Cambridge: Society of Biblical Literature, 1974), 118–21.

4. Related material is included in Michael E. Stone, "An Armenian Tradition Relating to the Death of the Three Companions of Daniel," *Le Muséon* 86 (1973): 111–23.

5. Barseł Sarghissian, Ուսումնասիրութիւնք Հին Կտակարանի Անվաւեր Գրոց Վրայ (*Studies on the Uncanonical Books of the Old Testament*) (Venice: Mekhitarist Press, 1898), 255–57.

6. Here and in the next phrase we have instances of the participle being used as a finite verb. The whole passage is impregnated with language from Prov 1:2, traditionally the first verse of the Bible translated into Armenian after the invention of the alphabet. It reads: 1:2 Ճանաչել զիմաստութիւն և զխրատ, իմանալ զբանս հանճարոյ, "For learning wisdom and counsel; For understanding words of discernment."

7. See Prov 4:10 and 4:20. Here an instrumental ending is put on the end of the last word of a phrase.

13. PRAISE OF THE PROPHETS

Being a child in body and aged in mind, vessel of the Holy Spirit, having been informed by God, the holy and great Solomon commands saying.[8]

Մովսէս Մարգարէն

Հայր մարգարէից եւ անմիջող բարեկամն Աստուծոյ, պարագլուխն տեսանողաց եւ հաւատարիմ հազարապետն խորոցն Աստուծոյ, օրինակս եւ առաջնորդ ժողովրդեան Իսրայէլի, հաւատարիմն ի վերայ տանն Աստուծոյ հեզայհոգի մարգարէն Մովսէս հրամայէ ի բանս իւր. «Հայեաց ի քեզ, կուցէ մոռայնացես»:d

The Prophet Moses

Father of prophets and unmediated companion of God, the leader (chief) of seers, and faithful general[9] of the deep things of God, this example and leader of the people of Israel, the faithful one over the house of God, the humble prophet Moses commands in his words, "Take heed lest you forget...."[10]

Եսայի Մարգարէն

Լցեալն ի շնորհաց հոգւոյ սրբոյ, իմաստացեալն յԱստուծոյ եւ կայծակնամաքուր[11] եւ համարձագականեւս մարգարէն Եսայի հրամ<այ>է ի բանս իւր. «Տէր, բարձր ես, եւ բազուկ քո հզօր»:

The Prophet Isaiah

Filled with grace of the Holy Spirit, made wise by God and purified by coal,[12] the most daring[13] prophet Isaiah commands in his words, "Lord, you are high and your arm is mighty."[14]

Դաւիթ Մարգարէն

Գովելին ի գումարս ամենայն մարգարէից եւ ցանկալին ի դասս թագաւորաց, բանաւ<ո>րն քնարն, քաղցրախօս ամենայն հանճար

---

8. It is not recorded here.
9. Literally: commander of a thousand, chiliarch.
10. Deuteronomy 8:11 taken from the Armenian Bible.
11. This word, missing from the dictionaries, seems to be corrupt for կայծակնամաքուր. This is an epithet of Isaiah, drawing from the events described in Isa 6: 5–7.
12. This refers to the coal mentioned in Isa 6:6 which cauterised his impure lips.
13. This word, not in the dictionaries, seems to be a derivative of համարձակ "daring, bold" and խել "crazy." Perhaps this refers to Isaiah's volunteering for the divine mission; see Isa 6:8.
14. Psalm 135:13 with some minor changes; compare Isa 26:11.

հոգւոյն, անյագապէս ուսանող բաղձանս սիրոյ առ Տէր եւ արարիչն իւր մարգարէն Դաւիթն հրամայէ ի բան իւր ողորմութեամբ:

Of the Prophet David
The most praiseworthy of the assemblies of all prophets and the most desirable in the ranks of the kings, the intelligent harp, sweetest-speaking of all intelligences through the Spirit, insatiable student of longing of love to his Lord and Creator, the prophet David, commands in his merciful words.[15]

The rest of the document deals with Paul and the Evangelists

---

15. The contents of David's commandment are not given.

14. THE SHORT STORY OF THE PROPHET ELIJAH

NOTES ON THE TEXTS IN M6092 AND M101

Above I presented as text no. 7 the work *Brief History of Joshua* from M6092, fols. 343v–351v, 353r.[1] In the introductory remarks there, I noted that the leaves of the exemplar from which of M6092 was copied were in disarray, causing the Joshua text to start in medias res. It also finishes in midstream on fol. 351v, where the Joshua text breaks off and an Elijah text starts.

This Elijah text, which runs from fol. 351v to fol. 353r, is an extract from the published apocryphon *A Short History of the Prophet Elijah* (henceforth *Short History of Elijah*).[2] It begins with text equivalent to Yovsēpʻianc̒, *Uncanonical Books*, 337, line 19 and concludes on 353r with text equivalent to Yovsēpʻianc̒, 338, line 21. It has neither a clear beginning nor a marked end. In the course of the story of Joshua, M6092 switches into the Elijah story (fol. 351v). Immediately after its end we find the last section of *Brief Story of Joshua son of Nun* which reads:

> M6092 68/... եւ եդին ընդ նմա գուրպն քայլախազեա, որով թլխատեաց զորդիսն Իսրայէլի. եւ Քրիստոսի մարդասիրին փառք յաւիտեանս ամէն:

> 68/ ... And they put with him a sharp flint, with which he circumcised the children of Israel. And glory to Christ, lover of humans, forever. Amen.

This text is very close to the last words of §68 in *The Brief History of Joshua Son of Nun*, but is not quite identical. The Elijah narrative text includes the

---

1. This is discussed fully in the introductory remarks to *Brief History of Joshua*, above pp. 58–59.

2. Yovsēpʻeanc̒, *Uncanonical Books*, 337–38 which corresponds to Issaverdens, *Uncanonical Writings*, 178–79.

story of Elijah and Ahab up to Ahab's asking Elijah to pray for rain. I decided to publish it here because it is likely to be missed because of the disarray of the manuscript.

Finally, I remark that there are numerous unpublished manuscript copies of *Short History of Elijah*, and the textual character and relationship of these two extracts will remain unclear until a broader sample of the witnesses is studied. It is also to be observed that in a number of manuscripts, *Short History of Elijah*, occurs directly following *Brief History of Joshua, Son of Nun*.[3] This conjunction should be studied at the time when all copies of *Short History of Elijah* are gathered and listed.

During the years past, I have noted copies of the *Short History of Elijah* in the following manuscripts, and these are but a few of the numerous copies that survive:

M0503, 1601 CE, 223r-234v; M0706, 1680 CE, 2r-9v; M0843, 1714-1716 CE; M2242, seventeenth century, 52r-74v; M2245, 1689 CE, 24v-34v; M6995, sixteenth century; M8093, eighteenth century; M8239, 1615 CE; J393, *notrgir*, pp. 169-86; J631, seventeenth century, pp. 300-310; J669, 1694 CE, 357r-382; J730, *notrgir*, 101r-129v.

Edition of the Extract in M6092

22/ վասն որոյ ասաց նմայ Տէր. «Երթ, երեւես գԱքայաբու, եւ տաց անձրեւ ի վերայ երկրի»: Եւ նայ ոչ երկեաւ Եզբելա, այլ զնաց երեւեցո նախ Աբիդու յիսնապետին Աքայաբու, զի / fol. 352r / ելեալ էին ի քաղաքէն եւ շրջէին յեզր գետոյ եւ առուաց գտանել խոտ անասնոց՝ ձիոց եւ ջորոց: Եւ ասէ Եղիայ գԱբ{ջ}իդու.[4] «Գնա, պատմեա զզայլուստ իմ թագաւորին»: Եւ ասէ Աբիդու. «Ընդէր առնես զիս զխապարտ թագաւորին, զի ձառայ քո երկիւղած ի Տեառնէ»:

23/ Եւ պատմեաց Աբիդու վասն Ճ. (100) մարքարէիցն, զոր կերակրեաց Աբիդու եւ պահեաց ձածուկ այրի միում ի Սիովդի անդ. իբրեւ եզաբել եւ կամէր կոտորել զնոսա, փոխեաց զնոսա Աբիդու այլ՝ խորագոյն այրս: Այլ եւ պատմեաց վասն Ճ. մարքարէիցն, զոր էսպան Եզաբել: Իբրեւ լուաւ / fol. 352v / Եղիայ, ասէ. «Մի՛ հոգար. ես առնեմ զվրէժ արեան մարքարէիցն՝ կոտորելով զմարքարէսն Բահադու: Բայց դու երբ պատմեա թագաւորին»: Եւ ասէ Աբիդու. «Կենդանի է Տէր, որ ոչ եկիր զիդ եւ քաղաք եւ անապատ, որ ոչ խնդրեա<ց> զքեզ թագաւորն»: Եւ ասաց. «Թէ ես երթամ պատմեմ, թէ՝ ահա Եղիա,

---

3. See, e.g., J631, J694, and J730.
4. Error for Աբիդու.

14. THE SHORT STORY OF THE PROPHET ELIJAH

զուցէ առնու զքո հոգին եւ տարցէ ցայլ անապատ տեղիս, որպէս ի հեղեղատն, եւ ես սուտ լինիմ եւ մահապարտ»:

24/ Եւ ասէ Եղիա. «Կենդանի է Տէր, որ ոչ փախչիմ եւ ոչ թաքչիմ ես, այլ դու երթ պատմեա»: Յայնժամ գնաց Աբիդու առ թագաւորն եւ ասաց. «Ահայ / fol. 353r / Եղիայ»: Իբրեւ լուաւ բեկաւորդն⁵ նորա, եւ եկն ընդ առաջ Եղիայի: Արդ թէպէտ ընդ առաջ գովելով, թվեր, թէ պա<ու>տէ զմարքարէն, այլ բանիւ բերանոյ իւրոյ անարգեաց զնայ: Իբրեւ էտես զԵղիայ ասէ. «Սուտ է՝ զայս խանգարիչ տանն Իսրայէլի»: Եւ ասէ Եղիայ. «Խանկգարիչ՝ դու, եւ Տեառն հ<ո>ր քո: Անունդ ինձ կու տաս»: Եւ ապա սկսաւ թագաւորն աղաչել զնայ, զի տացէ անձրեւ ի վերայ երկրի, եւ ասէ. «Ոչ այտպէս. այլ իւրոյ»:⁶

22/ concerning which God said to him, "Go, appear to Ahab and I will give rain upon the earth."⁷ He was not afraid of Jezebel but went (and) first appeared to Obadiah,⁸ Ahab's commander of fifty,⁹ for they had gone forth from the city and gone around to the bank of the river and streams to find grass for the beasts, for horses and for mules.¹⁰ And Elijah said to Obadiah, "Go, tell the king of my coming." And Obadiah said, "Why do you make me guilty of a capital offence to the king? For (I am) your god-fearing servant."¹¹

23/ And Obadiah related concerning the one hundred prophets whom Obadiah had fed and kept secretly in a cave in Sio,¹² when Jezebel also wished to cut them down, Obadiah transterred them to other, deeper caves. Moreover, he related concerning the one hundred prophets whom Jezebel killed.¹³ When Elijah heard, he said, "Do not worry. I will take vengeance

---

5. Unusual word: բեկանեմ means "to break, dishearten."
6. The word իւրոյ is not in Yovsēpʻiancʻ.
7. First Kings 18:1: "After many days the word of the Lord came to Elijah, in the third year, saying, "Go, show yourself to Ahab; and I will send rain upon the earth."
8. See 1 Kgs 18:13–16.
9. Probably an interpretation of 1 Kgs 18:4: "Obadiah took a hundred prophets, hid them by fifties in a cave."
10. 1 Kgs 18:5.
11. 1 Kgs 18:14.
12. Unknown place name, not represented in the biblical text. Probably a corrupt toponym.
13. This appears to be an exegesis distinguishing two narratives of his act of hiding, one related in the biblical text in 1 Kgs 18:4 and the other in 18:13. In the biblical text both verses actually refer to the same event. The Bible does not specify that the number of prophets killed by Jezebel was one hundred.

for the blood of (my) prophets, cutting down the prophets of Baal. But you go, tell the king." And Obadiah said. "As the Lord lives, that you did not come to a village and a town and a desert in which the king did not seek you."[14] And he said, "If I go (and) tell, 'Behold Elijah,' perhaps he will take your life (you) and bring (you) to other desert places, just as if to a torrent. And I would become false and mortally guilty."[15]

24/ And Elijah said, "As the Lord lives, I will not flee and will not hide, but, you go and tell (him)." Then Obadiah went to the king and said, "Behold, Elijah!"[16] When he heard his ...[17] he came to greet Elijah.

Now although by meeting (him) with praise, it seemed that he honored the prophet, but by the word of his mouth he scorned him. When he saw Elijah, he said, "Is it a lie (that you come), troubler of the house of Israel?" And Elijah said, "You (are) a troubler even of the Lord of your <fat>her.[18] You give me your own name." And then the king began to beseech him, so that he would cause rain (to fall) upon the earth. And he said, "In actual fact, no, for what was his?"[19]

Extract from M101

A similar extract from *Short History of Elijah* occurs in M101, fols. 399r–402r. In this case, however, the Elijah material is a deliberate abbreviation of the *Short History of the Prophet Elijah*. In the manuscript it is treated as a distinct composition and is provided with a title, and with introductory and concluding phrases. It includes more of the *Short History of Elijah* than does the fragment in M6902. Here we give the beginning and end of the document in M101. The details of M101 are given below in the introductory remarks to text no. 17, *The Ninevehites*.

M101 *incipit*:
Title / Վասն Եղիայի մարքարէին եւ բանալ երկնիցս
Յորժամ եկն Եղիայ եւ իբրեւ լուաւ Աքայաբ ...

---

14. 1 Kgs 18:10.
15. This address of Obadiah's is more extensive here than in the biblical text.
16. Another expansion on the biblical text.
17. The meaning is unclear.
18. Again there are scribal slips in this sentence, producing corruptions. I would suggest to read: խանկգարիչ դու ես Տեառն հօր քո "You are a troubler of the God of your father," compare 1 Kgs 18:18.
19. I.e., "his (the king's) sin."

14. THE SHORT STORY OF THE PROPHET ELIJAH

title / Concerning the Prophet Elijah and the opening of the heavens
When Elijah came, and when Ahab heard ...

The text continues as in Yovsēp'ianc', *Uncanonical Books,* 338, line 12. It concludes as follows:

M101 *explicit*:
Եւ կալան զնոսա. Եւ իջոյց զնոսա Եղիա ի հղեհատն Քիտրոնի եւ կոտորեաց զնոսա անդ:

and he seized them. And Elijah brought them to the Kidron stream and cut them down there.

The ending of the parallel text is on Yovsēp'ianc', *Uncanonical Books,* 341 line 14. It is followed by two verses from 1 Kgs 18:41–42. It is clear, therefore, that this is an edited extract from the longer work, *Short History of Elijah* and, unlike the segment found in MS M6092, in M101 the passage has been molded so as to form a discrete work.

15. Hezekiah and Manasseh

Introductory Remarks

This document is found in manuscript M4618 on fols. 142v–143v, written in the same hand as text no. 3, *Construction of Noah's Ark*. The manuscript is of the seventeenth century and contains a number of apocryphal texts.[1] The work I am presenting here is a retelling of the histories of Kings Hezekiah and Manasseh of Judah. Both narratives center around incidents of sin, repentance, and redemption.

In the narrative about Hezekiah, stress is put upon the event narrated in 2 Kgs 20:1–11.[2] The biblical narrative simply states, "In those days Hezekiah became sick and was at the point of death," while *Hezekiah and Manasseh* provides a cause for his illness, saying in §1: "The pious and God-loving king Hezekiah, suddenly fell into sin. The Lord was wrath with (him) and wished to kill him. And God said to Isaiah the prophet, 'Go, warn Hezekiah!' " This addition increases the symmetry of Hezekiah story with the following story of Manasseh and at the same time provides a reason for Hezekiah's illness. Hezekiah wept and prayed and the Lord announced to Isaiah that he would heal him. In 2 Kgs 20:9 a sign is granted Hezekiah as a surety, that the sun will go back ten degrees or steps on Ahaz's sundial. *Hezekiah and Manasseh* has basically the same plot, but *Hezekiah and Manasseh* makes Hezekiah's healing the result of his repentance of his sins. This provides an etiology for his illness, for in general Hezekiah was regarded as a good king, even as an in some ways ideal one. [3] Note, however, Hezekiah's pride and subsequent self-abasement related in 2 Chr 23:25–26. This is surely related to the attempt to understand Hezekiah's illness. Indeed, *Hezekiah and Manasseh* throughout, as our references will show, is drawing substantially on 2 Chronicles.

---

1. See the introductory remarks to text no. 2 for details of the manuscript.
2. The relevant chapters, 2 Kgs 18–20, also occur in Isa 36–39. We quote them here from 2 Kings.
3. Compare 2 Chr 31:20.

The second incident relates to his son Manasseh who is portrayed as the opposite of Hezekiah. His sinfulness is well documented in the Bible, where he is indicted for idolatry and following "the abominable practices of the nations" (2 Kgs 21:2). His wicked acts are enumerated in 2 Kgs 21:2–9, and the innocent blood he spilt is mentioned in 2 Kgs 21:16. To the biblical story, *Hezekiah and Manasseh* adds the theme of idolatry caused by a woman. This is perhaps inspired by the stories of Solomon and of his love of foreign women who tempted him into idolatry. In addition to Solomon, perhaps the figure of Jezebel also contributed to the picture of wicked, idolatrous women at this point.[4]

Manasseh's long reign of fifty-five years when seen together with his wicked conduct demanded explanation and 2 Chr 33 expands the story told in the Book of Kings and adds an incident to the narrative in Kings, the tale of Manasseh's exile and repentance related in 2 Chr 33:11–20. Thus, we read in 2 Chr 33:11–13:

> Therefore the Lord brought upon them the commanders of the army of the king of Assyria, who took Manasseh with hooks and bound him with fetters of bronze and brought him to Babylon. **12** And when he was in distress he entreated the favor of the Lord his God and humbled himself greatly before the God of his fathers. **13** He prayed to him, and God received his entreaty and heard his supplication and brought him again to Jerusalem into his kingdom. Then Manasseh knew that the Lord was God.

Hezekiah and Manasseh expands and elaborates upon the circumstances of Manasseh's sin, exile, imprisonment, and the miraculous divine intervention which is granted to him as a result of his repentance and prayer. Nothing is made of the different characters of Hezekiah and Manasseh, for it is the sin, repentance and miraculous intervention that are at the center of the author's interest. The narrative concludes with Manasseh's restoration to his throne in Jerusalem.

The narrative of these events is followed on the rest of fol. 143v by a different work, an exhortation to fasting and prayer, illustrated by biblical examples such as Adam, Noah, Abraham, etc. and continuing on fol. 144r with Joiakim and Anna, the Virgin, John, etc. This paradigmatic material is supplemented with further discussion of fasting, including refraining from

---

4. See 1 Kgs 11:4–6 and 11:6–8. Moreover, the Armenian apocryphal Solomon texts published in this volume also develop the attribution of idol worship to Solomon, instigated by his foreign wives.

wicked speech and concludes with assurances of reward and freedom from Hell's punishments.

Hezekiah and Manasseh as an individual work is known to date only in this single manuscript. As we said, the story is based on the narrative in 2 Kings, which is supplemented for Hezekiah and Manasseh from 2 Chronicles. Part of the diction is drawn from these works and from other biblical sources. The author excerpts two verses holus-bolus: In §13 he introduces a verse drawn from 2 Kgs 21:16, and in §25, he cites Pr Man 1. He also knows the tradition of Isaiah being sawn in two inside a tree at Manasseh's command. This tradition is alluded to in Heb 11:37 and later apocryphal, Rabbinic and Christian sources.[5] In addition to these clear citations the work depends on its biblical sources for quite a lot of content and for some of its wording.

As well as these direct literary sources, the work utilizes a number of *topoi* current in Jewish and Christian writing based on or expanding the Bible. So observe:

(1)	The admonitory death-bed speech or testament	§§6–7
(2)	Manasseh's sexual sins caused idolatry	§§9
(3)	A theme from Hellenistic literature: a female figure takes drugs to cause her illness to lead a central male figure astray	§10
(4)	An idol made in the form of a beloved figure	§13
(5)	A woman using her feminine wiles and drunkenness, gets her own way. Usually she is a positive figure: here she is negative	§§11, 23–24
(6)	A fast lasting forty days and forty nights	§25
(7)	Resurrection of dead animals as a sign of redemption	§28
(8)	The pagan king's recognition of God	§32

Thus, the work is an apocryphal writing, utilizing biblical sources and designed to fill out details "omitted" by the biblical text or to address problems created by a reading of that text. In doing this the author uses a combination of citation, biblical diction, and much of his own language. In the construction of the plot and its events, he uses well-known apocryphal traditions (such as Manasseh sawing Isaiah in two) and a number of standard biblical, postbiblical, and Hellenistic topoi. As well as promoting repentance and its reward, the work gives a significant place to lament, prayer, fasting, and penitence

---

5. See §21 and notes there.

15. HEZEKIAH AND MANASSEH

as works leading to repentance and forgiveness. These particular virtues are often stressed by Armenian Christian texts.

A number of letters are illegible due to loss of ink or other damage.

Text

M4168 1/ /fol. 142v / Բարեպաշտ եւ աստուածասէր թագաւորն Եզեկիա յանկարծ ի մեղս անկաւ։ Եւ բարկացաւ Տէր ի վերայ եւ կամէր սատակել զնա։ Եւ ասաց Աստուած մարգարէին յԵսայեա. «Երթ զգուշացոյ զԵզեկիա»։

2/ Եւ եկեալ մարգարէն յայտնեաց թագաւորին զմեղս իւր եւ զբարկանալն Աստուծոյ եւ զմահն իւր՝ մինչեւ ի մտանել արեգականն։ Յայն մահու անկաւ ի վերայ Եզեկիա։

3/ Յայնժամ թագաւորն ի պահս ապաւինեցաւ եւ յաղօթքն⁶ յուսացաւ։ Սուքն արին դարձաւ, եւ պիտեր յետ Գ ժամուց մեռանէր։⁷ Եկն Եսայի մարգարէ եւ ասէ. «Ահա էտես Աստուած զարտասուս աչաց քոց եւ զդառնութիւն սրտի քոյ եւ ողորմեցաւ քեզ։ Եւ այլ ոչ մեռանիս, եւ ԺԵ. (15) տարի եւս կեանս շնորհեաց քեզ, զի երկեար յինէն եւ ազատեցեր զծառայս քո եւ ողորմեցար աղքատաց եւ եդուր բաժին տանն Աստուծոյ»։

4/ Եւ ասէ Եզեկիա. «Որպէ՛ս հաւատամ բանից քոց, զոր ասես»։ Ասէ Եսայի. «Ահա արեգակն տասն աստիճան յառաջ երթից, զի լաւատասցես խօսից իմոց»։ Ասէ Եզեկիա. «Ոչ, այլ յետո դարձցի»։ Նոյնժամայն յետս դարձաւ։ Մեծ զարմանք էր, զի ի զկզբանէ⁸ արարածոց ոչ էր եղեալ այնպէս։ արեգակն ի մուտս էր, ի տեղի Թ. (9) ժամուն եկն կանգնեցաւ։

5/ Իսկ մարգարէն Եսայի եկեալ երանեաց եւ գովեաց զթագաւորն եւ ասաց, զի «ահա Տէր Աստուած հաշտեցաւ ընդ քեզ, զի ահա ԺԷ. (17)⁹ տարի եւս ապրիս վասն երկիւղածութեան քոյ»։

6/ Այսպէս պահքն եւ աղօթք հաշտեցոյց զԱստուած ընդ թագաւորին։ Զնոյն ԺԷ. (17) տարին պահօք եւ աղօթիւք եւ արտասուօք եկաց Եզեկիա։

---

6. An example of changed use of the Ancient Armenian nom. pl. ending, common in the Middle Ages.

7. Stone and Hillel, "Index of Variants," no. 117.

8. Sic!

9. For the common corruption of ե/է, see Stone and Hillel, "Index of Variants," no. 222. It also occurs in the next section. Here it should be "fifteen" as is clear from 2 Kgs 20:6.

Իսկ յօր մահուան խրատեաց զորդին իւր զՄանասէ եւ ասաց. «Եթէ կամիս մեծանալ եւ թագաւորել յաշխարհս, Աստուծոյ պատուիրանին հնազանդ կաց, պահօք եւ աղօթիւք անցո՛ զկեանս քո եւ մաքուր կաց ի պոռնկութենէ այլազգաց։ Թէ պահես զխրատս իմ եւ զպատուիրանն Աստուծոյ, մեծանաս քան զամենայն թագաւորս երկրի, եւ այլ ոչ ոք կարէ ընդ քեզ թշնամանութիւն առնել։

7/ Ապա եթէ ոչ պահես զխրատս իմ եւ զպատուիրանն Աստուծոյ, առանց թշնամւոյ՝ եւ առանց պատերազմի ի ձեռաց ընտանեաց եւ ծառայից քոց անկանիս ի գերութիւն։ Եւ ապա փոշիմանիս եւ յիշես զխրատն իմ»։ Զայդ ասաց եւ աւանդեաց զհոգին։

8/ Եւ թագաւորեաց որդի նորա Մանասէ եւ մոռացաւ զխրատ հօրն եւ ոչ պահէր զպատուիրանն Աստուծոյ։ Եւ եղեւ յոյժ մեծ թագաւոր եւ ահարկու ի վերայ ամենայն թագաւորաց, որք ամենեքեան հնազանդեցան եւ հարկու տային նմա։ Եւ խնդրեաց ի կռապաշտիցն զտ..գ.ցս եզագ.կ..ի[10] ի ծառայութիւն իւր։

9/ Եւ թագաւորն կռապաշտից ընտրեաց գեղեցիկ աղջկունս եւ արու տղայս՝ եւ առաքեաց Մանասէի։ Եւ Մանասէ շնայր ընդ մանկունս եւ ընդ աղջկունս կռապաշտից։ Իսկ աղջիկ մի յոյժ գեղեցիկ էր, եւ զնա խիստ սիրէր, եւ այնքան, մինչ զի թագուհին արար զնայ, եւ այնքան, որ զիշերն ճրագ վառէր մինչ ի լոյս եւ յերեսն հայէր։

10/ Եւ կինն օր մ[ի] դեղեաց զինքն եւ անկաւ հիւանդ։ Թագաւորն տեսաւ զերեսս նորա ... նած[11] դեղնաց, եհարց, թէ՝ «Զի՞նչ գայ ունիս»։ Ասաց կինն. «Ցաւ չունիմ. յորժամ զիմ հօր[12] կուռքն ի մտսւ բերեմ, նեղիմ, հալիմ եւ մաշիմ։ Եթէ կամիս՝ առողջանամ, արա ինձ կուռք մի ոսկեղէն, որ պաշտեցից զնա. ահա առո[ղ]ջանամ»։

11/ Յայնժամ թագաւորն շինեաց կուռք մի յոսկւոյ կնոջ սիրոյն։ Ասէ կինն. «Սիրե՞ս զիս»։ Ասէ թագաւորն. «Այո՛, սիրեմ զքեզ»։ Ասէ կինն. «Ուրեմն երկիր պագ կռոցն»։ Եւ երկիր եպագ թագաւորն։[13]

12/ Այլ / fol. 143r / եւ շինեաց զբարձունս եւ կանգնեաց զկուռս, զոր Եզեկիա եբարձ։ Եւ կռապաշտեցաւ ընդ կնոջն, եւ պաշտէին զկուռս։ Եւ առնէր անիրաւութիւն եւ կախարդութիւն, զոր հայր իւր խափանեաց։

13/ Եւ բազում անպարտ արիւն եհեղ եւ զերուսաղէմ անպարտ արեամբ ծայր ի ծայր ելից։ Եւ թէպէտ խրատէր Եսայի, սակայն ոչ

---

10. These two words are only partly legible, apparently referring to the girls and boys presented to him according to the next paragraph.

11. Partly legible.

12. in margin p.m.

13. ասէ կիննն1°–թագաւորն2° in lower margin p.m.

լսէր նմա։ Եւ մեռաւ կինն այն։ Թաղեաց զպիղծն եւ կանգնեաց ի վերայ գերեզմանի նորա կուռք` նորա պատկերի նման։ Եւ պաշտեալ ետ ամենայնի զպատկեր կնոջն։

14/ Եւ էառ այլ կին ի կռապաշտ թագաւորաց դստերացն` յոյժ գեղեցիկ իբրեւ զնա։ Եւ կանգնեաց այլ կուռք այն կինն, եւ պաշտէին ինքն եւ թագաւորն։

15/ Եւ կայր թագաւորին թագ մի ի հօրէ մնացած։ Ակ[ն] մի կայր ի վերայ, որ իբրեւ զճրագ վառէր։

16/ Յաւուր միում ասաց կինն. «Եթէ սիրես զիս, դիր զթագն ի գլուխ կօրցս»։[14] Ասէ թագաւորն. «Այս թագս ի հօրէս է մնացեր, եթէ դնեմ ի գլուխս իմ եւ ոստիմ յատեան յաթոռ ի մէջ ամենեցուն։ Այժմ եթէ դնեմ ի գլուխ կօրցն, ամենեքեան իմանան եւ թշնամի լինին եւ սպանեն[15] զիս»։

17/ Ասէ կինն. «Գիշերն դիր ի գլուխ կօրցն, զի պաշտեցցուք, եւ ցերեկն դիր ի գլուխ քո եւ նիստ յատենի»։ Ասէ թագաւորն. «Դոնապանք աստուածապաշտ են. եթէ իմանան, կու պատմեն իշխանացն»։

18/ Ասէ կինն. «Երբ այդպէս է, փոխէ զդռնապանքն,[16] ի մեր ազգէն դիր»։ Հրամայեաց թագաւորն, եւ փոխեցին զդռնապանքն։

19/ Քանզի[17] լուեալ կռապաշտիցն ..գն,[18] եթէ Մանասէ կռապաշտեցաւ, եւ վասն որսայոյ զնա գրեցին թէ. «Ընդէր առնես սուգ անմխիթար վասն միոյ կնոջ։ Այլ գեղեցիկ քան զնա առաքեմք ի դստերաց մերոց»։ Եւ խրատեալ զդուստրն այն ուղարկեցին առ Մանասէ, զի ի դիպող խմու գողացցի զնա։

20/ Դարձեալ եկն Եսայի մարգարէ առ Մանասէ եւ ասէ. «Ընդէր թո[ղ]եր զՏէր Աստուած կենդանի եւ պաշտես զզարշելի պատկերս կնոջ եւ զձեռագործս։ Մինչեւ յերբ անհրաւիս առ Աստուած քո։ Ահա այսպէս ասէ Տէր ամենակալ.[19] «.ո՞չ զքեզ ի ձեռն բռնաւորին բաբիլացւոց եւ պատառեցից զթագաւորութիւն քո, զի բազումս մեղար եւ ոչ երկեար յինէն»։

21/ Ասէ Մանասէ. «Որդի Ամովսայ, դու զի՞արդ իշխեցեր խօսիլ զայս բան առաջի իմ։ Արդ կալէք զդա եւ սպանէք առաջի իմ»։

---

14. Written over another, illegible word.
15. For սպանանեն.
16. This section contains two more instances of the changed usage of the Ancient Armenian nom. pl. ending.
17. քանզի is a marginal correction p.m. of եւ.
18. The first letters of this word are illegible.
19. This word is mostly illegible.

Յայնժամ ծառն, յորս յեցեալ էր մարգարէն, պատառեցաւ յերկուս եւ եկուլ զԵսայի ընդ մէջ: Ասէ Մանասէ. «Խիզար բերէք եւ կտրեցէք ընդ մէջն»: Եւ այնպէս սղոցեցին զԵսայի ընդ ծառին:

22/ Եւ վասն այն յոյժ բարկացաւ Տէր եւ ձգեաց ի սիրտ թագաւորին Մանասարայ որսալ զՄանասէ եւ ի բանտ արկանել: Եւ յղեաց թագաւորն զօմն իշխան ԳՃ. մարդով, ամենեքեան երկաթալ զզէստաւէք[20] զաղտ: Եւ յայտնի յԵրուսաղէմ. եւ եկեալ բանակեցաւ արտաքոյ քաղաքին, որ գիտելով Մանասէ: Ազդ եղեւ կնոջն, եւ նա ասէ. «Ոչ է ձեզ փոյթ. ես բերից զՄանասէ յոտս ձեր»:

23/ Եւ կինն յայսմ գիշերի արբոյց[21] թագաւորին եւ քնեցոյց: Եւ ի մէջ գիշերի գողացան զՄանասէ, հանին յիրանէն: Տվին ի ձեռս կռապաշտիցն գերի եւ տարան ի Բաբելօն, առաջի թագաւորին Մանասարայ: Եւ թագաւորն եդ կապանք երկաթի ի յոտն եւ ի վիզն եւ ի ձեռն: Եւ արարին կոճղ եւ արկին ի հոր, որ էր Խ կանգուն, եւ դրին ջաղացքար մի ի բերան հորոյն եւ գնացին:

24/ Յայնժամ Մանասէ եբեր ի միտ զխրատ հօրն եւ յիշեաց զմեղս իւր: Վայ տայր անձինն՝ եւ ծեծեր զգլուխն եւ ճար ոչ գտանէր[22]: Ապաւինեցաւ յԱստուած եւ սկսաւ լալ եւ աղօթել:

25/ Եւ ասեր ողբաձայն. «Տէր ամենակալ, Աստուած Աբրահամու, Իսահակայ, Յակոբայ եւ զաւակի նոցա արդարոց, ամենակալ Տէր, թող զմեղս իմ»: Խ. օր, Խ. գիշերոյ լալով եւ ողբով ասաց զՏէր ամենակալ եւ զԱստուած աղաչէր:

26/ Եւ յամէն օր կանգուն բարձրանայր ի հորէն, մինչեւ Խ. օրն ելաւ Մանասէ ի բերան հորին: Եւ հրեշտակ Աստուծոյ երեւեալ ումեմն ազդեաց / fol. 143v / զկենդանութիւնն Մանասէի:

27/ Իսկ թագաւորն Մանասար նստեալ ի սեղան ընդ իշխանացն՝ ուտին եւ ըմպէին: Հապք բազումք կային խորովեալ ի սեղան առաջի թագաւորին:

28/ Յորժամ ասէին, թէ Մանասէ կենդանի է, ծիծաղեցաւ թագաւորն եւ ասէ. «Թէ այդ հաւերս[23] կենդանի են, Մանասէ այլ կենդանի է»: Յայնժամ խորովեալ հաւերն երամ առեալ եւ թռեան:

29/ Հիացաւ զարմացաւ թագաւորն եւ ամենայն մեծամեծքն եւ իշխանքն եւ ելեալ գնացին ի բերան հորոյն: Վերացուցի[ն] զքարն եւ տեսին զՄանասէ պայծառ դիմօք: Երբ կանգնեցաւ յոտից, ինքնին լուծան կապանք վզին, ձեռացն եւ ոտիցն:

---

20. ԳՃ—զզէստաւէք in margin p.m.
21. One word erased.
22. Reading uncertain.
23. Middle Armenian plural.

30/ Ասէ թագաւորն կռապաշտ. «Այդ ի՞նչ սքանչելի է, զոր տեսանեմ ի քէն»։ Ասէ Մանասէ.²⁴ «Ո՛չ եթէ ես առնեմ զսքանչելիս, այլ Աստուած հարցն մերոց՝ Աբրահամու, Իսահակայ եւ Յակոբայ. նա առնէ զսքանչելիս»։

31/ Ասէ Մանասար թագաւորն. «Երբ դուք այսպէս զօրաւոր եւ մեծ Աստուած ունէք, ընդէ՞ր երեւտ²⁵ զքեզ ի գերութիւն մեր»։ Ասէ Մանասէ. «Զի ես մոռացայ զԱստուածն իմ եւ մոռացայ զխրատ հօր իմոյ եւ ոչ պահեցի զպատուիրանս Աստուծոյ իմոյ։

32/ Վասն այն բարկացաւ եւ ետ զիս ի ձեռս քո։ Բայց յորժամ անկայ ի բանտ հօրոյս, յիշեցի զխրատ հօրն իմոյ, աղաչեցի զԱստուածն իմ, աղաղակեցի եւ լացի։ Լուաւ ձայնի աղօթից իմոց եւ եհան զիս ի զրոյս եւ արձակեաց զկապանս իմ։ Եւ այժմ դու գիտես՝ ընդ Աստուածն իմ։ Որպէս հաճեցգէ քեզ, այնպէս արա»։

33/ Ասէ Մանասար. «Թողեմ զքեզ վասն Աստուծոյն քո»։ Իսկ մեծամեծքն եւ իշխանքս խորհեցան ընդ թագաւորին եւ ասացին, թէ՝ «Սրբա ի հօրէ եւ ի պապէ թշնամի են մեր ազգին. ոչ կամիմք, եթէ ազատես զդա»։

34/ Եւ ի գիշերն, մինչդեռ խորհէր թագաւորն, որպէս արասցէ, երեւեցաւ նմա Տէր Աստուած եւ ասէ. «Առաք զՄանասէ ի տեղն իւր։ Եթէ ոչ, քակեմ ի ժամուս յայս զթագաւորութիւն քո եւ սատակեմ զքեզ»։

35/ Զարթեաւ [ի տես]լենէն²⁶ Մանասար թագաւորն եւ ի մեջ գիշերին կոչեաց զՄանասէ եւ ասէ. «Մեծ է Աստուածն քո, քանզի իշխանք իմ չար խորհեցան քեզ, եւ Աստուածն քո յայտնի արար ինձ արձակել զքեզ։ Այժմ առաքեմ զքեզ ի ծածուկ, զի մի գիտասցեն իշխանքն իմ»։

36/ Եւ արձակեաց զՄանասէ ի գիշերին մեծաւ պատուով եւ հաւատարիմ ծառայիւք, զոր առեալ տարան հասուցին ի քաղաքն Երուսաղէմ։ Եւ նստաւ յաթոռն իւր եւ պատմեր զսքանչելիսն Աստուծոյ, զոր արար ընդ նմա՝ վասն մեղացն եւ վասն զղջմանն։ Եւ որք լսէին, զարմանային եւ փառս տային Աստուծոյ։

---

24. These two words in margin p.m.
25. երեւտ is a Middle Armenian form.
26. The first part of the word is illegible.

Translation

1/ The pious and God-loving king Hezekiah, suddenly fell into sin. The Lord was wrath with (him) and wished to kill him.[27] And God said to the prophet Isaiah, "Go, warn Hezekiah!"[28]

2/ And the prophet came and informed the king of his sins, and that God was wrathful, and that his death would take place before the sun set. The pain of death fell upon Hezekiah.[29]

3/ Then the king sought safety in fasting and set his hopes upon prayer. His mourning turned to blood,[30] and he was to die after three hours.[31] Isaiah the prophet came and said, "Behold, God has seen the tears of your eyes and the bitterness of your heart and he has had mercy upon you.[32] And, furthermore, you will not die and he has granted you fifteen (more) years of life, for you feared me and freed your slaves[33] and had mercy upon the poor, and you gave the portion of God's house.[34]

4/ And Hezekiah said, "How shall I believe your words that you say?" Isaiah said, "Behold the sun will go ten degrees[35] forward, so that you believe my words," Hezekiah said, "No, but let it turn backwards." At that very moment it turned backwards. It was a great wonder, for such a thing had not happened

---

27. Hezekiah's sin is added to provide a rationale for his illness. Second Kings 20:1 gives no explanation for the illness, but his prideful acts are clearly referred to in 2 Chr 32:25–26.

28. This is not in 2 Kgs 20.

29. Second Kings 20:1 says that the prophet came to him and told him he was going to die. All the rest of this section is an addition.

30. Translating սուրն as սուղն. This is an odd expression, not paralleled in the Bible. It is an authorial addition to the biblical text.

31. The "three hours" go back, perhaps, to the "three days" of Hezekiah's healing. 2 Kgs 20:5 says, "behold, I will heal you; on the third day you shall go up to the house of the Lord." Compare also v. 8 there. These events are also briefly recounted in 2 Chr 33:24.

32. Hezekiah's repentance and prayer are referred to in 2 Kgs 20:2–5.

33. This is an addition by the author. The celebration of freeing of slaves is not a theme commonly encountered in Armenian religious compositions.

34. Cf. 2 Kgs 20:6. The additions to the biblical story made here by *Hezekiah and Manasseh* highlight the theme of repentance. It is odd that God's promise to deliver the king from the Assyrians (Isa 38:6) is not mentioned; see n. 39 below.

35. Or: steps. Compare 2 Kgs 20:9.

from the beginning of creation. The sun was in the west[36] and it came to stand at place of the ninth hour.[37]

5/ Then the prophet Isaiah came and blessed and praised the king and said, "Behold, the Lord God is pleased with you, for behold! you will live <fifteen> more years,[38] on account of your piety."[39]

6/ Thus, the fasts and prayers reconciled[40] God with the king. Hezekiah spent[41] those very <fifteen> years in fasts and prayers and tears.[42]

Then on the day of (his) death, he counseled his son Manasseh and said, "If you wish to be great and to rule over this land,[43] be obedient to God's commandment, pass your life in fasts and prayers,[44] and be pure of licentiousness of the Gentiles. If you observe my counsel and God's commandment, you will be greater than all the kings of the earth and, moreover, no-one will be able to carry out hostile acts against you.[45]

7/ "Then, if you do not keep my counsel and God's commandments, without enemy and without war you will fall into captivity at the hands of

---

36. I.e., the sun was setting. See 2 Kgs 20:9–11. Here the author regards this as concerning a sundial, which seems to be correct. This is, of course, implied by the biblical text which uses "shadow." Many Armenian churches have sundials set in their outside walls.

37. This is additional, both in content and in wording. Of course, in a famous incident, the sun stood still for Joshua; see Josh 10:12–13. On the hours in the Armenian tradition, see Stone, *Angels and Biblical Heroes*, Texts 1.1 and 1.2, with further references there and Eynatyan and Tēr-Vardanean, *Ancient Armenian Calendar*. Here this specific hour is an addition to the biblical text both in content and wording, and the significance of the ninth hour is unclear.

38. 2 Kgs 20:6. The reading seventeen, instead of fifteen in Isaiah is due to the graphic corruption of ե/է. The same is true in the next section.

39. The content here is parallel to 2 Kgs 20:5–6 but there is little verbal similarity. The political dimension, exemplified in "I will deliver you and this city out of the hand of the king of Assyria" (2 Kgs 20:6) is absent from 2 Chronicles and from *Hezekiah and Manasseh*. The miraculous, though present in 2 Kings and Isaiah, is omitted from the parallel material in 2 Chronicles.

40. A plural verb would be expected.

41. Literally: was.

42. This material has no biblical parallel. Note this Christian, ascetic ideal of piety, which is promoted throughout the present document. It complements the theme of repentance.

43. Or: this world.

44. There is no biblical parallel. Observe, once more, this Christian ideal of piety and ascesis.

45. Literally: hostility. This deathbed address is not found in the Bible and is an addition by the author. Hezekiah's death and Manasseh's accession are related in 2 Kgs 20:21, 2 Chr 32:33.

your household and your servants.⁴⁶ And then you will repent and remember my counsel."⁴⁷ He said that and gave up his soul.

8/ And his son Manasseh became king and he forgot his father's counsel and did not observe God's commandments.⁴⁸ And he became a very powerful king and cast his fear upon all kings, who all became vassals and gave him tribute. And he sought from the idol-worshippers *two illegible words* for his service.

9/ And the king of the idolaters selected beautiful girls and boys⁴⁹ and sent (them) to Manasseh. And Manasseh fornicated with the children and the girls of the idolaters.⁵⁰ Then one girl was very beautiful and he loved her greatly, to the point where he made her queen and (he loved her) so much that at night he lit a candle until dawn⁵¹ and gazed upon her countenance.

10/ And o[ne] day, the woman medicated herself and fell ill.⁵² The king saw her ... yellow countenance. He asked, "Which pain (illness) do you have?" The woman said, "I have no pain (illness). When I think of my father's idols, I am afflicted, I melt, and I pine. If you wish me to become healthy, make me a golden idol so that I may worship it. Lo, (thus) I will become healthy."⁵³

11/ Then the king built an idol of gold for his beloved wife. The woman said, "Do you love me?" The king said, "Yes, I love you." The woman said, "Then, bow down to the idol." And the king bowed down.⁵⁴

---

46. As indeed happens when his Gentile wife delivers him to King Sanasar; see §23. The whole address is designed so as to coordinate with the narrative that is to follow.

47. This is fulfilled in §§24 and 31.

48. Manasseh's sins are detailed in 2 Kgs 21:2–7 and 2 Chr 33:2–7.

49. արու means "male." It seems to be superfluous here. Were it the similar and cognate word արի, it would mean "brave, valorous."

50. These sexual sins are not mentioned in 2 Kings or 2 Chronicles. They are required for the plot.

51. Literally: light.

52. A analogous incident involving medication or a magical preparation and seduction is related in *T. Jos.* 6:1–2, compare *T. Reu.* 4:9; see the Hellenistic parallels adduced in a note in Harm W. Hollander and Marinus de Jonge, *The Testaments of the Twelve Patriarchs: A Commentary*, SVTP 8 (Leiden: Brill, 1985), 382. *Testaments of the Twelve Patriarchs* was often included in Armenian Bible manuscripts.

53. Second Kings 21:7 records that Manasseh set up an Asherah. Historically and from archeological evidence, this is a pole or a tree, but this knowledge was lost and it could have been understood by our author as an image or an idol. A generally similar course of events is related about King Solomon in 1 Kgs 11:1–10.

54. This course of events is repeated in §§14–18. Manasseh became a worshipper of idols according to 2 Kgs 21:3 and 2 Chr 33:3.

12/ He also built high places and set up the idols that Hezekiah had removed.[55] And he worshipped idols with his wife, and they served the idols.[56] He did lawless things and magic that his father had prevented.[57]

13/ And he spilt much innocent blood, and he filled Jerusalem with innocent blood from end to end.[58] And although Isaiah rebuked (him), nonetheless he did not hearken to him. And that woman died; he buried the abominable one[59] and he set up an idol on her grave resembling her appearance. And he caused all to worship his wife's image.[60]

14/ And[61] he took another wife from the daughters of the idolatrous kings, very beautiful like her. And that woman set up another idol, and she and the king worshipped (it).[62]

15/ And the king had a crown left by his father. There was a jewel upon (it) which burned like a candle.[63]

16/ One day the woman said, "If you love me, put the crown on my idol's head." The king said, "This crown was left by my father so that I (should) put it on my head and sit in court on a throne, in the midst of all. Now, if I put it on the idol's head, all will know[64] and become enemies, and they will kill me."

17/ The woman said, "At night set (it) on the idol's head so that we may worship (it) and in the morning place it on your head and sit in court." The king said, "The doorkeepers are worshippers of God; if they learn (about this), they will tell the princes."[65]

18/ The woman said, "If this is the case, change the doorkeepers. Set (doorkeepers) from among our people." The king issued a command and they changed the doorkeepers.

---

55. Dependent on 2 Kgs 18:22 and 2 Chr 33:3.
56. Or: idol.
57. 2 Kgs 21:6. His father is not mentioned there. At this point, the language of *Hezekiah and Manasseh* is unlike 2 Kgs.
58. This is a citation of 2 Kgs 21:16. The rest of the section has no biblical basis.
59. Or: the abomination.
60. In some respects, this resembles the Euhemeristic narrative of the origins of idolatry found in *Wis* 14:14–21.
61. The incident related in this section is not in 2 Kings.
62. Note the consistent accusation of women as those who lead men astray into idolatry.
63. Such stories of wondrous gems are not uncommon. This incident in §§13–20 is added to the biblical narrative. This incident is concluded with the tradition of Isaiah's hiding in a tree and Manasseh's sawing of the tree in the middle. See n. 69.
64. Literally: apprehend. That is, "they will learn that I am idolater."
65. §§16–19 are the author's composition and have no basis or parallel in the Bible.

19/ Because the idol-worshippers ... heard that Manasseh had worshipped idols, and, in order to catch him, they wrote, "Why do you mourn inconsolably on account of one woman. We will send (you) another from among our daughters, more beautiful than her." And having instructed that daughter, they sent (her) to Manasseh, so that at a time of drinking, she might steal him.[66]

20/ The prophet Isaiah[67] came again to Manasseh and said, "Why have you abandoned the Lord, the living God, and you venerate the abominable image of a woman, which is manufactured? How long will you act lawlessly towards your God? Behold, thus says the omnipotent Lord, 'I will [ ] you at the hands of the Babylonian tyrant, and I will rend your kingdom,[68] for you committed many sins and did not fear me.'"

21/ Manasseh said, "Son of Amoz, how do you have the right to speak this word before me? Now, seize him and kill (him) before me. Then the tree upon which the prophet was leaning split in two and swallowed up Isaiah inside. Manasseh said, "Bring a saw and cut (it) in two." And thus they sawed Isaiah with the tree.[69]

22/ [70]And because of that the Lord was extremely angered and he cast into the heart of King Sanasar[71] to catch Manasseh and the throw him into

---

66. I.e., for idolatry.

67. Second Kings 21:10–15 records that "the prophets" (unnamed) rebuked Manasseh. The actual words, beyond the general idea of a catastrophe to come, do not resemble those in our document.

68. 1 Sam 15:28. Samuel says to Saul, "The Lord has torn the kingdom of Israel from you this day." The language of tearing used in both instances is striking.

69. This tradition is old and well established both in Jewish and Christian sources. The reference in Heb 11:37 to prophets being sawn in two most probably refers to Isaiah. Compare *b. Yebam.* 49b; *y. Sanh.* 10; *Ascen. Isa.* 1:9, 5:2, 14; this version of his death also occurs in the *Vita Isaiae* in the *Lives of the Prophets*. In many Armenian manuscript Bibles, the *Vita* of Isaiah occurs directly following the Book of Isaiah. The same tradition is found in *Names, Works and Deaths of the Holy Prophets* and see the notes on this in Stone, *Patriarchs and Prophets,* 160–61. A substantial discussion of variant forms of this tradition is to be found in Ginzberg, *Legends of the Jews,* 6:103–4.

70. At this point the story of Manasseh's exile by an unnamed "King of Assyria" and his subsequent return to Jerusalem, commences. It is found in 2 Chr 33:11. The text of *Hezekiah and Manasseh* here is the author's composition, with no source known to me, though such might well exist, still unidentified.

71. In *Hezekiah and Manasseh* the king is called Sanasar. In the Armenian Bible at 2 Kgs 19:37 "Sanasar" is the name of Sharezer, son of Sennacherib, king of Assyria. According to the Bible in 2 Kgs 19:37 and parallel in Isa 37:38, Sharezer killed Sennacherib and fled "into the land of Ararat." Under his Armenian name Sanasar he came to play quite a role in Armenian tradition, providing certain Armenian noble houses with a biblical

15. HEZEKIAH AND MANASSEH

prison. And the king secretly dispatched a certain prince[72] with three hundred men, all in iron armor. And he (the prince) came openly and encamped outside the city, which Manasseh knew. It was reported to the woman and she said, "Have no worry; I will send Manasseh to your feet."[73]

23/ And[74] on that night the woman, got the king drunk and put (him) to sleep.[75] And in the middle of the night they took Manasseh by stealth[76] (and) brought him out of his own place. They gave him into the hands of the idol worshippers as a captive. And they brought him to Babylon, before King Sanasar.[77] And the king put him in iron shackles, on his feet and on his neck and on his hands.[78] And they made a log.[79] And they cast him into a pit that was forty cubits deep, and placed a millstone on the mouth of the pit and went away.

24/ Then Manasseh recalled his father's counsel to mind and remembered his own sins. He bewailed[80] his soul, and beat his head, and found no way (out). He put his trust in God and began to weep and pray.

25/ And he said in a voice of lament, "Lord Omnipotent, God of Abraham, Isaac, and Jacob and their righteous seed,[81] Omnipotent Lord, forgive

---

anchor for their genealogy. See, as a typical case, the references and discussion in Thomson, *Moses Khorenats'i*, 108–9 n. 209, 140 n. 90. The name also appears in Armenian as Sarasar.

72. Or: nobleman.

73. First, note that similar stories are related about Jael, Esther, and Judith. Second, the woman is a sort of inverse form of Jael, Judith, and Esther. Jael having lured Sisera to sleep, hammered a tent peg into his head (Judg. 4:18, 21–22). Jael served as a model for Judith (Jdt 12:20, 13:7–8). The use of wine in a similar situation is also described in both the cases of Judith (12:17–13:2) and Esther (7:2). Of course, in those three incidents the women's aims were praiseworthy, while in *Hezekiah and Manasseh* the woman is intent on betraying Manasseh.

74. The following incidents and details relating to Manasseh's capture, imprisonment, and delivery from the pit are not found in other sources.

75. This incident is recorded nowhere else. It is notable for the continued negative presentation of the Gentile woman. We have observed this tendency of the author above.

76. Literally: stole.

77. See above, n. 69.

78. This description comes from *Pr. Man.* 10, "I am weighted down with many an iron fetter" and from 2 Chr 33:11 where the fetters are of bronze. The difference of the metals indicates that *Prayer of Manasseh* (iron) and not 2 Chronicles (bronze) is the source exploited at this point by the author of the present work. *Prayer of Manasseh* is printed at the end of the Zohrab Bible of 1805.

79. Apparently meaning that they shackled Manasseh to a log or tree trunk.

80. Literally: gave alas to.

81. This is drawn directly from Pr Man 1: "O Lord Almighty, God of our fathers,

my sins." For forty days and forty nights,[82] weeping lamenting tearfully he said "The omnipotent Lord"[83] and beseeched God.

26/ And each day he ascended one cubit from the pit,[84] until the twentieth day. Manasseh climbed to the mouth of the abyss and an angel of God appeared to somebody and notified that Manasseh was alive.[85]

27/ Then King Sanasar was seated at table with his princes. They were eating and drinking.[86] Many roasted birds were on the table before the king.

28/ When they said that Manasseh was alive, the king laughed derisively and said, "If these birds are alive, Manasseh too is alive." Then the roasted birds formed a flock and flew off.[87]

29/ The king and all the grandees and the princes looked (and) were astounded, and going forth they went to the mouth of the pit. They removed the stone and saw Manasseh with a shining face.[88] When he stood up on his own feet the shackles around his neck, hands and feet were released.[89]

---

of Abraham and Isaac and Jacob and of their righteous posterity." The Armenian in both sources is the same.

82. This is a stereotypical length of time; see Gen 7:12, 17, 8:6 (length of Flood); Exod 34:28, Deut 9:9, 18, etc. (Moses on the mountain); and Matt 4:2, Luke 4:2 (Jesus's fast in the desert), among others. Compare *4 Ezra* 14:44.

83. This tag is the opening words of Prayer of Manasseh, to which the author refers here.

84. Which was forty cubits deep, see §23. Apparently when he mounted to a depth of twenty cubits, he was able to climb from the hole. The numbers do not fit. He fasted for forty days and nights, but could leave the pit after twenty days!

85. Literally: the "aliveness" of Manasseh. The text does not make explicit who was notified.

86. The scene is reminiscent of Belshazzar's banquet in Dan 5 and Ahasuerus's feast in Esth 1:3–4. The royal feast is a common feature of court tales, such as in *Epistle of Aristeas*, and in the Zerubbabel story in 1 Esdras.

87. This incident is reminiscent of the resurrection of the calf reported in Stone, *Abraham*, Texts no. 8.29 and 15.29. Compare also the eagle's resurrection of a dead man in *Para Jer* 7.18 though that instance is somewhat different.

88. Shining countenances are a mark of divinity or sanctity. See already Exod 34:29 and also Qoh 8:1 (of the wise), Matt 17:2, Rev 1:16 and many other sources. Observe the studies by Andrei Orlov of "glory" which is associated with light, such as *From Apocalypticism to Merkabah Mysticism: Studies on the Slavonic Pseudepigrapha*, JSJSupl 114 (Leiden: Brill, 2007), especially 327–42.

89. See §23 above.

30/ The idolatrous king said, "What is this marvel that I see (coming) from you?" Manasseh said, "It is not that I do this marvel, but the God of our fathers Abraham, Isaac, and Jacob does this marvel."[90]

31/ King Sanasar said, "If[91] you have such a powerful and great God, why did he give you into our captivity?" Manasseh said, "Because I forgot my God and I forgot my father's counsel and did not observe my God's commandments.[92]

32/ "Because of that he was angry and gave me into your hands. But, when I was put down into the prison of the abyss, I remembered my father's counsel, I beseeched my God, I cried out and wept. He listened to the voice of my prayers and brought me forth from this pit and released my shackles. And now you know (that this took place) through my God. Accordingly, act as it pleases you."

33/ Sanasar said, "I pardon you for the sake of your God."[93] But the grandees and the princes took counsel with the king and said, "These ones[94] from their father's (time) and from their grandfather's (time) are an enemy of our people. We do not wish you to free him."

34/ And in the night, while the king considered how to act, the Lord God appeared to him and said, "Send Manasseh to his place. If not, I will demolish your kingdom in this very hour, and kill you."

35/ King Sanasar awoke <from his vi>sion.[95] In the middle of the night he called Manasseh and said, "Your God is great.[96] Because my princes plotted evil against you, and your God revealed to me to send you free, now I send you secretly lest my princes learn (of it)."[97]

---

90. Such statements of modesty and attribution of extraordinary deeds to God are often to be found in the Bible; see, e.g., Gen 40:8, Dan 2:20–22, 27–28, etc. The expression here "God of our fathers Abraham, Isaac, and Jacob" is probably influenced by *Pr. Man.* 1; compare §35 above.

91. Literally, "when," which word often introduces a conditional clause.

92. This sentence take up themes from Hezekiah's admonition, reported in §6 above.

93. The pagan king's recognition of God forms a major theme in the stories of Daniel, including the apocryphal story of the Dragon. See Dan 2:47; 3:28; 4:37; 6:26–27; 14:41. Sanasar is presented in a notably positive way.

94. The pronoun is plural as is the verb "are," and it seems that the implied subject is Manasseh and his ancestors.

95. Restoring ȗtȗu̞tȗut̞u "from / through a vision / dream." The word is partly illegible.

96. Compare n. 93.

97. Observe the unexplained secrecy in a similar mission described in §23.

36/ And he sent King Manasseh in the night with great honor and with trustworthy servants. They took him, led him and brought him to the city of Jerusalem. And he sat on his throne and he related God's marvels, which he had done with him, concerning his sins and concerning his repentance. And those who heard wondered and gave glory to God.

16. Jeremiah, Susanna, and the Two Elders

Introductory Remarks

This document occurs in manuscript M5607 on fols. 308r–309r, copied in the year 1278 in the Monastery of Vankʻun. Its thirteenth century date makes it a quite early manuscript source for apocryphal texts. The same manuscript also contains a work on the construction of the Tower of Babel.[1] In the manuscript the writing has no title and no versification, and I have introduced a simple pattern of numbering.

This work connects the two wicked elders of Susanna (Dan 13) and the two false prophets whose death is prophesied in Jer 29. The main point of the text is to show that the details in Jer 29 can be harmonized with the specific details transmitted in Susanna. It is, therefore, to be characterized as a school work of harmonization rather than as an apocryphal narrative.

Text

M5607 1/ / fol. 308r / Ի յիշատակի սուրբ մարգարէին Երեմիայի երանելոյն եւ Եպիփանու եպիսկոպոսի կիպրացւոյ, ի մեկնութենէ երկոտասան ականցն, ի բանէն, որ առ Իսրայէլի զիր իորեանա:

2/ Բայց քննեալ գտաք զԵրեմիաս զայս ասելով, զի Հ. (70) ամս ս[ահ]մանեցաւ ժողովրդեան քում ի գերութեան:

3/ Եւ զայս ինչ ասա[ս]ցես որդոցն Իսրայէլի յերկրին բաբելացւոց. «Առէք ձեզ կանայս, եւ եղիցին ձեզ որդիք։ Տնկեցէք այգիս եւ կերայք զպտուղ նորա»:

4/ Եւ յետ այսորիկ ասէ. «Ածցեն զտրակս զայս յերկրին բաբելացւոց ասելով. «Զայս ինչ արասցէ քեզ Տէր եւ զայս ին[չ] յաւելցէ, որպէս արար Սեդեկիա եւ Աքիա, զորս տապակեաց թագաւորն բաբելացւոց»:

---

1. *Short Catalogue* 2, 124.

5/ Վասն որդ առնէին գանաւր[էյ]նութիւն² եւ շնային ընդ կանայս քաղաքացեաց իւրեանց եւ բանս սուտս խաւսէին ի վերայ անուան իմոյ, զոր ոչ հրամայեցի ն[ո]գ[ա], ասէ Տէր»:

6/ Բայց աստ եւ զծերոցս զայս անուանս ասացից քեզ, քանզի մինն Սեղեկիա, իսկ միւսն Աքիա: Բայց անուանք նոցա ոչ բերին ի Դանիելի, բայց բերին ի գա/ fol. 308v /դտնի ուրեմն, զ[ ]ն³ ոչ են Դանիելի յայտնութիւն, այլ ա[ ]ուցեալ զանուանս զայնոսիկ, քանզի անդ են գրեալք՝ մինն Սաբա, իսկ միւսն Ադա:

7/ Բայց Երեմիա ի դատաս[տա]նն⁴ այսպէս ասաց. «Տապակումն», ասաց, «գտանջանս նոցա»: Իսկ ի Դանիէլի այսպէս ասէ. «Յարեաւ ամենայն ժողովուրդն ի վերայ նոցա՝ առ ի քարկոծել զնոսա, որպէս գրեալ է յաւրէնսն»:

8/ Բայց գտաք յայլում թարգմանութեանն Դանիէլի՝ յայլում աւրինակի, եթէ զաւագան հրեղէն անկաւ յերկնից ի մէջ ծերոցն եւ խանձատեաց զնոսա, այլ ոչ նոյնժամայն էսպան: Իսկ զիա՞րդ եղիցի այս կատարեալ, յորժամ այլ եւ այլպէս կայ իւրաքանչիւր աւրինակս գրոց:

9/ Այլ ամենայն ինչ դիւրին է եւ ոչ դժուար, քանզի յայտակն իրացս այսոցիկ ունի ըստ այսմ աւրինակի. եղին քարկոծել զնոսա, իսկ Աստուծոյ կամեցեալ ցուցանել զսրբոյն Դանիէլէ վկայութիւն ճշմարիտ գոլ՝ առ ի քարկոծել զնոսա, մինչեւ մեռեալ էին, զաւագան հրեղէն ընկէց ի մէջ նոցա եւ խանձատեաց զնոսա, եւ դեռ եւս կենդանի էին:

10/ Իսկ լուեալ Նաբուզողդոնոսորա վասն այսր սքանչելեաց եւ նախանձայոյզ եղեալ, յափշտակեաց զնոսա եւ տապակեաց: Եւ այսպէս ամենայն ինչ կատարեցաւ՝ ըստ աւրինացն քարկոծումն իսկ ըստ նախանձու Աստուծոյ, զաւագան հրեղէն՝ խանձատիչ, որ վկայ է Դանիէլ արդար դատողին, իսկ ըստ թագաւորին նախանձու՝ տապակումն:

11/ Կատարեալ տանջանք նոցա, ի վախճան {եկայ} գործով՝ ի ձեռն Երեմիայի աւրինացն կոչեցելոյն մարգարէութիւն, որպէս զի երզակցէ, որ ի Դանիէլն կա: Ըստ գրեցելոցն Երեմիայի մարգարէութեանն, որ ասէ ի սկզբանն. «Սուտ խաւսեցան ի վ[երայ] անուան իմոյ, ասէ Տէր»:

12/ Չի մի ինչ թողցուք պատմել: Հարկ է մեզ ասել, քանզի այսպէս ծերքն այն կեղծաւորք, անժույժք ումանք եղեա[լ],/ fol. 309r / [ ]

---

2. The letter է is reconstructed, its loss being due to a worm hole in the page. A similar hole affects ն[ն]գ[ա] at the end of this section.

3. Letters abraded.

4. Worm hole.

16. JEREMIAH, SUSANNA, AND THE TWO ELDERS 199

զկանայսն խաբէին սուտ իմն պատ[գամ]աւք ստեղծաբանեալ, ասելով ընդ նոսա, եթէ՝ «Ոչ ծնցի Քրիստոսն, ոչ փրկի մեր գերութիւնս, բայց Քրիստոսն ոչ այլուստեք ծնանի, այլ ի մէնջ՝ ի մեծամեծացս Իսրայելի եւ ի ծերունեացս։ Վասն որ հաւանակից լեր մեզ»։

13/ Իւրաքանչիւր ոք ի նոցանէ ասելով. «Եւ խառնակեա ընդ իմ՝ ոչ վասն խանդարատական ցանկունեանց, զի տեսանես, զի ծեր եմ, այլ վասն ողորմութեան Աստուծոյ եւ փրկութեան ամենայն ժողովրդեանս, եւ ընկալցիս զվարձուց այսօցիկ զհատուցումն»։

14/ Իսկ նոքա ի պատրանս անկեալք[5] տային զինքեանս ի մեղս, որպես յանդիմանէ զայս պատճառս սուրբն Դանիէլ ասելով. «Այսպես առնէիք դստերաց Իսրայելի։ Եւ նոքա երկուցեալ խառնակէին ընդ ձեզ, այլ դուստրդ Յուդա ոչ համբերեաց անարդեունեանց ձերոց»։

15/ Եւ այսպես Երեմիայի ասացուածն երզակցէ մեզ, եթէ՝ «Վասն զի առնէին անարդենութիւն եւ շնային ընդ կանայս քաղաքացեաց իւրեանց եւ բանս սուտս խաւսէին ի վերայ անուան իմոյ, զոր ոչ հրամայեցի նոցա ես, ասէ տէր»։ Վասն զի ասէին նոցա, եթէ տէր ասաց ի զաւակի նոցա յարուցանել զՔրիստոսն։ Չի այսպես ասէին կանանցն, եթէ տէր հրամայեաց նոցա։

16/ Եւ վասն այնորիկ եցոյց Աստուած զիւր նախանձն հրեղէն զաւազանին եւ վրէժխնդրութեանն Նաբուզոդոնոսրա եւ յանդիմանութեան սուրբ մարգարէի Դանիէլի։

17/ Այլ զայս ասացի ի ձեռնականս այսորիկ կարգեցելոյ։ Եւ զպատճառսն, որ յառաքելումն ասացաւ՝ եթէ թագաւորեաց մահ յԱդամայ մինչեւ ի Մովսես եւ ի վերայ չմեղուցելոցն։ Բայց աստ Դանիէլ ասէ. «Որպես եւ գրեալ է յարդեաս»։ Արդ եւ զԵրեմիա[յ]ս Տեառն ասէ, որպես եւ յաւետարանիս ասէ Տէրն եթէ աւրէնք մինչեւ ցՅովաննես։

---

5. Deletion mark over ք.

Translation

1/ For a memorial of the holy blessed prophet Jeremiah and of Epiphanius bishop of Cyprus, from the commentary on the twelve stones,[6] which (is) from the book of Iorean of Israel.[7]

2/ But having investigated, we found Jeremias[8] saying this, that seventy years were prescribed for your people in captivity.[9]

3/ And you shall say this to the children of Israel in the land of the Babylonians, "Take wives for yourselves and have children.[10] Plant vineyards and eat its fruit."[11]

4/ And after this it says, "Let them take this parable/simile to the land of the Babylonians saying, 'This is what the Lord will do to you and to this he will add,[12] as he did to Zedekiah and Akʻia whom the king of the Babylonians roasted.'"[13]

---

6. That is, Epiphanius's treatise *de Gemmis*. This work was widely known in Armenian and editions of versions of it were prepared by Robert P. Blake, *Epiphanius De Gemmis*, SD 2 (London: Christophers, 1934); Stone, "Armenian Epitome of *De Gemmis*"; Felix Albrecht and Arthur Manukyan, *De Duodecim Gemmis Rationalis: Über die zwölf Steine im hohepriesterlichen Brustschild nach dem Codex Vaticanus Borgianus Armenus 31* (Piscataway, NJ: Gorgias, 2014).

7. Iorean seems to be a proper name, but remains mysterious. The last phrase is not clear.

8. Observe the Latin / Greek ending of Jeremias.

9. Jeremiah 29:1 is closely related to this: "These are the words of the letter which Jeremiah the prophet sent from Jerusalem to the elders of the exiles, and to the priests, the prophets, and all the people, whom Nebuchadnezzar had taken into exile from Jerusalem to Babylon."

10. Jer 29:6.

11. Jer 29:5–6. The Armenian has նորա "its" where a plural, նոցա "their" would be expected.

12. A biblical phrase, found in 1 Sam 3:17; 2 Sam 19:13 (14). The sentiment of this section is found in Jer 29:22a; 1Kgs 2:23.

13. The Bible has "Ahab" and Աքիարայ in the Armenian of Jer 29:22 which is cited here. This curse is adapted from a rather differently worded context in Jeremiah, which reads, "Արասցէ զքեզ Տէր՝ որպէս արար Սեդեկեայ եւ Աքիարայ, զորս տապակէ աց արքայն Բաբելացւոց ի հուր:" That verse reads in NRSV: "The Lord make you like Zedekiah and Ahab, whom the king of Babylon roasted in the fire." These two men were false prophets whom Jeremiah attacked bitterly in chap. 29.

16. JEREMIAH, SUSANNA, AND THE TWO ELDERS

5/ "This was[14] since they did iniquity and committed adultery with the wives of their fellows,[15] and they spoke lying words against[16] my name, which I did not command them, said the Lord."[17]

6/ But here I will also tell you the names of these elders, because one was Zedekiah and the other Ak'ia.[18] But their names are not adduced in Daniel, but are adduced secretly, indeed, [ ] Daniel's revelation, but [ ] those names, because there they are written, the one as Saba and the other as Ada.[19]

7/ But Jeremiah said thus in judgment,[20] "The roasting," he said, "(is) their punishment." However, in Daniel it said thus, that, "All that people rose up against them to stone them as is written in the Law."[21]

---

14. Literally: On account of which (that).

15. This is from Jer 29:23. The word we translated "fellows" is actually "fellow-citizens," reflecting Greek τῶν πολιτῶν. The Hebrew means "friends, fellows." The citation is very close to the text of the Armenian Bible, for this verse refers to the false prophets Zedekiah and Ahab.

16. The biblical texts all have "in my name."

17. The text continues to quote Jer 29:23. It does not include the last words of the verse.

18. See above n. 13 on this name. The two false prophets mentioned in Jer 29:22 are understood to be the two elders in the story of Susanna. The surface of the manuscript had been damaged and there are what seem to be worm holes, which on occasion produce a lacuna that cannot be restored.

19. These names do not occur in Susanna, or in the book of Daniel. The basis of this assertion is unclear. The name Adah is found in the references to Cainite Lamech's two wives in Gen 4:19, 23. The relevance of that passage to the present section, if any, is unclear.

20. Or: their trial.

21. The discussion of the ensuing fate of the two elders builds on the existence of two translations of Daniel; see §8 below. However, two Armenian translations of Daniel do not exist as far as I know, although Peter Cowe found indication of an earlier translation of Daniel having existed before the present mid-fifth-century translation from Greek. See S. Peter Cowe, *The Armenian Version of Daniel*, UPATS 9 (Atlanta: Scholars Press, 1992), 229–89. The survival of this earliest text into the Middle Ages does not seem unlikely *prima facie*, but it is not known to have taken place. Consequently, just what "the other translation" of Daniel is, from an Armenian perspective, remains mysterious. Perhaps somehow the author is referring to the two texts of Greek Daniel, Old Greek, and Theodotion. The Old Greek of *Sus* 61 simply says that the people killed the elders according to the Law of Moses. The punishment of an adulterous woman and her partner is death according to Lev 10:20 and Deut 22:22. Theodotion, however, has a somewhat different text of these verses of Susanna that speaks of the two elders being cast into a ravine. If the text was translated from Greek or Latin (note in §2 the use of the name "Eremias," with a Latin or Greek ending), of course, the "other translation" might mean the Old Greek, except that the material here is not found in the Old Greek either. *Non liquet*.

8/ But we have found in the other translation of Daniel, in another copy,[22] that a fiery staff fell from heaven between the old men and moved them to compassion, but it did not kill (them) at that same time. But how did this happen[23] when each copy of the book is different?[24]

9/ But everything is easy and not difficult, because according to this copy, it has clearly of these matters: they went forth to stone them, but God, wishing to show concerning holy Daniel's that his is true, in order to stone them before they died, he cast a fiery staff in their midst and burnt them while they were still alive.[25]

10/ Then Nebuchadnezzar,[26] having heard about this miracle, and having become zealous, seized them and roasted (them). And thus everything came to fulfillment—stoning according to the Law and[27] according to God's zeal; a burner—the fiery staff, which witnesses to Daniel as a just judge; then the roasting in accord with the king's zealotry.[28]

11/ Their punishment having been carried out, it <came>[29] to an end by an act, through Jeremiah's summoning of the prophecy[30] of the law, so that it should be in harmony[31] with what there is in Daniel.[32] (This is) according to the writings of Jeremiah's prophecy, which says initially: " 'they spoke falsely [against] my name,' says the Lord."[33]

12/ For we are allowed to relate one thing. It is incumbent on us to say that because those elders were so false, they became unrestrained (and) deceived the women through certain false pre[dic]tions that they made up, deceiving (them) by saying to them, "If Christ will not be born, our captivity will not

---

22. That is, another manuscript.
23. Or: was this carried out.
24. Literally: differently. This means, when the mode of their death is different in the different copies of the book.
25. The author thus accounts for the different means of death in both his sources.
26. In Jer 29:21 Nebuchadnezzar is said to be destined to kill the false prophets.
27. Literally, "but." Stoning is not explicit as the punishment for adultery.
28. Jer 29:22.
29. Here I translate as if the text were եկաւ. The reading եկայ comes from կապանեմ "to shackle," which is difficult in context.
30. I.e., the inspired discourse, compare Jer 29:19.
31. Literally: "sing a duet."
32. See Sus 62 (Dan 13:62).
33. This is dependent on, but not letter for letter identical with, Jer 29:21 and 29:23. The expression also occurs in Jer 14:14, 23:25. In none of these instances can a word be found that might fit the lacuna. Its initial, surviving letter might be վ or ք.

16. JEREMIAH, SUSANNA, AND THE TWO ELDERS

be redeemed. However, Christ will not be born of anywhere[34] but from us, from us grandees of Israel and elders. Therefore, be persuaded of this by us."

13/ Each one of them said, "Lie also with me, not because of compassionate desires, for you see that I am old, but for the sake of God's mercy and the salvation of all our people, and you will receive the recompense of this reward."

14/ Then they, falling into deceit,[35] gave themselves to sin. Just as the holy Daniel opposed this argument,[36] saying, "Were you doing thus to the daughters of Israel? And they, being afraid, were lying with you, but this daughter of Judah did not abide your iniquities."[37]

15/ And thus Jeremiah's discourse harmonizes[38] for us, that "because they did lawlessness and committed adultery with their fellows' wives and spoke false things against my name, which I did not command them, says the Lord."[39] Because they said to them that the Lord said (that) he was going to raise up Christ in their seed, they said to the women, that thus the Lord commanded them.

16/ And because of that God showed his zealousness through[40] the fiery staff and through Nebuchadnezzar's vengeance and in the reproach of the holy prophet Daniel.

17/ And I said this through arranging this ordained one. And the reasons why the mission was spoken of were that from Adam to Moses death ruled also over those who did not sin. But here Daniel says, "As it is written in the Law." Now also Jeremiah says [*the Law*][41] of the Lord. (This is) just as the Lord says in the Gospel, that the Law (continues) up to John.[42]

---

34. I.e., of any source,
35. I.e., being deceived.
36. Or: reason.
37. *Sus* 57 (Dan 13:57). The narrative of §§12–13 is thus integrated with Susanna.
38. Or: "is harmonized."
39. This is a quotation of Jer 29:23 and the point is that the story retailed above fits both with Susannah and Daniel. Therefore this explanation "harmonizes."
40. Literally "of the fiery etc."; the nouns are in the genitive case depending on "vengeance."
41. This is this editor's speculation.
42. Matt 11:3 and Luke 16:16.

17. THE NINEVEHITES

INTRODUCTORY REMARKS

This short text is taken from among a group of similarly brief pieces in Erevan, Matenadaran manuscript no. M101, fol. 401v. It is followed on fol. 401v by an extract from the *Physiologus*, the section on the Phoenix,[1] and a passage on the Dragon-serpent (*višap*).[2] This second short piece is followed by another text on the Ninevehites, attributed to St. Ephrem.[3] We are not publishing the latter, attributed text, but only the anonymous one that precedes it.

Manuscript M101 is a *Miscellany* that was copied in Constantinople and T'oxat' in 1740.[4] It is discussed above, see introductory remarks to text no. 13, *Praise of the Prophets*. In addition to the works mentioned above, it contains: *Concerning the 72 Translators*[5] and *Concerning Elijah*.[6]

As is pointed out in the annotation, the text contains several unusual elements. These include the three-days' fast, Nineveh's location on a lake or perhaps an inlet, and the statements about the prior sin of the city and its corruption. It seems that the author thought that Nineveh had been worthy of destruction because of the Ninevehites' promiscuity. It has been saved by repentance and remained built for three hundred years after this event. This text does not mention Jonah and his preaching, but apparently the penitence that saved the city was that which followed on Jonah's teaching.

---

1. Muradyan, *Physiologus*, 102–5.
2. Gohar Muradyan informs me that the passages on the Phoenix and on the serpent are also found in the second recension of *The Physiologus*, which she has published in "Physiologus (*Baroyakhos*): Armenian Recensions," *Banber Matenadarani* 23 (2016), 312–13, 314–15.
3. For further Ephrem references in Armenian apocryphal texts, see text no. 12, *King Solomon: Four Short Texts*, above pp. 145 n. 12, 147 n. 29.
4. See *Complete Catalogue*, 1.419–30.
5. Published in Stone and Ervine, *Armenian Texts of Epiphanius of Salamis*, 73, but not from this particular manuscript.
6. Fols. 394–401; see text no. 14, *The Short History of the Prophet Elijah*.

17. THE NINEVEHITES

Nineveh's recidivation and its eventual submersion until only its walls and perhaps "its battlements[7] are visible"[8] are events that took place three hundred years after the repentance.[9] In fact, Nineveh was destroyed in 612 BCE as we know from sources outside the Bible. However, the Book of Jonah does not give a date and so it was possible to date his story quite early. This idea of the sin, repentance, and the subsequent renewal of sinning and punishment has not been observed elsewhere, though there is tension between Nineveh's repentance and its overall biblical image as a wicked city; see Nah 2:9 and 3:7.

There are other Jonah works extant among the Armenian parabiblical writings. We may note the following:

(1) Քարոզ Յովնանու Մարգարէի որ ի Նինուէ քաղաքին (*Sermon of Jonah the Prophet which (was) in the City of Nineveh*) (Yovsēpʻiancʻ, *Uncanonical Books*, 345–47; Issaverdens, *Uncanonical Writings*, 185–91).

(2) Այս է Պատմութիւն Նինուէի եւ Յովնանու (*This is the Story of Nineveh and Jonah*) (Stone, *Angels and Biblical Heroes*, 266–76).

(3) The Pseudo-Philonic *de Jonah*, the Armenian text of which was published by Hans Lewy in part 1 of *The Pseudo-Philonic De Jona*, SD (London: Christophers, 1936); an English translation was prepared by Gohar Muradyan and Aram Topchyan and published in "Pseudo-Philo, 'On Sampson and On Jonah,'" in *Outside the Bible: Ancient Jewish Writings Related to Scripture*, ed. Louis H. Feldman, James L. Kugel, and Lawrence H. Schiffman (Philadelphia: Jewish Publication Society, 2013), 1:750–803.

(4) My notes from over the years also include a brief notice of a Jonah work in manuscript M59, 9v–11r. Diligent work in manuscript catalogues would doubtless increase the number of works known from manuscripts.

Text

M101 Յաղագս Նինուէացւոցն

---

7. Is this what զէն means here? See n. 13, below.

8. See n. 14 below.

9. Compare Nah 2:7 and Zeph 2:13, both of which prophesy the destruction of Nineveh but do not mention submerging it in a lake or inlet.

/ fol. 401v / Յորժամ Նինուէացիք իւրեանց քաղաքին կործանումն լուան, այնպէս զղջացան, որ երեք աւուր[10] ապաշխարութեանն պատճառ է, յորս դարձան առ Տէր զղջմամբ մեծաւ՝ խորգով եւ մոխրով: Երեք հարիւ<ր>ք ամ շէն եւ հաստատ մնաց քաղաքն, իսկ յետ այնորիկ մոլորեցան եւ դարձան յառաջին պոռնկութիւնն: Եւ ծովակն, որ մօտ կայր, հեղեղեաց եւ ծածկեաց զնոսա: Եւ երեւի գլուխ պարսպին եւ զինուածոցն ի մէջ ջրոյն այնմիկ:

TRANSLATION

Concerning the Ninvehites

When the Ninevehites heard of the destruction of their city, they so repented that it was the cause of three days' penitence,[11] on which they returned to the Lord with great repentance in sackcloth and ashes.[12] For three hundred years the city remained built and firm, but after that they strayed and returned to their former promiscuity. And the lake that was close by flooded and concealed them, and the top of the wall and the battlements[13] are visible in the midst of that water.[14]

---

10. Above line p.m.

11. The three days' penitence in not mentioned in the book of Jonah. In Jonah 3:4 forty days' penitence are mentioned. The figure of "three days" may derive from Jonah 3:3 which describes Nineveh as "three days' journey in breadth." The same is to be found in *Angels and Biblical Heroes*, 4.13 §1.

12. Jonah 3:5.

13. The meaning of զինուածոցն is more precisely "armament." However, that would be odd here, and perhaps it signifies something like "battlements."

14. This element is not mentioned in other sources we have seen. The word ծովակն which we have translated "lake" could also mean a delimited part of the sea. In *Angels and Biblical Heroes*, 273, n. 1247 we discussed the geographical anomaly of Nineveh being on the sea, which could also be inferred from the biblical book, Jonah 3:1.

18. Story of Daniel

Introductory Remarks

The document published here is, according to its title, an epitome of Daniel's visions prepared by one T'ovma (Thomas) *vardapet*. So far, this is the only copy encountered of this work, and it is preserved in M1134, a *Miscellany* of 1695, fols. 81r–84r.[1] I have chosen to publish the segment dealing with the story of Susanna, which is thematically connected with text no. 16, *Jeremiah, Susanna, and the Two Elders* published above from M5518. We refer to the text of the biblical apocryphon as *Susanna*, but it also occurs as the thirteenth chapter of Daniel. In the manuscript copy of *Story of Daniel*, *Susanna* is followed by reworkings of other parts of Daniel, the sections dealing with Daniel's three companions following that on Susanna.

Manuscript M1134 is a *Miscellany* copied in 1695, of unknown provenance.[2] In this manuscript, the Daniel material runs from fol. 81r to fol. 125r. A typological work ensues, comparing Moses as depicted in the Book of Exodus with Christ. A number of theological works and sermons follow that. This passage dealing with Susanna suffices to illustrate this author's method of work. Clearly, a full study of these Daniel writings is a *desideratum*, though it cannot be done here.

This is not the only Daniel apocryphon existing in Armenian. There is a *Life of Daniel* in the *Lives of the Prophets*,[3] and another brief biographical summary in *Lives, Works and Deaths of the Holy Prophets*.[4] In addition, Yovsēp'ianc' included an apocalypse called *The Seventh Vision of Daniel* in his

---

1. *Short Catalogue* 1, 481. The manuscript does not preserve any further texts belonging to the "Uncanonical" category.

2. See in more detail *General Catalogue* 4, 395–98.

3. The standard Armenian translation is published in Yovsēp'ianc', *Uncanonical Books*, 222–23; Issaverdens, *Uncanonical Writings*, 150–51. See no. 13, *Praise of the Prophets* (p. 171 above) on this and other similar works.

4. Stone, *Patriarchs and Prophets*, 164–65.

Uncanonical Writings and that was translated into English by Issaverdens.[5] In the present manuscript this work follows the apocryphal Daniel retelling. Shortly after Yovsēpʻianc''s edition, *The Seventh Vision of Daniel* was edited and translated into German as the first number of a series of Armenian apocrypha by Kalemkiar.[6] This work has received some attention recently: La Porta published a new English translation with introduction,[7] and it is the subject of an excellent article by DiTommaso.[8] In general for Armenian Daniel Apocrypha, see the helpful list compiled by DiTommaso in his exhaustive work on the Daniel apocryphal writings in various traditions.[9] S. Peter Cowe discussed the development of the figure of Daniel in Armenian tradition and lists a number of works, still unpublished, surrounding this figure.[10] Daniel attracted a plethora of traditions and writings in many Christian and Jewish language traditions.

---

5. Yovsēpʻianc', *Uncanonical Books*, 237–53 and Issaverdens, *Uncanonical Writings*, 249–64.

6. Gregoris Kalemkiar, "Die Siebente Vision Daniel's: Armenischer Text mit deutscher Übersetzung," *WZKM* 6 (1892): 109–36. It was also published as a separate work by the Mekhitarist Press.

7. Sergio La Porta, "The Seventh Vision of Daniel: A New Translation and Introduction," in *Old Testament Pseudepigrapha: More Noncanonical Scripture*, ed. Richard Bauckham, James R. Davila, and Alexander Panayotov (Grand Rapids, MI: Eerdmans, 2013), 410–34.

8. Lorenzo DiTommaso, "The Armenian Seventh Vision of Daniel and the Historical Apocalyptica of Late Antiquity," in *The Armenian Apocalyptic Tradition: A Comparative Perspective*, ed. Kevork Bardakjian and Sergio La Porta, SVTP 25 (Leiden: Brill, 2014), 126–48. See also DiTommaso, "The Early Christian Daniel Apocalyptica," in *Apocalyptic Thought in Early Christianity*, ed. Robert J. Daly (Grand Rapids: Baker Academic Press, 2009), 269–86.

9. Lorenzo DiTommaso, *The Book of Daniel and the Apocryphal Daniel Literature*, SVTP 20 (Leiden: Brill, 2005). He deals with the Armenian works on pp. 499–503. There are a number of other works associated with Daniel in Armenian manuscripts, but my field notes lack details and I hope to publish details of them at a later date. There are also hagiographic writings dealing with Daniel's Three Companions (also known as the Three Hebrews). See concerning that tradition: G. Garitte, "L'Invention géorgienne des Trois Enfants de Babylone," *Le Muséon* 72 (1959): 1–32; Garitte, "Le Texte arménien de l'Invention des Trois Enfants de Babylone" *Le Muséon* 74 (1961): 91–108; Stone, "An Armenian Tradition," 111–23. In addition, the Three Companions in the furnace is a favorite subject of Armenian miniature painters.

10. S. Peter Cowe, "The Reception of the Book of Daniel in Late Antique and Medieval Armenian Society," in *The Armenian Apocalyptic Tradition: A Comparative Perspective*, ed. Kevork Bardakjian and Sergio La Porta, SVTP 25 (Leiden: Brill, 2014), 81–125. He mentions unpublished works on p. 83, and the body of that essay traces the influence of

18. STORY OF DANIEL

At the base of this part of the tradition in M1134 lies an identification of the two lascivious elders who feature in Susanna with the two false prophets excoriated by Jeremiah in chap. 29. The fictional temporal frame of Susanna overlaps with Jeremiah's prophecies against the false prophets in Babylon. We read in Jer 29:21:

> Thus, says the LORD of hosts, the God of Israel, concerning Ahab son of Kolaiah and Zedekiah son of Maaseiah, who are prophesying a lie to you in my name: I am going to deliver them into the hand of King Nebuchadrezzar of Babylon, and he shall kill them before your eyes.

This identification constitutes the central axis around which the retelling of Susanna in M1134 revolves. It is also discussed in the scholastic text, no. 16 above, *Jeremiah, Susanna, and the Two Elders*.

Text

M1134 Title/ Պատմութիւնս ի տեսեան Դանիէլի մարգարէ.[11] մեկնութիւն եւ կարծ ի կարձոյ ի Թովմայ վարդապետէ:

1/ Եւ էր այր մի բնակիչ ի Բաբելոն, եւ անուն նորա Յովակիմ:

2/ Եւ էառ իւր կին՝ անուն Շուշան, դուստր Քեղքեա, գեղեցիկ յոյժ եւ երկիւղած ի Տեառնէ:

3/ Եւ ծնողք նորա էին արդարք եւ ուսուցանէին զդուստր իւրեանց ըստ օրինաց Մովսեսի:

Պարտ է գիտել, զի Երեմիայ մարգարէն ասաց ի գիրս իւր, եթէ «Հ. ամ Իսրայէլ», ասացի, «ի գերութիւն մնալոց է»:

4/ Իսկ Յովակիմ յազգէ Յուդայ մեծատուն, քան ամենայն Իսրայէլ: / fol. 81v /

5/ Արար բուրաստանս ինքեան եւ ադբիւր ի մէջ նոցա: Եւ Շուշան մտեալ լուանայր[12] ի տօթամու, եւ Բ. (2) ադախնայք նորին փակեցին զդուռն եւ զբանալիք անդ եդին:

6/ Իսկ Բ. (2) ծեր՝ չար եւ դատաւորք, կամէին մեղանչել ընդ նմա: Միոյն անուն Աքիաբ՝ որդի Կովդա, եւ միոյն՝ Սեւեկիա, որդի Մասիա:

Daniel (with the so-called "additions") on Armenian culture, from liturgy, to art, poetry, and historical understanding.

11. This should be մարգարէի.
12. յ below line, p.m.

7/ Զոր[13] բազում անգամ խաբեալ էին զզդստերս որդոցն Իսրայէլի, թէ՝ «Մեսիա ի մէնջ ծնանելոց է», եւ սուտ մարգարէութիւնս պատմէին, զոր յառաջագոյն խոսեցաւ Աստուած ի ձիրս Երեմիա մարգարէին։ Եւ ասաց. «Տամ զնոսա ի ձեռն Նաբուգոդոնոսրայ, զի ստակեցցէ զնոսա»։

8/ Իսկ ծերքն ադին զայն յինքեան եւ ասեն. «Ահայ / fol. 81v / ... [14]

9/ ... / fol. 82r / դրունք փակեալ են, եւ ոչ ոք է, որ տեսանէ ի բրա,[15] թէ ոչ Աստուած, որ քնէ զսիրտս եւ զերիկամունս, որ եւ յանդիմանելք եղեն յողջախոհէն։ Լաւ է ինձ մեռանել ի ձեռաց բոց, քան թէ մեղայց առաջի Տեառն՝ տեսողին զամենայն»։

10/ Եւ ճչեաց օգնել[16] իւրն, զոր լուեալ Աստուծոյ, պահեաց զօգնելն ի դիպող ժամն։ Իսկ ընդանիքն պատառեցին ընդ դուռն, այլ ընդ որմովն անցանէին։

11/ Զի ծերոց ադալակն կից Շուշանա ծածկեաց զբանն, որք ասէին. «Օգնեցէ՛ք. պատանի ումն էր ընդ Շուշանա եւ փախեաւ»։ Եւ եղեւ օր մի ժողովոյ, եւ գործեցաւ ատեան, եւ ծերքն եկին անայրէն մոք սպանանել զՇուշան, եւ ոչ ըստ օրինաց։

12/ Եւ վկայեցին / fol. 82v / սուտ. եւ հրամայէին հողանի առնել, քանզի ձեռս եդին ի վերայ գլխոյ նորին՝ իբր ըստ օրինացն առնել, իբր թէ զոհ մատուցեն Աստուծոյ։ Եւ դարձեալ, թէ սուտ լինիցի ինքն, լիցի արիւն ապարտ։

13/ Ադալակեց Շուշան ի ձայն մեծ. «Աստուած ծածկազէտ, դու գիտես, զի սուտ վկայեն»։ Որում լուաւ արդարադատն Աստուած, զի զկամս երկիւղածաց եւ աղօթից նոցա լսէ։

14/ Զարթոյց Աստուած հոգին զերկայնմտութիւն իւր՝ ի վրէժխնդրութիւն ի վերայ մանկան միոյ տղայի՝ ապրեցուցանել զՇուշան։[17] Որպէս խսսամեաց[18] զմեռեալն Իսահակա եւ սէրն Աստուծոյ առ Աբրահամ, յայտնի եղեւ։

15/ Առեալ տանէին ի քարկոծումն, եւ ամենայն ընդանիքն լայով եւ ձանօթք զհետ երթային։ Գոչեաց դարձեալ ադ/ fol. 83r /աղակելով.

---

13. The prefix զ- is superfluous, as often happens in medieval texts. In Ancient Armenian it is either a preposition or the *nota accusativi*.

14. Apparently a folio was missing here from the *Vorlage* of M1134.

15. Unintelligible word: perhaps a corruption of բուրաստան, see above, §4.

16. Abbreviation mark over the first syllable.

17. *Sus* 45.

18. The reading here is not altogether clear.

18. STORY OF DANIEL

«Անպարտ եմ ես յարենէ դորա, եւ դուք՝ անմիտ եւ անիրաւք,[19] ընդէր ոչ քննեցիք զիրաւն[20] եւ զսուտն»։

16/ Եւ հայեցեալ ի Դանիէլ տեսին զերեսն՝ որպէս Մովսեսի եւ իբրեւ գնախա<վ>կային Ստեփանոսի։ Յորմէ բանէ գահի հարեալ յեսու դարձան։ Եւ ներեցին յանդիմանութեան, որ <ան>միստ կոչեաց գնոսա։

17/ Եւ եկեալ նստուցին զդարձեալ[21] ի յատան։ Եւ որպէս Սողոմոն արար դատաստան Բ. (2) կանանց, ասէ. «Մեկնեցէ՛ք զդոսա ի միմեանց»։ Եւ ասէ. «Ա՛յ հնացեալ աւուրք չարութեան, ընդ որով ծառով տեսեր զդա»։[22] Եւ նայ ասէ. «Ընդ հերձեալ[23] ծառով»։ Եւ ասէ. «հերձէ քեզ հրեշտակ Աստուծոյ»։ Եւ հրեշտակ Տեառն եհար գնայ հրեղեն սրով։

18/ Եւ ասէ գմիոյն։[24] «Ա՛յ հնացեալ աւուրք չարութեան, որդի Քանանու եւ ոչ Յուդայ, դու՛ ուխտեցեր»։ / fol. 83v / Եւ ասէ. «Ընդ սղոցեալ ծառովն»։ Եւ ասէ. «Սղոցէ քեզ հրեշտակ Աստուծոյ»։ Եւ հրեշտակն սղոցածեւ սրով կիսամահ արարեալ գնոսա։ Եւ ասեն. «Ծառն էր հերձատերեւ բղոր, եւ սղոցածեւ տերեւն՝ երկայն»։

19/ Դարձեալ. «Հերձել էին եւ պատուաստեալ, եւ այլք զգոս ծառոյ ծայրս կատարեալ էին»։

20/ Եւ ժողովուրդն ի ձայն մեծ էտուն փառս Աստուծոյ, որ ոչ է թողեալ գնոսա ի ձեռաց զերութեան ժամանակին։ Եւ ամենայն ժողովուրդ քարակոծ արարին գնոսա։ Եւ զուքն, որ փորեցին ինքնեանց լցին։

21/ Զոր լուեալ Նաբուզուտոնոսոր, եղ գնոսա ի սան պղնձի, տապակեաց ի հուր։ Եւ վայթեցին ի հող՝ ըստ բանին Տեառն, զոր խոսեցաւ ի ձեռն Երեմիայ մարգարէին։

22/ Եւ եղեն յանէձս զինքաւք. անիծանէին զվիճակակիցսն սալով. «Արասց/ fol. 84r /է քեզ Աստուած, որպէս արար Բ. (2) ծերոցն՝ Աքիաբա եւ Սեկիդիայ»։[25]

---

19. A preceding զ- has been erased.
20. The last four words are added p.m. in the margin
21. The meaning of the prefixed զ- is unclear; see n. 13, above.
22. In the margin with correction mark.
23. The scribe wrote the word զդա by error in the middle of this word, but he bracketed it and marked it with omission signs.
24. Perhaps this is corrupt for գմիւսն "the other (of two)."
25. Corrupt for Սեդեկիա, the transliteration of Zedekiah.

23/ Եւ փոխեցան արտասուք նոցա եւ ամօք հօր եւ մօր Շուշանայ ի խնդութիւն եւ յուրախութիւն։ Եւ բացաւ բերան նոցա ի փառաբանութիւն Աստուծոյ եւ յօրհնութիւն։

24/ Եւ հաստատեցան ի հաւատս եւ ի գործս արդարութեան։

25/ Եւ մեծեցաւ դարձեալ յայս ամենայն մարդկան, որ մեծ էր առաջ քան լինելն աշխարհի։

Additional Note

Յովակիմն առաջին ի զիրս Դանիէլ. եւ Յովակիմ {առաջին} ի տնօրէնութիւն Տեառն՝ մայրն սուրբ կուսին Մարիամ:²⁶

TRANSLATION

Title/ Stories of the Vision of the Prophet Daniel, a commentary and very shortly, by Tovma *vardapet*²⁷

1/ And there was a man, an inhabitant of Babylon, and his name of Joiakim.²⁸

2/ And he took as wife Helkiah's daughter named Susanna, his sister's daughter, very beautiful and fearing the Lord.²⁹

3/ And her parents were righteous and they taught their daughter in accordance with the Law of Moses.

It needs to be known that the prophet Jeremiah said in his book, "Israel," I said, "was destined to remain in captivity for seventy years."³⁰

4/ Joiakim, then, was of the tribe of Judah, wealthier than all Israel.³¹

5/ He made gardens for himself with a spring in them. And Susanna entered and would bathe in the hour of heat³² and her two maidservants closed the gate and placed the key there.³³

---

26. մր in Armenian, with no abbreviation mark. We read as Մարիամա "Mariam, Mary."

27. This person cannot be identified further.

28. Armenian Յովակիմ. *Sus* 1. The chapter and verse references are to parallels, not sources.

29. *Sus* 2.

30. See Jer 29:10.

31. "Then—wealthier," *Sus* 4.

32. I.e., in the hour when the day was hottest.

33. This detail is added by the author.

6/ Then two evil old men, judges[34] wished to sin with her.[35] The name of one was Ahab son of Kolaia and of the other Zedekiah son of Maaseiah.[36]

7/ Who had often deceived the daughters of the children of Israel[37] (saying) "The Messiah will be born of us,"[38] and they would tell (i.e., the women) this false prophecy, which previously God spoke in the book of Jeremiah the prophet.[39] And he (that is, God) said, "I will give them into the hands of Nebuchadnezzar, so that he may slaughter them."[40]

8/ Then the old men took that for themselves and said, "Behold ...[41]

9/ ... the gates are closed and there is no one who sees into (the garden)[42] except God who tests hearts and reins,[43] which are reproached by a modest person. It is better for me to die at your hands than to sin before the Lord who sees all."[44]

10/ And she cried out for help.[45] God, hearing this, kept the help for the fitting time. Then her household[46] rent the gate[47] and they also passed through the walls.[48]

---

34. "Then—judges," Sus 5.
35. This phrase summarizes Sus 7-14,
36. Armenian: Աքիաբ որդի Կովղա and Սեդեկիա որդի Մասիա. Here the two old men are identified with two false prophets named in Jer. 29:21; see the introductory remarks to this document.
37. Expansion of Jer 29:23a.
38. Authorial expansion based on Jer 29:21b. Note the unusual term Մեսիա "Messiah," which indicates that this text might have been translated from another language. See text no. 16.
39. There is no such prophecy in the Book of Jeremiah. False prophets are a frequently encountered theme in Jeremiah. See, e.g., Jer 2:8. 5:13, 31, 6:31, 8:10, etc. No specific condemnation of false prophecies of a Messiah are encountered. The words from "I will give—them 2°" are taken from Jer 29:21b.
40. Jer 27:6-8 is a likely reference, but the exact words do not appear in the Book of Jeremiah.
41. Apparently a folio was missing here from the *Vorlage* of M1134.
42. Sus 20 is reapplied in Susanna's speech here. Unintelligible word, րրա perhaps a corruption of բուրաստան:
43. This is an addition drawing on Jer 11:20, compare 17:10; Ps 7:10(9); 26:2.
44. This resumes after the lacuna with a speech by Susanna. This verse corresponds to Sus 23.
45. Literally: for herself to be helped.
46. Or: family, compare the Greek: οἱ ἐκ τῆς οἰκίας.
47. That is, "broke down the gate."
48. That is, "went inside the walls." The sentence is based on Sus 26, with expansions.

11/ For[49] the cry of the old men against Susanna concealed the affair. They were saying, "Help! A certain youth was with Susanna and he fled." And it came to pass on one day of assembly, court was held[50] and the old men came with the lawless intention to kill Susanna, and not according to the Law.[51]

12/ And they gave false witness.[52] And they commanded to uncover her head because they laid hands on her head, as if acting in accordance with the Law, as if they were offering a sacrifice to God.[53] And moreover, if she herself were lying, the blood would be blameless.[54]

13/ Susanna cried out loudly, "God, knower of secrets,[55] you know that they bear false witness."[56] The justly judging God heard her, for he hearkens to the desires of the pious and to their prayers.[57]

14/ God aroused his spirit of longsuffering[58] for vengeance, (and set it) upon one young boy, to deliver Susanna. In the same fashion, he cared for dead Isaac[59] and God's love towards Abraham became evident.[60]

15/ They took (her) and brought (her) to be stoned[61] and all her household and friends were following weeping.[62] He again called, beseeching, "I

---

49. This section is a summary of *Sus* 24.
50. In Susanna there is no explicit mention of a court being convened.
51. The author has added "and not according to the Law" to the verse.
52. This section expands the text of *Sus* 34 by introducing two additional elements. First the laying of hands on Susanna's head is connected with sacrificial ritual and second, the phrase "according to the Law" is added, as it was also in the preceding verse.
53. *Sus* 32–34.
54. This is the old men's statement.
55. *Sus* 42 is the source of this phrase. The last sentence of the section is an addition to the biblical text.
56. This phrase is drawn from *Sus* 43.
57. The last sentence is expanded from *Sus* 44.
58. This is somewhat unclear. The word զերկայնմտութիւն "long-suffering" is an accusative but that is difficult to understand in context. I have translated as if it were a genitive.
59. This is referring to the Binding of Isaac (Gen 22). Actually, Isaac did not die, but was destined to die and God gave him a reprieve.
60. The point is that it God's was pity on Isaac that made God's love of Abraham evident. Here, pity and anger at the injustice being done to Susanna made God's love of Daniel evident.
61. This is a development of *Sus* 46. Stoning is not mentioned in Susanna.
62. This phrase is not in Susanna.

am innocent of her blood⁶³ and you, foolish and unjust ones, why do you not examine truth and falsehood?"

16/ And looking at Daniel, they saw his face like Moses's and like the first martyr Stephen's.⁶⁴ They were frightened by this speech (and) turned back. And they overlooked the reproach, that he called them foolish.⁶⁵

17/ And having come they seated (him) once more in court.⁶⁶ And just as Solomon did the judgment of the two women,⁶⁷ he said: "Separate them from once another." And he said, "Woe, you who have grown old⁶⁸ in wickedness:⁶⁹ under which tree did you see her?" He⁷⁰ said, "Under a split tree."⁷¹ And he said, "The angel of God splits you." And an angel of the Lord smote him with a fiery sword.

18/ And he (Daniel) said to the (other) one,⁷² "Woe, you who have grown old⁷³ in wickedness.⁷⁴ Son of Canaan and not of Judah, did you swear?"⁷⁵ And he said, "Under the sawn tree."⁷⁶ And he said, "The angel of God will saw you."⁷⁷ And the angel half killed (them) with a saw-shaped

---

63. *Sus* 46. The following text, down to the end of the section, is a periphrasis of *Sus* 48.

64. Moses's face shone according to Exod 34:29, 30, 35. Acts does not say that Stephen's face shone, but it does say, "Stephen, full of grace and power, did great wonders and signs among the people" (Acts 6:8). The phrase in our text is an embroidery on the text of *Sus* 47 and explains why they turned back hastily, as related in *Sus* 50.

65. Here I have emended the Armenian from մխոս to ամախոս, for which reading, compare §13.

66. I.e., as judges.

67. First Kings 3:16–27 tells the story of the judgment of Solomon.

68. Literally: being old of days. This reflects the Greek text of *Sus* 52: Πεπαλαιωμένε ἡμερῶν κακῶν.

69. This is a genitive in Armenian.

70. One of the old men.

71. Thus, literally. The Greek text of Susanna, both OG and Th., has the tree name σχῖνον "mastik tree" and the Armenian translator has taken this as derived from σχίζω "to split." The Greek texts of *Sus* 55 have the same wordplay, for example when OG reads, ὁ γὰρ ἄγγελος κυρίου σχίσει σου τὴν ψυχήν σου. This wordplay was retained by the Armenian translator.

72. Literally: the one.

73. Literally: being old of days. This reflects the Greek text of *Sus* 52: Πεπαλαιωμένε ἡμερῶν κακῶν.

74. See §17 above for the same expression.

75. I.e., to give true evidence.

76. I.e., the question once more.

77. Compare *Sus* 59.

sword. And they said, "The tree was split-leaved (and) round, and the leaf was sword-shaped and long."[78]

19/ Again, they (said, "The leaves) had been split and grafted; and others had grown out of the dried-up tree's extremities."[79]

20/ And the people loudly glorified God, who had not abandoned them from his hands in the time of exile.[80] And all the people stoned them. And the pit which they had dug[81] for themselves, they filled.[82]

21/ When Nebuchadnezzar heard this, he put them into a copper cauldron, he heated it on the fire and they (were) poured out onto the ground according to the Lord's word which he spoke through the prophet Jeremiah.[83]

22/ And they themselves were under curses; [people] use to curse those sharing the(ir) situation:[84] "God will do to you as He did to the two old men Ahab and Ze<de>kiah."[85]

23/ And the tears and shame of Susanna's father and mother were changed into happiness and rejoicing, and their mouths[86] were opened in glorification of God and in blessing.[87]

24/ And they became firm in faith and in deeds of justice.[88]

---

78. At the end of §18, the two old men attempt to reconcile their conflicting evidence. This is an expansion based on the reading of σχῖνον as derived from σχίζω; see n. 71 above.

79. I am indebted to Gohar Muradyan's learning at this point.

80. This is based on *Sus* 60.

81. That is, for Susanna.

82. This is an addition not found in Susanna, nor is stoning mentioned there.

83. This strange detail is not found in Susanna. Conceivably, the reference is to Jer 1:13: "The word of the Lord came to me a second time, saying, 'What do you see?' And I said, 'I see a boiling pot, facing away from the north.'" In any case, Nebuchadnezzar's killing of the two false prophets is prophesied in Jer 29:22. There it is said that they are to be "roasted in the fire." Various biblical verses refer to cooking flesh of sacred offerings in cauldrons in diverse contexts, see 2 Chr 35:12. This fate is prophesied of the enemies of God in Ezek 11:3, 7, 11 and Micah 3:3.

84. The phrase is problematic. Gohar Muradyan suggested the translation given here based on an emendation of սալվ > ասելով.

85. Here the language of Susanna, "old men" is combined with the names of the two false prophets drawn from Jer 29.

86. Singular in Armenian, as is normal usage.

87. The last phrase comes from *Sus* 63.

88. This sentence is not in Susanna but seems to have been added to the story by the author.

25/ And He was again magnified in the eyes of all men,[89] He who was great before the world came into being.

Additional Note

The first Jehoiakim (is) in the book <of> Daniel.[90] And {the first} Jehoiakim (was) in the Lord's household,[91] the mother of the holy Virgin Mary.

---

89. *Sus* 64.
90. This refers to Susanna's husband; see *Sus* 1–2.
91. So in the apocryphal *Gospel of the Infancy*; see E. Tayecʻi, Անկանոն Գիրք Նոր Կտակարանաց (*Uncanonical Books of the New Testament*) (Venice: Mekhitarist Press, 1898), index s.v. The statement here is unclear: one would expect "the father" not "the mother."

19. Ezra Salathiel

Introductory Remarks

Matenadaran manuscript M724 is a *Miscellany* composed of two different parts. The texts to be discussed here are in the first part of the manuscript, copied in Jerusalem and Bethlehem in 1736.[1] In addition to the Ezra texts presented below, it preserves a number of documents appertaining to Armenian biblical retellings. These include *Names of the Forefathers, Prophets, Apostles, and Doctors* on fols. 19v–20r; fols. 158r–169v hold an Ezra text, of which the incipit is identical with Ezra 1:1 and it may be that work, and might even include Nehemiah. The documents edited below follow this Ezra text, designed, apparently to enrich it by the addition of further Ezra documents. In the manuscript a number of patristic works intervene between the onomastic texts on fols. 19v–20r and the *Book of Ezra*. Later on fols. 178r–180r contain the *Stories of Asaph* and *of Nathan*, which have been published.[2] This part of the manuscript ends on fol. 197v. The second part, of a different date, does not contain anything of interest to the present enquiry.

That the figure of Ezra played a significant role in the Armenian tradition is evidenced by the frequent inclusion of *Fourth Ezra* in biblical manuscripts. A brief note on an additional copy of *Fourth Ezra* is added following the three texts being published here from M724.[3]

1. Ezra-Salathiel in the Synaxarion

In M724 on fols. 169v–173v are three passages associated with Ezra. Two of these passages are allied with the entries for Ezra in the Armenian *Synaxari-*

---

1. See the description of this manuscript in *General Catalogue* 3, 475–84.
2. See Stone, *Angels and Biblical Heroes*, 263–65.
3. For a detailed discussion of the text-critical situation of the Armenian version of *Fourth Ezra*, see Michael E. Stone, "Textual History of the Armenian Version of 4 Ezra," in *Textual History of the Bible*, ed. Armin Lange, Frank Feder, and Matthias Henze (Leiden: Brill, forthcoming).

on.⁴ The *Synaxarion* also formed the basis of the treatment of Ezekiel that precedes that of Ezra. The feasts of these two prophets were celebrated on the same day.⁵

Here we present all the material associated with Ezra on these folios of M724. Following the two entries from the *Synaxarion* is a text of Recension B of *Questions of Ezra*. A description of the texts follows, preceding the edition and translation of them.

(1) M724 171v. This text differs from the published Ezra entries in two recensions of the *Synaxarion*, but is allied with, or adapted from them.

(2) M724, fols. 171v–172r bears a general relationship to the fourth recension of the *Synaxarion*, but has considerable individual material and quite a lot of variants. The author's editorial activity is illustrated by his giving this second hagiographic form of the prophet's entry immediately following the preceding.

(3) M724, fols. 172r–173v contain a copy of *Questions of Ezra*. To date, two forms of this work are known. Recension A is included in the collection of Armenian apocrypha published in 1896 by Fr. Sargis Yovsēpʻianc̔.⁶ He drew it from a single manuscript, Venice Mekhitarist V570, *Ritual* copied in 1208 CE. The text in M724 is, however, not a witness to this recension, but to Recension B, which is included in the fourth recension of the Armenian *Synaxarion*. This is a fourth witness now known to this recension, of which three witnesses have been published.⁷

TEXT 1

M724 1/ Իսկ Եզր մարգարէ եւ քահանայ:⁸

---

4. The texts are available easily in Stone, *Armenian Version of IV Ezra*, 38–39. On the recensions of the Armenian *Synaxarion*, see Jean Mécérian, "Introduction à l'étude des Synaxaires arméniens," *Bulletin Arménologique* in *Mélanges de l'Université de St. Joseph* 40 (1953): 99–185.

5. See M724, fol 169v. The date in the fourth recension of the *Synaxarion* is for 4 Areg and 12 March. The text concerning Ezekiel is published in full with some variants in Wright, Satran, and Stone *The Apocryphal Ezekiel*, 118–20.

6. Yovsēpʻianc̔, *Uncanonical Books*, 300–303.

7. The most recent edition is Stone, "Questions of Ezra." A German translation, with introduction and notes was prepared by Jutta Leonhardt-Balzer, *Fragen Esras*, JSHRZ 1.5 (Gütersloh: Gütersloher Verlagshaus, 2005). Very likely, other copies of this work exist, included in manuscripts of the fourth recension of the *Synaxarion*.

8. The title of this and the next work are rubricated.

Ծնեալ եղեւ ի Բաբելոն ի Սաղաթիէլէ։ Եւ անդէն աճեալ զարգացաւ, եկն ընդ Զորաբաբելի յԵրուսաղէմ.

2/ Ետես զշինուածս տաճարին եւ զամենայն բարութիւնն, զոր արար Աստուած ժողովրդեան Իսրայելի։

3/ Սա գրեաց զգիրս Զորաբաբելին եւ զԴարեհին՝ զգալն Գովգայ եւ զկոտորումն նորա։

4/ Սա մեռաւ յԵրուսաղէմ. եւ թաղեցաւ անդէն։

Translation

1/ Then Ezra, a prophet and a priest.[9]
He was born in Babylon, of Salathiel.[10] And there he grew up and developed.[11] And he came to Jerusalem with Zerubbabel.

2/ He saw the building[12] of the Temple and all the good things which God did for the people of Israel.

3/ He wrote the letters to Zerubbabel and that to Darius (concerning) the coming of Gog[13] and his being cut down.[14]

4/ He died in Jerusalem and was buried there.

Text 2

M724 1/ Իսկ միւս Եզրն, որ Սաղաթիէլ կոչեցաւ։[15]

---

9. The development of the figure of Ezra is set forth in Robert A. Kraft, "'Ezra' Materials in Judaism and Christianity," *ANRW* 19.1:119–36. See also Michael E. Stone, "The Metamorphosis of Ezra: Jewish Apocalypse and Mediaeval Vision," *JTS* 33 (1982): 1–18.

10. On the identity of Salathiel, see n. 19 below.

11. Literally: growing, he developed.

12. This word is plural in the text.

13. Armenian Գովգ.

14. There is an unpublished Armenian work on Gog and Magog, eschatological rulers who with their people who will attack Israel. This idea's primary source is surely Ezek 38 and 39. Their exact identification is debated. However, in later texts, usually they are described as coming to presage the eschaton and the battle with them is part of the final confrontation of good and evil. In the Jewish tradition, "Armageddon" is called "the wars of Gog and Magog." See Emil G. Hirsch and Mary W. Montgomery, "Gog," *JE* 6:19–20, where a Scythian identification is suggested and the developments of the legend are traced. Such letters are not mentioned in the Bible, though there are other letters preserved in the biblical Book of Ezra. Likewise, the role of the Byzantine period Daniel apocalypse in Armenian, *The Seventh Vision of Daniel*, should be brought into account; see above, p. 208, nn. 5–8.

15. Rubricated to here.

19. EZRA SALATHIEL

Եւ նա եւս էր ի Բաք/ fol. 172r /իլոն։ Եւ սուգ ունէր վասն աւերածուն[16] յԵրուսաղեմի,[17] վասն որոյ եւ Տէր առաքեաց զհրեշտակ իւր, եւ մխիթարեաց զնա։

2/ Եւ հոգովն Աստուծոյ գրեաց նա գօրէնս եւ զմարգարէսն ամենայն, զոր եղծեալ էր եւ ապականեալ ի հուր եւ ի ջուր[18] ձեռամբ անօրինացն։

3/ Սա արար նոր գիր եւ ուսոյց ժողովրդեանն։ Եւ եւեւ զդարձ գերելոցն եւ մխիթարեցաւ։

4/ Սա ետ պատարել զորովայն յոյի կանանցն ի սեմանց այլազգեացն, որոյ հաւանեալ ամենայն ժողովրդեանն։ Արարին ըստ կամաց նորա։

5/ Սա մեռաւ յԵրուսաղէմ եւ թաղեցաւ անդ։

Translation

1/ Then, the other Ezra who was called Salathiel.[19]

And he too was in Babylon. And he was mourning over the destruction of Jerusalem, [20] on account of which the Lord also sent his angel, and he comforted him.[21]

---

16. Late form.

17. Initial ʝ is superfluous. The addition and omission of this initial letter is so common in manuscripts that Stone and Hillel ("Index of Variants," no. 4) simply note frequency of its occurrence.

18. These two nouns are in the accusative case, which is not clear here. Perhaps a locative or an instrumental would have read more naturally.

19. See n. 10 above. This reflects the idea that there were two Ezras, one was Ezra the Scribe and the other was Ezra Salathiel the author of the apocalypse known as *4 Ezra*. This development is discussed in Michael E. Stone, *Fourth Ezra: A Commentary on the Book of Fourth Ezra*, Hermeneia (Minneapolis: Fortress, 1990), 55–56 and in the older papers by Montague Rhodes James, "Ego Salathiel qui et Ezras," *JTS* 18 (1917): 167–69 and James, "Salathiel qui et Esdras," *JTS* 19 (1918): 347–49. Text 1 makes him father of Ezra, but in text 2, as in the much older *4 Ezra*, both Ezra and Salathiel are regarded as names of the same individual. Observe the consequently different roles of Salathiel in these two documents. There is ambiguity about Salathiel and his role from quite early times: See further Stone *Fourth Ezra*, 55–57 on the origins of this equivalence in a misread biblical phrase.

20. This sentence picks up phrasing from Armenian *4 Ezra* 3:2.

21. Clearly alluding to *4 Ezra* 4:1.

2/ And through the spirit of God he wrote all the Law and the Prophets, which had been destroyed and corrupted by fire and water[22] at the hands of the wicked.

3/ He made a new Scripture and taught the people.[23] And he saw the return of the exiles and was comforted.[24]

4/ He caused the bellies of women pregnant from the seed of gentiles to be split open, at which he persuaded all the people. They did according to his will.[25]

5/ He died in Jerusalem and was buried there.[26]

Text 3. Questions of Ezra

This text, preserved in M724, fols. 172r–173v is a copy of recension B of *Questions of Ezra*, with some variants. I have collated it with the text and apparatus published in 1995 and republished in 2006.[27] The lemma is that text and the variant is M724. I have added in the equivalent variants from the other known copies:

---

22. The regnant tradition is that in the burning of the temple, the Torah was destroyed, see *4 Ezra* 14:21. However, in the same chapter, the twenty-four books of the Hebrew Bible are referred to and the seventy esoteric writings. Twenty-four is the traditional number of books of the Hebrew Bible; see Stone, *Fourth Ezra*, 441. The expression "Law and Prophets" in the gospels denotes Hebrew Scriptures as far as they had crystallized at that time. On these issues, see Stone, *Ancient Judaism*, 122–50. It is of course used in the gospels.

23. This and the preceding two sentences clearly refer to *4 Ezra* 14. The word "water" is not derived from that passage, however, for the fire was the instrument of destruction of the Temple. Perhaps the pair "fire" and "water" as used in *4 Ezra* 7:7 are being referred to, or conceivably the two floods, one of fire and one of water, that were expected at the end of days has influenced this section. On the two floods see *History of the Forefathers* 41 and 43 (Stone, *Armenian Apocrypha Relating to Adam and Eve*, 199–200 and discussion on p. 198). The issue of which books it was that were destroyed, according to legend, in the destruction of the Temple and which Ezra restored, is discussed in n. 22 above.

24. This might reflect the biblical chronology, placing Ezra in the time of the return. It might also reflect *4 Ezra* 13:47–48, talking of the return of the Ten Tribes.

25. See Ezra 9:12 and 10:3. The book of Ezra only mentions "putting away" the foreign wives and not the cutting open of their wombs. The acceptance of Ezra's words on the subject is related in Ezra 10:2–4. Indeed, this matter is at the heart of chaps. 9–10 of the book of Ezra.

26. Ezra's place of death is not mentioned in early sources, but is presumably inferred from the many references to his actions in Jerusalem.

27. See n. 7 above.

19. EZRA SALATHIEL

Y   The Yaysmaurkʻ (*Synaxarion*, ed. 1730).
O   Oxford Bodleian Marsh 438, vol. 3, fol. 402r.
V   Vienna, Mekhitarist MS 10, sixteenth century.[28]

Title] om 774
1/ գրեշտակն Աստուծոյ] գրեշտակ Տեառն = OV
յաշխարհէս] ի յաշխարհէս
2/ կեանք] եւ կեանք
տանջանք անվախճան "unending tortures"] հուրն եւ խաւարն եւ դժոխք յաւիտենական "fire and darkness and eternal hell" = OV : cf. A3
3/ իցէ] է
երկնից] յերկնից
4/ ամենայն] զամենայն = OV
ուր] ուր եւ
դատի] դատէ
5/ զհոգիս մարդկան] զմարդու հոգին
տանիս] + զնոսա
6/ յողս] ի յողդ = O
մեղաւորացն] մեղաւորաց
յողս] յող
7/ երք] յերք
8/ եթէ] թէ
ի յաշխարհիս բարի յիշատակ] բարի յիշատակ ի յաշխարհիս = V
աղօթիւք եւ ողորմութեամբ] ∞
10/ եւս] եւ = O
յիշատակ] + իւր
11/ զալուստ] զալուստն = OV
12/ ձեռացն] ձեռաց
յողիցդ] յողիցն
13/ մարմին հոդացեալ] ∞ = OV
14/ առաջ] յառաջ
գործոց] + նոյն ինքն ողորմեցի իւր հաւատացելոցն ամենեցուն "he himself will have mercy upon those who believe in him"
Colophon differs.

---

28. Hagovpos V. Dashian, *Catalog der armenischen Handschriften in der Mechitaristen-Bibliothek zu Wein*, Haupt-Catalog der Armenischen Handschriften 1.2 (Vienna: Mekhitarist Press, 1895), 79–80.

Text 4. The Oldest Manuscript of *4 Ezra*

In addition to the above three documents, there is a fourth item on Ezra that I wish to present briefly here. In 1979 I published a full, critical edition of *4 Ezra*, based on the twenty-two manuscripts known at that time. There existed at least one further manuscript of which I knew, then in the possession of the late H. Kurdian of Wichita, Kansas. That library was left after Mr. Kurdian's death to the Mekhitarist Monastery in Venice. I saw this manuscript briefly in 1965 and a summary description is to be found in my edition of the *Armenian Version of IV Ezra*, 32 n. 17.[29] I have not yet had an opportunity to examine it in any detail. What is striking is that all these manuscripts are Bibles. This contrasts with the situation of the works similar to *4 Ezra* and equally on the fringes of the Armenian Bible, such as *Joseph and Aseneth* and *Testaments of the Twelve Patriarchs*. Those works were preserved not only in Bibles, but also in other manuscripts of religious character.[30]

A substantial number of further manuscripts are known to me today that contain *4 Ezra* and were not included in the edition. These are listed and discussed in my forthcoming essay on the Armenian version of *4 Ezra*.[31]

Most notable among them is Matenadaran M5607 of 1278,[32] which preserves a long extract from *4 Ezra*: 7:10–9:16C on fols. 67r–81r. This is a significant find for two reasons: First, it is the oldest copy of *4 Ezra* to be found in a nonbiblical manuscript. That manuscript is a *Miscellany* containing a variety of works, a few possibly of apocryphal character, but others belonging to various theological genres. Second, not only is it the second instance known to date of the transmission of Armenian *4 Ezra* in a nonbiblical manuscript, it is also the oldest copy of any part of Armenian *4 Ezra*. Previously, the oldest known manuscript was Erevan, Matenadaran 1500, the famous manuscript copied by the savant, Mxit'ar of Ayrivank' (1222–1290?), which also includes a whole Bible and is still the most important single witness to the Armenian version of *4 Ezra*.

I collated two segments of manuscript M5607 comparing their text with the critical text based on two manuscripts published in my edition,[33] and

---

29. Stone, *Armenian Version of IV Ezra*.
30. See the editions of Christoph Burchard (*A Minor Edition of the Armenian Version of Joseph and Aseneth*, HUAS 10 [Leuven: Peeters, 2010]) and Stone and Hillel (*Armenian Version of the Testaments of the Twelve Patriarchs*).
31. See Stone, "Armenian Text of *4 Ezra*."
32. See *Short Catalogue* 2, 144–45.
33. In Stone, *Armenian Version of IV Ezra*, I have presented the various arguments for the priority of this text type.

with the recension represented by the majority of manuscripts, dubbed ψ and also printed at the end of that critical edition. I give only a preliminary report here, and a full textual study must await the future. On the whole, Aa (M5607) resembles witnesses Wψ, and rarely occurs alone with manuscript H (M1500, mentioned above), which is the base manuscript of the critical edition. It is often related to manuscript W (J2558).[34] It already has the special Armenian expansions, such as that in chapter 9:16A–16I, which corroborates the earlier finding that Agathangelos (fifth century) already cites the reworked recension underlying the text of the critical edition.[35]

Sample Readings and Stemmatic Discussion

In this section, I use the sigla employed in Stone, *Armenian Version of IV Ezra*.[36] I also list a number of readings that serve to show the chief affinities of M5607 and conjecture its position on the stemma given in Stone, *Armenian Version of IV Ezra*, 12.

Among the selected readings given below, taken from the collation of the first and last surviving verses of *4 Ezra* in MS Aa, the instances listed below, occurring in the text of 7:14–26 and 8:27, 9:1–16D, are notable. From them we learn that:

(1) Aa has unique corruptions. This shows that it is not the direct ancestor of any of the manuscript groups.

(2) The group Aa ψ occurs quite often and in significant readings. Therefore, Aa and group ψ share an ancestor.

(3) Aa W ψ is a rather common grouping. W is closest to ψ, but shares some readings with H. The occurrence of Aa together with ψW indicates that its readings are, on the whole, derived from the hypothetical ancestor of what may now be called Recension II.

(4) H Aa :: ψ W occurs rarely. These groupings illustrate that, though all four groups share a common archetype, Aa has no special relationship with H or with the special readings of W.

Thus, we may infer that Aa, the oldest known copy of 4 Ezra, is not the ancestor of H but shares an ancestor with it. Observe that, of course, the conjunctive readings of W ψ and some others as well, contradict these posited relationships. Further such readings may occur in other parts of the surviv-

---

34. See the next section.
35. On all these matters see Stone, *Armenian Version of IV Ezra*, 1–25. That work presents both the critical text and a diplomatic edition of recension ψ.
36. Stone, *Armenian Version of IV Ezra*, xv.

ing text, and conflation and contamination always threaten a stemma based on samples. As has already been noted, W has a series of anomalous readings indicating conflation and this unique character of W is borne out by the variants involving it and Aa.[37]

Aa must share a hyparchetype with H and ψ. Because of Aa ψ also seem to share an ancestor, and H has a different ancestor, readings of the groups H Aa and H ψ are likely to be original. As for W, this manuscript's relationships are complex, sometimes reading with Aa ψ and sometimes with Aa H as well as with H alone. From this it follows that there is a bifurcation between H and Aa ψ W and the ancestor of Aa ψ W split from the archetype at the same level as the ancestor of H. As for unique readings of W, these should now be assessed individually.

The readings listed here are all of such character as to show conjunction or disjunction. Certain common variants are not listed and not regarded as probative nor are minor unique readings of Aa, but those cited are more than sufficient to support the argument being forwarded here.[38] The lemma is the text of the critical edition, and the variant is the reading of M5607 (Aa).

(1) Unique corruptions / readings of Aa[39]

7:16	է] om Aa	
7:19	քաղցր] om Aa	
7:20	արհամարհեցին] աւրէնսն Aa	
7:25	դու] om Aa	
	սողեցի] սողացի Aa	
8:27	գործս] գործոց	
8:27–63	long omission running from զմատլ in 8:27 to մտալ in 9:1] Aa	
9:1	ամենային] զամենայն following կատարել Aa	
9:3	նենգութիւն] նենգութիւնք Aa	
9:8	տեսէ W ψ] գտցէ Aa om H	
9:9	իմ] om Aa	
9:16B	այնպէս] om Aa	
9:16B	եւ 1°] om Aa	
9:16C	համարատութք] om Aa	
9:16D	կրել] + քեզ	

---

37. Stone, *Armenian Version of IV Ezra*, 13–14.
38. Stone, *Armenian Version of IV Ezra*, 23–25.
39. The unique variants of H W and ψ are given in Stone, *Armenian Version of IV Ezra*, 11–13.

19. EZRA SALATHIEL

These readings are decisive and show that Aa is not the ancestor of any surviving manuscript.

(2) Readings Aa ψ: H W

7:17   ասացի] եւ ասացի Aa ψ
9:2   հաւատող] հաւատոյ Aa ψ

less certain is:

7:16   արտի] om W մտի Aa ψ

These readings are not a strong indication of a textual relationship.

(2) Readings Aa ψW : H

7:12   այնորիկ] այսորիկ Aa W ψ
7:14   զայս աշխարհս] զաշխարհս Aa W^{m}ψ
7:16   հպեալ] հպեայ (հպեա W ψ) Aa W
7:18   կեցին] անցուցանեն Aa W ψ
7:19   իբրեւ] պան W* Aa ψ
7:26   եւ1°] om Aa W ψ
9:1   ինձ] + տէր Aa W ψ
9:2   այունգ] յայունգ Aa W ψ
9:3   ժողովրդեան] ժողովրդոց Aa W ψ
9:3   մոլորութիւն] մոլորութիւնք Aa W ψ^m
9:3   այունգ] յայունգ Aa W ψ
9:8   եւ պատրաստեցի — ժառանգութիւն] om Aa W ψ
9:16B կարէ] կարացէ Aa W ψ
9:16D սիրեցիս] սիրեցեա Aa W ψ

(3) Readings of Aa W : H ψ

9:9   այնորիկ] այսորիկ W Aa
9:16A բազումք] բազում W Aa
9:16A ապրեալք] ընտրեալք Aa W

(4) Readings of Aa H : W ψ

7:22   շարեաց] ոչ շարեաց H Aa
7:25   ունայնութիւն] ունայն Aa H

BIBLIOGRAPHY

Adjémian (Ajamian), Chahé. *Grand Catalogue des manuscrits arméniens de la Bible.* Bibliothèque arménienne de la Fondation Calouste Gulbenkian. Lisbon: Gulbenkian Foundation, 1992.

Albrecht, Felix, and Arthur Manukyan, *De Duodecim Gemmis Rationalis: Über die zwölf Steine im hohepriesterlichen Brustschild nach dem Codex Vaticanus Borgianus Armenus 31.* Piscataway, NJ: Gorgias, 2014.

Alexander, P. S. "Incantations and Books of Magic." Pages 342–79 in vol. 3.1 of *The History of the Jewish People in the Age of Jesus Christ.* Edited by Géza Vermès, Fergus Millar, Martin Goodman, and Emil Schürer. Edinburgh: T&T Clark, 1986.

Ananyan, Shahé. "La Figure de Salomon et les livres sapientiaux dans la tradition arménienne." *REArm* 34 (2012): 29–39.

Beer, Bernhard. *Leben Abrahams nach Auffassung der Jüdischen Sagen.* Leipzig: Leiner, 1859.

Bezold, Carol. *Die Schatzhöhle, syrisch und deutsch herausgegeben.* Leipzig: Hinrichs, 1888.

Blake, Robert P. *Epiphanius De Gemmis.* SD 2. London: Christophers, 1934.

Bogharian, Norayr. *Մայր ցուցակ ձեռագրաց Սրբոց Յակոբեանց* (*Grand Catalogue of St. James Manuscripts*). 11 vols. Jerusalem: St. James Press, 1966–1991.

Brinner, William M. *The Children of Israel.* Vol. 3 of *The History of Al-Tabari (Tar'arik al-Rusul wal-Muluk).* Albany: State University of New York Press, 1991.

Brock, Sebastian P. "The Queen of Sheba's Questions to Solomon: A Syriac Version." *Le Muséon* 92 (1979): 331–45.

Burchard, Christoph. *A Minor Edition of the Armenian Version of Joseph and Aseneth.* HUAS 10. Leuven: Peeters, 2010.

Clements, Ruth A. "A Shelter amid the Flood: Noah's Ark in Early Jewish and Christian Art." Pages 277–99 in *Noah and His Books.* Edited by Michael E. Stone, Aryeh Amihay, and Vered Hillel. EJL 28. Atlanta: Society of Biblical Literature, 2010.

Cowe, S. Peter. *The Armenian Version of Daniel.* UPATS 9. Atlanta: Scholars Press, 1992.

———. "The Reception of the Book of Daniel in Late Antique and Medieval Armenian Society." Pages 81–125 in *The Armenian Apocalyptic Tradition: A Comparative Perspective.* Edited by Kevork Bardakjian and Sergio La Porta. SVTP 25. Leiden: Brill, 2014.

Curley, Michael J. *Physiologus.* Austin: University of Texas Press, 1979.

Dashian, Hagovpos V. *Catalog der armenischen Handschriften in der Mechitaristen-bibliothek zu Wein.* Haupt-Catalog der Armenischen Handschriften 1.2. Vienna: Mekhitarist Press, 1895.

DiTommaso, Lorenzo. "The Armenian Seventh Vision of Daniel and the Historical Apocalyptica of Late Antiquity." Pages 126–48 in *The Armenian Apocalyptic Tradition: A*

Comparative Perspective. Edited by Kevork Bardakjian, and Sergio La Porta. SVTP 25. Leiden: Brill, 2014.

———. *The Book of Daniel and the Apocryphal Daniel Literature*. SVTP 20. Leiden: Brill, 2005.

———. "The Early Christian Daniel Apocalyptica." Pages 269–86 in *Apocalyptic Thought in Early Christianity*. Edited by Robert J. Daly. Grand Rapids: Baker Academic Press, 2009.

Dorfmann-Lazarev, Igor. "The Cave of the Nativity Revisited: Memory of the Primeval Beings in the Armenian Lord's Infancy and Cognate Sources." Pages 285–333 in *Mélanges Jean-Pierre Mahé*. Edited by Aram Mardirossian, Agnès Ouzounian, and Constantin Zuckerman. Travaux et Mémoires 18. Paris: Association des Amis de Centre d'Histoire and Civilization de Byzance, 2014.

Duling, Dennis C. "The Testament of Solomon: Retrospect and Prospect." *JSP* 2 (1988): 87–112.

Eynatyan, Juliet. *The Ancient Armenian Calendar (7th–15th cc.)*. Translated by Gohar Muradyan and Aram Topchyan. Erevan: Magaghat, 2002.

Fabricius, Johann A. Vol. 1 of *Codex Pseudepigraphus Veteris Testamenti*. Hamburg: Liebezeit, 1713.

Feydit, Frédéric. *Amulettes de l'Arménie chrétienne*. Bibliothèque arménienne de la Fondation Calouste Gulbenkian. Venice: St. Lazare, 1986.

Frank, K. Suso. *ΑΓΓΕΛΙΚΟΣ ΒΙΟΣ: Begriffsanalytische und Begriffsgeschichtliche Untersuchung zum "Engelgeleichen Leben" im frühen Mönchtum*. BGAMB 26. Münster: Aschendorf, 1964.

Garitte, G. "L'Invention géorgienne des Trois Enfants de Babylone." *Le Muséon* 72 (1959): 1–32.

———. "Le Texte arménien de l'Invention des Trois Enfants de Babylone." *Le Muséon* 74 (1961): 91–108.

Ginzberg, Louis. *The Legends of the Jews*. 7 vols. Philadelphia: Jewish Publication Society of America, 1909–1938.

Goehring, James E. *Ascetics, Society, and the Desert: Studies in Early Egyptian Monasticism*. SAC. Harrisburg, PA: Trinity Press International, 1999.

Goldin, Judah. *The Fathers according to Rabbi Nathan*. YJS 10. New Haven: Yale University Press, 1955.

Grünbaum, Max. *Neue Beiträge zur Semitischen Sagenkunde*. Leiden: Brill, 1893.

Harutʻyunyan, Sargis. Հայ հմայական և ժողովրդական աղոթքներ (*Armenian Incantations and Folk Prayers*). Erevan: Erevan State University Press, 2006.

Himmelfarb, Martha. *Tours of Hell: An Apocalyptic Form in Jewish and Christian Literature*. Philadelphia: University of Pennsylvania Press, 1983.

Hirsch, Emil G., and Mary W. Montgomery. "Gog." *JE* 6:19–20.

Hollander, Harm W., and Marinus de Jonge. *The Testaments of the Twelve Patriarchs: A Commentary*. SVTP 8. Leiden: Brill, 1985.

Issaverdens, Jacques, trans. *The Uncanonical Writings of the Old Testament Found in the Armenian Mss. of the Library of St. Lazarus*. 2nd ed. Venice: Mekhitarist Press, 1934.

James, Montague Rhodes. "Ego Salathiel qui et Ezras." *JTS* 18 (1917): 167–69.

———. "Salathiel qui et Esdras." *JTS* 19 (1918): 347–49.

Kalemkiar, Gregoris. "Die Siebente Vision Daniels: Armenischer Text mit deutscher Übersetzung." *WZKM* 6 (1892): 109–36.

Kévorkian, Raymond H. et al., *Manuscrits arméniens de la Bibliothèque nationale de France: Catalogue*. Paris: Bibliothèque Nationale and Calouste Gulbenkian Foundation: 1998.
Koen-Sarano, Matilda. *King Solomon and the Golden Fish: Tales from the Sephardic Tradition*. Detroit: Wayne State University Press, 2004.
Kohler, Kaufmann, and Louis Ginzberg. "Asmodeus." *JE* 5:217–20.
Kraft, Robert A. "'Ezra' Materials in Judaism and Christianity." *ANRW* 19.1.119–36. Part 2, *Principat*, 19.1. Berlin: de Gruyter, 1979.
Kulik, Alexander. *3 Baruch: Greek-Slavonic Apocalypse of Baruch*. CEJL. Berlin: de Gruyter, 2010.
La Porta, Sergio. "The Seventh Vision of Daniel: A New Translation and Introduction." Pages 410–34 in *Old Testament Pseudepigrapha: More Noncanonical Scripture*. Edited by Richard Bauckham, James R. Davila, and Alexander Panayotov. Grand Rapids, MI: Eerdmans, 2013.
Leonhardt-Balzer, Jutta. *Fragen Esras*. JSHRZ 1.5. Gütersloh: Gütersloher Verlagshaus, 2005.
Lewy, Hans. Part 1 of *The Pseudo-Philonic De Jona*. SD. London: Christophers, 1936.
Lipscomb, W. Lowndes. *The Armenian Apocryphal Adam Literature*. UPATS 8. Atlanta: Scholars Press, 1990.
Loeff, Yoav. "Four Texts from the Oldest Known Armenian Amulet Scroll: Matenadaran 115 (1428) with Introduction, Translation." MA thesis, Hebrew University of Jerusalem, 2002.
McCown, Chester Charlton. *The Testament of Solomon*. Leipzig: Hinrichs, 1922.
Mécérian, Jean. "Introduction à l'étude des Synaxaires arméniens." *Bulletin Arménologique in Mélanges de l'Université de St. Joseph* 40 (1953): 99–185.
Muradyan, Gohar. *Physiologus: The Greek and Armenian Versions with a Study of Translation Technique*. Translated by Aram Topchyan. HUAS 6. Leuven: Peeters, 2005.
———. "Physiologus (*Baroyakhos*): Armenian Recensions." *Banber Matenadarani* 23 (2016): 291–329.
Muradyan, Gohar, and Aram Topchyan, trans. "Pseudo-Philo, 'On Sampson and On Jonah.'" Pages 750–803 in vol. 1 of *Outside the Bible: Ancient Jewish Writings Related to Scripture*. Edited by Louis H. Feldman, James L. Kugel, and Lawrence H. Schiffman. 3 vols. Philadelphia: Jewish Publication Society, 2013.
Orengo, Alessandro. *Owrbat'agirk' (Il Libro del Venerdì)*. Atti della Accademia Nazionale dei Lincei 388. Rome: Accademia Nazionale dei Lincei, 1991.
Orlov, Andrei A. *From Apocalypticism to Merkabah Mysticism: Studies on the Slavonic Pseudepigrapha*. JSJSup 114. Leiden: Brill, 2007.
Quinn, Esther C. *The Quest of Seth for the Oil of Life*. Chicago: University of Chicago Press, 1962.
Robinson, Stephen Edward. *The Testament of Adam: An Examination of the Syriac and Greek Traditions*. SBLDS 52. Chico, CA: Scholars Press, 1982.
———. "Testament of Adam." Pages 989–95 in *Apocalyptic Literature and Testaments*, vol. 1 of *The Old Testament Pseudepigrapha*. Edited by James H. Charlesworth. Garden City, NY: Doubleday, 1983.
———. "The Testament of Adam: An Updated *Arbeitbericht*." *JSP* 5 (1989): 95–100.
Sarghissian, Barseł. Ուսումնասիրութիւն Հին Կտակարանի Անվաւեր Գրոց Վրայ

(*Studies on the Uncanonical Books of the Old Testament*). Venice: Mekhitarist Press, 1898.

———. *Grand Catalogue des manuscrits arméniens de la bibliothèque des Pp. Mekhitaristes de Saint-Lazare*, vol. 1. Venice: Mekhitarist Press, 1914. (Armenian)

Seymour, St. John Drelinc. *Tales of King Solomon*. London: Oxford University Press, 1924.

Srjuni, A. H. "Սրբոյն Եփրեմի ի Յովսեփի վասն եւթն Վահանկի (St. Ephrem's 'On the Seven Vahangs of Joseph')." *Sion* 47 (1973): 26–37, 137–44.

Stone, Michael E. *Adam's Contract with Satan: The Legend of the Cheirograph of Adam*. Bloomington: Indiana University Press, 2002.

———. *Adam and Eve in the Armenian Tradition, Fifth through Seventeenth Centuries*. EJL 38. Atlanta: Society of Biblical Literature, 2013.

———. "Adam, Eve and the Incarnation." *St. Nersess Theological Review* 2 (1997): 167–79. Repr. in *Apocrypha, Pseudepigrapha and Armenian Studies: Collected Papers*, 1:213–25. Edited by Michael E. Stone. 2 vols. OLA 144–145. Leuven: Peeters, 2006.

———. *Ancient Judaism: New Visions and Views*. Grand Rapids, MI: Eerdmans, 2011.

———. *Apocrypha, Pseudepigrapha and Armenian Studies: Collected Papers*. 2 vols. OLA 144–145. Leuven: Peeters, 2006.

———. *Armenian Apocrypha Relating to Abraham*. EJL 37. Atlanta: Society of Biblical Literature, 2012.

———. *Armenian Apocrypha Relating to Adam and Eve*. SVTP 14. Leiden: Brill, 1996.

———. *Armenian Apocrypha Relating to Angels and Biblical Heroes*. EJL 45. Atlanta: Society of Biblical Literature, 2016.

———. *Armenian Apocrypha Relating to Patriarchs and Prophets*. Jerusalem: Israel Academy of Sciences, 1982.

———. "Armenian Canon Lists III: The Lists of Mechitar of Ayrivank' (c. 1285)." *HTR* 69 (1976): 289–300.

———. "An Armenian Epitome of Epiphanius' *De Gemmis*." *HTR* 82 (1982): 467–76.

———. "An Armenian Tradition Relating to the Death of the Three Companions of Daniel." *Le Muséon* 86 (1973): 111–23.

———. "An Armenian Translation of a Baraitha in the Babylonian Talmud." *HTR* 63 (1970): 151–54.

———. *The Armenian Version of IV Ezra*. UPATS 1. Missoula, MT: Scholars Press, 1979.

———. "The Book of Esdras." *JSAS* 4 (1988): 209–12.

———. "The Cedar in Jewish Antiquity." Pages 66–82 in *The Archaeology and Material Culture of the Babylonian Talmud*. Edited by Markham J. Geller. IJS Studies in Judaica 16. Leiden: Brill, 2015.

———. "Concerning the Penitence of Solomon." *JTS* 29 (1978): 1–19.

———. "The Death of Adam: An Armenian Adam Book." *HTR* 59 (1966): 283–91.

———. "The Document Called 'Question.'" Pages 295–300 in *La diffusione dell'eredità classica nell'età tardoantica e medievale: Il "Romanzo di Alessandro" e altri scritti*. Edited by Rosa Bianca Finazzi and Alfredo Valvo. Alessandria: Orso, 1999.

———. *Fourth Ezra: A Commentary on the Book of Fourth Ezra*. Hermeneia. Minneapolis: Fortress, 1990.

———. *A History of the Literature of Adam and Eve*. EJL 3. Atlanta: Scholars Press, 1992.

———. "The Metamorphosis of Ezra: Jewish Apocalypse and Mediaeval Vision." *JTS* 33 (1982): 1–18.

———. "The Months of the Hebrews." *Le Muséon* 101 (1988): 5–12.

———. "A New Edition and Translation of the Questions of Ezra." Pages 293–316 in *Solving Riddles and Untying Knots: Biblical, Epigraphic, and Semitic Studies in Honor of Jonas C. Greenfield*. Edited by Ziony Zevit, Seymour Gitin, and Michael Sokoloff. Winona Lake, IN: Eisenbrauns, 1995.

———. "The Questions of St. Gregory: The First Recension." *Le Muséon* 131 (2018): 141–71.

———, ed. *Selected Studies in the Pseudepigrapha with Special Reference to the Armenian Tradition*. SVTP 9. Leiden: Brill, 1991.

———. *Signs of the Judgment, Onomastica Sacra and the Generations from Adam*. UPATS 3. Chico, CA: Scholars Press, 1981.

———. "Some Armenian Angelological and Uranographical Texts." *Le Muséon* 105 (1992): 147–57.

———. "Some Further Armenian Angelological Texts." Pages 427–35 in vol. 1 of *Apocrypha, Pseudepigrapha, and Armenian Studies: Collected Papers*. OLA 144 Leuven: Peeters, 2006.

———. "Some Observations on the Armenian Version of the Paralipomena of Jeremiah." *CBQ* 35 (1973): 47–59. Repr. in *Selected Studies in the Pseudepigrapha with Special Reference to the Armenian Tradition*, 77–89. Edited by Michael E. Stone. SVTP 9. Leiden: Brill, 1991.

———. "Textual History of the Armenian Version of *4 Ezra*." In *Textual History of the Bible*. Edited by Armin Lange, Frank Feder, and Matthias Henze. Leiden: Brill, forthcoming.

———. "Three Apocryphal Fragments from Armenian Manuscripts." Pages 939–46 in *A Teacher for All Generations: Essays in Honor of James C. Vanderkam*. Edited by Eric F. Mason et al. 2 vols. JSJSup 153. Leiden: Brill, 2012.

———. "Three Armenian Accounts of the Death of Moses." Pages 118–21 in *Studies on the Testament of Moses: Seminar Papers*. Edited by George W. E. Nickelsburg, SBLSCS 4. Cambridge, MA: Society of Biblical Literature, 1973.

———. "Two Stories about the Ark of the Covenant." Pages 257–71 in *Sion, Mère des Églises: Mélanges liturgiques offerts au Père Charles Athanase Renoux*. Edited by Michael Daniel Findikyan, Daniel Galadza, and André Lossky. Semaines d'Études Liturgiques Saint-Serge 1. Münster: Aschendorff, 2016.

Stone, Michael E., and David Amit. "Report on the Survey of a Medieval Jewish Cemetery in Eghegis, Vayots Dzor Region, Armenia." *JJS* 53 (2002): 66–106.

———. "The Second and Third Seasons of Research at the Medieval Jewish Cemetery in Eghegis, Vayots Dzor Region, Armenia." *JJS* 57 (2006): 99–135.

Stone, Michael E., and Roberta R. Ervine. *The Armenian Texts of Epiphanius of Salamis: de mensuris et ponderibus*. CSCO 583. Leuven: Peeters, 2000.

Stone, Michael E., in collaboration with Vered Hillel. *The Armenian Version of the Testaments of the Twelve Patriarchs: Edition, Apparatus, Translation and Commentary*. HUAS 11. Leuven: Peeters, 2012.

———. "Index of Variants." Pages 421–46 in *The Armenian Version of the Testaments of the Twelve Patriarchs: Edition, Apparatus, Translation and Commentary*. By Michael E. Stone and Vered Hillel. HUAS 11. Leuven: Peeters, 2012.

Stone, Michael E., and M. E. Shirinian, eds. *Pseudo-Zeno, Anonymous Philosophical Treatise*. PhA 83. Leiden: Brill, 2000.

Stroumsa, Gedaliyahu G. "Le Couple de l'ange divin et de l'esprit: Traditions juives et chrétiens." *RB* 88 (1981): 42–61.

Tatʻewacʻi, Grigor. Գիրք Հարցմանց (*Book of Questions*). Repr. ed. Jerusalem: St. James Press, 1993.

Tayecʻi, E. Անկանոն Գիրք Նոր Կտակարանաց (*Uncanonical Books of the New Testament*). Venice: Mekhitarist Press, 1898.

Tēr Vardanyan, Gēorg. Vol. 7 of Մայր ցուցակ հայերէն ձեռագրաց Մաշտոցի անուան Մատենադարանի (*General Catalogue of Armenian Manuscripts of the Maštocʻ Matenadaran*). Erevan: Nairi, 2012.

Thomson, Robert W. *Moses Khorenatsʻi: History of the Armenians*. Rev. ed. Ann Arbor: Caravan, 2006.

Torijano, Pablo A. *Solomon the Esoteric King: From King to Magus, Development of a Tradition*. JSJSup 72. Leiden: Brill, 2002.

Weil, Gustav. *Biblische Legenden der Muselmäner*. Frankfurt am Main: Literarische Anstalt, 1845.

Wright, Benjamin G., David Satran, and Michael E. Stone. *The Apocryphal Ezekiel*. EJL 18. Atlanta: Society of Biblical Literature, 2000.

Wright, J. Edward. *The Early History of Heaven*. New York: Oxford University Press, 2000.

Wutz, Franz Xaver. *Onomastica Sacra: Untersuchungen zum Liber Interpretationis Nominum Hebraeorum des Hl. Hieronymus*. TU 41.2. Leipzig: Hinrichs, 1915.

Yovsēpʻiancʻ, Sargis. Անկանոն գիրք Հին Կտակարանաց (*Uncanonical Books of the Old Testament*). Venice: Mekhitarist Press, 1896.

Index of Subjects

This index contains chief subjects, names of ancient and modern persons and places, and names of works of which there is substantive discussion. Names of works are italicised. The list is in alphabetic order.

4 *Ezra*, Armenian, sample collations and stemmatics, 225–27

Aaron, 84
   staff of, 126
Abel, killing of, 12
Abimelech, 18
Abiram, 97
Abraham, 17, 42, 49, 85, 181, 195
Abraham and the Idols, 148
Abraham
   dispute of, with God, 27
   intercession or supplication of, 45, 46, 49, 53
   love of, 27, 48, 53
   recognition of God, 21
   recovers prisoners, 49
   saga of, 57
   ten trials of, 15
Achan, 60, 99, 100, 101
   punishment of, 101
   sin of, 103
Adam, 4, 5, 181
   children or house of, 97, 98
   garment of, 6
   Testament of, 5, 6
   treasury of, 6
adamant. *See* stone, adamant, 95
Adrianopolis (Edirne), 1
Adriazar, king of Edom, 161
Ahab, king, 97, 176, 177, 209
Ahab, son of Kolaiah false prophet, 200, 213

Ahiman, 95
Ai, 95
   destruction of, 100, 102
   king of, 99
Ajamian (Adjémian), Shahe, Archbishop, ix, 145, 146, 148, 159
Akʻia, false prophet, 200
Akʻor, valley of, 99
al-Tabari, 167
Albanians, Caucasian, 7
Albrecht, Felix, 200
Alexander, Phillip S., 129
alloy, 96
Amalek, 102
Amit, David, 139
Amorites, 87, 88, 91, 100
Anak, son of Ham, 95
Ananyan, Shahe, 150
angel(s), 3, 27, 48, 51, 53, 82, 165, 215
   beauty of, 27, 49, 50
   bodiless, 82
   commander, 93, 94
   delivers prayers, 44
   function of, 94
   guardian, 43, 165
   nine classes of, 1, 3
   ranks and/or classes of, 1, 43, 45
   supplication of, 43, 45
   twelve classes of, 2, 3
   vision of, 121
angelic life, 82
Anna, 181

antichrist will open the Ark and eat the manna, 124, 127
Apostles, twelve, 87, 91
Arba (person), 95
archangels, 3
    guardian, 43, 44
Arevšatyan, Sen, ix
Ark of the Covenant, 57, 89, 96, 116
    and the Tent of Meeting, 116, 126
    antichrist opens to eat manna, 124
    captivity of, 124, 127
    construction of, 110, 114, 126
    dimensions of, 60, 126
    disasters attendant to captivity of, 121
    divine speech from, 116, 124, 126, 127
    feeds people with manna, 121
    hiding of, 121, 124, 127
    image or type of the cross, 90, 126
    in the Temple, 124
    Joshua beseeches, 119
    oracular function, 116, 117, 119
    placed beneath the altar, 127
    powers of, 89, 110, 118, 121, 124, 126
    prophecy from, 116
    symbol of Church, 121
    taken to battle, 117, 118
    will burn antichrist, 124, 127
    wind issues from, 119
    wonders of, 118, 119, 121, 124
    wonders of, cease, 121
Ark, Noah's, 8, 11, 12
    construction of, 14
    door of, 12
    shape of, 12
Armageddon, 220
Armenian language, dialects of, 24
Armenian Patriarchate of Jerusalem, ix
Armenians, Noachic ancestry of, 18
armour, 96
Arsaces and Arsacids, 18
ascetic ideal, ascetics, 56, 189
Asher, 19
Ashtoreth, 161
Assyrians, 127
Astarte, 161
astronomy, 11
Ayalon, Vale of, 104

Azan of Bethel, 97
Azotos (Ashdod), 127

Baal, prophets of, 178
Babylon, 221
Babylonia, 200
Bahl, 18
Baptism, 92
Bardakjian, Kevork, 208
basket, Rahab's, type of the mystery of the Church, 88
Bauckham, Richard, 208
beastiality, 48, 54
Beer, Bernhard, 21
Belshazzar, banquet of, 194
Benjamin, 19
Bethlehem, 218
Beth Shemesh, 127
Bezold, Carl, 6
Bible
    Armenian, xiii, 96
    embroidered, 57, 96, 103, 189
binding, magical, 104
Biqlis, 167
birds, shade Solomon, 169
Blake, Robert P., 200
blind and lame, parable of, 44
blood, of goat, 96
body, Edenic, 126
Bogharian, Norayr, Archbishop, ix, 145, 147, 148, 151, 157, 158
Book of Ezra, 218
Book of the Watchers, 9
books
    burning of Solomon's, 156, 161, 162
    divine, 55
    inspired, 156
Brief History of Joshua, 148
brimstone, 53
Brinner, William M., 167
Brock, Sebastian P., 133, 143
Bubu bird, 167
    brings report to Solomon, 169
    carries Solomon's letter 169
Buller, Bob, x
Burchard, Christoph, 224
burning, punishment, 53, 54

INDEX OF SUBJECTS

Cain, begetting of, 12
Cain, sons of, 13
Caleb, 83, 95
Canaan, conquest of, 60
Canaanites, 49, 83, 87, 91, 95, 100, 103, 107, 108, 126, 154
    kings of, 104, 106
    seven nations of, 106
Carmi, 72, 99
carob, 22
cauldrons, 216
cavalry, Israelite, 117
cave, prophets hidden in, 177
cedars, 161, 162, *See also* Temple, built of cedars
censer, golden, 116, 126
chastity, 54
Cherubs, 3
Chiefs, angelic class, 3
Christ, 5, 23, 93, 105, 107
    blood of, 88
    guardian, 43
    mystery of, 106
chronological texts, 129
circumcision, 18, 92, 93, 97
cities of refuge, 60
    forty-eight, 107
Clements, Ruth, 12
cloud, divine, 82
Commentary on the Twelve Stones (de Gemmis), 200
Communion, 55, 121
Concerning the Writings of Solomon 2, 148
Constantinople, 137
constellations
    names of, 105
    twelve, 105
copper, 96
Coulie, Bernard, xiii
court of law, 214
covenant, 108
Cowe, S. Peter, 201, 208
cross, 99, 105, 107, 126
    wood of, 2
crown, 55, 133
    Manasseh inherits, 191
crows. *See* ravens

crucifixion, 88
Curley, Michael J., 95

Dagon, 127
Daly, Robert J., 208
Dan, 19
Daniel, Book of, 201, 217
    differing copies of, 202
Daniel
    examines evidence, 215
    face like Moses's, 215
    face like Stephen protomartyr's, 215
    figure of, 208
    judgement by, 215
    Old Greek translation, 201
    reproaches elders, 203
    second translation of, 202
    Theodotion translation, 201
    two translations of, 201
    young boy, 214
Daniel, Seventh Vision of, 208
Darius, 220
Dashian, Hagovpos V., 223
David, 55, 103, 118, 124, 127, 154, 155
    praise of, 174
    prophet and king, 174
Davila, James R., 208
Day of Atonement, 44
Day of Judgement, 55, 93
Dead Sea, 11, 32, 54, 90
death
    pain of, 188
    rules from Adam to Moses, 203
delay for repentance, 101
demon, replaces Solomon on throne, 163, 165
demon(s), demonology, 43, 129, 163, 165, 166, 169
desert, 178
diasporas, Armenian and Jewish, 139
Dinah, 19
DiTommaso, Lorenzo, 208
dittography, 112
divinity
    in angelic commander, 95
    in thorn bush, 95
doctors, of soul, 135

dog, 55
Doitch, Tomer, x
Dominions, angelic class, 3
donkey, 55
Dorfmann-Lazarev, Igor, 5
Duling, Dennis C., 129

earth, corpse-eating, 47
Easter, 89
Ebal, Mount, 103
Eghegis, Armenia, Jewish cemetery in, 139
Egypt, 84, 100
Egyptians, 93, 94
elders
    cursed, 216
    deceived women by false prophecy, 202–3, 213
    false witness of, 214
    lay hands on Susanna, 214
    two adulterous, 213
    two wicked, 213
    wicked, boiled, 216
Eleazar, priest, 82, 84
elements, 43, 45
elenchic. *See* erotapokrisis
Eli
    death of, 121, 127
    priest and judge, 119, 120
    rebukes sons, 120
    Life of Eli, 171
Elijah, 176, 177
    confrontation with Ahab, 178
    Life of Elijah, 171
Emmanuel, Michal, x
Ephraim, tribe, 81
Ephrem, St., 106, 145, 204
    works connected with, 145
Epiphanius of Cyprus, 200
erotapokrisis, erotapokriseis, 8, 9–11, 25, 54, 55, 101, 102
Ervine, Roberta R., 134, 204
Esau, 19
Esther, 193
Ethiopia, wise woman from, 155
evidence, rules of, 42, 43
Exodus, 100,000 people, 83
exorcism, 4

Eynatyan, Juliet, 106, 189
Ezekiel, 172
    Pseudo-, 44
    text concerning, 219
Ezra
    prophet and priest, 220
    two persons so named, 221

Fabricius, Johann A., 129
faith, 51
false prophets, adultery of, 201
fasting and prayer, 188, 189
Feder, Frank, 218
feet of woman, bad, 170
Feydit, Frédéric, 2, 4
fiery staff, 202, 203
fifty, significance of, 89
Finazzi, Rosa Bianca, 123
Findikyan, Michael, 58
fire, 26, 50, 54
    and water, 222
    punishment by, 54, 98, 135
    rain of, 53, 54, 87
fishermen, 165
five kings, 53
flint, symbol of hearts, 92
flint knife, 92
    buried with Joshua, 108
Flood, generation of, 55
forty days and nights, Manasseh weeps, 194
forty years, 81
forty-day fast, 82
forty-five, significance of, 47
Frank, K. Suso, 82

Gad, 19, 95
    tribe, 85
Galadza, Daniel, 58
Garden of Eden, 53, 126, 135
garden, closed gates of, 213
Garitte, G., 208
garlic, 93
gates, heavenly, 44
geography, ignorance of, 22, 90, 206
Gerizim, Mount, 103
giants, 107

INDEX OF SUBJECTS

Gibeath-ha'aralot, 92
Gibeon, 104, 119
Gibeonites, 60, 103, 154
    ruse of, 103–4
Gilgal, 92, 118
Ginzberg, Louis, 21, 129, 163, 167, 192
Gittin, Seymour, 9
glory, 55, 56, 165
    garment of, 90
    of God, 91
    studies of, 194
gluttony, 13
God
    determines human fates, 165
    friend of, 56
    glorified, 216
    heathen worship of, 88
    justice of, 46
    king of Israel, 119
    knowledge of, 42
    living, designation, 88, 95, 108
    mercy of, 44, 46, 54, 188
    name of, 100
Goehring, James E., 82
Gog, coming of, 220
Gog and Magog, 220
    wars of, 220
gold, on the Ark, 116
Goldin, Judah, 137, 139
Good Friday, 107
Goodman, Martin, 129
Gospel, 90
graphic corruption, 72, 89
greed, 102
Grigor Tat'ewac'i, *Book of Questions*, 8, 10
Grigor, scribe, 7
Grünbaum, Max, 167

Hadad the Edomite, 161
Hagar, 18
Ham, 12, 14, 95
hand, right, 99
Haran (Abraham's brother), 17
    death of, 15, 19
Haran (place), 17–19
Harut'unyan, K'nar, 7
Harut'unyan, Sargis, 2, 4, 163

Hayk, 18
heart, circumcision of, 92
heavens, Abraham's contemplation of, 21
Hebrews (people), 96, 97
Hebron, 95
heifers, 121
Helkiah, Joiakim's brother-in-law, 212
Hell, 93, 95, 97
    depths of, 91
    descent to, 98
    divisions of, 98
    punishments of, 182
Henze, Matthias, 218
Hezekiah, king, 7, 171, 180
    companions of, 150, 162
    counsels Manasseh on deathbed, 189
    reason for illness of, 180
    pride of, 180
    sin of, 188
Hezekiah and Manasseh
    character of, 182
    composition of, 182
Hiel of Bethel, 97
Hillel, Vered, 30, 81, 149, 150, 183, 221, 224
Himmelfarb, Martha, 98,
Hiram, King, 155
Hirsch, Emil G., 220
Hollander, Harm W., 190
holy spirit, 162
homiletics, 57, 87, 130
homoeoarchton, 114
homoeoteleuton, 114
homosexuality, 27, 28, 44, 47, 50, 54,
honey, 22
    varieties of, 23
Hophni, son of Eli, 119, 120
hospitality, 48, 49
    rules of, 50
humans, ideal age of, 47
humility, 85
hyssop, 162

idol-worshippers, 190
idolatry, 87
    caused by a woman, 181, 190, 191
idols, falling of, 21, 22
Ierianos, 162

Ignatius of Amida, scribe, 7
Infancy Gospel, 5, 123
infertility, 98
Iorean of Israel, Book of, 200
iron, 95, 96
Isaac, 195, 214
    binding of, 214
    birth of, 18
    death of, 19
Isaiah, Life of, 192
Isaiah, prophet, 180, 188, 189
    praise of, 173
    sawn in half, 182, 191,
Isaiah, (Story of), 7
Ishmael, birth of, 18
Israel Academy of Sciences and Humanities, ix
Israel Science Foundation, ix
Israel, country, 107
Israelites, 121, 126, 155, 167, *See also* Hebrews
    lose battle, 120
Issachar, 19
Issaverdens, Jacques, 132, 143, 144, 147, 150, 171, 175, 207, 208

Jacob, 19, 195
    marriages of, 19
Jael, 193
James, Montague Rhodes, 221
Japheth, 12, 14
javelin, 102
Jehoiakim, first, 217
Jehoikim, 181
Jeremiah, prophet, 200, 201, 202, 203, 212, 213
    captured by Assyrians, 127
Jeremiah, Susanna, and the Two Elders, 209
Jericho, 57, 59, 60, 95, 97, 100, 101, 103, 118
    attack on, 60
    circumambulation of, 118
    circumambulation of, type of Psalter, 99
    cursing of, 60, 97, 98
    fortress, 117
    idols on the walls of, 117
    image or type of Hell, 95, 98, 126
    king of, image of Satan, 126
    sins of, 98
    walls of, 95, 96, 97
Jerusalem, 119, 121, 127, 128, 133, 141, 221
Jesus, blood of, 97
Jesus, true, 89
Jezebel, 177
Joad, Life of, 171
John, 181
John the Baptist, 22
    food of, 22–23
Joiakim, 212
Jonah works, list of, 205
Jonah, Book of, 205
Jonge, M. de, 190
Jordan, 32, 54, 85, 88, 92
    crossing of, miracles attending, 59
    flow of, 89
    splitting/crossing of, 59, 90, 117, 126
Joseph, 19, 55, 81
Joseph and Asenath, 224
Josephus, 163
Joshua, 57, 81, 88, 92, 93, 95, 97, 99–105, 117, 126
    abstinence of, 83, 88
    age of at death, 108
    appointed leader, 84
    death of, 61, 108
    dream of, 59
    dream trial of, 82
    encounters angel, 60
    fast of, 59
    fast of, forty-six days, 82, 83
    humble, 85
    image of true Jesus, 126
    Moses's disciple, 59, 81–82
    name of, 57, 59, 81, 83
    origins of and office, 59
    stretches out arm, 102
    type of Christ, 83, 90
    valour of, 83
    vision of, 93
Joshua, Brief History of, 8, 10, 11, 58, 61, 175
Judah, 19
    country, 107

INDEX OF SUBJECTS 241

son of Simon, 103
tribe, 97, 101, 212
Judea, 23
judgement, rules for, 42, 43
Judith, 193

Kalemkiar, Gregoris, 208
Kēosēyan, Y., 146
Kēoškeryan, A., 146
Keturah, 18
Kévorkian, Raymond H., 128
kings
    five, hanged, 99
    thirty-two, 126
    three, 119
    three, attack Israel, 118
Kiriath Jearim, Ark in, 127
Koen-Sariano, Matilda, 165
Kohler, Kaufman, 163
kor (measure), 134
Kulik, Alexander, 44
Kurdian, H., 224

land
    allotment of, 60, 83–85, 107,
    called holy, 95
    character of, 93
    promise of, 85
Lange, Armin, 218
LaPorta, Sergio, 208
Law continues up to John, 203
Law of Moses, 212
law, second, 91
lead, 96
    molten, 96
leaders, dual, 84, 85
Leah, 19
Lebanon, wood of, 133, *See* cedar
legal procedures, 42, 43
legs, hairy, become white, 167
Lent, 107
Leonhardt-Balzer, Jutta, 219
letter of God, 5
Levi, 19
life, vanity of, 135
light, eternal, 56
Limbo, Descent into, 126

Lint, Theo M. van, ix
Lipscomb, Lowndes W., 7, 9, 13
locusts, 22, 121
lodestone, 95
Loeff, Yoav, 4
Lord, living. *See* God, living
Lossky, André, 58
Lot, 18, 27, 47, 49, 51, 52, 53
    daughters of, 51, 52, 53
    wife of, 27, 28, 47, 51
lots, cast, 101
luminaries, worship of, 105

Maccabees, Books of, 96
magic, 51, 190
magnetic stone, 95
male children, 93
Malkhasyan, Armen, 148
man is angel, 93
Manasseh, king, 171, 180
    arises from pit, 194
    besotted with girl, 190
    betrayed by woman, 193
    Isaiah rebuked, 191, 192,
    magical acts of, 191
    praises God, 195
    repentance of, 181
    restoration of, 196
    sex with girls and boys, 190
    shackles fall off, 194
    shining face of, 194
    sinfulness of, 181
    taken captive to Babylon in chains, 193
    weeps forty days and nights, 194
    wickedness of, 190
    worships idols, 190, 191
Manasseh, tribe, 85
manna, 89, 93, 116
manna, cessation of, 85
manslaughter, 107
Manukean, Tat'ewik, 64
Manukyan, Arthur, 200
Mardirossian, Aram, 5
martyrs, 56
Mary, Virgin, 217
Mason, Eric F., 99

mastik tree, 215
Maštocʻ Matenadaran, ix
McCown, Chester Charlton, 129
Mécérian, Jean, 219
Mekhitarist Monastery, Venice, 224
mercilessness, 48
mercy, gate(s) of, 44, 48
mice, 121
Michael, archangel, 163
Millar, Fergus, 129
miracles in Temple, ten, 137
Mishnah, 137
modius (measure), 134
Mokkʻ, 148, 159
Montgomery, Mary W., 220
moon, stands still, 11
Moses, 55, 82, 83–85, 88, 89, 102, 103, 108, 121, 154
   death of, 84
   father of prophets, 173
   law(s) of, 103, 155, 161, 201
   Life of Moses, 172
   mediator, 115–16
   praise of, 173
   prophet, 115, 126
mountain people, 107
movement, six-fold, 47
mule, begetting of, 19
Muradyan, Gohar, ix, 45, 48, 88, 95, 106, 204, 216
murderer, 45
Mxitʻar Ayrivanecʻi, 146, 151, 156, 224
mystery, divine, 89

Nahor, 17, 19
Names, Works, and Deaths of the Holy Prophets 172, 192
Naphtali, 19
Nathan, Life of, 171
nations, twelve believing, 91
Nativity, 89
natural law, 54
nature, word indicates the body, 90, 126
Nebo, Mount, 84
Nebuchadnezzar, 202, 203, 213, 216
Nebuchadrezzar (Nebuchadnezzar), 209
Nerṙn (antichrist, Nero), 127

Nersēs, craftsman of Noah's Ark, 12
Nickelsburg, George W.E., 172,
Nineveh, 205
   flooded, 206
   recidivation of, 206
   survives three hundred years, 206
   walls of, 205
Noah, 8, 181
   chastity of, 12, 13, 14
   founder of humanity, 13
   sons of, marriage of, 14
Noah's Ark. *See* Ark, Noah's
Noemzara, 14
numerology, 47

Obadia, commander of fifty, 177
omniscience, 100
On Measures by Anania of Shirak, 134
onion, 93
onomastics, 53, 57, 83, 92, 118
oracle, 116
Orengo, Alessandro, 4, 5
Orlov, Andrei, 194
orphan, 45
orthography, 38, 58, 64, 131, 151
Ouzounian, Agnès, 5

Pʻaran (place), 22
Pahlavunis, 18
palace, of Pharaoh's daughter, of gold, 161
Palestine, 18
Panayotov, Alexander, 208
Paralipomena Ieremiou, 147
Paralipomena of the Greeks, 147
paralipomena, title, 146, 147, 154
parchment, luminous, 5
Passover, 93
pearl, from clouds, 169
penitence, hope for, 51
penitence, three days of, 206
Pharaoh, 18
Philo of Alexandria, ix, 9
Philo
   Quest. Exod., 9
   Quest. Gen., 9
Phineas, 82, 119, 120
phoenix, 204

Physiologus, 204
pilgrims, 119
pillar, 89
    inscribed with covenant, 108
Pinhas. *See* Phineas
pit, 216
pitcher, golden, 126
Polycrates, 163
poor, 45
power(s), 3, 88, 97
    two, 48
prescience, 51
priest, and prophet, 119
priest, burned, 118
priests
    settling of, 107
    priests, seven, 89, 96
    twelve, with Ark, 117
primogeniture, 19
princes, twelve, 134
promiscuity, 13, 44, 55
prophet, 116
prophet and priest, 119
prophets
    false, 213
    one hundred, hidden, 177
punishment, 55
purification, three days, 89

Queen of Sheba, 132, 167
Queen of the South, 132
Questions and Answers. *See* erotapokrisis
Quinn, Esther C., 2

Rabbinic sources, used by Armenians, 139
Rachel, 19, 101
Rahab, 60, 85, 86, 97, 118, 154
    basket, type of mystery of the Church, 88
    hides spies, 85
    house of, 87, 118
    red sign of, 97
    type of the Church, 87
Rausnitz, Samuel, x
Ravens, 21
Rebecca, 19
recompense, future, 56

Red Sea, 8, 89, 91
red sign, of Rahab, 97
red, symbolism of, 88
repentance, 180
    refusal of, 103
resolution of contradictions, 202, 203
rest, 56
Reuben, 19
    tribe, 86
riddle, 23
ring, swallowed by fish, 163, 165
roasted fowl, resurrected, 194
Robinson, Stephen E., 5
rules, angelic class, 3

Sabaoth, 163
Sabbath, 96
sacrifice, 214
saints, 85, 136
Salathiel, 220, 221
salt
    metaphor of, 107
    pillar of, 26, 51
Sanasar, king, 192, 194, 195
    positive presentation of, 195
    receives night vision, 195
Sarah (Sara), 18
Sarasar. *See* Sanasar
Sarghissian, Barseł, 151, 162, 172
Satan, 4, 6, 20, 95, 98–99, 126
satan, (adversary), 161
Satran, David, 44, 171
Saul, king, son of Kish, 103, 119
scholasticism, 10, 139
Schürer, Emil, 129
seduction, 190
Segub, 97
Sennacherib, 192
Serag (Segub), 98
Seraphs, 3
Seth, sons of, 13, 14
seventh era, 93
Seventh Vision of Daniel, 220
seventy elders, 82
seventy years' captivity, 200, 212
Seymour, St. John D., 23, 129, 163
Sharezar, 192

Sheba, Queen of, 155
Shem, 12, 14
Sheshai, 95
Shinar, 99
shining face, 194, 215
Shirinian, Manea E., 47
shoes, taken off, 94
Short History of Elijah, manuscripts of, 176, 204
Shulberg, Guy, x
Sidon, 161
sign, 54
Simeon, 19
Sinai, Mount, Ark deposited in, 121, 127
sins, debt of, 108
six, meaning of, 47
Sodom, 25, 47, 48, 49, 51
  booty of, 18
  destruction of, 11
  wickedness of, 27
Sodomites, 45, 50, 55
Sokoloff, Michael, 9
Solomon, 190
Solomon, king, 23, 124, 127, 129, 130, 154
  burning of books, 156, 161, 162
  deceived by women, 155
  food of, 134
  garments of, 133
  glory of, 133
  God punished, 161, 166
  grief and weeping of, 156, 162
  in Gospel, 132
  judgement of, 215
  king for forty years, 132
  literature of, 139–40
  magical traditions of, 145, 163, 169
  many writings of, 149, 162
  number of wives of, 154,
  pride of, 165, 166
  replaced on throne by demon, 163
  ring of, 163, 165
  sends letter to woman by bird, 167
  sets up idols, 155
  sin and repentance of, 149, 154, 161, 162, 165
  talks with birds and animal, 167
  texts concerning, 143, 144, 181
  toilet habits of, 165
  wisdom of, 172
  wonderworking of, 129, 167
Solomon and the Bubu Bird, traditions shared with Al-Tabari, 167
Solomon Text 2, 144, 147–50
spheres, seven, 106
spies, 85
spirit of knowledge, 162
spirit, prophetic, 101
stars, five, 105
stereotypical translation, 126
Stone, Michael E., *passim*
Stone, Nira, x
stone tablet, 116, 126
stone, adamant, 95, 117
stones
  hail of, 104
  twelve, 90, 91, 117
stoning, 101, 216
Stroumsa, Gedaliyahu G., 93
sulphur, 26
sun and moon stand still, 11, 104, 105, 119
  mechanics of, 105,106
sun
  goes back, 180, 188
  stood at ninth hour, 189
sundial, 189
Susanna, 209
Susanna
  niece of Joiakim, 212
  trial of, 214
sword, 93, 94, 106
Synaxarion, 219

Talmai, 95
Tamrazyan, Hrachea, ix
Tayecʻi, E., 217
Temple
  building of, 129
  built of cedars of Lebanon, 161
  construction of, 133
  list of wonders in, 141
  rebuilding of, 220
ten, 47
Tent of Witness, 81
Tēr-Ghevondyan, Vahan, ix

INDEX OF SUBJECTS

Tēr-Vardanean, Gēorg, ix, 64,
Terah, 17, 19, 21
    maker of idols, 21, 22
Terian, Abraham, ix, 3, 168
testament, 5
Testament of Solomon, 129, 163
Testaments of the Twelve Patriarchs, 190, 224
Tetrakys, Pythagorean, 47
textual clusters, 149, 156
Theotokos, 23
thirty, 47
thirty days travel between constellations, 105
thirty thousand, size of army, 117
thirty years, 12
Thomson, Robert W., 18, 193
thorn bush, 94
three hundred and sixty days, 105
Three Young Men (Children), Life of 172
Thrones, 3
tin, 96
Titus, 141
Topchyan, Aram, ix, 106
topoi, narrative, 182
Torah, burned, 222
Torijano, Pablo, 23, 129, 163
T'ovma *vardapet* (author), 207, 212
Tower of Babel, 7, 97, 197
Transfiguration, 89
Treasures, Cave of, 6
tribes, twelve, 134
Trinity, 48, 136
Trishagion, 136
trumpets, 96
Tsabari, Shir, x
Tsabari, Yael N.M., x
Turk' (individual), 19
Turkish language, 22
Turks, 18
twelve spies, 83, 91
twenty, 47
two false prophets, 197
two wicked elders, 197
typology, 57

unleavened bread, Lot prepares, 50

Urbat'agirk', xi xii 4
urn, golden, 165
    with manna, 116

Valvo, Alfredo, 123
Van, 148, 159
Vanakan *vardapet* Taušec'i, 10
Vank'un, monastery, 197
Vardan *vardapet*, scribe, 7
Venice (place), 4
Vermès, Géza, 129
Vespasian, 141
vineyard, keeper of, 44
Virgin, the, 181, *See* Theotokos
Vitae Prophetarum, 171

wages, witholding of, 45
wall melts, 96, 118
water, black, 32, 54
water, woman crosses, 170
weeping and gnashing of teeth, 135
weeping and prayer, 195
Weil, Gustav, 167
Werline, Rod, x
widow, 45
wind, brings woman to Solomon, 169
Wisdom of Solomon, 149
women of Balaam, 155
wood, not rotting, 116, 129
word-play, 50
world, end of, 91
worms, undying, 135
Wright, Benjamin D., 44, 171
Wright, J. Edward, 44
writings. *See* books
Wutz, Franz Xavier, 83, 92, 118

Xačatur *erēc'*, scribe, 128
Yaacov-Avni, Noga, x

Yereknazan, wife of Noah's son, 14
Yovsēp'ianc', Sargis, 132, 143–48, 150, 154, 157, 158, 171, 175, 179, 207, 208, 219

Zanazan, wife of Noah's son, 14
Zarmanazan, wife of Noah's son, 14
Zebulun, 19

Zechariah (1), Life of 171
Zechariah (2), Life of 172
Zedekiah
    false prophet, 200
    son of Maaseiah, 209, 213
Zerubbabel, 220
    story of, 194

Zevit, Ziony, 9
Zilpah, 19
Zoar, 53
    meaning of, 53
Zohrab Bible, 193
zones, seven, 105
Zuckerman, Constantine, 5

Index of Ancient Sources

Hebrew Bible

Genesis

Reference	Page
1:24	47
3:3	100
3:9	100
3:24	135
4:10	42
4:19	201
4:23	201
5:31	13
6:14	12
6:15	12
6:16	12
6:19	13
7:6	13
7:12	194
7:17	194
8:6	194
10:6	95
10:15–20	95
11:8	97
11:31	17
12:1–13:11	18
12:4–5	18
12:29–32	46
13:10	25, 53
14	25, 53
14:2	46
14:14–16	52
14:16	49
14:22–23	18
16:16	18
17:2–13	18
17:24	18
18	48
18:1–16	18
18:2	48, 49
18:22	45
18:22–23	46
18:23	46
18:25	46
18:28	46
18:32–33	48
19:1	48
19:2	49
19:3	50
19:5	50
19:6	50
19:8	51
19:9	51
19:10	51
19:11	51
19:12	47
19:13	42
19:14	52
19:17	52
19:18	52
19:19	53
19:20a	53
19:20b	53
19:26	52
19:30–36	52
20:2–18	18
21:5	18
21:12	18
21:14	18
21:21	22
22:2–13	18
23:1	18
24:67	19
25:1–2	18
25:7–8	19
25:20	19
25:25–26	19

25:33	19	Numbers	
31:44	101	7:89	116
35:1	19	10:21	22
35:23	19	10:35	117
35:28	19	11:25	82
40:8	195	12:16	22
		13:3–16	83
Exodus		13:8	81
1:1–4	19	13:16	81, 83
3:5	82, 94	14:1–4	83
4:25	92	14:7–9	83
9:23–24	87	14:30	84
12:12	48	26:25	84
12:23	48	27:17	62, 84
12:37	83	32:12	84
13:21–22	89	32:28	84
17:9–11	121	32:33–34	86
17:9–13	83	34:17	84
17:11	102	35:6–7	107
17:13	83	35:28	107
19:11	82	35:30	42
24:10	110		
24:13	82	Deuteronomy	
24:16	82	3:28	84
24:18	82	3:32	84
24:35	215	5:26	86
25:10	126	7:2	161
25:15–18	110	8:11	173
25:22	116	9:9	194
27:21	126	9:18	194
33:7	116	10:16	92
33:11	82	11:23	85
33:61	116	11:39	103
34:28	194	20:10–15	103
34:29	194	20:16–17	103
34:29–30	215	20:18	103
37:1	126	20:38	84
38:26	83	22:22	201
		30:6	92
Leviticus		31:6	85
10:20	201	31:7	84, 85
19:13	25, 45	31:23	84, 85
25:1–38	47	32:44	84
25:10	47	32:48–52	84
25:32–34	107	34:9	84

INDEX OF ANCIENT SOURCES 249

Joshua
1:1	81, 85	6:25	99
1:3	85	6:26	97
1:11	85, 86, 89	7:1	72, 99
1:17	85	7:3	100
2	86	7:5	10, 100
2:2	86	7:6	100
2:3	86	7:7	100
2:4	86	7:9	100
2:6	86	7:10	100
2:10–11	87	7:12	101
2:12–13	87	7:15	101
2:16–19	65	7:16–18	101
2:18	87	7:18–26	99
2:19	87	7:20	101
2:24	87	7:21	100
3:4	89	7:22–23	101
3:7	85	7:24–26	101
3:10	86	7:25	101
3:11–4:7	117	7:26	101, 102
3:16	90	8:3	102, 117
4:3	90, 117	8:3b–6	102
4:7	118	8:10–13	102
4:8	90	8:14–17	102
4:9	117	8:18	102
4:12	86	8:19	102
4:21–24	91	8:20	102
5:1	90, 91	8:22	102
5:2–3	92	8:26	102
5:3	92	8:29	99
5:9	92, 118	8:30–35	103
5:10	93	9:1–2	103
5:11–12	85, 86	9:3	103
5:12	93	9:3–5	103
5:13	94	9:6–13	104
5:13–6:5	94	9:12–15	103
5:14	94	9:21–22	104
5:15	94	10	91, 119
6	89, 117	10:1–6	104
6:6–13	117	10:3	118
6:9	96	10:6	104
6:17–18	118	10:11	104
6:19	99	10:12	104
6:20	96, 118	10:12–13	119, 189
6:21	118	10:25	85
6:23	99	11:15	85
6:23–26	97	11:21–22	107
		11:23	85

12:9	87	4:16–17	120
14:1	84	4:18	119
14:9	85	11:8	117
15:4	95	12:12	119
17:4	84	15:24	103
18–21:45	86	15:28	192
18:7	86		
19:51	83, 84	**Second Samuel**	
20–21	107	6	118
20:2–6	107	6:1	117
20:6	107	6:6–7	118
21:1	84	19:3	200
21:4–8	107		
21:13–40	107	**First Kings**	
21:40	107	2:1–4	155
22:1–6	86	2:23	200
22:5	155	3:16–26	215
23	108	4:7	134
23:4	90	4:22 (5:2)	134
23:7	108	4:22–23 (5:2–3)	134
24:14–15	108	4:27	134
24:16–18	108	4:32	149
24:19–20	108	4:32–33	162
24:21	108	4:33	162
24:21–22	108	4:34 (5:14)	133
24:24	108	5:15(29)	133
24:25	108	5:29	133
24:26–27	108	5:30	133
		6:17	89
Judges		7:8	161
4:18	193	9:24	161
4:21–22	193	10:6–8	133
20:27–28	117	11:1–10	190
		11:4	149
First Samuel		11:4–6	181
2:7	165	11:5	161
2:12	119	11:6	155
2:13–17	119	11:6–8	181
2:22	119	11:14	161
2:23–25	120	11:23	161
3:17	200	16:34	97
4:2	120	17:26	86
4:3	120	17:36	86
4:4–5	117	18:1	177
4:10	117, 120	18:4	177
4:12	120	18:5	177
4:12–18	121	18:13	177

18:13–16	177	8:10	213
18:14	177	11:20	42, 213
18:18	178	14:14	202
18:41–42	179	17:10	213
		23:25	202
Second Kings		27:6–8	213
2:19–22	98	29	200, 209, 216
18:22	191	29:1	200
19:16	86	29:5–6	200
19:37	192	29:6	200
20	188	29:10	212
20:1–11	180	29:19	202
20:1	188	29:21	202, 209, 213
20:2–5	188	29:21b	213
20:5–6	189	29:22	201, 202, 216
20:5	188	29:22a	200
20:6	188, 189	29:23	201, 202, 203
20:9–11	189	29:23a	213
20:9	180, 188		
20:21	189	Ezekiel	
21:2–7	190	16:49	25, 46
21:2–9	181	36:26	92
21:2	181	38–39	220
21:3	190	41:2	89
21:7	190	47:20	90
21:10–16	192		
21:16	181, 182, 191	Jonah	
23:13	161	3:1	206
		3:3	206
Isaiah		3:4	206
6:5–7	173		
6:8	173	Micah	
26:11	173	1:4	118
29:7	14		
35:10	136	Nahum	
37:38	192	2:7	205
38:6	188	2:9	205
38:11	95	3:7	205
51:11	136		
61:1	47	Zephaniah	
		2:13	205
Jeremiah			
2:8	213	Psalms	
4:4	92	6:6	156
5:13	213	7:9(10)	42
5:31	213	7:10(9)	213
6:31	213	22:14	118

26:2	213	4:37	195
68:2	118	5	194
73(72):20	14	6:26–27	195
74(73):9	141	7:10	3
78(77):51	48	14:41	195
90(89):5	14		
97:5	118	Nehemiah	
106(105):35	103	10:29	155
116(114):9	95		
135:13	173	First Chronicles	
142:5 (141:6)	95	32:7	85

Proverbs
		Second Chronicles	
1:2	172	23:25–26	180
4:10	172	31:20	180
4:20	172	32:25–26	188
25:1	150, 162	32:33	189
		33:2–7	190

Job
		33:3	190, 191
1:21 (22)	165	33:11	192, 193
6:6	107	33:11–13	181
20:8	14	33:24	188
41:24	92	35:12	216

Song of Songs

NEW TESTAMENT

1:6	44		
2:15	44	Matthew	
3:9–11	133	1:5	97
3:10	130, 133	3:4	22
3:11	131, 133	4:2	194
5:11	161	5:13	107
		6:23	130
Qohelet		6:28–29	133
1:2	134	8:12	135
2:12–13	134	11:3	203
2:12	134	12:42	132
8:1	194	13:42	135
		13:50	135
Esther		17:2	194
1:3–4	194	20:1–5	44
7:2	193	22:13	135
		24:51	135
Daniel		25:34–36	135
2:20–22	195	26:30	135
2:27–28	195	27:3	103
2:47	195		
3:28	195		

INDEX OF ANCIENT SOURCES

Mark		*4 Ezra*	9, 218
1:6	22	*4 Ezra* 3:2	221
2:17	46	*4 Ezra* 3:9–11	13
9:50	107	*4 Ezra* 4:1	221
		4 Ezra 7:7	222
Luke		*4 Ezra* 7:10–9:16C	224
4:2	194	*4 Ezra* 8:31–33	46
5:32	46	*4 Ezra* 9:12	222
11:31	132	*4 Ezra* 10:2–4	222
13:28	135	*4 Ezra* 10:3	222
14:24	107	*4 Ezra* 13:47–48	222
16:16	203	*4 Ezra* 14	222
		4 Ezra 14:21	222
Acts		*4 Ezra* 14:37–42	82
6:8	215	*4 Ezra* 14:44	194
		Apoc. Ab. 1–3	21
Epistles		*Ascen. Isa.* 1:9	192
2 Cor 3:3	92	*Ascen. Isa.* 5:2	192
2 Cor 11:32	65, 88	*Ascen. Isa.* 5:14	192
Col 1:13	135	*Jub.* 4:33	14
Col 2:14	108	*Jub.* 11:28	17
Col 4:6	107	*Jub.* 12:12	18
Heb 9:4	165	*Jdt* 12:17–13:2	193
Heb 10:27	54	*Jdt* 12:20	193
Heb 10:31	54	*Jdt* 13:7–8	193
Heb 11:30	118	*Pen. Adam* 44.17.1	165
Heb 11:37	182, 192	*Paralipomena Ieremiou* 3:10	127
Jas 5:4	45	*Paralipomena Ieremiou* 3:18–19	127
		Paralipomena Ieremiou 7:18	194
Revelations		*Pr. Man.* 1	182, 195
1:16	194	*Pr. Man.* 10	193
		Sus 1	201, 212
APOCRYPHA AND PSEUDEPIGRAPHA		*Sus* 1–2	217
(IN ALPHABETICAL ORDER)		*Sus* 2	212
		Sus 4	212
1 En. 22	98	*Sus* 5	213
1 Macc. 2:34	96	*Sus* 7–14	213
1 Macc. 2:40	96	*Sus* 20	213
1 Macc. 2:41	96	*Sus* 24	214
2 Macc. 2:4–5	121	*Sus* 26	213
2 Macc. 2:4–6	127	*Sus* 32–34	214
2 Macc. 5:25	96	*Sus* 34	214
2 Macc. 8:26	96	*Sus* 42	214
3 (Greek Apoc) Baruch	9	*Sus* 43	214
3 (Greek Apoc) Bar 12	44	*Sus* 44	214
3 (Greek Apoc) Bar 12:1–13:7	44	*Sus* 46	214, 215
4 Baruch	147	*Sus* 48	215

254 ARMENIAN APOCRYPHA RELATING TO BIBLICAL HEROES

Sus 52	215
Sus 57 (Dan 13:57)	203
Sus 59	215
Sus 60	216
Sus 62 (Dan 13:62)	202
Sus 63	216
Sus 64	217
T. Ab. 1	94
T. Ab. 2	94
T. Ab. 3	94
T. Jos. 6:1–2	190
T. Reu. 4:9	190
T. Sol. 1:6–7	163
Wis. 2:24	95
Wis. 7:20	169
Wis. 14:14–21	191

Armenian Pseudepigrapha
(in alphabetical order)

Abraham and Terah, Story of	21
Abraham Text 2	6, 8
Abraham, Concerning	10, 15
Abraham, Genealogy of	10, 15
Abraham, Story concerning	8
Abraham, Story of Father	21, 25
Adam and Eve, History of	7
Adam and his Grandsons, History of	12
Adam Fragments	2
Adam Story 1	123
Adam Story 2	123
Adam, Death of	147
Adam, Deception of	7
Adam, Eve and the Incarnation	24
Adam, Generations from	1
Adam, Words of, to Seth	2
Angelology Text 2	1
Angels, Praise of the	1
Angels, Fall of the	1
Angels, Number and Twelve Classes of	11
Apostles, Names of	123
Archangels, Question concerning	1
Ark of God, Concerning	58, 61, 123
Ark of the Covenant, Story of	58, 61
Ark of the Testaments §21b	127
Ark of the Testaments, Concerning the Story of	58, 123
Ark, Dimensions of	58
Ark, Noah's, Construction of	10, 19, 148
Ark, Noah's, Question concerning	11
Asaph, Story of	218
Biblical Paraphrases	8
Biblical Paraphrases §9	97
Christ, Flight of, to Egypt	7
Daniel, Life of	207
Daniel, Seventh Vision of	207
Daniel, Story of	207
Eleven Periods	123
Elijah, Concerning	204
Elijah, Short History of	175
Ezra, Questions of	9, 98, 219, 222
Flood, Sermon concerning the	8, 24
Forefathers, History of	222
Forefathers, Memorial of	58
Forefathers, Names of	123, 218
Gems, Names of	123
Gog and Magog, Story of	123
Gregory, St., Questions of	9
Hell, Concerning the Places of	8
Hezekiah and Manasseh	8, 180
Hezekiah and Manasseh §§ 8–12	149
History of the Forefathers § §41, 43	222
Jeremiah, Concerning the Prophet	128
Jeremiah, Susanna, and the Two Elders	207
Jewels of Aaron's Ephod, Names of the	123
Jonah the Prophet, Sermon on	205
Joseph and Asenath	224
Joseph, Third Story of	1, 24
Joshua, Brief History of	148
Joshua, Brief History of §46	118,
Joshua, History of (in Biblical Paraphrases)	58
Joshua, Short History of	58
Millennia, Concerning, II	8
Nathan, Story of	218
Nineveh and Jonah, This is the Story of	205
Ninevehites, The	145, 178, 204, 205
Noah, Story of	13, 89
Oil, Found in Albanian Books	7
Praise of the Prophets	207
Pseudo-Philo, On Jonah	205
Queen, Questions of	23, 132, 143
Satanel and Adam, Fall of	7

INDEX OF ANCIENT SOURCES

Seth, Concerning the Good
  Tidings of   9, 12, 13,
Seventy-Two Translators, Concerning   204
Six Millennia, Concerning   123
Sodomites 1–4   106
Sodomites and Gomorreans,
  Supplication about   11
Solomon and the Bubu Bird   144, 145, 149
Solomon, Concerning King
  (two recensions)   8, 23, 143, 144, 146, 165
Solomon, Concerning the
  Writings of   143, 144, 165
Solomon, Concerning, and the
  Building of the Temple   144, 145
Solomon, King, Four Short Texts   7
Solomon, King, Ring of   144, 145, 149
Solomon's Temple, Concerning
  the Wonders of   128, 144
St. Gregory, Questions of   1, 7, 9
Temple, Signs and Wonders of   128, 137
Testaments of the Twelve Patriarchs   224
Three Youths, Sermon concerning   24
Tower, Concerning the   7
Twelve Literate Nations   20

RABBINIC LITERATURE

m. Abot 1:1   82
m. Abot 5:7   137, 138
m. Ber. 6.3   22
b. Mak. 10a   107
b. Yebam. 49b   192
y. Sanh. 10   192
y. Shelamim 6:1 49d   82
'Abot de Rabbi Nathan   138
Tanḥuma Lek Leka 2.2   21

OTHER ANCIENT SOURCES

11QMelch 2:6–10   47
1Q20 (Genesis Apocryphon) 6:7   14
Agathangelos 3   90
Movsēs Xorenacʻi 2.1   18
Movsēs Xorenacʻi 2.8   18
Pseudo-Zeno §4.3.4   47
Herodotus 3.40–43   163
Josephus, *AJ* 8.46–48   163
Maimonides, *Mishneh Torah,*
  Murder 8.5   107

Index of Manuscripts

Armenian Patriarchate of Jerusalem

J393	176
J631	176
J652	xi xii, 148, 151, 157, 159
J669	176
J730	176
J652	xi xii, 148, 151, 157, 159
J1761	145
J2558	xii, 145, 147, 157

Erevan, Maštocʻ Matenadaran

M43	145
M59	205
M101	xi, xii, 175, 178, 204
M268	20
M503	176
M533	172
M537	20
M605	20
M682	xi, 15
M706	176
M724	xi, xii, 218, 219
M843	176
M1134	xi, xii, 207
M1495	137, 139
M1500	xi, xii, 143, 145, 146, 150, 156, 157, 176
M2168	xi, xii, 58, 79, 91
M2242	xi, xii, 24, 38
M2245	xi, xii, 1, 176
M2679	20
M3854	58
M4231	58
M4618	xi, xii 7, 20, 58, 59, 61, 91, 144, 147–51, 154, 157–59, 167, 180
M5531	xi, xii, 171
M5571	xi, xii, 24, 38
M5607	xi, xii, 197, 224–27
M5933	xi, xii, 137
M6092	xi, xii, 58, 59, 73, 74, 77, 79, 101, 175, 178
M6340	xi, xii, 58, 109, 114
M6349	58
M8093	176
M8239	176
M8494	20
M9100	xi, xii, 58, 123
M10561	145
M10986	xi, xii, 128, 143, 146

Istanbul, Armenian Patriarchate

Galata 54	58, 126

London, British Library

Egerton 708	xii, 58, 123

Paris, Bibliothèque Nationale de France

P121	20
BnF 128	128

Venice, Mekhitarist Fathers

V176	172
V280/10	150, 151
V570	219
V927	4
V1260/1095	150, 158
V1957	xii

www.ingramcontent.com/pod-product-compliance
Lightning Source LLC
Chambersburg PA
CBHW020610300426
44113CB00007B/582